TRUST, COURTS AND SOCIAL RIGHTS

Trust, Courts and Social Rights proposes an innovative legal framework for judicially enforcing social rights that is rooted in public trust in government or 'political trust'. Interdisciplinary in nature, the book draws on theoretical and empirical scholarship on the concept of trust across disciplines, including philosophy, sociology, psychology and political theory. It integrates that scholarship with the relevant public law literature on social rights, fiduciary political theory and judicial review. In doing so, the book uses trust as an analytical lens for social rights law – importing ideas from the scholarship on trust into the social rights literature – and develops a normative argument that contributes to the controversial debate on how courts should enforce social rights. Also global in focus, the book uses cases from courts in Africa, Europe, Latin America and North America to illustrate how the trust-based framework operates in practice.

DAVID VITALE is Associate Professor at the University of Warwick, School of Law. He holds law degrees from the UK (London School of Economics and Political Science), the US (New York University) and Canada (Osgoode Hall Law School), and a degree in psychology (University of Toronto). He has also worked as a judicial clerk in Canada and Israel, held various research positions globally and practised as a litigator in Canada.

CAMBRIDGE STUDIES IN CONSTITUTIONAL LAW

The aim of this series is to produce leading monographs in constitutional law. All areas of constitutional law and public law fall within the ambit of the series, including human rights and civil liberties law, administrative law, as well as constitutional theory and the history of constitutional law. A wide variety of scholarly approaches is encouraged, with the governing criterion being simply that the work is of interest to an international audience. Thus, works concerned with only one jurisdiction will be included in the series as appropriate, while, at the same time, the series will include works which are explicitly comparative or theoretical – or both. The series editors likewise welcome proposals that work at the intersection of constitutional and international law, or that seek to bridge the gaps between civil law systems, the US, and the common law jurisdictions of the Commonwealth.

TRUST, COURTS AND SOCIAL RIGHTS

A Trust-Based Framework for Social Rights Enforcement

DAVID VITALE

University of Warwick

CAMBRIDGE
UNIVERSITY PRESS

CAMBRIDGE
UNIVERSITY PRESS

Shaftesbury Road, Cambridge CB2 8EA, United Kingdom

One Liberty Plaza, 20th Floor, New York, NY 10006, USA

477 Williamstown Road, Port Melbourne, VIC 3207, Australia

314–321, 3rd Floor, Plot 3, Splendor Forum, Jasola District Centre, New Delhi – 110025, India

103 Penang Road, #05-06/07, Visioncrest Commercial, Singapore 238467

Cambridge University Press is part of Cambridge University Press & Assessment,
a department of the University of Cambridge.

We share the University's mission to contribute to society through the pursuit of education, learning and research at the highest international levels of excellence.

www.cambridge.org
Information on this title: www.cambridge.org/9781009098557

DOI: 10.1017/9781009089654

First published 2024

A catalogue record for this publication is available from the British Library

Library of Congress Cataloging-in-Publication Data
Names: Vitale, David, author.
Title: Trust, courts, and social rights : a trust-based framework for social rights enforcement / David Vitale, University of Warwick.
Description: Cambridge, United Kingdom ; New York, NY : Cambridge University Press, 2024. | Series: Cambridge studies in constitutional law | Includes bibliographical references and index.
Identifiers: LCCN 2023038112 (print) | LCCN 2023038113 (ebook) | ISBN 9781009098557 (hardback) | ISBN 9781009096331 (paperback) | ISBN 9781009089654 (epub)
Subjects: LCSH: Social rights. | Human rights. | Courts. | Trust.
Classification: LCC K3239.8 (print) | LCC K3239.8 (ebook) | DDC 342.08/5–dc23/eng/20231003
LC record available at https://lccn.loc.gov/2023038112
LC ebook record available at https://lccn.loc.gov/2023038113

ISBN 978-1-009-09855-7 Hardback

CONTENTS

ACKNOWLEDGEMENTS

I thank all those who have helped and supported me through the book-writing process.

This book started as a PhD thesis at the London School of Economics and Political Science (LSE) Law School. I thus begin by thanking my supervisors, Tom Poole and Jo Murkens, for recognising promise in the topic of trust and social rights, challenging me to think critically about the topic, offering me invaluable guidance and providing encouragement. I am also grateful for their mentorship and support since completing the PhD. Thanks also to the academic and administrative staff at the LSE Law School, including the then-directors of the PhD programme (Linda Mulcahy and Susan Marks), my upgrade readers (Martin Loughlin and Grégoire Webber) and my fellow students, with special thanks to Velimir Živković, Wend Teeder, Bernard Keenan and Geetanjali Ganguly. I am also indebted to my examiners, Colm O'Cinneide and Aoife Nolan, who provided detailed feedback on my thesis, from which this book has benefited tremendously.

Next, I thank the various colleagues who have generously read draft chapters (or portions of draft chapters) and provided valuable feedback on them: Catherine Briddick, Mara Malagodi, Virginia Mantouvalou, Vanessa Munro, Tom Poole, Sharifah Sekalala and Ioanna Tourkochoriti. I am also appreciative to the two anonymous referees during the commissioning of this book.

Additionally, portions of this book were presented at various international conferences and benefited from feedback that I received from colleagues at those events: the Economic and Social Rights Academic Network: United Kingdom & Ireland (ESRAN-UKI) Workshop at the Irish Centre for Human Rights, National University of Ireland, Galway (June 2021); the Constitutional Works-in-Progress Workshop at the UCD Sutherland School of Law, Dublin (June 2019); the European Junior Faculty Forum at the LSE Law School (jointly organised by the European University Institute and WZB in Berlin) (June 2019); the

'Fiduciaries and Trust: Ethics, Politics, Economics and Law' Workshop at Melbourne Law School (December 2018); the McGill Law Graduate Conference, Montreal (May 2018); the 'New Voices in Administrative Justice' Workshop at the University of Sheffield, School of Law (September 2017); the Social Justice Speaker Series at the University of Ottawa, Faculty of Law (September 2016); the International Society of Public Law (ICON-S) Conferences in Berlin and New York (June 2016 and July 2015); the Public Law Doctoral Research Colloquium at the LSE Law School (October 2015); and the Society of Legal Scholars (SLS) PhD Conference at the York Law School (September 2015).

Although rewritten for the book, some of the material was first published as the following publications: David Vitale, 'A Trust Network Model for Social Rights Fulfilment' (2018) 38 *Oxford Journal of Legal Studies* 706; David Vitale, 'Political Trust as the Basis for a Social Rights Enforcement Framework' (2018) 44 *Queen's Law Journal* 177; and David Vitale, 'The Relational Impact of Social Rights Judgments: A Trust-Based Analysis' (2022) 42 *Legal Studies* 408.

For providing funding at the doctoral and post-doctoral stages, I am grateful to the LSE Law School, the Social Sciences and Humanities Research Council of Canada (SSHRC) and the Minerva Center for the Rule of Law under Extreme Conditions, University of Haifa. For their assistance throughout the process, thanks also to the editorial team at Cambridge University Press. I am also appreciative to Clet Abraham for kindly providing the book's cover art.

Lastly, my greatest debt is to my family and my friends (in Canada, the UK and elsewhere) who continue to offer me love and support. This book would not have been possible without you.

TABLE OF CASES

Canada

Auton (Guardian ad litem of) v. British Columbia (Attorney General), 2004 SCC 78
Eldridge v. British Columbia (Attorney General) [1997] 3 SCR 624
Gosselin v. Québec (Attorney General), 2002 SCC 84
R v. Kapp, 2008 SCC 41

Colombia

Corte Constitutional de Colombia (2008) Sala Segunda de Revisión, T-760

Germany

Asylum Seekers Benefits, 132 BVerfGE 134
Hartz IV, 125 BVerfGE 172

India

Hassan v. National Insurance Institute [2012] HCJ 10662/04
Olga Tellis and Others v. Bombay Municipal Corporation [1985] 2 Supp SCR 51
State of Maharashtra through CBI, Anti Corruption Branch, Mumbai v. Balakrishna Dattatrya Kumbhar [2012] 9 SCR 601
Vineet Narain and Others v. Union of India and Another, (1998) 1 SCC 226

Kenya

Governing Body of the Juma Musjid Primary School and Others v. Essay N.O. and Others [2011] ZACC 13
John Kabui Mwai and Others v. Kenya National Examination Council and Others [2011] eKLR

Latvia

Disbursement Law, Case No. 2009-43-01

South Africa

AllPay Consolidated Investment Holdings (Pty) Ltd. and Others v. Chief Executive Officer, South African Social Security Agency and Others [2013] ZASCA 29
AllPay Consolidated Investment Holdings (Pty) Ltd. and Others v. Chief Executive Officer, South African Social Security Agency and Others [2013] ZACC 42
AllPay Consolidated Investment (Pty) Ltd. and Others v. Chief Executive Officer, South African Social Security Agency and Others (no. 2) [2014] ZACC 12
Black Sash Trust v. Minister of Social Development and Others (Freedom Under Law NPC Intervening) [2017] ZACC 8
Black Sash Trust v. Minister of Social Development and Others (Freedom Under Law NPC Intervening) [2017] ZACC 20
Black Sash Trust v. Minister of Social Development and Others (Freedom Under Law NPC Intervening) [2018] ZACC 36
City of Johannesburg Metropolitan Municipality v. Blue Moonlight Properties 39 (Pty) Ltd. and Others [2011] ZACC 33
Glenister v. President of the Republic of South Africa and Others [2011] ZACC 6
Government of the Republic of South Africa and Others v. Grootboom and Others [2000] ZACC 19
Khosa and Others v. Minister of Social Development and Others [2004] ZACC 11
Madzozo and Others v. Minister of Basic Education and Others [2014] ZAECMHC 5
Minister of Basic Education and Others v. Basic Education for All and Others [2015] ZASCA 198
Minister of Health and Others v. Treatment Action Campaign and Others [2002] ZACC 15
National Coalition for Gay and Lesbian Equality and Another v. Minister of Justice and Others [1998] ZACC 15
Occupiers of 51 Olivia Road and Others v. City of Johannesburg and Others [2008] ZACC 1
Residents of Joe Slovo Community v. Thubelisha Homes and Others [2009] ZACC 16
Section 27 and Others v. Minister of Education and Another [2012] 3 All SA 579

Uganda

Centre for Health, Human Rights and Development and Others v. Attorney General, Constitutional Petition No. 16 of 2011

United Kingdom

Nzolameso v. City of Westminster [2015] UKSC 22

R (on the application of Good Law Project Ltd.) v. Secretary of State for Health and Social Care [2021] EWHC 346 (Admin)

R (on the application of Good Law Project Ltd. and EveryDoctor) v. Secretary of State for Health and Social Care [2022] EWHC 46 (TCC)

R v. Cambridge Health Authority [1995] EWCA Civ 49, [1995] WLR 898

R v. North West Lancashire Health Authority, ex parte A, D and G [1999] EWCA Civ 2022, [2000] 1 WLR 977

1

Introduction

Social rights have become a central component of the modern constitution. The vast majority of constitutions globally contain at least one social (or economic) right.[1] And the general trend is towards more of these rights. In 2016, for instance, 51 constitutions had more social and economic rights than they did in 2000, whereas only four had less.[2] Where social rights are not expressly protected in constitutions (e.g., in older constitutional documents), it is commonplace for courts to read social rights into general constitutional provisions like the rights to life and human dignity.[3]

Despite this global pattern of greater protection of social rights constitutionally, the role of the courts in enforcing these rights against government actors remains unresolved. Jurists and politicians have long engaged in a conversation regarding the judicial enforcement of social rights. This conversation has come to pass in a series of waves.[4] In its

[1] Courtney Jung, Ran Hirschl and Evan Rosevear concluded in a 2014 study that 90 per cent of 195 constitutions then in force contained at least one 'economic and social right', with rights to education, health care and social security (the rights which, as I note later, I am including under the category of 'social rights') being especially prevalent: Courtney Jung, Ran Hirschl and Evan Rosevear, 'Economic and Social Rights in National Constitutions' (2014) 62 *American Journal of Comparative Law* 1043, 1053. See also Evan Rosevear, Ran Hirschl and Courtney Jung, 'Justiciable and Aspirational Economic and Social Rights in National Constitutions' in Katharine G. Young (ed.), *The Future of Economic and Social Rights* (Cambridge: Cambridge University Press, 2019), pp. 37–65.

[2] Rosevear et al., 'Justiciable and Aspirational', p. 46.

[3] For example, see the social rights protected under the right to dignity in Israel's Basic Law: Human Dignity and Liberty: Aeyal Gross, 'The Right to Health in Israel between Solidarity and Neoliberalism' in Colleen M. Flood and Aeyal Gross (eds.), *The Right to Health at the Public/Private Divide* (Cambridge: Cambridge University Press, 2014), p. 165. See also relevant cases from the German Constitutional Court and the Indian Supreme Court: *Hartz IV*, 125 BVerfGE 172; *Olga Tellis and Others v. Bombay Municipal Corporation* [1985] 2 Supp SCR 51.

[4] For this terminology of 'waves', see Richard Stacey, 'Dynamic Regulatory Constitutionalism: Taking Legislation Seriously in the Judicial Enforcement of Economic

'first wave', the conversation centred on justiciability – that is, whether social rights are enforceable by the courts. That wave reached its peak during the late 1980s to early 1990s when the new democracies of the 'Global South' and the former Soviet Union sought to decide whether to include express, and enforceable, social rights provisions in their constitutions. Now in its 'second wave', the conversation's focus is different. Many new democracies, after intense debate, opted for the inclusion of express and enforceable social rights provisions in their constitutions.[5] Consequently, most jurists and politicians, with the passage of time, have come to accept that social rights are indeed justiciable. And the conversation now centres on the question of how the courts should enforce social rights.

Given the prevalence of constitutionalised and justiciable social rights globally, this question demands an answer. And the urgency of answering it intensifies with the corresponding proliferation – or as some scholars have described it, the 'explosion' – of social rights litigation.[6]

In this book, I address the above question using a concept that has received much attention recently – in academic circles and the media. That concept is public trust in government or what I call 'political trust'. In broad terms, this book examines social rights law from the perspective of political trust.[7] It uses the concept as an analytical lens for this area of law, addressing, among other things, what it means to trust one's government with respect to social rights, how trust functions in the context of social rights and what we can reasonably expect the impact of different modes of social rights adjudication to be on the public's trust in government actors. My principal objective in this book, however, is more

and Social Rights' (2017) 31 *Notre Dame Journal of Law, Ethics and Public Policy* 85, 85–86.

5 Rosevear et al., 'Justiciable and Aspirational', p. 62. See also Adam Chilton and Mila Versteeg, *How Constitutional Rights Matter* (Oxford: Oxford University Press, 2020), pp. 172–173, 176.

6 Daniel M. Brinks and Varun Gauri, 'The Law's Majestic Equality? The Distributive Impact of Judicializing Social and Economic Rights' (2014) 12 *Perspectives on Politics* 375, 376. See also Octàvio Luiz Motta Ferraz, 'The Right to Health in the Courts of Brazil: Worsening Health Inequities?' (2009) 11 *Health and Human Rights* 33; Chilton and Versteeg, *How Constitutional Rights Matter*, p. 198. In 2009, for example, Malcolm Langford noted that '[i]f we were to speculate on the total number of decisions that have invoked constitutional and international [social] rights, a figure of at least one to two hundred thousand would be in order': Malcolm Langford, 'Domestic Adjudication and Economic, Social and Cultural Rights: A Socio-Legal Review' (2009) 6 *International Journal on Human Rights* 91, 91.

7 By 'social rights law', I mean the law pertaining to constitutional social rights, including their judicial enforcement.

precise: that objective is to advance a normative argument regarding the judicial enforcement of constitutional social rights. I propose that the courts, when they are enforcing these rights against government actors, should focus their analysis on political trust. They should aim, I suggest, to promote the trustworthiness of government actors – specifically vis-à-vis their provision of social goods and services to the public. And following on from this, I employ political trust as the basis for a new legal framework for judicially enforcing social rights.

1.1 Political Trust and Public Cooperation

As a starting point, we may ask: why political trust? That is, why should we examine social rights law from the perspective of political trust? And why should political trust provide the basis for a legal framework for judicially enforcing social rights? Owing to the complex and multi-layered nature of these two questions, answering them will be an ongoing process in the book. I will begin, however, by considering the relationship between political trust and public cooperation which provides, I submit, a central reason why political trust is of significance to social rights law.

Dating back at least 50 years, scholars across disciplines have stressed the importance of public trust in government to well-functioning democracies. They have theorised about the consequences of political trust, arguing that it is tied to such valuable ends as social stability, economic welfare and effective governance.[8] This tie is explained as follows. When the public has greater trust in government, it is more likely to regard government actions as legitimate and to cooperate with them, tolerating the political regime and voluntarily complying with laws and government demands. Such cooperation is critical because it allows the state to focus

[8] See Christina Boswell, *Manufacturing Political Trust: Targets and Performance Measurement in Public Policy* (Cambridge: Cambridge University Press, 2018); Russell J. Dalton, *Democratic Challenges, Democratic Choices: The Erosion of Political Support in Advanced Industrial Democracies* (Oxford: Oxford University Press, 2004); Pippa Norris, 'Conclusion: The Growth of Critical Citizens and Its Consequences' in Pippa Norris (ed.), *Critical Citizens: Global Support for Democratic Government* (Oxford: Oxford University Press, 1999), pp. 257–272; Bo Rothstein, *Just Institutions Matter* (Cambridge: Cambridge University Press, 1998). In addition to the instrumental value of political trust, it has also been argued that political trust is intrinsically valuable: see Matthew Harding, 'Trust and Fiduciary Law' (2013) 33 *Oxford Journal of Legal Studies* 81; Colleen Murphy, *A Moral Theory of Political Reconciliation* (Cambridge: Cambridge University Press, 2010).

its limited resources for coercion on the relatively few disobedient.[9] As Russell Dalton has said, 'democracy functions with minimal coercive force because of the legitimacy of the system and the voluntary compliance of the public. Declining feelings of political trust and political support can undermine this relationship and therefore the workings of democracy'.[10] As voluntary compliance with laws and government demands becomes the norm in a democracy, public cooperation translates into social stability.[11]

The link between political trust and public cooperation finds significant support in empirical research. Tom Tyler, for instance, has consistently demonstrated that individuals' trust in authority figures increases their cooperation with those figures. Based on data collected in a series of interviews, Tyler has convincingly shown that trust increases individuals' willingness to accept authority decisions, their feelings of obligation to obey organisational rules and laws and their performance evaluations of those in positions of authority.[12] These findings have been replicated across a range of contexts and groups.[13] Similarly, Dalton, using the 1995–98 World Values Survey, has shown a positive correlation between levels of political support (a concept closely tied to political trust) and people's willingness to obey the law.[14] Building on a categorisation developed by David Easton, Dalton divided political support into four categories: institutional support (support for the institutions of governance), authority support (support for those who control the institutions), support for democratic values, and community support (support for the nation or the political system in broad terms). Dalton found that all four categories correlate in a positive direction with willingness to obey the

[9] Russell Hardin, 'Trust in Government' in Valerie Braithwaite and Margaret Levi (eds.), *Trust and Governance* (New York: Russell Sage Foundation, 1998), p. 10.

[10] Dalton, *Democratic Challenges, Democratic Choices*, p. 159. Some writers have described this benefit of trust as reduced 'transaction costs' for governments: Dalton, *Democratic Challenges, Democratic Choices*, p. 159; Eva-Maria Trüdinger and Uwe Bollow, 'Evaluations of Welfare State Reforms in Germany: Political Trust Makes a (Big) Difference' in Sonja Zmerli and Marc Hooghe (eds.), *Political Trust: Why Context Matters* (Colchester: ECPR Press, 2011), p. 189.

[11] Dalton, *Democratic Challenges, Democratic Choices*, p. 165.

[12] For a summary, see Tom R. Tyler and Peter Degoey, 'Trust in Organizational Authorities: The Influence of Motive Attributions on Willingness to Accept Decisions' in Roderick M. Kramer and Tom R. Tyler (eds.), *Trust in Organizations: Frontiers of Theory and Research* (Thousand Oaks, CA: Sage Publications, 1996), p. 336.

[13] Tom R. Tyler and Yuen J. Huo, *Trust in the Law: Encouraging Public Cooperation with the Police and Courts* (New York: Russell Sage Foundation, 2002).

[14] Dalton, *Democratic Challenges, Democratic Choices*, pp. 165–166.

law, with institutional and community support having the strongest correlation. Lastly, Sofie Marien and Marc Hooghe, in a study much like that of Dalton but using the European Values Survey 1999–2001, obtained similar findings to those of Dalton.[15] They found that respondents with higher levels of political trust, specifically trust in political institutions, were significantly less likely to have permissive attitudes towards law-breaking (the inverse of the 'willingness-to-obey-the-law' measure that Dalton used in his study)[16] than those with lower levels of political trust. Marien and Hooghe found that this relationship held even controlling for variables like the respondents' age, gender, education level and religious practice.[17]

This link between political trust and public cooperation is significant for social rights law owing to two inter-related reasons. First, public cooperation manifests itself as public willingness to pay taxes – a source of revenue that is critical to financing the state's fulfilment of social rights.[18] Social rights reflect constitutional entitlements to social goods and services that one needs to lead a decent life, with the state having a corresponding obligation to provide the public with those goods and services.[19] The state's provision of these goods and services, however, depends on resources which the public itself provides. The public pays taxes to the state and, using the revenue collected from those taxes, the

[15] Sofie Marien and Marc Hooghe, 'Does Political Trust Matter? An Empirical Investigation into the Relation between Political Trust and Support for Compliance' (2011) 50 *European Journal of Political Research* 267.

[16] Dalton used the same type of survey items but used those items to create what he calls a 'willingness-to-obey-the-law index': Dalton, *Democratic Challenges, Democratic Choices*, p. 166.

[17] For further empirical support, see Martin Lindstrom, 'Social Capital, Political Trust and Purchase of Illegal Liquor: A Population-Based Study in Southern Sweden' (2008) 86 *Health Policy* 266; Norris, 'Conclusion'.

[18] Laurence E. Lynn, Jr., 'How Do Trust and Confidence Affect the Governing of America?' in Sue Llewellyn, Stephen Brookes and Ann Mahon (eds.), *Trust and Confidence in Government and Public Services* (Abingdon: Routledge, 2013), p. 21; Joseph S. Nye, Jr., 'Introduction: The Decline of Confidence in Government' in Joseph S. Nye, Jr., Philip D. Zelikow and David C. King (eds.), *Why People Do Not Trust Government* (Cambridge, MA: Harvard University Press, 1997), p. 4; Bo Rothstein, Marcus Samanni and Jan Teorell, 'Explaining the Welfare State: Power Resources vs. the Quality of Government' (2012) 4 *European Political Science Review* 1, 10–11; Stefan Svallfors, 'Introduction' in Stefan Svallfors (ed.), *The Political Sociology of the Welfare State: Institutions, Social Cleavages and Orientations* (Stanford, CA: Stanford University Press, 2007), pp. 1–29.

[19] Cécile Fabre, *Social Rights under the Constitution: Government and the Decent Life* (Oxford: Oxford University Press, 2003), p. 7; Jeff King, *Judging Social Rights* (Cambridge: Cambridge University Press, 2012), p. 17.

state administers social programmes. Public taxes are therefore a prerequisite to state-provided social goods and services. In the words of Eric Uslaner, '[t]axes are the economic glue of social programs, the source of government's ability to transfer resources – and, indeed, to function at all'.[20] And for this reason, it has been argued that the 'future of the welfare state is likely to hinge on the ability for nation states to levy taxes . . . on their populations'.[21]

Given the above-described link between political trust and public cooperation, writers have argued that the public's willingness to pay taxes, as a form of public cooperation, depends on the public's trust in government.[22] The public, it has been suggested, is less likely to pay taxes if it does not trust its government. This jeopardises the state's ability to provide the public with social goods and services. At the same time, the public's unwillingness to pay taxes, it has also been suggested, can generate a vicious, self-perpetuating circle: if the state cannot provide social goods and services to the public owing to the public's unwillingness to pay taxes, this will lead the public to become even less trusting of its government – and thus, even less willing to pay taxes.[23] And '[s]uch a cumulative downward spiral', as Joseph S. Nye, Jr. has claimed, tying the concept of political trust to social stability, 'could [ultimately] erode support for democracy as a form of governance'.[24]

The relationship between political trust and public willingness to pay taxes (or public tax compliance) similarly finds support in empirical research. John Scholz and Mark Lubell, for instance, have shown a positive relationship between political trust and public tax compliance using a US Internal Revenue Service survey which asked a sample of taxpayers in New York about tax compliance and civic values.[25] In an

20 Eric M. Uslaner, 'Tax Evasion, Trust, and the Strong Arm of the Law' in Nicolas Hayoz and Simon Hug (eds.), *Tax Evasion, Trust and State Capacities* (Bern: Peter Lang, 2007), p. 19.

21 Nathalie Morel and Joakim Palme, 'Financing the Welfare State and the Politics of Taxation' in Brent Greve (ed.), *The Routledge Handbook of the Welfare State* (Abingdon: Routledge, 2013), p. 407.

22 Norris, 'Conclusion', p. 264.

23 Nye, Jr., 'Introduction', p. 4; Eric M. Uslaner, 'Corruption, the Inequality Trap and Trust in Government' in Zmerli and Hooghe, *Political Trust*, pp. 141–142.

24 Nye, Jr., 'Introduction', p. 4.

25 John T. Scholz and Mark Lubell, 'Trust and Taxpaying: Testing the Heuristic Approach to Collective Action' (1998) 42 *American Journal of Political Science* 398. See also John T. Scholz, 'Trust, Taxes, and Compliance' in Braithwaite and Levi, *Trust and Governance*; John T. Scholz and Neil Pinney, 'Duty, Fear, and Tax Compliance: The Heuristic Basis of

analysis of that survey data combined with in-person interviews, Scholz and Lubell found that trust in government significantly increased the likelihood of respondents' tax compliance. This relationship persisted even after they controlled for the influence of self-interested fear of getting caught and an internalised sense of duty to pay taxes. Based on their results, Scholz and Lubell concluded that 'trust in government … significantly influence[s] tax compliance'.[26] Additionally, Steven Sheffrin and Robert Triest, in a study analysing the same survey data as Scholz and Lubell, found that respondents' attitudes towards government, including a belief that tax money is wasted by government, was the best predictor of underreporting income and overstating deductions.[27] Such attitudes were even a better predictor than the probability of detection and whether fellow members of the public paid their fair share.[28]

Secondly, in addition to public willingness to pay taxes, public cooperation manifests itself as overall public support for governmental social policies. Accordingly, writers have argued that the public's support for its government's social policies likewise depends on its trust in government: if the public does not trust its government, it will not support the policies that its government develops and implements, including social policies that fulfil social rights.[29] It has been suggested that trust functions as a cognitive heuristic that the public relies on when forming opinions about

Citizenship Behavior' (1995) 39 *American Journal of Political Science* 490. While tax compliance was self-reported in the study and thus not directly measured (a point which Scholz and Lubell acknowledge (402)), as Dalton, *Democratic Challenges, Democratic Choices*, p. 169 and Uslaner, 'Tax Evasion, Trust', p. 22, emphasise, it is difficult to objectively measure compliance with government regulations.

26 Scholz and Lubell, 'Trust and Taxpaying', 412.

27 Steven M. Sheffrin and Robert K. Triest, 'Can Brute Deterrence Backfire? Perceptions and Attitudes in Taxpayer Compliance' in Joel Slemrod (ed.), *Why People Pay Taxes* (Ann Arbor: University of Michigan Press, 1992), pp. 193–222.

28 For further empirical support, see Ho Fai Chan, Mohammed Wangsit Supriyadi and Benno Torgler, 'Trust and Tax Morale' in Eric M. Uslaner (ed.), *The Oxford Handbook of Social and Political Trust* (Oxford: Oxford University Press, 2018), pp. 497–534; Dalton, *Democratic Challenges, Democratic Choices*; Christoph Kogler et al., 'Perceptions of Trust and Power Are Associated with Tax Compliance: A Cross-cultural Study' (2023) 11 *Economic and Political Studies* 365; Margaret Levi and Audrey Sacks, 'Legitimating Beliefs: Sources and Indicators' (2009) 3 *Regulation & Governance* 311; Kristina Murphy, 'The Role of Trust in Nurturing Compliance: A Study of Accused Tax Avoiders' (2004) 28 *Law and Human Behavior* 187.

29 See Jonas Edlund, 'Trust in the Capability of the Welfare State and General Welfare State Support: Sweden 1997–2002' (2006) 49 *Acta Sociologica* 395.

social policies.[30] Faced with the complex institutional arrangements of the welfare state and the uncertain consequences of social policies, the public turns to trust: '[o]ther things equal, if people perceive the architect of policies as untrustworthy, they will reject its policies; if they consider it trustworthy, they will be more inclined to embrace them'.[31] And if the public does not support governmental policies, those policies are not likely to succeed. In particular, political trust is necessary to grant governments the flexibility they need to effectively carry out their policies. The more the public trusts its government, the more likely the public will grant what Margaret Levi has termed 'contingent consent'.[32] That is, the public is more likely to support a governmental policy, or at least to tolerate that policy, even if the likely outcome of that policy is perceived to be personally unfavourable to the individual.[33] For example, a public who trusts its government is more likely to agree to a tax increase in support of a policy or to a proposed reform of that policy. For this reason, it is said that aside from its relevance as an influence on the public's provision of critical resources in the form of tax money, political trust is furthermore, as a heuristic linked to public support for social policies, in and of itself 'a critical resource for government'.[34]

The above-noted claim that political trust can impact the public's support for its government's social policies is likewise backed by empirics. Virginia Chanley and colleagues have offered convincing evidence here.[35] Using US survey data specifically, their study examined the relationship between public trust in government and what they refer to as 'policy mood' (a measure reflecting 'the extent of public support for increased government spending and activity across a range of domestic

[30] Marc J. Hetherington, *Why Trust Matters: Declining Political Trust and the Demise of American Liberalism* (Princeton, NJ: Princeton University Press, 2005); Thomas J. Rudolph, 'Political Trust, Ideology, and Public Support for Tax Cuts' (2009) 73 *Public Opinion Quarterly* 144, 144–145; Trüdinger and Bollow, 'Evaluations of Welfare State', p. 191. For a summary, see Thomas J. Rudolph, 'Political Trust as a Heuristic' in Sonja Zmerli and Tom van der Meer (eds.), *Handbook on Political Trust* (Cheltenham: Edward Elgar, 2017), pp. 197–211.

[31] Hetherington, *Why Trust Matters*, p. 51.

[32] Margaret Levi, *Consent, Dissent and Patriotism* (Cambridge: Cambridge University Press, 1997).

[33] Oscar W. Gabriel and Eva-Maria Trüdinger, 'Embellishing Welfare State Reforms? Political Trust and the Support for Welfare State Reforms in Germany' (2011) 20 *German Politics* 273, 275.

[34] Trüdinger and Bollow, 'Evaluations of Welfare State', p. 189.

[35] Virginia A. Chanley, Thomas J. Rudolph and Wendy M. Rahn, 'The Origins and Consequences of Public Trust in Government' (2000) 64 *Public Opinion Quarterly* 239.

policy areas, including education, health care, welfare, aid to cities, and the environment').[36] They found a positive correlation: greater trust in government correlated with greater policy mood. Chanley and colleagues have concluded that their findings are 'consistent with theoretical expectations concerning the importance of trust in government for public willingness to commit public resources for policy ends'.[37] A study conducted by Stefan Svallfors using Swedish survey data yielded similar findings to those of Chanley and colleagues.[38] In fact, contrary to what one may expect, Sven Steinmo has persuasively argued that the difference in the size of the welfare state in Sweden as compared with that of the United States is attributable to a difference in political trust, rather than a difference in citizen want for government spending.[39] In interviews he conducted with citizens of Sweden, the United Kingdom and the United States, Steinmo found that the vast majority – including Americans – said they would agree to an increase in their taxes if they 'could be guaranteed that increased government spending would be efficiently and effectively used to address society's problems'.[40] He found, however, that American respondents were especially likely to follow up their responses saying that they did 'not believe that revenue from higher taxes would be used efficiently or effectively and therefore they would not approve tax increases'.[41] In parallel, Eva-Maria Trüdinger and Uwe Bollow have demonstrated a positive relationship between political trust and support for welfare state reforms.[42] In their interviews with over 1,800 Germans, respondents were asked to report the level of trust they had in various political institutions or actors, and to evaluate the

36 Ibid, p. 245.

37 Ibid, p. 253.

38 Stefan Svallfors, 'Political Trust and Support for the Welfare State: Unpacking a Supposed Relationship' in Bo Rothstein and Sven Steinmo (eds.), *Restructuring the Welfare State: Political Institutions and Policy Change* (London: Palgrave MacMillan, 2002), pp. 184–205.

39 Sven Steinmo, *Taxation and Democracy: Swedish, British and American Approaches to Financing the Modern State* (New Haven, CT: Yale University Press, 1993). See also Sven H. Steinmo, 'American Exceptionalism Reconsidered: Culture or Institutions?' in Lawrence C. Dodd and Calvin Jillson (eds.), *The Dynamics of American Politics: Approaches and Interpretations* (Boulder, CO: Westview Press, 1994), pp. 106–131. For a more recent, but relevant, consideration of this area, see Sven H. Steinmo (ed.), *The Leap of Faith: The Fiscal Foundations of Successful Government in Europe and America* (Oxford: Oxford University Press, 2018).

40 Steinmo, *Taxation and Democracy*, p. 199.

41 Ibid, p. 199.

42 Trüdinger and Bollow, 'Evaluations of Welfare State'.

direction of recent reforms on health care, pension and family policy. Trüdinger and Bollow 'found significant effects of political trust': the more respondents trusted government, the more likely they were to agree with the reforms.[43]

The public tax compliance and social policy support that follow from political trust are especially important today given present circumstances that make the public funding and delivery of social goods and services ever-more challenging. In 2001, Paul Pierson wrote that the welfare state in affluent democracies faces a context of 'permanent austerity'.[44] By this he meant that owing to a set of circumstances that have generated much fiscal stress for countries – including changes in the global economy, a slowdown in economic growth, aging populations and reduced fertility rates – it is increasingly difficult for governments to finance previously made commitments to social goods and services. Contrary to then-popular beliefs, Pierson prophesied that given persistent public support for the welfare state, the result of these pressures would not be the welfare state's dismantling, but, rather, moderate cost-cutting efforts by governments. For him, 'neither the alternatives of standing pat or dismantling are likely to prove viable in most countries'; instead, 'we should expect strong pressures to move towards more centrist – and therefore more incremental – responses' with '[t]hose seeking to generate significant cost reductions while modernizing particular aspects of social provision … [holding] the balance of political power'.[45]

Over the past 20 years, we have witnessed the sort of cost-cutting efforts that Pierson prophesied – in both affluent and developing democracies alike.[46] In fact, owing to the 2008 global financial and economic crisis, the COVID-19 public health crisis and the follow-on cost-of-living

[43] Ibid. For further empirical support, see Eun Young Nam and Myungsook Woo, 'Who Is Willing to Pay More Taxes for Welfare? Focusing on the Effects of Diverse Types of Trust in South Korea and Taiwan' (2015) 44 *Development and Society* 319. For a relatively recent summary, see Jack Citrin and Laura Stoker, 'Political Trust in a Cynical Age' (2018) 21 *Annual Review of Political Science* 49, 61–62.

[44] Paul Pierson, 'Coping with Permanent Austerity: Welfare State Restructuring in Affluent Democracies' in Paul Pierson (ed.), *The New Politics of the Welfare State* (Oxford: Oxford University Press, 2001).

[45] Ibid, p. 417.

[46] James Connelly, 'Conclusion: Remaining the Welfare State?' in James Connelly and Jack Hayward (eds.), *The Withering of the Welfare State: Regression* (London: Palgrave Macmillan, 2012), pp. 208–216; Staffan Kumlin, 'Overloaded or Undermined? European Welfare States in the Face of Performance Dissatisfaction' in Svallfors, *The Political Sociology of the Welfare State*, pp. 80–116.

or socio-economic crisis, austerity has become the 'new normal'.[47] Although the global financial and COVID-19 crises did, at least initially, lead to periods of fiscal expansion, those expansion periods were short-lived (limited to one or two years) and were followed by long periods of fiscal austerity, with the current period of fiscal austerity expected to last until 2025.[48] In both cases, many governments globally reduced public spending, frequently on social goods and services.[49]

Given the current state of events, it seems that now, more than ever, governments need the public to pay taxes and to support social policies. If not, the lack of cooperation in this regard, coupled with the circumstances that have given rise to 'permanent austerity' and the string of recent crises, will seriously endanger the ability of states to provide social goods and services to the public. The significance of political trust to social rights law, I therefore submit, is undeniable.

1.2 The Book's Objectives

Owing, at least in part, to the above link between trust and cooperation, there have been a growing number of scholarly calls for greater attention to be paid to trust in our study of law.[50] As Frank Cross once commented: '[t]he importance of trust should surely command the attention of lawmakers be they legislators, administrators, or judges. Trust, obviously essential to successful interpersonal relationships, is also of great significance to national economic well-being and governance.'[51] The concept of trust is not new to law, however. Legal scholars, in fields ranging from contracts and trusts to medical and fiduciary law, have

[47] See Aoife Nolan, 'Introduction' in Aoife Nolan (ed.), *Economic and Social Rights after the Global Financial Crisis* (Cambridge: Cambridge University Press, 2014), pp. 1–4; Isabel Ortiz and Matthew Cummins, 'Austerity: The New Normal: A Renewed Washington Consensus 2010–24' (Initiative for Policy Dialogue, Working Paper, October 2019) http://policydialogue.org/files/publications/papers/Austerity-the-New-Normal-Ortiz-Cummins-6-Oct-2019.pdf, accessed 16 November 2022, 9; Isabel Ortiz and Matthew Cummins, 'End Austerity: A Global Report on Budget Cuts and Harmful Social Reforms in 2022–25' (Initiative for Policy Dialogue, September 2022) https://assets.nationbuilder.com/eurodad/pages/3039/attachments/original/1664184662/Austerity_Ortiz_Cummins_FINAL_26-09.pdf?1664184662, accessed 16 November 2022, 8–15.

[48] Ortiz and Cummins, 'End Austerity', 8, 9.

[49] Ibid, 8.

[50] See Matthew Harding, 'Manifesting Trust' (2009) 29 *Oxford Journal of Legal Studies* 245; Tom R. Tyler, 'Trust and Law Abidingness: A Proactive Model of Social Regulation' (2001) 81 *Boston University Law Review* 361.

[51] Frank B. Cross, 'Law and Trust' (2005) 93 *Georgetown Law Journal* 1457, 1459.

recognised the importance of trust to law, and have used the concept to better understand and advance their respective fields.[52] Matthew Harding, for instance, in his work using trust to study fiduciary law, has proposed that legal scholars' frequent references to the concept of trust 'suggests that trust may be an important organizing idea when thinking about what law is, what effect it has and what it ought to be doing'.[53]

Trust is likewise not new to public law. Not only is the concept deeply embedded in the writings of many political philosophers,[54] trust additionally has gained prevalence in modern public law scholarship. For example, there is a growing body of work that emphasises the fiduciary foundations of public authority – a body described as 'fiduciary political theory'.[55] Legal scholars in this camp have argued that various relationships in the political realm – including those between political representatives and the people, judges and the people, and administrative agencies

52 Anthony J. Bellia, Jr., 'Promises, Trust, and Contract Law' (2002) 47 *American Journal of Jurisprudence* 25; Margaret M. Blair and Lynn A. Stout, 'Trust, Trustworthiness, and the Behavioral Foundations of Corporate Law' (2001) 149 *University of Pennsylvania Law Review* 1735; Roger Cotterrell, 'Trusting in Law: Legal and Moral Concepts of Trust' (1993) 46 *Current Legal Problems* 75; Cross, 'Law and Trust'; Mark A. Hall, 'Law, Medicine, and Trust' (2002) 55 *Stanford Law Review* 463; Mark A. Hall, 'The Importance of Trust for Ethics, Law, and Public Policy' (2005) 14 *Cambridge Quarterly of Healthcare Ethics* 156; Harding, 'Manifesting Trust'; Matthew Harding, 'Responding to Trust' (2011) 24 *Ratio Juris* 75. See also the various chapters in Paul B. Miller and Matthew Harding (eds.), *Fiduciaries and Trust: Ethics, Politics, Economics and Law* (Cambridge: Cambridge University Press, 2020).

53 Harding, 'Manifesting Trust', 245. See also Matthew Harding, 'Contracts, Fiduciary Relationships and Trust' in Miller and Harding, *Fiduciaries and Trust*, pp. 55–73.

54 See Deborah Baumgold, 'Trust in Hobbes' Political Thought' (2013) 20 *Political Theory* 1; Patti Tamara Lenard, 'The Political Philosophy of Trust and Distrust in Democracies and Beyond' (2015) 98 *The Monist* 353. See also the various chapters in Lazlo Kontler and Mark Somos (eds.), *Trust and Happiness in the History of European Political Thought* (Leiden: Brill, 2017).

55 As a representative sample, see Evan J. Criddle, 'Fiduciary Foundations of Administrative Law' (2006) 54 *UCLA Law Review* 117; Evan Fox-Decent, 'The Fiduciary Nature of State Legal Authority' (2005) 31 *Queen's Law Journal* 259; Evan Fox-Decent, *Sovereignty's Promise: The State as Fiduciary* (Oxford: Oxford University Press, 2011); Ethan J. Leib, David L. Ponet and Michael Serota, 'A Fiduciary Theory of Judging' (2013) 101 *California Law Review* 699; D. Theodore Rave, 'Politicians as Fiduciaries' (2013) 126 *Harvard Law Review* 671. The terminology of 'fiduciary political theory' was coined by Ethan J. Leib, David L. Ponet and Michael Serota, 'Translating Fiduciary Principles into Public Law' (2013) 126 *Harvard Law Review Forum* 91, 91.

and the people – are fairly characterised as fiduciary in nature. Of particular note, for many of these fiduciary political theory scholars, it is trust that lies at the core of this fiduciary characterisation.

Trust has never been used, however, to advance the study of social rights law. This book seeks to fill that gap in the literature. As I outlined earlier, I use the concept of political trust to build, in particular, a normative argument about the appropriate role of the courts in enforcing constitutional social rights. That argument is the one identified at the outset: that the courts, when enforcing these rights against government actors, should focus their analysis on political trust, aiming specifically to promote the trustworthiness of government actors vis-à-vis their provision of social goods and services to the public. And in tandem with that argument, I develop a new legal framework, rooted in political trust, for judicially enforcing social rights. To develop this normative argument and trust-based legal framework for social rights enforcement, I use political trust as an analytical lens for social rights law – that is, I analyse the law, especially the judicial enforcement of social rights, with reference to theoretical and empirical research on the concept of trust from various disciplines, including philosophy, sociology, psychology and political theory.

In developing this normative argument and trust-based legal framework, I centre my analysis on a specific relationship: the relationship that exists, in constitutional, social democracies, between citizens and the representative or elected branches of government, particularly with respect to social rights (what I refer to as the 'citizen–government relationship'). Before proceeding, I will clarify a few terms. First, by 'constitutional, social democracies', I mean democratic states where (i) state actors, including the courts, are bound by a constitution that grants and constrains those actors' powers, and (ii) citizens are provided by the state with a subset of social goods and services, following on from social rights that are guaranteed in the constitution. Next, by 'representative or elected branches of government', I mean the legislature and the executive, the latter of which includes civil servants and the administrative agencies relevant to social welfare. Lastly, by 'citizens', I do not mean it in the sense of citizenship as legal status. I use the term, rather, to refer to those individuals guaranteed social rights under the relevant constitution. So, depending on the jurisdiction, the term may include residents and individuals of other legal status.

In constitutional, social democracies, there exists a relationship between citizens and the representative or elected branches of government with respect to social rights. To repeat, citizens pay taxes to the state and using the revenue collected from those taxes, the state provides citizens with a range of social goods and services by delivering social programmes. Constitutional social rights afford citizens constitutional protections vis-à-vis those goods and services, and establish corresponding state obligations.[56] Hence, it is this relationship around which my analysis revolves.

I have chosen this relationship owing to the literature to which I seek to contribute. This book's focus is on the longstanding conversation among jurists and politicians about the judicial enforcement of social rights. That conversation, including its 'first wave' on justiciability, is premised on a distinction between the legislature and the executive – as elected bodies – and the judiciary – as an unelected body. As I explain in Chapter 4, this distinction has been used by some commentators to challenge the legitimacy of the courts in deciding social rights matters. At the same time, it has been used by other commentators to argue for greater judicial involvement in this area because courts, being unelected, are arguably in a better position to protect the interests of low-income citizens not adequately represented in the political and democratic processes. There is thus an orthodoxy in the social rights literature to focus on the tripartite relationship between citizens, these representative or elected branches, and the courts. For this reason, I have chosen to exclude the courts from the citizen–government relationship. I have also chosen to collapse the legislature and the executive into one body (what I refer to as the 'elected branches'). While I recognise that there is an important distinction to be drawn between the legislature and the executive, I do not want that distinction to overshadow the distinction between the elected branches and the courts, which is more central to my analysis. Where the distinction between the legislature and the executive is relevant to my analysis, however, I consider the two independently.

1.3 The Book's Scope

In the interests of greater clarity, I will take a moment here to outline the scope of the book.

[56] Such rights may guarantee citizens the social goods and services themselves or they may guarantee citizens 'access' (or some equivalent) to the social goods and services.

1.3.1 *Defining Constitutional Social Rights*

First of all, I think that the term 'constitutional social rights' requires some clarification. As Jeff King has helpfully catalogued, there are many different senses in which we may use the term 'social rights'.[57] Not only are there both moral and legal senses to the term, but when social rights are used in their legal sense, they may have different sources, including international law, national legislation and national constitutions. In this book, my focus is national constitutions. So, when I refer to 'social rights' in this book, unless otherwise stated, I mean such constitutionalised social rights. In particular, I am concerned mainly with a defined, but rather large, subset of constitutional social rights: rights to health, housing, education and social security.[58] Additionally, in referring to constitutional social rights, I do not mean only those rights set out expressly in a constitutional document. In using the term, I also refer to social rights that have been read into general constitutional provisions (e.g., rights to life, human dignity or security of the person) by the courts. Lastly, it is well recognised that social rights give rise to a tripartite set of duties on governments: to respect (a duty of non-interference), to protect (a duty to prevent interference or denial by third parties) and to fulfil (a duty to positively provide).[59] It is the duty to fulfil that is my primary concern in this book as it raises the greatest issues of public resource allocation, making it the main reason why the enforcement of constitutional social rights by the courts is so contentious. Therefore, 'social rights', as used in this book, also refers specifically to positive social rights of this nature.

1.3.2 *Political Trust, Not Social Trust*

In the political arena, the literature on trust has recognised four categories of relationships in which trust operates: the trust of citizens in their

[57] King, *Judging Social Rights*, pp. 18–19.

[58] For a study with a similar focus, see ibid. In line with a well-established orthodoxy in the social rights literature, I am not concerned with labour rights (or what are often termed 'economic' rights). Also, while some commentators prefer the language of the 'right to health care', I use the 'right to health', which also appears often in the literature.

[59] Henry Shue, *Basic Rights, Subsistence, Affluence, and U.S. Foreign Policy* (Princeton, NJ: Princeton University Press, 1980), p. 52; Henry Shue, 'The Interdependence of Duties' in Philip Alston and Katarina Tomasevski (eds.), *The Right to Food* (Leiden: Martinus Nijhoff Publishers, 1985), p. 86. See also David Bilchitz, *Poverty and Fundamental Rights: The Justification and Enforcement of Socio-economic Rights* (Oxford: Oxford University Press, 2007), p. 184; King, *Judging Social Rights*, p. 35.

fellow citizens (what is often referred to as 'social trust'); the trust of citizens in state actors, including both political and legal institutions, as well as the individuals who staff them (what is often referred to as, and what I am calling, 'political trust'); the horizontal trust among state actors; and the top-down vertical relationship where state actors form beliefs and expectations about the behavioural dispositions of citizens.[60] This book does not address the category of social trust. It focuses predominantly on political trust, particularly citizens' trust in legislative and executive actors, and to some extent, the other two. While I acknowledge that social trust and political trust are related, as many writers have argued, there are also significant differences between the two types of trust, including with respect to their underlying foundations and consequences.[61] Hence, I leave the concept of social trust aside for the purpose of this book.

In focusing on political trust, I want to emphasise that I am not concerned, at least not per se, with citizens' trust in the courts. I say 'not per se' because some of the claims that I make do rest on an assumption, to some extent, that citizens trust the courts. This is the case, for example, with my claim in Chapter 4 that the courts, via their enforcement of social rights, can foster trust in the citizen–government relationship. As I explain there, for social rights enforcement to promote the elected branches' trustworthiness with respect to social rights, and foster citizens' trust in the elected branches, citizens must trust the courts. Specifically, they must trust the courts to hold the elected branches accountable where those branches do not fulfil citizens' trust in them.

The assumption that I make of citizens' trust in the courts is not baseless. Empirical studies have consistently shown across jurisdictions that relative to the elected branches of government, the courts benefit from a high level of public support or trust.[62] Of course, there are

60 See Claus Offe, 'How Can We Trust Our Fellow Citizens?' in Mark E. Warren (ed.), *Democracy and Trust* (Cambridge: Cambridge University Press, 1999), p. 44.

61 For a consideration of the difference between social trust and political trust, see Kenneth Newton, 'Social and Political Trust in Established Democracies' in Norris, *Critical Citizens*, p. 179.

62 For relevant surveys, see, for example, OECD: OECD, 'Building Trust to Reinforce Democracy: Summary Brief Presenting the Main Findings from the OECD Trust Survey' (2022), www.oecd.org/governance/trust-in-government/oecd-trust-survey-main-findings-en.pdf, accessed 7 March 2022, 2 (with 56.9 per cent of respondents across 22 countries in 2021 having trust in the courts, compared to 41.4 per cent for national

circumstances in which the public does not trust the courts. For instance, in some jurisdictions, recent years have seen a decline in the public's support or trust in the courts, especially with the COVID-19 public health crisis.[63] Likewise, in jurisdictions where judicial corruption is widespread (as I discuss in Chapter 7), the public is less likely to trust the courts. And these circumstances may seem to undermine the above claim as well as the trust-based framework that I propose. This may be true. But in these circumstances, I think the same can be said for any approach to social rights enforcement. Owing to the link between political trust and public cooperation, public trust in the courts is central to the rule of law, necessary for public respect of the law and compliance with court decisions.[64] No matter which approach to social rights enforcement is adopted, it will be undermined by the public's lack of

government and 39.4 per cent for national legislatures); South Africa: Afrobarometer, 'South Africans' Trust in Institutions and Representatives Reaches New Low' (24 August 2021), https://news.gallup.com/poll/4732/supreme-court.aspx, accessed 7 March 2022, 7 (with 42 per cent of respondents in 2021 indicating that they had 'a lot' of trust or 'somewhat' trusted the courts, compared to 38 per cent for the President and 27 per cent for Parliament; and these numbers were significantly higher in previous years); UK: Office for National Statistics, 'Trust in Government, UK: 2022' (2022), www.ons.gov.uk/peoplepopulationandcommunity/wellbeing/bulletins/trustingovernmentuk/2022, accessed 7 March 2022 (with 68 per cent of respondents in 2022 indicating trust in the courts and legal system, compared to 35 per cent for national government and 42 per cent for local government); US: Gallup, 'Trust in Government' (2022), https://news.gallup.com/poll/5392/trust-government.aspx, accessed 7 March 2022 (with 47 per cent of respondents in 2022 indicating a 'great deal' or 'fair amount' of trust in the judicial branch, compared to 43 per cent for the executive branch and 38 per cent for the legislative branch). For scholarship in this area, see Gregory A. Caldeira and James L. Gibson, 'The Etiology of Public Support for the Supreme Court' (1992) 36 *American Journal of Political Science* 635; Gregory A. Caldeira and James L. Gibson, 'The Legitimacy of the Court of Justice in the European Union: Models of Institutional Support' (1995) 89 *American Political Science Review* 356; James L. Gibson, Gregory A. Caldeira and Vanessa A. Baird, 'On the Legitimacy of National High Courts' (1998) 92 *American Political Science Review* 343; James L. Gibson, Gregory A. Caldeira and Lester Kenyatta Spence, 'Measuring Attitudes toward the United States Supreme Court' (2003) 47 *American Journal of Political Science* 354; James L. Gibson and Gregory A. Caldeira, *Citizens, Courts, and Confirmations* (Princeton, NJ: Princeton University Press, 2009).

63 See Gallup, 'Supreme Court Trust, Jobs Approval at Historical Lows' (29 September 2022), https://news.gallup.com/poll/402044/supreme-court-trust-job-approval-historical-lows.aspx, accessed 7 March 2022 (indicating a 20-percentage-point drop in trust for the judicial branch in the US between 2020 and 2022); Afrobarometer, 'South Africans' Trust' (indicating that, for the first time, public trust in the courts has fallen below 50 per cent); Anne Wallace and Jane Goodman-Delahunty, 'Measuring Trust and Confidence in Courts' (2021) 12 *International Journal for Court Administration* 1.

64 Wallace and Goodman-Delahunty, 'Measuring Trust and Confidence in Courts'.

trust in the courts. I therefore submit that where the assumption does not hold – and citizens do not, in fact, trust the courts – we must remedy citizens' lack of trust. Remedying that lack of trust in the courts, however, is not something I address in this book.

1.3.3 Political Trust, Not Political Satisfaction

As well, political trust in this book should be distinguished from what may be termed 'political satisfaction'. There is a tendency among lay-people and writers on trust alike to conflate citizens' trust in government actors and their satisfaction with the outcomes that the government produces. As I elaborate in Chapter 2, this conflation follows on from what I suggest are erroneous definitions of trust as a concept. Some writers on trust define the concept in terms of outcome – that is, I trust you if I expect that you will produce an outcome that is favourable to me. By this definition, if I am satisfied with the outcomes that you have produced in the past, I should expect you to produce outcomes that are favourable to me in the future, and it necessarily follows on from that expectation that I trust you. For reasons that I describe in that chapter, however, such a definition of trust is problematic. Instead, trust is better understood, I suggest, in procedural terms – that is, I trust you if I expect that you will follow a defined procedure in your interaction with me. I define the relevant procedure in much greater detail in the forthcoming chapters. Accordingly, in this book, I maintain a distinction between political trust and political satisfaction.

As a necessary implication of this, the trust-based framework that I propose draws a distinction between the procedure followed by the elected branches in making decisions about social goods and services, and the outcome of that decision-making. Under the framework, the courts, in enforcing social rights, focus on the former rather than the latter. Granted, the procedure-outcome distinction is not clear-cut;[65] but at this point, I simply want to flag that the framework leans heavily towards procedure. This idea is discussed in detail in Chapters 2 and 4.

[65] Colm O'Cinneide, 'Legal Accountability and Social Justice' in Nicholas Bamforth and Peter Leyland (eds.), *Accountability in the Contemporary Constitution* (Oxford: Oxford University Press, 2013), p. 392.

1.3.4 'Warranted' or 'Intelligent' Trust, Not Blind Trust

Not all trust in government is good. As I highlight in Chapter 4, some scholars have pointed out that political trust may in fact be detrimental (i.e., where government is not trustworthy); and in these cases, citizen distrust or scepticism is beneficial because it 'keeps constituents alert, and thus public officials responsive'.[66] I do not dispute that argument. I do, however, draw a distinction between blind trust, and 'warranted' or 'intelligent' trust.[67] I elaborate on the distinction between these types of trust in Chapter 4. Thus, when I reference the recognised value of political trust (i.e., following on from the link between political trust and public cooperation), I mean the latter.

1.3.5 Theoretical Arguments, Not an Empirical Investigation

I also want to say something about the nature of the claims that I make in this book. Like most fields of study, the literature on trust is composed of two principal categories. First, there is a body of theoretical work. Scholars across disciplines have conceptualised what trust is, have theorised how we can expect trust to function, and have made theoretically grounded predictions on the consequences of increased and decreased trust. Secondly, scientists have conducted empirical investigations of trust. In an effort to test untested theoretical arguments or to understand more generally the social determinants and consequences of trust, they have examined the relationship between trust and many variables. The approach I adopt in this book falls into the former category. I do not offer an empirical investigation of political trust. I advance, rather, theoretical arguments regarding political trust and the judicial

[66] Karen S. Cook, Russell Hardin and Margaret Levi, *Cooperation without Trust?* (New York: Russell Sage Foundation, 2005), p. 165; Margaret Levi, 'A State of Trust' in Braithwaite and Levi, *Trust and Governance*, pp. 95–96; Onora O'Neill, *A Question of Trust* (Cambridge: Cambridge University Press, 2002); Onora O'Neill, 'Trust, Trustworthiness, and Accountability' in Nicholas Morris and David Vines (eds.), *Capital Failure: Rebuilding Trust in Financial Institutions* (Oxford: Oxford University Press, 2014), pp. 172–190; Onora O'Neill, 'Accountable Institutions, Trustworthy Cultures' (2017) 9 *Hague Journal on the Rule of Law* 401.

[67] Mark E. Warren, 'Introduction' in Mark E. Warren (ed.), *Democracy and Trust* (Cambridge: Cambridge University Press, 1999), p. 4; Mark E. Warren, 'Democratic Theory and Trust' in Warren, *Democracy and Trust*; Mark Warren, 'Trust and Democracy' in Eric M. Uslaner (ed.), *The Oxford Handbook of Social and Political Trust* (Oxford: Oxford University Press, 2018), pp. 75–94; O'Neill, 'Trust, Trustworthiness, and Accountability', p. 178.

enforcement of constitutional social rights. And in doing so, I import theoretical and empirical research on trust into this area of law.

To be clear, in using the term 'empirical', I seek to distinguish the theoretical arguments that I advance regarding trust, from the empirical studies that have been conducted in the social science scholarship on trust. I do not mean to suggest, however, that I will only be considering social rights enforcement in an abstract way without reference to cases and other jurisdiction-specific materials. As we will see later, particularly in Chapters 5–7, I use cases and constitutions from a wide range of jurisdictions, including Canada, Colombia, Germany, Kenya, Latvia, South Africa, Uganda and the UK, to illustrate how the trust-based framework operates in practice.

1.3.6 Restriction to Social and Constitutional Democracies

Lastly, I point out that the arguments advanced in this book are, at least technically, restricted to specific jurisdictions. First, owing to the book's focus on constitutional social rights and their enforcement by courts, its arguments are restricted to constitutional democracies, as I have defined that term, with a system of judicial review. Secondly, because the book is focused on social rights that are positive in nature – and the corresponding duty on governments to fulfil the rights in question – its arguments are also restricted to social democracies, as I have defined that term.

I say 'at least technically' because in my view, this book's arguments also have relevance for, and can be applied to, jurisdictions beyond these two categories. In particular, I want to highlight their relevance for jurisdictions that do not meet the definition of a social democracy. Technically speaking, the trust-based framework that I propose can only be applied by courts in jurisdictions where social rights have been constitutionalised. If a jurisdiction has not constitutionalised social rights, there are no rights to be enforced and consequently, nothing to which the framework can be applied. However, in jurisdictions where social rights have not been constitutionalised, the framework nonetheless offers the courts a recommendation about how, if their jurisdictions were to constitutionalise social rights (either via constitutional amendment or by the courts reading them into general provisions), they could, and I would put forward should, enforce the rights. And in cases where courts in these jurisdictions have been hesitant to read social rights into their constitutions' general provisions (as is the case in Canada, for example, as we will see in Chapter 5), to the extent that this hesitation is attributable to concerns about the drawbacks of existing enforcement frameworks, the trust-based framework may help allay these concerns.

1.4 A Cautionary Note about the Applicability of the Trust-Based Framework

Despite the above restrictions, the trust-based framework, I am thus suggesting, can be applied to a very large number of jurisdictions with different legal systems (e.g., common law and civil law), constitutional cultures, political climates and socio-economic structures. In making this suggestion, I recognise the problems with advocating a uniform legal approach across jurisdictions.[68] At the same time, however, owing to political trust's tie to social stability, economic welfare and effective governance – ends which are not jurisdiction specific – alongside the reasons that I present in Chapter 4 for why trust should provide the basis for a social rights enforcement framework, the trust-based framework, in my view, has broad currency. So, rather than take an overly cautious approach and restrict the framework to a small set of jurisdictions, I present the framework at a general level, leaving it to readers with expertise in their respective jurisdictions to determine more precisely how it applies to their jurisdictions, including any required modifications. However, I do want to stress that the framework cannot, and will not, apply in exactly the same manner across different jurisdictions. For instance, as I point out in Chapters 4 and 7, it will apply differently depending on constitutional text, including the language used in relevant social rights provisions.

Following on from the trust-based framework's broad applicability, I use a wide range of jurisdictions to illustrate the framework, particularly in Chapters 5–7. As I have mentioned, these include Canada, Colombia, Germany, Kenya, Latvia, South Africa, Uganda and the UK. I have chosen these jurisdictions for many reasons. First, I have done so because their respective courts have decided social rights cases which, in my view, are especially apt at demonstrating the trust-based framework. In some cases, the relevant jurisdictions do not meet the definitions of constitutional democracy and social democracy that I have set out (e.g., Canada

[68] See Colm O'Cinneide, 'The Problematic of Social Rights – Uniformity and Diversity in the Development of Social Rights Review' in Liora Lazarus, Christopher McCrudden and Nigel Bowles (eds.), *Reasoning Rights: Comparative Judicial Engagement* (Oxford: Hart, 2014), pp. 299–317.

and the UK). But as I explain later, these jurisdictions and their respective cases are nonetheless valuable to illustrate how the trust-based framework operates in practice. Secondly, I have chosen these jurisdictions for practical reasons. These include my linguistic limitations as an English-language speaker (with these jurisdictions' courts either publishing in English or having translations and academic commentary available in English), and my legal training and familiarity with many of these jurisdictions. Lastly, but related to my first point, I have also chosen many of these jurisdictions in the interests of clarity. Given the novelty of political trust, both as a concept and as a vocabulary for the area of social rights law, I think it makes sense to illustrate the framework with reference to familiar cases from familiar jurisdictions (e.g., South Africa, Germany and Canada). At the same time, however, given scholarly criticisms of the prevalent pattern in the social rights scholarship to focus on a limited set of jurisdictions, I have sought to balance my use of familiar jurisdictions with less familiar and under-represented ones in the scholarship (e.g., Kenya, Latvia and Uganda).[69]

1.5 Situating the Trust-Based Framework in Existing Frameworks

The trust-based framework that I propose aligns, in certain respects, with approaches that have either been employed by courts in different jurisdictions or proposed by other academic writers. This should not be too surprising since we should expect existing approaches, even if only done on an intuitive level, to promote the trustworthiness of government actors vis-à-vis their provision of social goods and services. And in detailing the framework in subsequent chapters, I will highlight the relevant alignments. However, the trust-based framework is also distinguishable from such approaches in many respects. In subsequent chapters, I will also point out these differences, and the corresponding limitations, in my view, of alternative approaches to social rights enforcement.

That said, as an introduction to the framework and its contribution to the literature, I will briefly outline some key differences. First, what distinguishes the trust-based framework from other approaches to social rights enforcement is its comprehensiveness. As we will see in Chapter 2, trust consists of three expectations – goodwill, competence and fiduciary

[69] See Ran Hirschl, 'From Comparative Constitutional Law to Comparative Constitutional Studies' (2013) 11 *International Journal of Constitutional Law* 1, 8–9.

responsibility. These expectations, when applied to the citizen–government relationship and used to develop the framework, incorporate into social rights enforcement several requirements, including government transparency, engagement or participation, equality, evidence-based policy-making and non-corruption. While each of these requirements has, to some extent, been advocated in the social rights literature and employed by various courts in their social rights cases, they have never been brought together to construct a unified legal framework. The trust-based framework does precisely this, with the aim of promoting the trustworthiness of government actors vis-à-vis their provision of social goods and services. Thus, in line with what Harding has argued vis-à-vis law more broadly, the concept of political trust, in the framework, serves as an organising idea for social rights law.

Secondly, owing to trust's procedural orientation, the trust-based framework – which focuses on the procedure followed by the elected branches in making resource allocation decisions – stands in contrast to approaches that focus on the outcome of that decision-making. This includes the individualised enforcement model prevalent in Latin American jurisdictions. As I explain in Chapter 4, that model is problematic – in terms of the separation of powers and equity. The trust-based framework, as a principally procedural approach, does not share these problems.

The trust-based framework instead aligns with procedural approaches to social rights enforcement, including the 'reasonableness review' standard used by the South African Constitutional Court in enforcing its social rights. That said, for reasons I explain in Chapter 4, the framework mitigates concerns that have been raised in the literature about such approaches.[70]

[70] David Bilchitz, 'Giving Socio-economic Rights Teeth: The Minimum Core and Its Importance' (2002) 119 *South African Law Journal* 484; Bilchitz, *Poverty and Fundamental Rights*, pp. 136–176; Danie Brand, 'The Proceduralisation of South African Socio-economic Rights Jurisprudence, or "What Are Socio-economic Rights For?"' in Henk Botha, Andre van der Walt and Johan van der Walt (eds.), *Rights and Democracy in a Transformative Constitution* (Stellenbosch: Sun Press, 2003), pp. 33–56; Marius Pieterse, 'Resuscitating Socio-economic Rights: Constitutional Entitlements to Health Care Services' (2006) 22 *South African Journal on Human Rights* 473; Marius Pieterse, 'Eating Socioeconomic Rights: The Usefulness of Rights Talk in Alleviating Social Hardship Revisited' (2007) 29 *Human Rights Quarterly* 796. There have also been more recent criticisms aimed at the 'proceduralisation' of social rights in terms of the court's adoption of engagement as an enforcement tool in social rights cases: for example,

1.6 The Book's Structure

Chapters 2 and 3 lay some necessary conceptual foundation. Chapter 2 draws on theoretical and empirical literature to offer a conceptualisation of trust in the social rights context. It first envisages trust as relational, meaning that trust may only arise in a relationship that contains three elements: control, discretion/uncertainty and vulnerability (a 'trust relationship'). Secondly, it defines trust in a trust relationship as a set of three expectations held by a truster about a trustee: an expectation that the trustee will exercise goodwill towards the truster ('expectation of goodwill'); an expectation that the trustee will exercise competence towards the truster ('expectation of competence'); and an expectation that the trustee will fulfil their fiduciary responsibility (if any) to the truster ('expectation of fiduciary responsibility'). The chapter then applies this conceptualisation to the citizen–government relationship, characterising it as a trust relationship and defining trust in it.

Chapter 3 adds a further layer of conceptual foundation by applying to the citizen–government relationship what I call the 'network conception of trust' from the scholarship on trust. In doing so, it makes a claim of how trust functions in the social rights context. According to this conception, trust arises in, and depends on, complex structures or networks of relationships. Applying this conception to the citizen–government relationship, the chapter therefore argues that in contemporary democracies, the citizen–government relationship exists in a network of relationships and that trust in the citizen–government relationship depends on the relationships that constitute the network – including, importantly, the relationship between citizens and the courts that arises out of the adjudication of social rights by courts. This argument adds nuance to our understanding of trust and lays foundation for my contention in Chapter 4 that the courts, via their enforcement of social rights, can foster citizens' trust in the elected branches.

Using the foundation laid in Chapters 2 and 3, Chapter 4 outlines four justifications for why political trust is not only a valuable perspective from which to examine social rights law but should also provide the basis for a social rights enforcement framework. The first justification relates to the value of political trust to well-functioning democracies. The second follows on from what I argue is the fiduciary nature of the citizen–

see Kirsty McLean, 'Meaningful Engagement: One Step Forward or Two Back? Some Thoughts on *Joe Slovo*' (2010) 3 *Constitutional Court Review* 223.

government relationship, in line with the growing fiduciary political theory literature. The third pertains to political trust's fit with social rights adjudication. By this I mean that political trust responds well to the challenges posed by social rights adjudication. And the final justification is linked to a traditional defence for constitutional review – that is, constitutional review's potential to support or enhance democracy. I suggest that consistent with this defence, the trust-based framework supports democracy. The chapter also lays the foundation for the final three chapters – Chapters 5–7 – by offering a brief overview of what a trust-based framework for the judicial enforcement of social rights involves.

Chapters 5–7 then proceed to develop the framework. Each chapter focuses on a constituent expectation of trust as applied to the citizen–government relationship: Chapter 5 on the expectation of goodwill; Chapter 6 on the expectation of competence; and Chapter 7 on the expectation of fiduciary responsibility. Each one also uses various social rights cases to illustrate.

2

Conceptualising Trust in the Social Rights Context

Writers on trust generally agree that trust is a context-specific concept.[1] Put simply, what trust means in one context may not necessarily hold in another. For this reason, Russell Hardin has stressed that it is inaccurate and unhelpful to provide an all-encompassing or 'true' definition of trust. He has warned: '[n]o matter how enticing it may sometimes be, to engage in that debate is foolish'.[2] My goal in this chapter is thus a modest one. Based on my reading of the theoretical and empirical literature on trust, I put forward 'a workable notion' of the concept, which is useable, I think, in the social rights context; and I apply that notion to the citizen–government relationship to define what it means for citizens to trust the elected branches with respect to social rights.[3]

2.1 Trust as a Relational Concept: Defining a 'Trust Relationship'

Following the lead of several prominent writers on trust, I choose to conceptualise trust as relational. By this I mean that trust is a property of a social relationship.[4] That relationship is of a three-part form comprising a trustee (A), a truster (B) and a good or service (X), where the relationship

1 Bernard Barber, *The Logic and Limits of Trust* (New Brunswick, NJ: Rutgers University Press, 1983), pp. 16–17; Karen S. Cook and Russell Hardin, 'Norms of Cooperativeness and Networks of Trust' in Michael Hechter and Karl-Dieter Opp (eds.), *Social Norms* (New York: Russell Sage Foundation, 2001), p. 331; Diego Gambetta, 'Can We Trust Trust?' in Diego Gambetta (ed.), *Trust: Making and Breaking Cooperative Relations* (Oxford: Basil Blackwell, 1988), p. 219; Trudy Govier, *Social Trust and Human Communities* (Kingston, ON: McGill-Queen's University Press, 1997), p. 6; Richard Holton, 'Deciding to Trust, Coming to Believe' (1994) 72 *Australian Journal of Philosophy* 63, 67; Matthew Harding, 'Manifesting Trust' (2009) 29 *Oxford Journal of Legal Studies* 245, 246; Karen Jones, 'Trust as an Affective Attitude' (1996) 107 *Ethics* 4, 5.

2 Russell Hardin, 'Conceptions and Explanations of Trust' in Karen S. Cook (ed.), *Trust in Society* (New York: Russell Sage Foundation, 2001), p. 9.

3 Ibid.

4 Cook and Hardin, 'Norms of Cooperativeness', pp. 330–331.

takes the form of 'B trusts A with respect to X'.[5] This relational view of trust is to be distinguished from a competing view of the concept which instead treats trust as a trait or a disposition of an individual actor (i.e., the truster).[6] I elaborate on this distinction in Chapter 3.

Based on my reading of the trust scholarship from various disciplines, I propose that three elements are essential for trust to arise in that relationship between A and B: (i) A must maintain control over a good or service (X); (ii) A must hold discretion in exercising their control over X, thus rendering B uncertain of how A will exercise that control; and (iii) B must need or want X, which coupled with A's control and discretion over X, renders B vulnerable to A. These three relational elements constitute a 'trust relationship'. To be clear, by 'trust relationship' I do not mean a relationship in which trust exists (what may be distinguished as a 'trust*ing* relationship'). I mean, rather, a relationship in which it is possible for trust to arise. Hence, although trust may theoretically arise in a trust relationship, it may or may not, in actuality, exist in the relationship.

In the social rights context, the identities of the trustee and the truster (A and B) as well as the definition of the good or service (X) depend on the specific sub-context. In my later consideration and application of trust to specific relationships, I will be able to address more closely the identities of A and B, as well as the precise definition of X. I will, however, make some general remarks now in order to provide some perspective for the discussion in this section.

The potential actors which A and B may represent include both individuals and institutions. This conclusion finds support in the positions adopted by several prominent writers on trust, including Rom Harré,[7] Guido Möllering,[8] Henry

[5] Karen S. Cook and Alexandra Gerbasi, 'Trust' in Peter Hedstrom and Peter S. Bearman (eds.), *The Oxford Handbook of Analytical Sociology* (Oxford: Oxford University Press, 2009), p. 220; Evan Fox-Decent, 'The Fiduciary Nature of State Legal Authority' (2005) 31 *Queen's Law Journal* 259, 263, citing Annette Baier, 'Trust and Antitrust' (1985) 96 *Ethics* 231, 236–237; Evan Fox-Decent, *Sovereignty's Promise: The State as Fiduciary* (Oxford: Oxford University Press, 2011), p. 105; Russell Hardin, 'The Street-Level Epistemology of Trust' (1993) 21 *Politics and Society* 505, 506; Holton, 'Deciding to Trust', 66.

[6] Hardin, 'Conceptions and Explanations'. See also Cook and Gerbasi, 'Trust', p. 220.

[7] Rom Harré, 'Trust and Its Surrogates' in Mark E. Warren (ed.), *Democracy and Trust* (Cambridge: Cambridge University Press, 1999), pp. 259–260.

[8] Guido Möllering, 'Understanding Trust from the Perspective of Sociological Neoinstitutionalism: The Interplay of Institutions and Agency' (Max Planck Institute for the Study of Societies, Discussion Paper 05/13, 2009), www.ssoar.info/ssoar/bitstream/handle/document/37397/ssoar-2005-mollering-Understanding_trust_from_the_perspective.pdf?sequence=1, accessed 19 November 2022, 15.

Farrell,[9] Jörg Sydow,[10] and Bernard Barber.[11] A and B may therefore represent both individuals (including individual citizens and residents, service providers, political officials and judges) and institutions (including not only the executive and legislative branches of government, and the courts, but also, as I describe in Chapter 3, the media and special interest groups). As for X, its definition depends on both the relationship and the social right at issue. In the citizen–government relationship, for example, X may represent any one of the many social goods and services that are the subject of social rights. Understandably, the precise nature of those social goods and services depends on the social right. Generally, though, X in the citizen–government relationship denotes physical goods, personnel, infrastructure, equipment and benefits or services. In the right to health, for instance, it includes pharmaceuticals (physical goods); trained doctors, nurses and other health-care providers (personnel); hospitals and clinics (infrastructure); machines and beds (equipment); and various medical procedures.

2.1.1 The Trustee's Control over a Good or Service

The first element of a trust relationship is that the trustee (A) maintains control over a good or service (X) (which the truster (B) needs or wants). Different circumstances may give rise to A's control over X. These circumstances include the cost of X (such that A but not B has the financial means to afford X), the scarcity of X (such that A but not B has access to X) and B giving control of X to A (such that B has given A the responsibility of taking care of X). Many writers on trust assume that A's control over X must stem from the third of these – that is, B giving A control. Hardin has criticised this assumption, identifying it as a slippage between the related concepts of 'trusting' and 'entrusting', where the third circumstance – B giving A control over X – is better captured by the concept of 'entrusting'.[12] I agree with Hardin's criticism.

[9] Henry Farrell, 'Institutions and Midlevel Explanations of Trust' in Karen S. Cook, Margaret Levi and Russell Hardin (eds.), *Whom Can We Trust? How Groups, Networks, and Institutions Make Trust Possible* (New York: Russell Sage Foundation, 2009), p. 133.

[10] Jörg Sydow, 'Understanding the Constitution of Interorganizational Trust' in Christel Lane and Reinhard Bachmann (eds.), *Trust within and between Organizations: Conceptual Issues and Empirical Applications* (Oxford: Oxford University Press, 1998), pp. 43–44.

[11] Barber, *The Logic and Limits*, p. 18.

[12] Hardin, 'Conceptions and Explanations', p. 17.

As he has said, 'I can trust you to do something that I have not (even could not have) entrusted to you ... trusting and entrusting are not equivalent or even parallel, although we might use the two terms as though they were interchangeable, especially in contexts in which both might apply'.[13] Therefore, although A must maintain control over X, the source of A's control does not need to be a grant of control from B.

Two forms of distinction are relevant here. First, the trustee may maintain direct or indirect control over the good or service (X). Direct control refers to situations where the trustee controls the good or service itself. Indirect control, in contrast, covers those circumstances in which the trustee does not control the good or service itself, but controls some means of gaining access to the good or service. In the citizen–government relationship, for example, the elected branches may maintain indirect control over social goods and services by operating social funding programmes. Secondly, the control maintained by the trustee may be exclusive or partial. This distinction relates to the availability of the good or service to the truster from some source other than the trustee. Whereas exclusive control denotes that the trustee is the truster's only possible source of obtaining the good or service, partial control, in contrast, means that the trustee is one of multiple sources.

2.1.2 The Trustee's Discretion in Exercising Control and the Truster's Corresponding Uncertainty

The trustee (A), in addition to maintaining control over the good or service (X), must also hold discretion in exercising that control. Although writers on trust describe this element in slightly different ways, the substance is the same: A must not be so constrained by external factors that they no longer have free will in exercising their control. Diego Gambetta, for instance, has said that trust necessitates that 'agents have a degree of freedom to disappoint our expectations' and that there 'be the possibility of exit, betrayal, defection'.[14] For Roger Cotterrell, trust requires discretion to act 'in unforeseen circumstances or in relation to new situations'.[15] And according to Matthew Harding, trust 'recognizes and responds to the freedom of individuals to make choices'.[16]

13 Ibid.

14 Gambetta, 'Can We Trust Trust?', pp. 218–219.

15 Roger Cotterrell, 'Trusting in Law: Legal and Moral Concepts of Trust' (1993) 46 *Current Legal Problems* 75, 77–78.

16 Harding, 'Manifesting Trust', 246.

A's discretion in exercising control over X creates corresponding uncertainty for B. Uncertainty reflects the inability of B to predict the outcome of their interaction with A.[17] Accordingly, B is uncertain whether they will obtain X from A. Discretion and uncertainty are directly related: more discretion afforded to A yields a wider range of possible courses of action for A in exercising their control over X, which in turn yields a greater degree of uncertainty for B.

By imposing external constraints on A, we reduce A's discretion and in turn reduce the degree of uncertainty for B: B is better able to predict the outcome of their interaction with A based on B's knowledge that A is constrained by external factors. Trust based on this knowledge has been called 'impersonal trust',[18] or 'secondary trust'.[19] Where no constraints have been imposed on A, however, B, in trusting A, must rely only on beliefs B holds about A's person or character. These beliefs will stem from information that B possesses about A such as A's past behaviours. Trust based on these types of belief has been called 'personal trust',[20] or 'primary trust'.[21]

The range of possible courses of action available to A may be referred to as the 'sphere' of discretion.[22] This sphere understandably lies along a spectrum. At one end, A may have no external constraints imposed on them and so, have absolute or unfettered discretion. At the other extreme, A may have so many external constraints imposed on them so as to dictate the outcome of their interaction with B and leave A with no discretion. To be clear, the latter extreme (i.e., no discretion) is not trust. To repeat, for trust to arise, discretion and uncertainty (at least of some degree) must be present in the relationship. Uncertainty arises out of what Niklas Luhmann has called trust's 'problematic relationship with time'.[23] As he and other writers have emphasised, to trust is to anticipate or hypothesise future events. The future, however, cannot be accurately

[17] Carol A. Heimer, 'Solving the Problem of Trust' in Cook, *Trust in Society*, p. 42.

[18] Philip Pettit, 'Republican Theory and Political Trust' in Valerie Braithwaite and Margaret Levi (eds.), *Trust and Governance* (New York: Russell Sage Foundation, 1998), pp. 298–299.

[19] Piotr Sztompka, *Trust: A Sociological Theory* (Cambridge: Cambridge University Press, 1999), p. 87.

[20] Pettit, 'Republican Theory', p. 296.

[21] Sztompka, *Trust: A Sociological Theory*, pp. 46–47.

[22] Matthew Harding, 'Trust and Fiduciary Law' (2013) 33 *Oxford Journal of Legal Studies* 81, 83.

[23] Niklas Luhmann, *Trust and Power: Two Works* (Chichester: Wiley, 1979), p. 10.

predicted. In Luhmann's words, 'the future contains far more possibilities than could ever be realized in the present and hence be transferred into the past. The uncertainty that is bound to exist is simply a consequence of the very elementary fact that not all futures can become the present'.[24] Given this prospect for multiple futures, trust is our response (or our 'solution' if you prefer) to uncertainty in the trust relationship. By trusting we anticipate 'an unknowable future'.[25] As Guido Möllering has helpfully described, a key idea to the concept of trust is that it 'requires a leap of faith'.[26] In other words, we trust in spite of the uncertainty in the trust relationship.

If the trustee's exercise of control is so constrained by external factors to the point of eliminating their discretion and dictating the outcome, trust has been removed from the equation. Without uncertainty in the relationship, there is no room left for trust: we no longer need to anticipate or hypothesise the future – we know it.[27] In the fitting words of Helen Nissenbaum: 'Where people are guaranteed safety, where they are protected from harm via assurances ... trust is redundant; it is unnecessary. What we have is certainty, security, and safety – not trust'.[28]

Of course, as the sphere of discretion lies along a spectrum, circumstances can and will fall in between the two extremes of absolute or unfettered discretion and no discretion. The trustee may have some external constraints placed on their exercise of control but nonetheless maintain some discretion in exercising that control. In these circumstances, the truster's ability to predict the outcome of their interaction with the trustee will be based on a mixture of the information the truster holds about the trustee and the truster's knowledge of the external constraints that have been imposed on the trustee. This intermediate position between absolute or unfettered discretion and no discretion is central to the normative argument that I advance in this book (described in detail in Chapter 4).

24 Ibid.

25 Jack Barbalet, 'A Characterization of Trust, and Its Consequences' (2009) 38 *Theory and Society* 367, 372.

26 Möllering, 'Understanding Trust', 7.

27 Helen Nissenbaum, 'Will Security Enhance Trust Online, or Supplant It?' in Roderick M. Kramer and Karen S. Cook (eds.), *Trust and Distrust in Organizations* (New York: Russell Sage Foundation, 2004), p. 173; Sztompka, *Trust: A Sociological Theory*, pp. 23–33.

28 Nissenbaum, 'Will Security Enhance Trust Online, or Supplant It?', p. 173.

2.1.3 *The Resulting Vulnerability of the Truster*

Lastly, the good or service (X) is something that the truster (B) either needs or wants. This fact, coupled with the other two elements, renders B vulnerable to the trustee (A). Since X is of necessity or value to B, its provision to B contributes to B's well-being. And because A has control and discretion over X, B is placed in a position of vulnerability: it is possible that A may act in a way which is in B's interests, so as to further B's well-being, but since A is a free agent with discretion, A may also act to harm B's interests in their interaction.[29] Put concisely, A may provide B with X (a good or service that B needs or wants); however, because A has discretion in exercising their control over X, it is also possible that A may not provide B with X.

The extent of B's vulnerability to A depends principally on two factors: the availability of X to B from sources other than A, and the personal attributes and life circumstances of B.[30] First, B's vulnerability depends on whether or not they can obtain X from sources other than A. This factor is linked with the control element in the trust relationship – and more specifically, the distinction drawn there between exclusive and partial control.[31] If A is B's only source of X, A maintains exclusive control over X. This exclusive control, depending on the extent of A's discretion in exercising that control, opens B up to extreme vulnerability to A. B is at the mercy of A with respect to X. Should A refuse to provide B with X, B is denied X – a good or service that B needs or wants. If B has the option of obtaining X from an alternative source, however, A's control over X is only partial, and B's vulnerability is less. In that case, should A refuse to provide B with X, B may suffer harm as a result of inconvenience, time or cost, for example, but B is not denied X. B has the option of turning to the alternative source of X.

It may be argued that what I am calling vulnerability is more accurately described as 'dependence'. This is probably true. The work of scholars, including Martha Albertson Fineman, Susan Dodds and Margaret Urban Walker, however, suggests that vulnerability and

29 Pettit, 'Republican Theory', p. 208.

30 Ibid, p. 240. See also Richard Emerson, 'Power-Dependence Relations' (1962) 27 *American Sociological Review* 31, 31–32.

31 Claus Offe, 'How Can We Trust Our Fellow Citizens?' in Warren, *Democracy and Trust*, p. 54.

dependence are closely connected.[32] In fact, both Dodds and Walker have defined dependence as a form of vulnerability. Both of them have drawn a distinction between vulnerability in a general sense (i.e., as a result of our embodiment) and vulnerability to a specific person given a certain relationship. Dodds and Walker have identified the latter type of vulnerability as dependence. For Dodds, '[d]ependence is vulnerability that requires the support of a specific person (or people) . . . In this way dependence can be contrasted with those vulnerabilities that do not involve immediate reliance on specific individuals'.[33] Similarly, Walker has distinguished between vulnerability in a general sense (what she has called 'vulnerability-in-principle') – which she has described as 'susceptibility to injury' or 'being under threat of harm' – and vulnerability to a particular actor (what she has called 'dependence-in-fact').[34] For Walker, in the case of dependence, the actor who 'holds control of the vulnerability stands in a particular sort of relation to the one who has the vulnerability'.[35] In a trust relationship, the vulnerability to which the truster is exposed is not of a general sort but, rather, is vulnerability to a specific actor – that is, the trustee. Although the trust literature uses the term vulnerability, I think that it is really dependence, as a form of vulnerability, in which we are most interested. Nevertheless, throughout this book, to be consistent with the trust literature, I will continue to use the broader term vulnerability, as opposed to dependence.

Secondly, the extent of B's vulnerability to A depends on certain personal attributes and life circumstances of B. These attributes and circumstances are those which have bearing on the extent to which B needs or wants X, like B's health, age, talents and socio-economic status.[36] These attributes and circumstances increase B's stakes in the transaction between B and A.[37] For example, let us consider a scenario where A is a health administrative agency that determines coverage

32 Susan Dodds, 'Dependence, Care, and Vulnerability' in Catriona MacKenzie, Wendy Rogers and Susan Dodds (eds.), *Vulnerability: New Essays in Ethics and Feminist Philosophy* (Oxford: Oxford University Press, 2013), pp. 181–203; Martha Albertson Fineman, 'The Vulnerable Subject: Anchoring Equality in the Human Condition' (2008) 20 *Yale Journal of Law and Feminism* 1; Margaret Urban Walker, *Moral Understandings: A Feminist Study in Ethics* (Oxford: Oxford University Press, 2008).

33 Dodds, 'Dependence, Care, and Vulnerability', pp. 182–183.

34 Walker, *Moral Understandings*, p. 90.

35 Ibid.

36 Fox-Decent, 'The Fiduciary Nature', 299.

37 Frank B. Cross, 'Law and Trust' (2005) 93 *Georgetown Law Journal* 1457, 1462.

under a government-funded health insurance plan, and X is a particular treatment such as a chemotherapy drug. The value of X to B in this scenario depends on B's health. Assume three potential trusters: B1 (an individual who has been diagnosed today with a malignant tumour), B2 (an individual who has been diagnosed today with a benign tumour), and B3 (an individual who was diagnosed a year ago with a malignant tumour, who has not responded to any drugs and who has been advised by their oncologist that they will likely not respond to X). Given their respective health statuses, the chemotherapy drug is of greater value to B1 and B3 than B2. Let us further assume that B3 is persuaded by their doctor's advice and therefore, X is of greater value to B1 than B3. Owing to the health statuses of the three trusters and the drug's value to each of them given the information from B3's doctor, B1 is most vulnerable to A followed by B3 and then B2.

Since this factor is tied to the identity of B, as opposed to the relationship or X itself (which was the case for the previous factor), it has the potential to discriminate. By this I mean that one truster may be rendered more vulnerable to a trustee than another even though the two are parties to the same relationship with A, involving the same good or service. B's attributes and circumstances may also overlap (e.g., health or race with socio-economic status) to exacerbate B's vulnerability to A, and further discriminate.[38] And further still, this second factor may interact with the first factor (the alternative availability of X) such that although two trusters may equally need or want X, they may unequally need or want X *from A*. For instance, let us consider a scenario where X is available from a source other than A but at a significant cost. Although X is technically available to B from an alternative source, in actuality, X is only available to B where B has the financial means to take advantage of that alternative source of X. To demonstrate, let us consider again the scenario of B1, B2 and B3, and the chemotherapy drug. Assume that in the scenario, a private insurance company offers plans that cover the drug for an annual charge. B1, B2 and B3 accordingly have access to an alternative source of X (the private insurance company) but only where they are in a financial position to afford to pay the annual charge levied by the company. One who is not in that financial position is more vulnerable to the health administrative agency and its coverage decision. So, if B1 is of a lower socio-economic status than B2 and B3, B1's socio-

[38] Mark E. Warren, 'Democratic Theory and Trust' in Warren, *Democracy and Trust*, p. 335.

economic status interacts with the availability of X such that, aside from B1's differential health status as discussed, they are more vulnerable to A than B2 and B3 because they are less able to afford what it costs to take advantage of the alternative source of X (the private insurance company).

2.2 The Citizen–Government Relationship: A Trust Relationship

The citizen–government relationship satisfies all three elements of a trust relationship. Before explaining how this is the case, let us first reconfigure the citizen–government relationship to fit the three-part form (i.e., the A–B–X relationship) that I outlined earlier. A and B (the trustee and the truster) represent the elected branches and citizens, respectively. The elected branches (A) include, as I have said, both the legislature and the executive. And X represents any one of the many social goods and services that I outlined previously as being the subject of social rights.

2.2.1 The Elected Branches' Control over Social Goods and Services

The first element of a trust relationship – control – is quite manifest in the citizen–government relationship. In any social democracy, the elected branches maintain some degree of control over social goods and services that citizens need or want. It will be recalled that social rights promise social goods and services that citizens need to lead a decent life.[39] I therefore proceed under the assumption that in this relationship, the social goods and services at issue are *needed* by citizens.

The elected branches' control over these social goods and services is exercised via various legislative and administrative steps. The legislative branch contributes amendments to and promulgates the primary legislation that defines the parameters of state-delivered social programmes.[40] It also endorses the budget that allows the state to fund, and accordingly to deliver, the programmes. The executive, in contrast, prepares the bulk of primary legislation, which is introduced to the legislature, and then, following that, supplements, amplifies and implements that legislation

[39] Cécile Fabre, *Social Rights under the Constitution: Government and the Decent Life* (Oxford: Oxford University Press, 2003), p. 7; Jeff King, *Judging Social Rights* (Cambridge: Cambridge University Press, 2012), p. 17.

[40] King, *Judging Social Rights*, pp. 41, 44.

through a broad range of administrative action.[41] These legislative and administrative steps, taken collectively, are prerequisites to the state-delivered social programmes that ultimately grant citizens access to the social goods and services that they need.

Granted, the nature of the elected branches' control is nuanced. First, the source of that control is debatable. There is a good argument that the source of the elected branches' control is citizens' taxes (following on from what I said in Chapter 1). Charles Reich argued long ago that owing to citizens' obligation to pay taxes to the state, social rights are best seen as property rights.[42] For Reich, since social goods and services are supported by taxes, they are best viewed as 'substitutes for, rather than supplements to, other forms of wealth'.[43] The tax money that citizens pay to the state 'is no longer available for individual savings or insurance. The taxpayer is a participant in public insurance by compulsion, and his ability to care for his own needs independently is correspondingly reduced'.[44] If we accept Reich's argument, citizens are giving the elected branches control over these social goods and services, entrusting them with the social goods and services that they need. As I explained earlier, however, while such giving of control, or entrusting, is one source of control – and so, sufficient for this element of a trust relationship – it is not a requirement. All that a trust relationship requires is that the elected branches, by whatever means, exercise control over the social goods and services. This is undoubtedly the case.

Secondly, the elected branches may maintain direct or indirect control over the social goods and services. In some jurisdictions and with some social rights, the elected branches maintain direct control over goods and services: they produce physical goods, employ personnel, own equipment and infrastructure, or administer benefits and services directly to citizens. In others, they maintain indirect control by operating funding programmes and via regulation.

Lastly, the elected branches' control may be exclusive or partial: the elected branches may be citizens' only possible means of obtaining social

[41] Ibid, pp. 44–48; Lorne Sossin, 'Boldly Going Where No Law Has Gone Before: Call Centres, Intake Scripts, Database Fields, and Discretionary Justice in Social Assistance' (2004) 42 *Osgoode Hall Law Journal* 363, 364–365.

[42] Charles A. Reich, 'The New Property' (1964) 73 *The Yale Law Journal* 733. See also John Allett, 'New Liberalism & the New Property Doctrine: Welfare Rights as Property Rights' (1987) 20 *Polity* 57.

[43] Reich, 'The New Property', 737.

[44] Ibid.

goods and services (exclusive control) or they may be one of multiple means (partial control). In contemporary social democracies, providers of social goods and services rarely find themselves confined to the public system; they usually have the option of offering their goods and services privately. The consequence of this option is that the elected branches only maintain partial control over the social goods and services that citizens need. That said, neither of the noted distinctions – direct/indirect and exclusive/partial – changes the critical fact that the elected branches do indeed maintain control over social goods and services.

The first element of a trust relationship is therefore satisfied in the citizen–government relationship: regardless of the nuanced nature of the elected branches' control, including that control's ultimate source and exact type, the elected branches in contemporary social democracies do maintain some degree of control over the social goods and services that citizens need.

2.2.2 *The Elected Branches' Discretion and Citizens' Uncertainty*

In any social democracy, the elected branches, on top of maintaining control over social goods and services, also hold discretion in exercising that control. In his influential book *Discretionary Justice*, Kenneth Culp Davis has defined 'discretion' in politics as follows. 'A public officer has discretion whenever the effective limits on his power leave him free to make a choice among possible courses of action or inaction.'[45] Under this definition, both branches exercise discretion.[46]

The legislature undoubtedly exercises significant discretion.[47] Both in exercising its power of the purse and in promulgating primary legislation,

[45] Kenneth Culp Davis, *Discretionary Justice: A Preliminary Inquiry* (Baton Rouge: Louisiana State University Press, 1969), p. 4. For other – but similar – definitions of discretion, see Denis J. Galligan, *Discretionary Powers: A Legal Study of Official Discretion* (Oxford: Clarendon Press, 1986), p. 21; Robert E. Goodin, *Reasons for Welfare: The Political Theory of the Welfare State* (Princeton, NJ: Princeton University Press, 1988), p. 186; Jeffrey Jowell, 'The Legal Control of Administrative Discretion' (1973) *Public Law* 178, 179.

[46] Goodin, *Reasons for Welfare*, p. 12. See also King, *Judging Social Rights*, pp. 250–286 on legislative and administrative 'flexibility'; Colm O'Cinneide, 'Legal Accountability and Social Justice' in Nicholas Bamforth and Peter Leyland (eds.), *Accountability in the Contemporary Constitution* (Oxford: Oxford University Press, 2013), p. 389. Note that, for the moment, I am leaving aside any constraints on the elected branches' discretion which may be imposed by the courts.

[47] Xenophon Contiades and Alkmene Fotiadou, 'Social Rights in the Age of Proportionality: Global Economic Crisis and Constitutional Litigation' (2012) 10 *International Journal of*

the legislature is, in Davis's words, left 'free to make a choice among possible courses of action or inaction'. Among other things, it can choose to approve (or not approve) the executive's proposed budget, and it can choose to promulgate (or not, or propose amendments to) legislation that is put before it. While the legislature's discretion can be restrained by constitutional limits, including express social rights language, given the vagueness with which social rights are often formulated, such restraint is likely to be minimal.[48]

The executive likewise has a wide margin of discretion.[49] Lorne Sossin has helpfully classified three levels of discretion which are exercised by administrative decision-makers.[50] The first is legal discretion, referring to legislative grants of authority in which administrative decision-makers are given an express choice. At this level, the legislature expressly delegates its discretion to administrative decision-makers because those decision-makers may be in a better position to make the decision at hand (although the legislature usually specifies an overall purpose). Secondly, administrative decision-makers exercise interpretive discretion. Unlike the first level, interpretive discretion is not expressly delegated by the legislature but arises from vague or ambiguous language in the relevant social welfare statutes. As explained by Henriette Sinding Aasen and colleagues, '[l]egislation pertaining to welfare is often formulated in general or vague terms and with broad object clauses, which leave room for a substantial degree of professional discretion in the application of the law'.[51] Administrative decision-makers are thus left with the discretion to interpret such general or vague statutory language. Finally, administrative decision-makers exercise discretion through what Sossin

Constitutional Law 660, 667–668; Goodin, *Reasons for Welfare*; King, *Judging Social Rights*.

48 For example, Jeff King has stressed that social rights are inescapably vague, owing to the fact that they often impose qualified obligations on the state: King, *Judging Social Rights*, pp. 100–106. See also Anders Molander, *Discretion in the Welfare State: Social Rights and Professional Judgment* (Abingdon: Routledge, 2016), p. 49.

49 Robert E. Goodin, 'Welfare, Rights and Discretion' (1986) 6 *Oxford Journal of Legal Studies* 232; Molander, *Discretion in the Welfare State*; Richard M. Titmuss, 'Welfare "Rights", Law and Discretion' (1971) 42 *The Political Quarterly* 113.

50 Sossin, 'Boldly Going'.

51 Henriette Sinding Aasen et al., 'Juridification and Social Citizenship: International Law, Democracy and Professional Discretion' in Henriette Sinding Aasen et al. (eds.), *Juridification and Social Citizenship in the Welfare State* (Cheltenham: Edward Elgar, 2014), p. 296.

has termed 'administrative choices'.[52] These choices include how a citizen applies for benefits, which documents must be produced and verified, how decisions on eligibility are reached by decision-makers, the requisite training and qualifications of decision-makers, and the extent of personal contact between decision-makers and applicants. At each of these three levels, decision-makers are, per Davis's definition again, given a 'choice among possible courses of action or inaction' – whether that choice is express, implicit or administrative.

The discretion exercised by both elected branches of government gives rise to inevitable uncertainty for citizens. This uncertainty likewise exists on multiple levels. Inescapably, whenever a political decision is made, there is the uncertainty that a citizen will not receive what they want from the political process. Governing necessarily involves balancing competing demands and setting priorities, and frequently one demand is fulfilled by the elected branches at the expense of another demand.[53] Conor Gearty has called this form of uncertainty the 'defect in politics'.[54] In social rights matters, there is a limited budget available to the elected branches in funding and delivering social goods and services to their citizens. Governments cannot fund and deliver every social good and service to every citizen.[55] Hence, as an inevitable consequence of such budget limitations, some citizens will be left unhappy or dissatisfied with the political process's outcome.

However, and in my view more importantly, there is an additional type of uncertainty: uncertainty regarding the overall procedure followed by the elected branches in making their decisions vis-à-vis social goods and services. Included among this is the uncertainty that a citizen's interests will be discounted, or worse, disregarded. In those cases where a citizen has not received what they want from the political process, it does not necessarily follow that their interests have been discounted or disregarded: the citizen's interests may have been duly considered by the elected branches but, in making their decisions in this regard, the elected

[52] Sossin, 'Boldly Going', 364–365.

[53] See Jane Mansbridge, 'Social and Cultural Causes of Dissatisfaction with U.S. Government' in Joseph S. Nye Jr., Philip D. Zelikow and David C. King (eds.), *Why People Do Not Trust Government* (Cambridge, MA: Harvard University Press, 1997), p. 134; Ben Seyd, 'Exploring Political Disappointment' (2016) 69 *Parliamentary Affairs* 327.

[54] Conor Gearty, 'Against Judicial Enforcement' in Conor Gearty and Virginia Mantouvalou (eds.), *Debating Social Rights* (Oxford: Hart, 2010), pp. 53–54.

[55] Warren, 'Democratic Theory and Trust', p. 311.

branches may have decided that what the citizen wanted was not the 'right' or 'best' decision. Nevertheless, because the elected branches do have the discretion I have just described, the reverse may be equally true: the citizen's interests may have been indeed discounted or disregarded. First, the elected branches may discount or disregard a citizen's interests in favour of their staff's own interests. As Margaret Levi has explained, both bureaucrats and politicians have their own interests when they make political decisions: for bureaucrats it is to maximise budgets and power, and for politicians it is to maximise votes.[56] When these actors' interests conflict with the interests of citizens (generally or a specific subset of citizens), there is the uncertainty that the elected branches' decisions will be made in a way which furthers these actors' interests.[57] Secondly, even if we assume good faith on the part of bureaucrats and politicians, these actors may nonetheless discount or disregard a citizen's interests because of neglect.[58] Owing to a lack of experience or to just basic ignorance on their part, bureaucrats and politicians may not be aware of or fully understand the plight of the citizen (or the group to which they belong) and so, may fail to protect the citizen's interests – albeit unintentionally.

Of note, the threat of a citizen's interests being discounted or disregarded by the elected branches is especially pronounced for low-income citizens. This is so because their interests are not likely to align with either bureaucrats or politicians. Bureaucrats' interests in maximising budgets and power are likely to run contrary to the interests of low-income citizens in maximising social welfare entitlements; the less money spent on social welfare, the more money that remains in the budget, and that may be used elsewhere. Politicians' interests in maximising votes means that they will cater to the interests of those who have political influence and can re-elect them into power. Unfortunately, those with low income are not likely to be part of this politically powerful cohort of citizens. Several social rights scholars have forcefully argued, supported by empirical studies, that low-income citizens do not exert much political influence – and consequently, are a marginalised group.[59] This

56 Margaret Levi, 'A State of Trust' in Braithwaite and Levi, *Trust and Governance*, p. 95.

57 Warren, 'Democratic Theory and Trust', pp. 311–313.

58 King, *Judging Social Rights*, pp. 166–167.

59 Sandra Fredman, *Human Rights Transformed: Positive Rights and Positive Duties* (Oxford: Oxford University Press, 2008), p. 34; King, *Judging Social Rights*, pp. 157–169; Paul O'Connell, *Vindicating Socio-economic Rights: International Standards and Comparative Experiences* (Abingdon: Routledge, 2013), p. 5; Kim Lane

marginalisation of low-income citizens follows a circular pattern. It is well recognised that governmental policy-making, to start, is heavily influenced by the wealthy through lobbying and interest groups.[60] As Colm O'Cinneide has noted, the reality of the situation is 'that those in most need of state support are often those least able to access the political system and press for change'.[61] Then, following on in large part from the wealthy's disproportionate political influence, those with low income tend to feel excluded from the democratic process and so, tend not to participate in it: they seldom register as voters and, when they do register, they are not organised voters generally.[62] Political parties accordingly rarely target low-income voters and therefore, low-income citizens lack representation which would give them a political voice to influence governmental policy-making.[63] As a result, the interests of low-income citizens – on top of being discounted or disregarded intentionally in the pursuit of political ambition – are also likely to be neglected unintentionally due to a lack of representation.[64] Bringing us full circle, the wealthy are therefore given even more political clout, leading low-income citizens to feel even further excluded and to their further marginalisation. On those rare occasions where a political party does target those with low income, it is often met with countervailing political forces from the wealthy lobbying and interest groups that prevent it from delivering on the social programmes it may have promised.[65] As Jeff King has pointed out, a strong welfare state – which entails regulation of commerce and redistributive tax spending – is '*diametrically opposed*

Scheppele, 'A Realpolitik Defense of Social Rights' (2004) 82 *Texas Law Review* 1921, 1926–1927.

60 King, *Judging Social Rights*, p. 157; Virginia Mantouvalou, 'In Support of Legalisation' in Gearty and Mantouvalou, *Debating Social Rights*, pp. 116–117; Gearty, 'Against Judicial Enforcement', p. 75. For empirical support of this claim, see also D.C. Freeman, 'Note: The Poor and the Political Process: Equal Access to Lobbying' (1969) 6 *Harvard Journal on Legislation* 369, 370, cited in King, *Judging Social Rights*, p. 157.

61 O'Cinneide, 'Legal Accountability', p. 405.

62 O'Connell, *Vindicating Socio-economic Rights*, p. 5; Scheppele, 'A Realpolitik Defense', 1926–1927.

63 O'Connell, *Vindicating Socio-economic Rights*.

64 Moreover, as O'Cinneide has pointed out, 'the daily operation of the welfare state is often a complex and impenetrable process, and there is not much political capital to be gained by elected politicians and other opinion-formers probing deeply into how the system treats marginalized individuals and groups': O'Cinneide, 'Legal Accountability', pp. 404–405.

65 Scheppele, 'A Realpolitik Defense', 1926–1927.

to the interests of the wealthy' and thus 'precisely the target of the well-resourced lobbying interests'.[66]

We may therefore fairly conclude that the citizen–government relationship also satisfies the second element of a trust relationship: in contemporary social democracies, the legislature and the executive hold discretion in exercising their control over social goods and services that citizens need; and correspondingly, citizens are left uncertain regarding how that control will be exercised.

2.2.3 Citizens' Vulnerability to the Elected Branches

Lastly, in the citizen–government relationship, citizens are vulnerable to the elected branches. Extrapolating from what I said earlier, citizens' vulnerability follows on from the combined effect of two features of the citizen–government relationship: first, the control and discretion that the elected branches have over social goods and services; and secondly, citizens' need for those social goods and services. As citizens need the goods and services, their provision to citizens contributes to citizens' well-being; and because the elected branches have control and discretion over those goods and services, the elected branches hold power over citizens. The elected branches, in exercising their control, may or may not choose to provide the social goods and services to citizens. Therefore, citizens may not be able to obtain those goods and services – at least not from the state.

Granted, citizens are not equally vulnerable to the elected branches. The vulnerability of an individual citizen to the elected branches depends on the two factors outlined earlier. In the citizen–government relationship, the first factor (the availability of the good or service from an alternative source) usually translates into whether the social good or service is available from a provider on the private market. To repeat, in contemporary social democracies, it is rare for the elected branches to maintain exclusive control over social goods and services: there is often available to citizens (at least those who can afford it) a private market for those goods and services. In other words, the elected branches maintain partial control. Where a citizen can access a social good or service through the private market, their vulnerability to the elected branches is less.

[66] King, *Judging Social Rights*, p. 157.

Secondly, a citizen's vulnerability depends on the personal attributes and life circumstances from earlier, including their health, age, talents and socio-economic status. A citizen in poor health, for instance, is in greater need of public health care than one who is in good health and so, is more vulnerable to the elected branches. A citizen with children has greater need for public education than one without children and so, is more vulnerable. Also recall that this second factor may interact with the first. In the citizen–government relationship, this interaction is an especially significant one. Citizens' socio-economic status, in particular, interacts with the availability of social goods and services from private sources to generate an inequality of vulnerability across citizens. Again, where a citizen can access a good or service through the private market, their vulnerability to the elected branches is less – or put another way, the relevant private providers mitigate citizens' vulnerability. However, only those citizens who have the financial means to turn to the private market (i.e., the relatively wealthy) may benefit from this opportunity for mitigated vulnerability. Their money makes the private market a practical alternative should their government refuse to provide, or place restrictions on the provision of, social goods and services in the public system. In other words, the latter category of citizens is not wholly dependent on their government for the social goods and services that they need. For low-income citizens, the public system is likely their only means of access. They do not have the financial resources necessary to make the private market a practical alternative. Low-income citizens are thus likely to be at the mercy of politicians and bureaucrats for the social goods and services that they need.[67]

I leave aside for now the inequality of vulnerability which follows on from these two factors and their interaction. While I acknowledge that this inequality does exist, the fact remains that all citizens are vulnerable to the elected branches, at least to some extent. If the social goods and services at issue are, generally speaking and on the whole, things that citizens need, and the elected branches have control and discretion over them, citizens are inevitably vulnerable. The citizen–government relationship hence satisfies this third and final element of a trust relationship.

2.3 Defining Trust

To recap: where the three elements of control, discretion/uncertainty and vulnerability are present in a relationship, trust may arise in that

[67] Offe, 'How Can We Trust Our Fellow Citizens?', p. 53.

relationship. These elements do not guarantee trust but set the stage for it to be possible. The citizen–government relationship, based on the above, offers an example. This does not explain, however, what trust is. In this part of the chapter, building on the three constituent elements of a trust relationship, I provide a definition of trust in the social rights context. This definition will serve as a key theoretical building block for the remainder of the book.

2.3.1 Cognitive versus Affective Trust

To develop this definition of trust, and for the purpose of clarity, I will start with a common categorisation used in the trust literature. Trust is frequently divided into two categories: affective and cognitive trust.[68] On the one hand, affective trust is emotional in nature.[69] It is a matter of our having 'trustful affects, emotions or motivational structures' towards another actor.[70] We can think of affective trust as sort of 'feeling' trust towards the trustee. Cognitive trust, on the other hand, is more conscious and reasoned in nature than affective trust.[71] It is a matter of our beliefs – or, as I explain shortly, our expectations – about how another actor will behave towards us.[72]

In most circumstances, trust will be a combination of these two categories.[73] That said, my focus in this book is on the category of cognitive trust. This is so for at least two reasons. First, as writers on trust have recognised, affective trust usually arises in relationships of shared interests between the truster and the trustee which can merge into a shared identity.[74] We see this kind of trust most commonly in parent–child or marital relationships, for example. Cognitive trust, in contrast, arises more in relationships that occur at a distance and lack the affective convergence of interests and identities, such as trust in professionals,

[68] Lawrence C. Becker, 'Trust as Noncognitive Security about Motives' (1996) 107 *Ethics* 43, 44–45. These components are not separated into watertight compartments; or as Becker has observed 'a fuzzy boundary' exists between them. However, it is worthwhile to maintain a distinction between them (44–45).

[69] Cross, 'Law and Trust', 1459.

[70] Becker, 'Trust as Noncognitive', 44.

[71] Cross, 'Law and Trust', 1459.

[72] Becker, 'Trust as Noncognitive', 44.

[73] Annette Baier, 'Trust and Its Vulnerabilities' in Annette Baier (ed.), *Moral Prejudices: Essays on Ethics* (Cambridge, MA: Harvard University Press, 1995), p. 132; Becker, 'Trust as Noncognitive', 44–45.

[74] Warren, 'Democratic Theory and Trust', p. 330.

authorities, political officials and institutions.[75] Given this book's emphasis on political trust and the citizen–government relationship, it is therefore appropriate to focus on the latter category of trust. Secondly, cognitive trust is more contingent than affective trust on external circumstances.[76] Our beliefs and expectations of others are likely to change depending on those circumstances. To assert that B trusts A cognitively suggests that B expects A will do C in situation S; to assert that B trusts A affectively suggests that B's emotional attitude towards A is trustful, regardless of the situation in which B finds themselves.[77] Accordingly, it should be possible to change B's cognitive trust in A by changing S (at least more so than affective trust which is less adaptable). Owing to this book's concern with the impact that social rights adjudication can reasonably be expected to have on political trust (as I describe in Chapter 4), it again makes sense for it to focus on cognitive trust.

2.3.2 *Trust as a Set of Expectations*

Many writers have defined trust, at least cognitively, in terms of the truster's expectations vis-à-vis the trustee's behaviour.[78] In this chapter, I do so as well. I propose that trust involves three specific expectations: (i) an expectation that the trustee will exercise goodwill towards the truster in exercising their control over the good or service ('expectation of goodwill'); (ii) an expectation that the trustee will exercise competence in so exercising their control ('expectation of competence'); and (iii) in relationships that are of a fiduciary nature, an expectation that the trustee will fulfil the fiduciary responsibility that they owe to the truster ('expectation of fiduciary responsibility').

First is the truster's expectation that the trustee will exercise goodwill towards the truster.[79] This expectation has been characterised differently by different writers on trust. Karen Jones has focused on how the trustee will respond to their being trusted, describing it as an 'expectation that,

75 Ibid, p. 330.
76 Cross, 'Law and Trust', 1468.
77 Becker, 'Trust as Noncognitive', 44–45.
78 Barbalet, 'A Characterization of Trust', 371–372; Barber, *The Logic and Limits*, pp. 15–21; Farrell, 'Institutions and Midlevel Explanations', pp. 128–129; Gambetta, 'Can We Trust Trust?', pp. 218–219; Niklas Luhmann, 'Familiarity, Confidence, Trust: Problems and Alternatives' in Gambetta, *Trust: Making and Breaking*, p. 97; Sztompka, *Trust: A Sociological Theory*, p. 26.
79 Barber, *The Logic and Limits*, p. 9.

when the need arises, the one trusted will be directly and favourably moved by the thought that you are counting on her'.[80] For John Dunn, it is an 'expectation of benign intentions in another free agent' thereby emphasising a lack of ill will on the part of the trustee.[81] Bernard Barber's account characterises it as an 'expectation of the persistence and fulfillment of the natural and the moral social orders' where those orders encompass an expectation that one will exercise goodwill towards another in the absence of reasons to the contrary.[82] I think that this expectation may be summed up in the following terms. It is an expectation that the trustee, in exercising their control over the good or service, will act in a way that we would expect an actor with good motives to act.

The second expectation by which trust is constituted is an expectation held by the truster that the trustee will exercise their control over the good or service with the requisite technical competence (i.e., knowledge and skills).[83] This expectation necessarily supplements the expectation of goodwill because as Jones has justifiably pointed out, 'optimism about goodwill is not sufficient, for some people have very good wills but very little competence, and the incompetent deserve our trust almost as little as the malicious'.[84] The trustee's competence may come from a number of different sources, including expert knowledge, technical facility or daily routine performance.[85] Competence helps explain, at least in part, why trust involves a three-part relationship revolving around a particular good or service (X). Although we may expect that an actor has the competence to deal with one good or service, this expectation does not necessarily carry over to a different good or service. Where X changes, B's expectations of A's competence may change and in turn from that, the extent to which B trusts A with respect to the new X may also change. Trudy Govier has vividly made the point by stating 'trust is often relative to particular contexts and ranges of action: we might trust someone in the role of snow-shoveller but not that of baby-sitter'.[86]

In addition to the expectations of goodwill and competence, which are universal, in fiduciary relationships, trust also comprises a third expectation. This expectation finds its roots in the sociological work of Barber.

[80] Jones, 'Trust as an Affective', 5–6.
[81] John Dunn, 'Trust and Political Agency' in Gambetta, *Trust: Making and Breaking*, p. 74.
[82] Barber, *The Logic and Limits*, p. 9.
[83] Ibid, p. 9.
[84] Jones, 'Trust as an Affective', 6–7.
[85] Barber, *The Logic and Limits*, p. 9.
[86] Govier, *Social Trust and Human Communities*, p. 6.

According to Barber, because there are cases where the truster may not be able to comprehend the trustee's technical competence, society instils a moral sense of fiduciary responsibility in those who possess special knowledge and skills, and following on from that, wield power.[87] Such trustees include parents, government officials, professionals and institutions. As Barber has pointed out, we can only monitor competent performance from these individuals and institutions 'insofar as it is based on shared knowledge and expertise'.[88] Where the trustee's knowledge and expertise are not shared by the truster, something more is necessary. Fiduciary responsibility is that something more. Trust by way of the fiduciary expectation is thus 'a social mechanism that makes possible the effective and just use of the power that knowledge and position give and forestalls abuses of that power'.[89] The expectation is that the fiduciary will fulfil the responsibility that society has instilled in the fiduciary. And that responsibility is, as Barber has described it, 'to demonstrate a special concern for others' interests above [the fiduciary's] own'.[90]

2.3.3 A Behavioural Aspect to Trust?

The definition of trust that I have set out above – as a set of expectations held by the truster about the trustee's behaviour – may lead us to ask: but is trust not also a behaviour on the part of the truster? Indeed, this is the case. In fact, it is well recognised in the trust literature that, affective trust aside, trust exists on two interconnected levels: one cognitive and the other behavioural.

Cognitive trust refers to an aspect of trust which is internal to the truster. As the term suggests, it occurs at the level of thoughts or beliefs held by the truster about the trustee and the trustee's behaviour. The definition of trust that I have set out in the previous section captures trust at a cognitive level. Behavioural trust, in contrast, is the outward manifestation of those thoughts or beliefs by the truster, in the form of actions. Behavioural trust signals to the trustee, as well as the world at large, that the truster trusts the trustee. Consequently, extrapolating from the definition of trust that I have set out, trust at the behavioural level may be defined as the truster's acting on the expectations of goodwill,

[87] Barber, *The Logic and Limits*, p. 9.
[88] Ibid, p. 15.
[89] Ibid, p. 15.
[90] Ibid, p. 14.

competence and fiduciary responsibility that the truster holds if, or perhaps when, they trust the trustee at a cognitive level, thereby manifesting their trust in the trustee.[91]

Some writers on trust argue, or at least seem to suggest, that both levels – cognitive and behavioural – are necessary for there to be trust at all.[92] I disagree with this suggestion. While trust at the cognitive level may surely be manifested in behaviour, and that behaviour could be rightfully included within the concept of trust, in my view, the absence of such behaviour does not mean that trust somehow ceases to exist. Why must I act on my expectations of goodwill, competence and fiduciary responsibility in order to 'trust' you? I can see no reason why this must be the case.

On the contrary, defining trust as requiring both the cognitive and behavioural levels has problematic consequences. It may lead, and in actuality has led, many writers to the erroneous conclusion that trust represents a 'choice' – that is, the truster chooses, at a cognitive level, to trust the trustee. This conclusion, as Hardin has stressed, is incorrect, however: one does not choose to trust at a cognitive level, but rather one chooses to act on cognitive trust. Hardin has explained: 'I do not typically choose to trust and therefore act; rather, I do trust and therefore choose to act'.[93] As a result, it is the truster's behaviour in response to their trust at a cognitive level (i.e., behavioural trust on the truster's part) that represents a choice. This error is not by itself insurmountable for the definition of trust. What is insurmountable, in my view, is the following: because the 'choice' characterisation attaches to the behavioural level of trust, as I have just explained, and these writers' definition of trust requires both levels for trust to exist, some writers have suggested that where the truster has no choice of behaviour, trust cannot exist.[94] In these writers' view, trust necessitates that it be 'possible for us to refrain from action. If it were only others who enjoyed freedom, while we had no alternative but to depend on them, then for us the problem of trust would not arise'.[95] In other words, choice, it has been suggested by these writers, is a requirement of trust.

[91] For a more fulsome consideration of trust at the behavioural level, see Harding, 'Manifesting Trust'.

[92] For a summary of this point, see Hardin, 'Conceptions and Explanations', pp. 9–12.

[93] Hardin, 'The Street-Level Epistemology', 516.

[94] Gambetta, 'Can We Trust Trust?', p. 219; Sztompka, *Trust: A Sociological Theory*, pp. 25–29.

[95] Gambetta, 'Can We Trust Trust?', p. 219.

This suggestion is problematic because it excludes from the ambit of trust, a number of relationships, including political relationships like the citizen–government relationship. In general, political relationships are characterised by little or no choice because citizens' subjection to governmental power is inevitable. As Philip Pettit has said, '[w]herever I choose to live, I will find myself subject to a government and in a position of vulnerability to government agents'.[96] Citizens thus have very limited choices: limited to choices in voting for their elected officials and whether to remain in their country.[97] Now, in the social rights context, relatively wealthy citizens do have a choice that low-income citizens do not: they have the option to turn to the private market for social goods and services. As I have already explained, low-income citizens are at the mercy of politicians and bureaucrats for social goods and services. To define trust as requiring both cognitive and behavioural levels, and choice necessarily present at the behavioural level, suggests that whereas relatively wealthy citizens can trust their elected branches with respect to social rights, for low-income citizens, trust is not possible. In my view, this conclusion cannot be correct. Despite having no choice but to rely on the elected branches for social goods and services, low-income citizens may nonetheless trust those branches at a cognitive level.

For these reasons, I have chosen to define trust as a cognitive concept, separate from its behavioural manifestation. In this choice I am again supported by prominent writers on trust.[98] To be clear, this does not mean that trust does not have a behavioural aspect. A truster may act on their expectations of goodwill, competence and fiduciary responsibility and, in so doing, manifest their trust in the trustee. What it means, rather, is that this behaviour is not a requirement of trust.

2.3.4 Trust's Focus on Procedure

The three expectations outlined above regard the manner in which the trustee exercises their control over the good or service – in other words, the procedure by which that exercise of control takes place. There is an additional expectation which the truster may hold, however: an expectation regarding the outcome of their interaction with the trustee. Put

96 Pettit, 'Republican Theory', pp. 299–300.

97 Luhmann, *Trust and Power*, p. 55.

98 Hardin, 'Conceptions and Explanations', pp. 9–12; Pettit, 'Republican Theory', p. 310.

simply, the truster may have an expectation about whether the trustee will provide the truster with the good or service that the truster needs or wants. These two expectations are undoubtedly interconnected. It makes sense that if I expect you to exercise goodwill, act competently and fulfil your fiduciary responsibility to me, I should be more likely to expect a favourable outcome from our interaction (i.e., that you will provide me with the good or service). The reverse should also be true: if I do not expect goodwill, competence and fulfilment of fiduciary responsibility, I should be less likely to expect a favourable outcome.

Despite the interconnection between these two expectations, it is imperative that we not conflate them so as to equate the latter – the expectation of a favourable outcome – with trust. To explain why I think that this is so, let us consider what it means to say that a trustee has 'abused' or 'breached' a truster's trust. Under the definition of trust that I have set out, where the trustee acts contrary to these expectations (i.e., the trustee does not exercise goodwill, act competently or fulfil their fiduciary responsibility), the trustee will have abused or breached the truster's trust in them. In my view, this conclusion is a reasonable one. Now, let us contrast that with a definition of trust as an expectation of a favourable outcome. This would mean that if the trustee acts contrary to that expectation by producing an unfavourable outcome – even though the trustee exercised goodwill, acted competently and fulfilled their fiduciary responsibility to the truster – the trustee will have abused or breached the truster's trust in them. I do not think that this conclusion is reasonable. The truster may be dissatisfied with the outcome, but it cannot reasonably be said that there has been an abuse or a breach of the truster's trust. It is for this reason, as will be recalled from Chapter 1, that I distinguish political trust (focusing on procedure) from the idea of political satisfaction (focusing on outcome).

My conclusion that trust focuses on procedure as opposed to outcome is also supported by empirical research. We know that the value of political trust is its link with public cooperation, including the public's willingness to accept authority decisions, its feeling obligated to obey laws and its performance evaluations of those in positions of authority. This link explains, in turn, why public trust in government is considered a means to the valuable ends of social stability, economic welfare and effective governance. However, and significantly, the work of scholars like Tom Tyler, Margaret Levi, John Hibbing and Elizabeth Theiss-Morse has shown that citizens' assessments of government legitimacy, and the cooperation following on from that legitimacy, are much more influenced by citizens' judgments of the procedure by which government actors make decisions than by the outcome of their decision-making.[99] They have concluded that, in fact, vis-à-vis legitimacy and cooperation, procedure is the 'central' or 'dominant' consideration for citizens.[100]

To be clear, the outcome of the interaction between citizens and government actors is not irrelevant. Outcomes are highly relevant, especially to citizens' satisfaction with government. However, the above empirical research supports the conclusion that outcomes have minimal importance to citizens' assessments of government legitimacy and their cooperation with government actors.[101] Because the principal basis for political trust's value to well-functioning democracies is public cooperation with government, it thus makes sense, I think, to conceptualise trust in terms of the three expectations above, which are procedural and whose connection with cooperation finds strong empirical support, rather than an expectation of a favourable outcome.[102]

99 Stephen J. Farnsworth, 'Congress and Citizen Discontent: Public Evaluations of the Membership of One's Own Representative' (2003) 1 *American Politics Research* 66; Amy Gangl, 'Procedural Justice Theory and Evaluations of the Lawmaking Process' (2003) 25 *Political Behavior* 119; John R. Hibbing and Elizabeth Theiss-Morse, 'Process Preferences and American Politics: What the People Want Government to Be' (2001) 95 *American Political Science Review* 145; John R. Hibbing and Elizabeth Theiss-Morse, *Stealth Democracy: Americans' Beliefs about How Government Should Work* (Cambridge: Cambridge University Press, 2002); Margaret Levi, Audrey Sacks and Tom Tyler, 'Conceptualizing Legitimacy, Measuring Legitimating Beliefs' (2009) 53 *American Behavioral Scientist* 354; Tom R. Tyler, *Why People Obey the Law* (New Haven, CT: Yale University Press, 1990); Tom R. Tyler, Jonathan D. Casper and Bonnie Fisher, 'Maintaining Allegiance toward Political Authorities: The Role of Prior Attitudes and the Use of Fair Procedures' (1989) 33 *American Journal of Political Science* 629; Tom R. Tyler and Peter Degoey, 'Collective Restraint in Social Dilemmas: Procedural Justice and Social Identification Effects on Support for Authorities' (1995) 69 *Journal of Personality and Social Psychology* 482; Tom R. Tyler and Peter Degoey, 'Trust in Organizational Authorities: The Influence of Motive Attributions on Willingness to Accept Decisions' in Roderick M. Kramer and Tom R. Tyler (eds.), *Trust in Organizations: Frontiers of Theory and Research* (Thousand Oaks, CA: Sage Publications, 1996), pp. 331–356.

100 Farnsworth, 'Congress and Citizen Discontent', 75; Gangl, 'Procedural Justice Theory and Evaluations', 136; Hibbing and Theiss-Morse, *Stealth Democracy*, p. 65; Tyler and Degoey, 'Trust in Organizational Authorities', pp. 335, 347.

101 Tyler, *Why People Obey the Law*, pp. 82–83.

102 It is noteworthy that the procedural judgments which these scholars have found to be connected with the public's assessments of government legitimacy and its cooperation with government actors largely pertain to what I have described as government goodwill, competence and fulfilment of fiduciary responsibility to citizens, including as I conceptualise those three expectations in later chapters in the specific context of the citizen–government relationship.

2.4 Applying the Definition of Trust to the Citizen–Government Relationship

In the citizen–government relationship, trust may thus be described, in broad terms, as a set of expectations held by citizens regarding the manner in which the elected branches will exercise their control over the social goods and services that citizens need. Since the expectations of goodwill and competence apply universally, trust in this relationship necessarily includes expectations that the elected branches, in exercising their control, will exercise goodwill towards citizens, and that they will act competently. I elaborate on these two expectations in Chapters 5 and 6, respectively.

What about the expectation of fiduciary responsibility, however? I submit that the citizen–government relationship is fiduciary in nature; and as a fiduciary relationship, trust in the citizen–government relationship necessarily includes an expectation of fiduciary responsibility. In so submitting, I rely on the growing body of fiduciary political theory literature.[103] In particular, I will employ Evan Fox-Decent's conceptualisation of a fiduciary relationship to demonstrate how the citizen–government relationship may be accurately characterised as fiduciary.[104] According to Fox-Decent, three conditions are necessary and sufficient for a fiduciary relationship to arise: (i) the fiduciary must have 'administrative', discretionary power over some set of the beneficiary's interests; (ii) the beneficiary must be 'incapable of controlling the fiduciary's exercise of power'; and (iii) the beneficiary's relevant interests must be 'capable of forming the subject matter of a fiduciary obligation'.[105] Each of these conditions is satisfied in the citizen–government relationship.

Fox-Decent's first condition has two sub-conditions: (a) the fiduciary must exercise discretionary power over a set of the beneficiary's interests

[103] As a representative sample, see Evan J. Criddle, 'Fiduciary Foundations of Administrative Law' (2006) 54 *UCLA Law Review* 117; Fox-Decent, 'The Fiduciary Nature'; Fox-Decent, *Sovereignty's Promise*; Ethan J. Leib, David L. Ponet and Michael Serota, 'A Fiduciary Theory of Judging' (2013) 101 *California Law Review* 699; D. Theodore Rave, 'Politicians as Fiduciaries' (2013) 126 *Harvard Law Review* 671.

[104] There is a difference of opinion in the literature as to what characterises a fiduciary relationship. I employ Fox-Decent's conceptualisation because there is significant overlap between his conceptualisation and those of others, it is rooted in case law and his work has been highly influential in the fiduciary political theory field.

[105] Fox-Decent, *Sovereignty's Promise*, pp. 93–94. These three conditions are consistent with what Leib, Ponet and Serota have identified as the three indicia of fiduciary relationships: discretion, vulnerability and trust: 'A Fiduciary Theory of Judging', 706.

and (b) that power must be 'administrative' in nature – that is, it must be 'institutional' (the exercise of power takes place in an institution which has its own substantive values and internal practices), 'purpose-laden' (the power is exercised for some purpose) and 'other-regarding' (that purpose involves a party other than the fiduciary).[106] Both sub-conditions are satisfied in the citizen–government relationship. As for (a), it will be recalled that the social goods and services that are the subject of social rights are things that citizens need; and as such, citizens have an interest in obtaining them. It will also be recalled that the elected branches exercise control over those social goods and services through the legislative and administrative steps outlined earlier in this chapter: the preparation, development and promulgation of primary legislation, the preparation and approval of the budget, and subsequent administrative action. Because in each of these steps, the elected branches exercise significant discretion, I think it is fair to say that the elected branches exercise discretionary power over a set of citizens' interests – that is, citizens' interests with respect to those social goods and services.

Regarding (b), I submit that the elected branches' discretionary power in this regard is also 'administrative' in nature. Its institutional character is fairly obvious. As for its being purpose-laden and other-regarding, it satisfies these elements for two reasons. The first is the overarching fact of sovereignty, which Fox-Decent has used to argue that the state's power over its subjects is purpose-laden and other-regarding.[107] According to Fox-Decent, because the state assumes sovereign powers, which it exercises through its institutions, subjects have no choice but to 'entrust the specification, administration, adjudication, and vindication of their rights to the state'.[108] For that reason, Fox-Decent has argued, the state exercises its powers for the purpose of benefiting its subjects. Included in those rights are social rights whose administration and specification citizens have no choice but to entrust to the state – and by extension, the elected branches which exercise its powers. Consequently, I think that Fox-Decent's argument may be fairly extended to the citizen–government relationship. Secondly, as will be recalled from earlier in this

[106] Fox-Decent, *Sovereignty's Promise*, p. 101.

[107] Ibid, p. 29. Owing to this overarching fact of sovereignty, Fox-Decent has recognised that 'with respect to the legislative, executive and judicial powers entailed by sovereignty, they each in their own familiar ways are institutional, purpose-laden, and other-regarding' (p. 112).

[108] Ibid, p. 111.

chapter, there is a good argument that citizens, via their payment of taxes to the state, specifically entrust social goods and services to the state – and again by extension, to the elected branches. Both of these points – the fact of sovereignty and citizens' specific entrustment of social goods and services to the elected branches via their payment of taxes to the state – support the same conclusion: that the elected branches' discretionary power over citizens' interests with respect to the relevant social goods and services is exercised for the purpose of benefiting citizens. And owing to that conclusion, their power may be fairly characterised as both purpose-laden and other-regarding.

Fox-Decent's second condition for a fiduciary relationship is that the beneficiary is incapable of controlling the fiduciary's exercise of power; and following on from that fact, the beneficiary is vulnerable to abuses of the fiduciary's power.[109] This condition is also satisfied in the citizen–government relationship. As Fox-Decent has argued for the state–subject relationship, '[p]rivate parties have no authority to . . . exercise the powers necessary to determine' their rights: 'they do not get to make laws that apply to others' and so, 'are juridically incapable of exercising public authority'.[110] This argument applies equally to the closely related citizen–government relationship. Aside from their limited voting power, citizens are incapable of controlling the elected branches' power over their interests with respect to the social goods and services that they need. They do not dictate the content of social welfare legislation, they do not decide what is and is not included in the budget, and they do not control the administrative action through which the legislation is implemented. Hence, citizens are vulnerable to abuses of the elected branches' power.

Lastly, the beneficiary's interests, for Fox-Decent, must be 'capable of forming the subject matter of a fiduciary obligation'.[111] The fiduciary relationship, as we know, has trust at its core. As Fox-Decent has explained, the fiduciary concept was 'born of a rich and complex legal history animated by a concern to protect the integrity of relations of trust'.[112] For Fox-Decent, in contrast to how the literature from other disciplines has conceptualised it, trust is a presumptive concept – that is, the fiduciary exercises their power 'on the basis of the beneficiary's trust' regardless of whether the beneficiary does anything to repose trust in

[109] Ibid, p. 101.
[110] Ibid, p. 111.
[111] Ibid, pp. 93–94.
[112] Ibid, p. 30.

them.[113] Fox-Decent has therefore argued that in the state–subject relationship, trust is both the basis for the state's authority over its subjects and its duty to them. As he has summarised, the law, via the fiduciary principle, 'entrusts the state to establish legal order on behalf of the people'; and the state in turn, 'exercises power on the basis of the people's trust . . . precisely because the fiduciary principle has entrusted the state with public powers on their behalf'.[114] The same reasoning may be applied to the citizen–government relationship. Regardless of citizens' actual trust in the elected branches with respect to social rights, the fiduciary principle entrusts the elected branches with the above power on citizens' behalf; and the elected branches exercise their power on the basis of citizens' trust. The citizen–government relationship therefore satisfies Fox-Decent's third and final condition for a fiduciary relationship.

My analysis above mirrors the reasoning of, and conclusion drawn, by Laura Underkuffler in her work on positive rights.[115] Underkuffler has grounded positive rights in fiduciary theory; and as an initial step, she has characterised the relationship between citizens and government (what she terms the 'government/citizen relationship') as fiduciary. To do so, she has relied, as I have, on Fox-Decent's conceptualisation of the fiduciary relationship, recognising it as the 'foundational contemporary work'.[116] Extrapolating from Fox-Decent's conceptualisation, Underkuffler has explained that 'fiduciary relationships are imposed by law in situations that involve relationships between stronger and weaker parties', where 'the stronger party is [often] imbued with power by virtue of a structured, institutional, hierarchical relationship, with all of the opportunities for overreaching that such relationships involve' and the weaker party's vulnerability has an 'element of incapacity about it'.[117] What underlies all of this, for her, is 'the beneficiary's consent (on some level) to the structural arrangement, and the idea of the beneficiary's trust'.[118] And applying Fox-Decent's three conditions to the government/citizen relationship, Underkuffler has concluded that 'the match between

113 Ibid, p. 105.

114 Ibid, p. 106.

115 See Laura S. Underkuffler, 'Property, Sovereignty, and the Public Trust' (2017) 18 *Theoretical Inquiries in Law* 329; Laura S. Underkuffler, 'Fiduciary Theory: The Missing Piece for Positive Rights' in Evan Criddle et al. (eds.), *Fiduciary Government* (Cambridge: Cambridge University Press, 2018).

116 Underkuffler, 'Fiduciary Theory: The Missing Piece', p. 109.

117 Ibid, p. 109.

118 Ibid, p. 109.

these characteristics and that relationship is obvious'.[119] Accordingly, my conclusion on the citizen–government relationship's fiduciary nature finds support in Underkuffler's work.

I recognise that fiduciary political theory has its critics.[120] For the reasons which scholars in this area have put forward, however, I think that the theory holds significant promise; and following on from this, I suggest that it can be applied to the citizen–government relationship.[121]

Furthermore, my suggestion that the citizen–government relationship is fiduciary in nature also finds support in Barber's sociological work.[122] As will be recalled from earlier in this chapter, Barber roots the expectation of fiduciary responsibility in the fact that in certain relationships, the trustee possesses special knowledge and skills which make the trustee's technically competent performance difficult to monitor by the truster. The citizen–government relationship satisfies Barber's description. In exercising their control over social goods and services, the elected branches possess special knowledge and skills which would make it difficult for citizens, as trusters, to monitor their technical competence. I elaborate on such competence in Chapter 6. Barber also specifically recognises the application of this expectation to the relationship between 'The Public and Its Leaders'.[123] There is therefore good reason to believe that Barber himself would have concluded that the expectation of fiduciary responsibility applies to the citizen–government relationship.

I thus propose that the citizen–government relationship is a fiduciary relationship – and so, that trust in the relationship includes, in addition to expectations of goodwill and competence, an expectation that the elected branches, in exercising their control over social goods and services, will fulfil their fiduciary responsibility to citizens. I elaborate on this expectation in Chapter 7.

[119] Ibid, p. 109.

[120] For example, see Seth Davis, 'The False Promise of Fiduciary Government' (2014) 89 *Notre Dame Law Review* 1145; Timothy Endicott, 'Equity and Administrative Behaviour: A Commentary' in P.G. Turner (ed.), *Equity and Administration* (Cambridge: Cambridge University Press, 2016); Ethan J. Leib and Stephen R. Galoob, 'Fiduciary Political Theory: A Critique' (2016) 125 *The Yale Law Journal* 1820.

[121] For a response to the above critiques, see Evan Fox-Decent, 'Challenges to Public Fiduciary Theory: An Assessment' in D. Gordon Smith and Andrew S. Gold (eds.), *Research Handbook on Fiduciary Law* (Cheltenham: Edward Elgar, 2018).

[122] Barber, *The Logic and Limits*.

[123] Ibid, pp. 80–81. Barber devotes an entire chapter of his book to such relationships.

Before concluding this chapter, I want to highlight one point. We may ask: what is the difference between the expectation of goodwill and the expectation of fiduciary responsibility? Based on my theorisation of these expectations up to this point, it may seem like there is significant overlap between the two. Depending on how we define 'fiduciary responsibility' for the purpose of the latter expectation, there may be a great deal of overlap. However, as we will see in Chapter 7, I define fiduciary responsibility in the context of the citizen–government relationship in narrow terms, specifically in terms of non-corruption. This gives the expectation of fiduciary responsibility a well-defined scope and differentiates it from the expectation of goodwill – which, as we will see in Chapter 5, involves expectations of procedural fairness and what I describe as 'good intentions'. Hence, while the two (and, in fact, all three expectations) are related, they are nonetheless different.

3

The Citizen–Government Relationship in a Network of Trust Relationships

Owing to the citizen–government relationship's characterisation in Chapter 2 as a trust relationship (i.e., a relationship in which the elements of control, discretion/uncertainty and vulnerability are present), we know that trust can arise in it. And I took steps there to describe what it means for citizens to trust the elected branches with respect to social rights. In this chapter, I expand on this description of trust in the citizen–government relationship using an idea from the scholarship on trust that I call the 'network conception of trust'. This conception posits that in contemporary societies, a trust relationship, like the citizen–government relationship, is embedded in a complex network of social relationships, and that trust in that relationship depends on the network of relationships in which it is embedded. So, applying this idea to the citizen–government relationship, I advance two claims in this chapter: first, that in contemporary social democracies, the citizen–government relationship is embedded in a complex network of social relationships among citizens, the elected branches, and other state and non-state actors; and secondly, that trust in the citizen–government relationship depends on the relationships that constitute the network.

In advancing these claims, this chapter adds needed nuance to our understanding of trust in the citizen–government relationship. It makes clear that the citizen–government relationship does not exist in a vacuum, with trust in that relationship being dependent on other relationships. However, more than offering such nuance, the claims advanced here are of key relevance to the principal argument of this book. As I explain shortly, one of the relationships that constitute the network within which the citizen–government relationship is embedded is the relationship between citizens and the courts that arises out of social rights adjudication (what I call the 'citizen–court relationship'). Following on from the claims advanced in this chapter, we can thus conclude that trust in the citizen–government relationship depends on the citizen–court relationship. And this conclusion, as we will see in

Chapter 4, lays the foundation for my contention in that chapter that courts, via their enforcement of social rights, can foster citizens' trust in the elected branches.

3.1 The 'Network Conception of Trust'

What I am calling the 'network conception of trust' does not belong to a single author or to a single discipline.[1] Rather, it is a broad idea that has been expressed by numerous writers on trust across a range of disciplines, including sociology,[2] economics,[3] philosophy,[4] political theory[5] and management.[6] Based on my reading, these writers' arguments (though dissimilar in some respects) share two fundamental features that

1 The expression 'network conception of trust' is drawn from Karen S. Cook and Russell Hardin, 'Norms of Cooperativeness and Networks of Trust' in Michael Hechter and Karl-Dieter Opp (eds.), *Social Norms* (New York: Russell Sage Foundation, 2001), pp. 327–347.

2 James Coleman, *Foundations of Social Theory* (Cambridge, MA: Harvard University Press, 1994); Karen S. Cook and Alexandra Gerbasi, 'Trust' in Peter Hedstrom and Peter S. Bearman (eds.), *The Oxford Handbook of Analytical Sociology* (Oxford: Oxford University Press, 2009), pp. 218–242; Cook and Hardin, 'Norms of Cooperativeness'; Mark S. Granovetter, 'The Strength of Weak Ties' (1973) 78 *American Journal of Sociology* 1360; Jocelyn Pixley, 'Impersonal Trust in Global Mediating Organizations' (1999) 42 *Sociological Perspectives* 647; Susan P. Shapiro, 'The Social Control of Impersonal Trust' (1987) 93 *American Journal of Sociology* 623; Susan Shapiro, 'The Grammar of Trust' in Jocelyn Pixley (ed.), *New Perspectives on Emotions in Finance: The Sociology of Confidence, Fear and Betrayal* (Abingdon: Routledge, 2012), pp. 99–118; Lynne Zucker, 'Production of Trust: Institutional Sources of Economic Structure, 1840 to 1920' (1986) 8 *Research in Organizational Behavior* 53.

3 Partha Dasgupta, 'Trust as a Commodity' in Diego Gambetta (ed.), *Trust: Making and Breaking Cooperative Relations* (Oxford: Basil Blackwell, 1988), pp. 49–72; Mark Granovetter, 'Economic Action and Social Structure: The Problem of Embeddedness' (1985) 91 *American Journal of Sociology* 481.

4 Annette C. Baier, *Moral Prejudices: Essays on Ethics* (Cambridge, MA: Harvard University Press, 1995).

5 Karen S. Cook, Russell Hardin and Margaret Levi, *Cooperation without Trust?* (New York: Russell Sage Foundation, 2005); Roger Cotterrell, 'Trusting in Law: Legal and Moral Concepts of Trust' (1993) 46 *Current Legal Problems* 75; Henry Farrell, 'Institutions and Midlevel Explanations of Trust' in Karen S. Cook, Margaret Levi and Russell Hardin (eds.), *Whom Can We Trust? How Groups, Networks, and Institutions Make Trust Possible* (New York: Russell Sage Foundation, 2009), pp. 127–148; Margaret Levi, 'A State of Trust' in Valerie Braithwaite and Margaret Levi (eds.), *Trust and Governance* (New York: Russell Sage Foundation, 1998), pp. 77–101; Charles Tilly, *Democracy* (Cambridge: Cambridge University Press, 2007).

6 Jörg Sydow, 'Understanding the Constitution of Interorganizational Trust' in Christel Lane and Reinhard Bachmann (eds.), *Trust within and between Organizations: Conceptual Issues and Empirical Applications* (Oxford: Oxford University Press, 1998), pp. 31–63.

I will use to define this conception of trust. The first is that in contemporary societies, relationships in which trust may arise are embedded in a rich social context – a social context that comprises complex structures or 'networks' of social relationships.[7] The second feature of this conception is that trust in a given trust relationship depends on the other relationships that constitute the network in which the former is embedded.

We can see this network conception of trust most clearly in the work of sociologists and political scientists Karen Cook and Russell Hardin.[8] Cook and Hardin have sought to build on, and apply to the concept of trust, the scholarship of sociologist Richard Emerson on the concept of power.[9] For Emerson, a key flaw in the sociological power research up to the point in time in which he was working (the 1960s) was 'the implicit treatment of power as though it were an attribute of a person or a group ("X is an influential person," "Y is a powerful group," etc.)'.[10] Breaking with this orthodoxy in the power literature, Emerson argued that power is better seen as 'a property of the social relation', thereby shifting the focus of analysis on power from the individual to the relationship.[11] Following on from his relational understanding of power, Emerson, in later work (alone and collaboratively), theorised that so-called power-dependence relationships (or what they broadly called 'exchange relations') 'connect' with one another to form an 'exchange network'.[12] By 'connect', Emerson and colleagues meant that two exchange relations were contingent on one another or interdependent. They noted: '[t]wo exchange relations between actors A-B and actors A-C are connected to

[7] Some writers, rather than using the term 'network' as I have, have opted for alternative terms, including 'system' or 'mosaic': see Coleman, *Foundations of Social Theory* for the former and Dasgupta, 'Trust as a Commodity' for the latter. However, the vast majority of writers have adopted the 'network' terminology.

[8] Cook and Hardin, 'Norms of Cooperativeness'. See also Cook et al., *Cooperation without Trust.*

[9] Richard M. Emerson, 'Power-Dependence Relations' (1962) 27 *American Sociological Review* 31; Richard M. Emerson, 'Power-Dependence Relations: Two Experiments' (1964) 27 *Sociometry* 282; Karen S. Cook and Richard M. Emerson, 'Power, Equity and Commitment in Exchange Networks' (1978) 43 *American Sociological Review* 721; Karen S. Cook et al., 'The Distribution of Power in Exchange Networks: Theory and Experimental Results' (1983) 89 *American Journal of Sociology* 275.

[10] Emerson, 'Power-Dependence Relations', 31.

[11] Ibid, 32.

[12] For a summary, see Karen S. Cook et al., 'Social Exchange Theory' in John DeLamater and Amanda Ward (eds.), *Handbook of Social Psychology* (New York: Springer, 2013), p. 64.

form the minimal network B-A-C to the degree that exchange in one relation is contingent on exchange (or nonexchange) in the other relation'.[13]

Cook and Hardin have proposed that Emerson's work on power provides an appropriate model for a theory of trust. As they have said, Emerson's work 'does for the concept, power, what can be done for the concept, trust. It shifts the framework surrounding the study of power from that of an attribute of an individual . . . to that of a property of a social relation'.[14] Following Emerson's lead, Cook and Hardin have adopted a relational understanding of trust.[15] They have defined trust, similar to the way I have, as a three-part relationship involving a truster (A), a trustee (B) and some relatively defined matter (*x*), with the relationship taking the form of 'A trusts B to do *x*'.[16] And they have suggested that trust necessarily depends on relational considerations (i.e., factors pertaining to the relationship), including the nature of the truster's interests, the trustee's interests, the two parties' knowledge of one another and other attributes such as the truster's gender, age or education level. At the same time, however, and the key point for present purposes, Cook and Hardin have also suggested that the 'commonplace discussion of trust between two individuals as though they were abstracted from their social context misses too much of what is at stake to make sense of social relations'.[17] They have argued, rather, that trust is best conceived of as 'embedded in a network of relations', and consequently, it also depends 'on the larger context of our social relations and the broader network of relations that surrounds us'.[18] Put simply, trust is 'a function of iterated or ongoing interactions' in which the truster and the trustee are involved.[19]

Sociologist James Coleman, in his highly influential book *Foundations of Social Theory*, has similarly developed what may be described as a network conception of trust. In line with Cook and Hardin, Coleman has conceived of trust as arising in a relationship between a truster and a

[13] Cook et al., 'The Distribution of Power in Exchange Networks', 275, 277.

[14] Cook and Hardin, 'Norms of Cooperativeness', p. 331.

[15] Ibid, p. 332. See also Cook et al., *Cooperation without Trust*, p. 2.

[16] Cook and Hardin, 'Norms of Cooperativeness', p. 331. Cook and Hardin have swapped 'A' and 'B' in their formulation and have adopted a slightly different role for 'x' (i.e., 'to do x').

[17] Ibid, p. 330.

[18] Ibid, pp. 330–331.

[19] Ibid, pp. 330–331.

trustee.[20] And he has proposed, much like Cook and Hardin, that trust relationships exist in structures that encompass groups of relationships – referred to by him as 'systems of trust'.[21]

Coleman has specifically identified three such systems of trust: mutual trust, intermediaries in trust and third party trust. He has suggested that within each of these systems, trust in a trust relationship depends on another trust relationship; or to put it in slightly different, more active language, one trust relationship impacts trust in another trust relationship. In the first category of system, a mutual trust system, two actors are in two trust relationships with one another, each actor occupying the role of truster in one of those relationships and the role of trustee in the other. Coleman has claimed that the mutual trust system fosters trust in a trust relationship by increasing the likelihood that the trustee in that relationship will keep the trust, out of fear that if the trustee does not keep their trust, the truster (who is the trustee in the second trust relationship) will not keep theirs.

In an intermediary in trust system, an actor outside the immediate trust relationship serves as both trustee for one party to the trust relationship and as truster for the other party, thereby acting as an intermediary between the two parties. Coleman has identified, in particular, three kinds of intermediaries: what he has called 'advisors', 'guarantors' and 'entrepreneurs'. I shall briefly elaborate on one intermediary – 'the advisor' – as it is relevant to my later analysis in this chapter. The advisor is an actor outside the immediate trust relationship who essentially advises the truster to trust the trustee. As Coleman has explained, the truster's relationship with the advisor fosters the truster's trust in the trustee because the truster 'trusts the advisor's judgment, leading him to place trust in the ability and integrity of the trustee . . . It is the trust[e]r's trust in an advisor's judgment that leads to placement of trust in the performance capability of the ultimate trustee'.[22] For instance, at the time that *Foundations of Social Theory* was published (the early 1990s), Coleman identified the mass media as an increasingly influential 'advisor' in the relationship between the public and its government in contemporary societies. He explained, as one example, that the mass media's exposure of 'defects in the trusted elites' can lead to the 'withdrawal of

[20] Coleman, *Foundations of Social Theory*, p. 96.
[21] Ibid, p. 177.
[22] Ibid, p. 181.

public trust in the elites'.[23]

Lastly, a third party system involves a situation where a truster accepts a promise from a third party to aid in the truster's transaction with the trustee. According to Coleman, the truster's relationship with the third party impacts their trust in the trustee as it allows the truster to transact with the trustee where they would not otherwise.

While the above two- and three-party systems are the focus of Coleman's analysis, he has recognised that trust also arises in larger systems (i.e., involving more parties). And this, once again, aligns with Cook and Hardin's suggestion of a network of relationships. In such larger systems, Coleman has said that the smaller systems of mutual trust, intermediaries in trust and third party trust act as 'building blocks' to construct the larger system.[24]

One final example of a network conception of trust is that of sociologist Susan Shapiro.[25] Like the above writers, Shapiro has conceived of trust as arising in a relationship – specifically an agency relationship 'in which principals … invest resources, authority, or responsibility in another [an agent] to act on their behalf for some uncertain future return'.[26] Shapiro's network argument, however, is much more targeted in scope than that of either Cook and Hardin or Coleman. She is focused on a specific type of network or system – one involving third parties who impose a variety of social control measures on the trustee in the trustee's relationship with the truster (e.g., professional associations, regulatory watchdogs and certified public accountants). Shapiro has called these third parties 'guardians of trust'. She has claimed that through social control measures, a guardian of trust – and more precisely, the guardian's relationship with the truster – fosters trust between the truster and the trustee, with the resulting trust being 'impersonal trust' (a term which will be recalled from Chapter 2).[27] Thus, Shapiro's understanding of trust, though targeted, parallels the conceptions of Cook and Hardin, and Coleman. Additionally, she has recognised, similarly to Coleman's suggestion regarding larger systems of trust, that such truster–guardian relationships rarely exist in isolation: as she has explained, they usually

[23] Ibid, p. 194.

[24] Ibid, p. 188.

[25] Shapiro, 'The Social Control'. See also Shapiro, 'The Grammar of Trust'.

[26] Shapiro, 'The Social Control', 626. As I noted in Chapter 2, I do not agree with this characterisation of a trust relationship as it necessitates that the trustee's control over the good or service results from the truster entrusting.

[27] Ibid, 636 (footnote 18).

form part of 'a complicated matrix of social-control strategies – that intervene at different points in the delivery of trust and scrutinize different roles, records, or organizational routines from different perspectives, for different purposes'.[28] Hence, for Shapiro (much like Coleman, as well as Cook and Hardin), trust in a trust relationship depends on the network of relationships (for her, truster–guardian relationships) in which it is embedded.

3.2 The Network Conception Follows on from a Relational View of Trust

As Cook and Hardin have made clear, the network conception of trust follows on from a relational view of the concept.[29] I noted in Chapter 2 that the relational view of trust is to be distinguished from a competing view which considers trust a trait or a disposition of an individual actor.[30] In the latter view of trust, the unit of analysis is the individual – that is, the truster. Focusing on the individual, that view envisages trust as depending on a single factor that is internal to the truster: whether the truster has a specific trait or a disposition towards trusting others. If the truster has this trait or disposition, we may say that the truster is a 'trusting' person and accordingly, that trust exists.[31] Trust, in that view, does not depend on the party whom the truster is 'trusting' (i.e., the trustee) or the circumstances surrounding that trust. In other words, trust is a *psychological* phenomenon.[32] In the relational view, in contrast, trust is treated as a property of a social relationship.[33] The unit of analysis is the relationship, not the individual truster, and so, trust depends on that relationship.[34] In other words, trust, in the relational view, is a *social* phenomenon. Now, of course, trust, in the relational view, depends on things that are internal to the relationship, including the nature of the

[28] Ibid, 644–645.

[29] Cook and Hardin, 'Norms of Cooperativeness', pp. 330–331.

[30] Russell Hardin, 'Conceptions and Explanations of Trust' in Karen S. Cook (ed.), *Trust in Society* (New York: Russell Sage Foundation, 2001). See also Cook and Gerbasi, 'Trust', p. 220.

[31] Hardin, 'Conceptions and Explanations of Trust', pp. 12–13.

[32] Reinhard Bachmann and Andrew C. Inkpen, 'Understanding Institutional-Based Trust Building Processes in Inter-Organizational Relationships' (2011) 32 *Organization Studies* 281, 282.

[33] Cook and Hardin, 'Norms of Cooperativeness', pp. 330–331. See also Cook and Gerbasi, 'Trust', p. 220; Cook et al., *Cooperation without Trust*, p. 2; Levi, 'A State of Trust', p. 78.

[34] Cook and Gerbasi, 'Trust', p. 220; Cook and Hardin, 'Norms of Cooperativeness', p. 331.

good or service at issue in the relationship and the truster's knowledge of or familiarity with the trustee.[35] For example, I made the point in Chapter 2 that where the good or service at issue in the relationship (i.e., X) changes, the truster's expectation of the trustee's competence may change and consequently, the extent to which the truster trusts the trustee may also change. However, at the same time, and as the above writers on trust have stressed, social relationships in contemporary societies are embedded in a rich social context. And because of this embeddedness, to use the words of sociologist Mark Granovetter, 'to construe them as independent [from each other] is a grievous misunderstanding'.[36] It is from the latter point which the network conception of trust stems. Trust, as a property of a social relationship, depends not only on factors that are internal to that relationship, but also on external factors – that is, on the network in which it is embedded.

As should be clear by this point, in this book, following the lead of many prominent writers on the concept, I have adopted a relational view of trust. Like Cook and Hardin, I have conceived of trust as arising in a three-part relationship between a truster, a trustee and some good or service (X). That relationship is built on the three elements described in Chapter 2 of control, discretion/uncertainty and vulnerability. Furthermore, it will be recalled that in Chapter 2, I characterised the citizen–government relationship as a trust relationship of this sort. From these two points, coupled with the foregoing discussion of the network conception of trust as following on from a relational view, I suggest that it follows, in turn, that the network conception of trust is appropriately applied to the citizen–government relationship. And applying the network conception of trust to the citizen–government relationship, I make two principal claims. First, I claim that in contemporary social democracies, the citizen–government relationship is embedded in a network of trust relationships that exist among citizens, the elected branches of government, and other state and non-state actors. As I explain in more detail in the next part of the chapter, these actors include, but are not limited to, private providers of social goods and services, the media and, importantly for the purpose of this book's principal argument, the courts. Secondly, I claim that trust in the citizen–government relationship depends on this network of relationships. This includes, again significantly for this book's principal argument, citizens' relationship with the

[35] Cook and Hardin, 'Norms of Cooperativeness', pp. 331, 334.
[36] Granovetter, 'Economic Action and Social Structure', 482.

courts that arises out of social rights adjudication. I now proceed with making out these two claims.

3.3 The Social Rights Network

I will begin with my first claim: that the citizen–government relationship is embedded in a network of trust relationships among citizens, state and non-state actors. To make out this first claim, I will take steps to demonstrate how the citizen–government relationship interconnects with several different parties and relationships to form a network configuration. I will therefore, in essence, walk the reader through the construction of this network (what I call the 'social rights network').

3.3.1 Defining the Boundaries of the Social Rights Network

Before so constructing, I will start by defining the boundaries of the social rights network. In contemporary social democracies, the fulfilment of social rights involves an ever-larger cast of characters and array of relationships. Because of increasing globalisation, privatisation and public interest litigation, courts and other decision-makers, extra-governmental parties such as private industry, lawyers, legal aid bodies, non-governmental and international organisations, as well as foreign governments, have come to play a role in the process of social rights fulfilment. In my view, all these parties and the relationships existing among them, citizens and the elected branches, would constitute the rich social context in which the citizen–government relationship is embedded and thus, the full network of relationships for social rights (i.e., the complete social rights network).

It would be impossible to analyse all these parties and the relationships among them in the limited space of this chapter. Fortunately, my aim is not to do so. Instead, my aim is merely to introduce the network conception of trust to social rights law for the specific purpose of my analysis in Chapter 4 on the proper role of the courts in enforcing constitutional social rights. Given this specific objective, I will limit my consideration of the social rights network to a subset of three parties in the network and the relationships among them. These parties are private providers of social goods and services, the media and the courts.[37] I have

[37] A caveat: my brief analysis of these parties should not be taken as a thorough analysis of their complex roles in the process of social rights fulfilment. I acknowledge that their

chosen these parties for a few reasons. First, they provide good illustrations by which I may introduce and apply the network conception to social rights law. Secondly, as I explain shortly, they play key roles in social rights matters and therefore, it makes sense to include them in any thoughtful analysis of this area. Lastly, I have obviously chosen the courts as they are the central focus of this book's argument.

Before turning to the first party, private providers of social goods and services, I will clarify one point. The relationships that exist among the above parties, citizens and the elected branches, are not merely social relationships (which is what the network conception of trust, as I understand it, posits) but may accurately be characterised as trust relationships (as I have defined the term in Chapter 2). In fact, I anticipate that most, if not all, the relationships in the social rights network may be characterised in this way. This is relevant because, as trust relationships, the extent to which a truster's trust in a trustee depends on another relationship of which the truster is part is likely to depend, in turn, on the extent to which the truster trusts the trustee in that second relationship. Put simply, the presence of trust in one relationship is likely to impact the level of trust in another relationship. Coleman, for instance, makes this point in his discussion of 'the advisor' as an intermediary in trust. He explains that the truster's relationship with the advisor impacts their trust relationship with the trustee because the truster trusts the advisor. If the truster does not trust the advisor, their relationship with the advisor will not impact their trust in the trustee. For this reason, in my analysis that follows, I briefly outline how each relationship would be expected to satisfy the three elements of a trust relationship from Chapter 2. That said, to be clear, there is no reason why trust in a trust relationship depends only on the trust relationships in its social network (as opposed to other social, but non-trust, relationships). It is thus conceivable that some of the relationships in the social rights network would not satisfy the three elements of a trust relationship. And their failure to so satisfy would not necessarily detract from their capacity to impact trust in a trust relationship.

respective roles in the process are significantly more complicated than I can accommodate in this chapter. As I have said, my analysis here is for the limited purpose of my analysis in Chapter 4 of the proper role of the courts in the enforcement of constitutional social rights.

3.3.2 *Constructing the Social Rights Network*

3.3.2.1 Private Providers of Social Goods and Services

The first party that I will describe here as forming part of the social rights network is private providers of social goods and services. In contemporary social democracies, the provision of social goods and services by the state is entirely dependent on those who directly provide those goods and services. Public health care, for example, depends on, among many others, physicians, nurses and medical technicians. Public education depends on teachers, teaching assistants, principals or head-teachers and other staff. Governments may either employ these providers or, as is more commonly the case in recent years, they may outsource to them.[38] At the same time, as I mentioned briefly in Chapter 2 with respect to the direct/indirect control distinction, these providers rarely find themselves confined to a single, public system. In the vast majority of cases, they, as an overall group, have the opportunity to offer their goods and services privately. A given provider may either have the option of offering their services concurrently in the public and private systems, or they may be compelled to choose one. In either case, there is likely to exist a cohort of providers who offer their goods and services privately. This cohort of providers is the focus of this section.

The existence of this cohort of private providers has an important consequence for citizens on the receiving end. It means the availability of a private market, the effect of which is that citizens (technically speaking) are not wholly dependent on the elected branches for the social goods and services that they need; they have the option of obtaining those social goods and services from sources alternative to the elected branches (i.e., private providers) who, much like the elected branches, maintain control over the goods and services. In Chapter 2, I referred to this state of affairs as the elected branches maintaining partial control. To make clear the consequence that this state of affairs has for citizens, I will refer to private providers from here forward as 'alternative sources'. Where a private market is available, in addition to the citizen–government relationship, citizens may also be said to have a relationship with the alternative source. By this I do not mean that citizens have opted for, or are even in a financial position to opt for, the alternative source over the elected branches (a point which will become relevant in the next part); I mean

[38] Stephen Goldsmith and William D. Eggers, *Governing by Network: The New Shape of the Public Sector* (Washington, DC: Brookings Institution Press, 2004), pp. 13–14.

simply that the alternative source is available to citizens, making it part of the rich social context or network in which the citizen–government relationship is embedded. Expanding on the three-part form that I developed in Chapter 2 (where the elected branches are the trustee (A), citizens are the truster (B), and X is the social good or service at issue), I will refer to the alternative source of X as C.

Consistent with what I suggested earlier, the relationship between citizens (B) and the alternative source (C) (what I call the 'alternative source relationship') may be characterised as a trust relationship. C, like the elected branches, maintains control over X, a social good or service that citizens need. This is what makes C an 'alternative source' in the first place. Furthermore, in the vast majority of cases, C also holds some discretion in exercising this control vis-à-vis citizens. In education, for example, private educational institutions have discretion over the standards for admission, who they admit, the courses they offer, the grading scheme and the awarding of diplomas. Of course, this discretion will vary from context to context and will depend on regulation, professional standards and ethical considerations. That said, C ultimately holds some discretion, leaving citizens uncertain about their interaction with the alternative source. Lastly, given the alternative source's control and discretion over X, coupled with citizens' need for X, citizens are vulnerable to the alternative source. Figure 3.1 reflects pictorially the citizen–government and alternative source relationships. The lines are the trust relationships, and the arrows indicate the direction in which trust flows in the relationship from truster to trustee.

To provide some level of concreteness to the scenario depicted in Figure 3.1, let us make X a defined good or service: primary education, continuing on with our previous example. Consistent with what I said earlier about the common concurrence of public systems and private markets, in most contemporary social democracies, primary education is available both publicly (through a public education system) and privately. The latter may be delivered by private educational institutions (e.g., institutions that are religiously affiliated or based on a particular theory of teaching) or by private tutors. In this example, C in Figure 3.1 represents one of these private institutions or private tutors, and citizens may have the option of sending their children to a public institution (as part of the public system) (A) or to the private institution or tutor (C).

As well, in contemporary social democracies, assuming a competitive market, it is unlikely that citizens would only have access to one alternative source of X. In our primary education example, we can expect

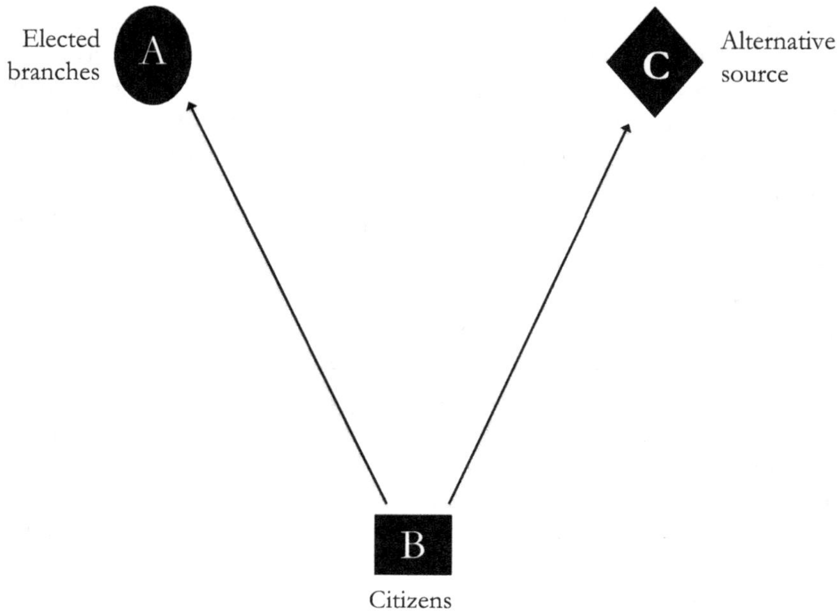

Figure 3.1 The citizen–government and alternative source relationships

citizens to have a range of alternative sources, including both multiple private institutions and private tutors. This means that citizens may not only have the option of turning to a source of X alternative to the elected branches, but additionally, in exercising this option, they may have a choice of alternative sources. For the purpose of illustration, let us say that citizens have a choice of three alternative sources: C1, C2 and C3. Assuming the same circumstances as before (satisfying the elements of control, discretion/uncertainty and vulnerability), the relationships between citizens and each of C1, C2 and C3 may be characterised as trust relationships. This choice of alternative sources is depicted in Figure 3.2.

The foregoing analysis has captured one category of relationships in social welfare: the relationships between the consumers of social goods and services (citizens) and their providers (the elected branches and alternative sources). For the purpose of this book, this category of relationships is the most fundamental. I would be remiss, however, in developing the network and in the interests of comprehensiveness, if I did not at least point out that these parties are also involved in another category of relationships. In contemporary social democracies, the

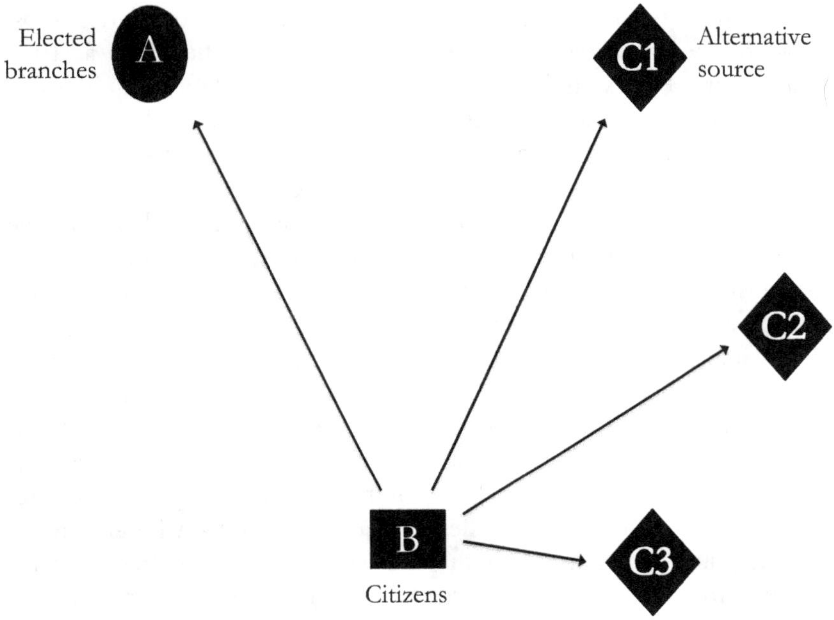

Figure 3.2 The choice of alternative source relationships

elected branches occupy dual roles: as a source of social goods and services to citizens (hence, the relationships I just described) and as a representative of citizens via the democratic process.[39] In their role as citizens' representative, the elected branches are also responsible for regulating the relationship between citizens and alternative sources: this may include licensing and setting standards of practice, overseeing the liberty of these alternative sources to set fees or select to whom they deliver their services, restricting the power of these alternative sources' professional associations to sanction their members, and imposing criminal liability on these alternative sources.[40] Given this role and its responsibilities, we may say that the elected branches, in addition to being in relationships with citizens, are likewise in relationships with the alternative sources.

[39] Varun Gauri and Daniel M. Brinks, 'Introduction: The Elements of Legalization and the Triangular Shape of Social and Economic Rights' in Varun Gauri and Daniel M. Brinks (eds.), *Courting Social Justice: Judicial Enforcement of Social and Economic Rights in the Developing World* (Cambridge: Cambridge University Press, 2010), pp. 10–11.

[40] Ibid, p. 10.

Like the citizen–government and alternative source relationships, I also think that it is fair to characterise these relationships as trust relationships. For example, we may conceive of the relationship between the elected branches and an alternative source as a trust relationship in which the elected branches are truster and the alternative source is trustee. This conception makes sense if we recognise, as Bernard Barber has, that the truster in a trust relationship does not necessarily need to be the direct recipient of the good or service which is at issue in the relationship.[41] For instance, a parent may be in a trust relationship with a third party for a good or service that their child will ultimately receive. This would be the case in our primary education example from earlier. So, how are the three elements of a trust relationship satisfied in this relationship? The alternative source continues to maintain control and discretion in exercising that control over X – a good or service that citizens, and by extension the elected branches, need. In this relationship, however, it is the elected branches, rather than citizens, who are uncertain: they are uncertain about the alternative source's interaction with citizens. And as the elected branches represent citizens, who are vulnerable to the alternative source as I described earlier, the elected branches are also vulnerable to the alternative source: unfavourable behaviour by the alternative source towards citizens opens the elected branches up to negative repercussions, including the possibility of being voted out of power by citizens. This specific group of trust relationships between the elected branches and each of the alternative sources (C1, C2 and C3) is depicted in Figure 3.3.

3.3.2.2 The Media

I turn next to a somewhat undervalued party in the social rights literature – the media. Scholars of both political science and media studies have recognised that in contemporary democracies, the media plays a fundamental role in the relationship between citizens and their governments.[42]

[41] Bernard Barber, *The Logic and Limits of Trust* (New Brunswick, NJ: Rutgers University Press, 1983), p. 17.

[42] Kees Aarts, Audun Fladmoe and Jesper Stromback, 'Media, Political Trust, and Political Knowledge' in Toril Aalberg and James Curran (eds.), *How Media Inform Democracy: A Comparative Approach* (Abingdon: Routledge, 2012), pp. 98–99; Kelly Blidook, 'Media, Public Opinion and Health Care in Canada: How the Media Affect "The Way Things Are"' (2008) 41 *Canadian Journal of Political Science* 355; Mark Bovens and Anchrit Wille, 'Falling or Fluctuating Trust Levels? The Case of the Netherlands' in Sonja Zmerli

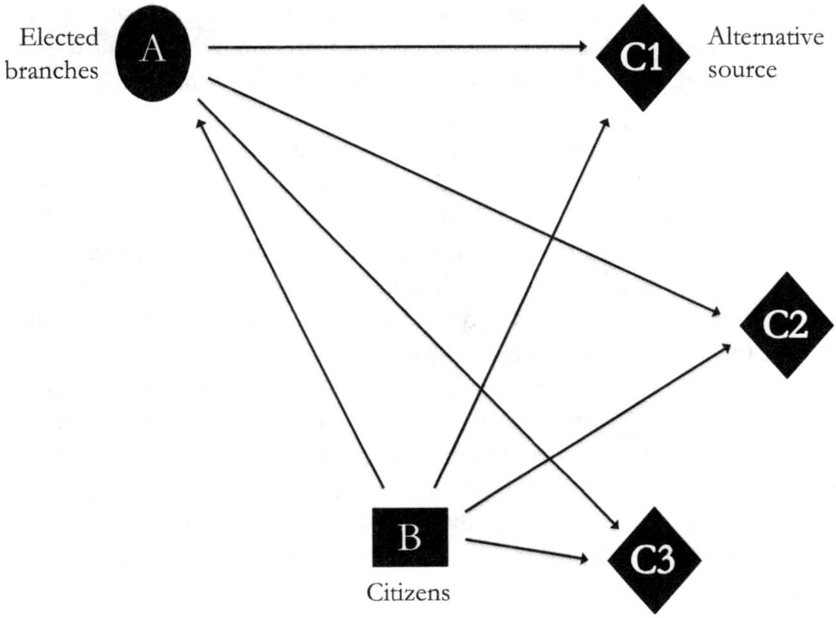

Figure 3.3 The trust relationships among the elected branches and alternative sources

It is beyond the scope of this book to comprehensively consider the media's role in the fulfilment of social rights, but I do wish to offer some elaboration in this regard to aid in applying the network conception to the citizen–government relationship. The media provides a critical, if not the primary, source of information for citizens about politics and current

and Marc Hooghe (eds.), *Political Trust: Why Context Matters* (Colchester: ECPR Press, 2011), p. 59; Jan Müller, *Mechanisms of Trust: News Media in Democratic and Authoritarian Regimes* (Frankfurt: Campus, 2013), p. 17; Patricia Moy and Muzammil M. Hussain, 'Media Influences on Political Trust and Engagement' in George C. Edwards III, Lawrence R. Jacobs and Robert Y. Shapiro (eds.), *The Oxford Handbook of American Public Opinion and the Media* (Oxford: Oxford University Press, 2011), pp. 222–223; Joseph S. Nye, Jr., 'Introduction: The Decline of Confidence in Government' in Joseph S. Nye, Jr., Philip D. Zelikow and David C. King (eds.), *Why People Do Not Trust Government* (Cambridge, MA: Harvard University Press, 1997), pp. 15–17; Joseph S. Nye, Jr. and Philip D. Zelikow, 'Conclusion: Reflections, Conjectures and Puzzles' in Nye, Jr. et al., *Why People Do Not Trust*, pp. 261–275; Orlando Patterson, 'Liberty against the Democratic State: On the Historical and Contemporary Sources of American Trust' in Mark E. Warren (ed.), *Democracy and Trust* (Cambridge: Cambridge University Press, 1999), p. 191.

affairs.[43] Social scientists have thus theorised and empirically shown that the media can and does have a significant impact on citizens' knowledge of and attitudes towards government actors and their policies.[44]

The relationship between citizens and the media may likewise be accurately characterised as a trust relationship. The media controls a good or service that citizens need (or want) – that is, political information. This control stems, in significant part, from its investigatory capabilities and its priority access to sources. However, the media is not simply a channel through which information flows: it has discretion in what information it conveys and how it conveys that information to the public. Owing to this discretion, it has been said, and empirically shown, that the media has both priming effects (based on how much attention it chooses to pay to a particular issue) as well as framing effects (based on the style in which it chooses to cover that issue) on citizens.[45] In fact, on the latter point, modern media coverage of political stories is more often journalists' opinions of political events as opposed to the substance of the events themselves.[46] For this reason, the media, it has been said, occupies a new 'interpretive' role in contemporary democracies, making it 'an unaccountable part of the political process'.[47] The media simultaneously has self-serving interests: it may be partisan to a particular political party or a particular ideology and, like any commercial industry that strives for self-preservation and profit, it has an interest in increasing the size of its audience. Given these interests, coupled with the media's control and discretion, citizens cannot be certain of their interaction with the media (i.e., what political information the media will convey and how it will convey it). Finally, citizens' need or want for political information – and more importantly, the impact the information has on their knowledge and attitudes – renders citizens vulnerable to the media. Expanding again on the three-part form of the citizen–government trust relationship developed in Chapter 2, I will refer to the media as D.

[43] Aarts et al., 'Media, Political Trust', pp. 98–99, 103–104; Patterson, 'Liberty against the Democratic State', p. 191; Nye, Jr. and Zelikow, 'Conclusion', p. 261.

[44] Richard Gunther and Anthony Mughan, *Democracy and the Media: A Comparative Perspective* (Cambridge: Cambridge University Press, 2000), pp. 16–20; Nye, Jr. and Zelikow, 'Conclusion', p. 274.

[45] Blidook, 'Media, Public Opinion', 356–358 (who cites a number of studies in support of these claims).

[46] Nye, Jr. and Zelikow, 'Conclusion', p. 274.

[47] Nye, Jr., 'Introduction', p. 17.

If we again assume a competitive market, it is inaccurate to conceive of the media as a single entity. Just as citizens have a choice of private providers of social goods and services or alternative sources, they have a choice of media sources: citizens may choose among different types of media (print, television, radio) as well as among different companies of any given type. For illustration purposes, let us say that citizens have a choice between two sources: D1 and D2.

Now, we may ask: what about the elected branches? Are they not also in a trust relationship with the media? After all, the elected branches, and their policies, are the subject of the political information that the media conveys; and most often, the media controls that information because the elected branches have granted them access to it, thereby entrusting them with that political information. Accordingly, the elected branches and the media are likewise in a trust relationship. The good or service over which the media has control is again political information. What the elected branches need or want, however, is for the media to convey that information in a way that portrays them positively. Otherwise, they may, again, suffer negative repercussions from citizens. As I have said, the media also has discretion both as to substance and style: therefore, the elected branches cannot be certain of what information the media will convey to the public or how it will convey that information. For instance, it may distort the story, omit positive aspects, take words uttered out of context or, as we see with recent allegations of so-called fake news, offer a story with no factual foundation. And because the information conveyed by the media has significant impact on citizens' political knowledge and attitudes, the elected branches are also vulnerable to the media. Figure 3.4 provides a pictorial representation that incorporates the media.

3.3.2.3 The Courts

Lastly, but certainly not least in this book, I come to the courts. Based on the book's argument up to this point, we already know that the role of the courts in enforcing constitutional social rights is contested. That is the reason why it is the central focus of this book in the first place. However, for the present purpose, I think that I may confidently draw a few, relatively uncontroversial conclusions that will enable me to establish the courts as forming part of the social rights network.

As I noted in Chapter 1, the justiciability of social rights was once the subject of an intense debate among jurists and politicians across the globe. In the last few decades, however, jurists and politicians have (for the most part) come to accept that courts have at least some role to play.

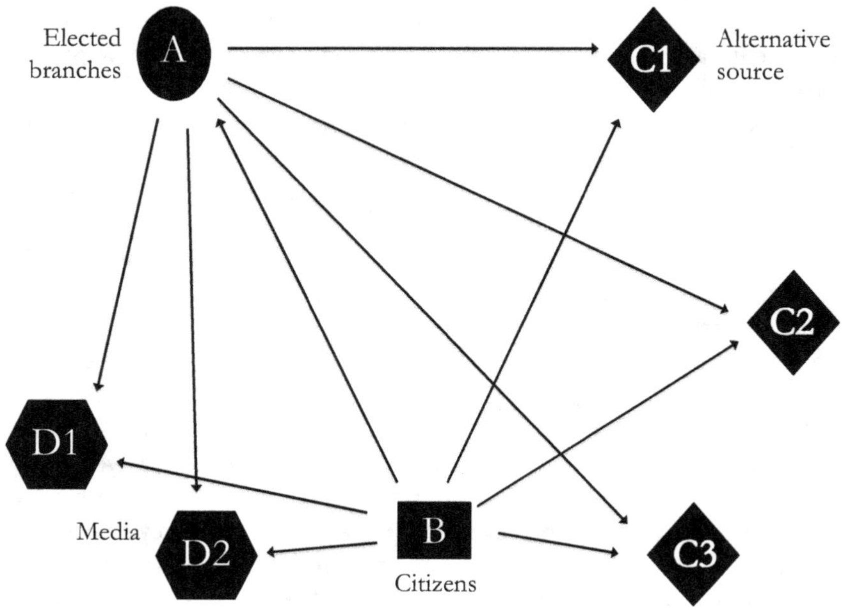

Figure 3.4 The trust relationships with the media

Such acceptance perhaps was inevitable given that an increasing number of constitutions now include express and justiciable social rights provisions, several courts have accepted their justiciability and, in many jurisdictions without express constitutional provisions, courts have recognised implicit constitutional protection for social rights.[48] It is thus not surprising that, as Anashri Pillay has summarised, '[t]he weight of academic, judicial and political opinion in this area has moved away from justiciability to a consideration of the most effective judicial approaches to' social rights.[49] David Landau has concurred in this point, noting, '[f]or all practical purposes, the debate about whether to include social rights in constitutions is over . . . Most of the more recent work in the field has focused on the specific question of *how* social rights should be enforced rather than the older question of *whether* they should be

[48] Xenophon Contiades and Alkmene Fotiadou, 'Social Rights in the Age of Proportionality: Global Economic Crisis and Constitutional Litigation' (2012) 10 *International Journal of Constitutional Law* 660, 673.

[49] Anashri Pillay, 'Economic and Social Rights Adjudication: Developing Principles of Judicial Restraint in South Africa and the United Kingdom' (2013) *Public Law* 599, 599.

included in constitutional texts in the first place'.[50] Accordingly, I contend that we should accept – as it appears most jurists and politicians have – that social rights are justiciable and that the courts have at least some role to play in the social rights arena. And if we do accept this point, we should likewise accept that the courts form part of the social context or network within which the citizen–government relationship is embedded.

Even if we do not accept such a role for the courts – that is, we do not agree that social rights are justiciable and that the courts should be intervening in such matters – the conclusion that the courts form part of the citizen–government relationship's social context follows, nevertheless. Regardless of what we may think the courts should be doing in this area of law, it is undeniable that over the last few decades, the courts have played a role in it: with increasing frequency, litigants have brought social rights cases before courts, and courts have decided the cases.[51] This proliferation of social rights litigation means that the courts do form part of the social rights network. As Daniel Brinks and Varun Gauri have said, 'for good or ill – or, more accurately, for good *and* ill ... – the language of rights, the mechanism of courts, the intervention of lawyers, and the cumbersome tools of the law have become a permanent and prominent part of the policy-making landscape'.[52] Therefore, setting aside the justiciability debate, there is inescapably a relationship between citizens and the courts that arises out of social rights adjudication of this sort.

Given the nature of the above-described social rights matters – which involve the courts reviewing a range of governmental decisions on social welfare – I suggest that it is accurate to say that the courts, at a minimum,

[50] David Landau, 'The Reality of Social Rights Enforcement' (2012) 53 *Harvard International Law Journal* 189, 190, 196. For a similar position, see also Colm O'Cinneide, 'The Problematic of Social Rights – Uniformity and Diversity in the Development of Social Rights Review' in Liora Lazarus, Christopher McCrudden and Nigel Bowles (eds.), *Reasoning Rights: Comparative Judicial Engagement* (Oxford: Hart, 2014), pp. 299–317.

[51] Daniel M. Brinks and Varun Gauri, 'The Law's Majestic Equality? The Distributive Impact of Judicializing Social and Economic Rights' (2014) 12 *Perspectives on Politics* 375, 376; Malcolm Langford, César Rodriguez-Garavito and Julieta Rossi (eds.), *Social Rights Judgments and the Politics of Compliance: Making It Stick* (Cambridge: Cambridge University Press, 2017).

[52] Daniel M. Brinks and Varun Gauri, 'A New Policy Landscape: Legalizing Social and Economic Rights in the Developing World' in Gauri and Brinks, *Courting Social Justice*, p. 303.

occupy a position in the social rights network between citizens and the elected branches. Such social rights matters usually involve citizens, either alone or relying on representatives (e.g., lawyers, non-governmental organisations, special interest groups), turning to the courts when they are dissatisfied with the process or the results of governmental decision-making. In cases to date, citizens have challenged, among other things: governmental decisions not to fund or deliver whole categories of social programmes; where funded or delivered, the eligibility criteria for those social programmes; and the implementation of those programmes.

Like the other relationships that I have considered up to this point in the chapter, the relationship between citizens and the courts may accurately be characterised as a trust relationship. The courts have control over something that citizens need: a judicial ruling in their favour vis-à-vis the social goods and services that they need. Put simply, that judicial ruling brings them closer to the relevant social goods and services. The courts also have discretion in delivering their rulings.[53] As Ronald Dworkin once said, 'the general proposition, that the exercise of judicial choice or discretion within areas circumscribed more or less tightly by rules is not an occasional misfiring but a characteristic feature of the legal process, is today almost a law school cliché'.[54] This discretion relates not only to the court's interpretation of social rights but also to its granting of remedies for social rights violations. Because of this discretion, citizens cannot be certain of how the courts will rule; and given their need for a favourable ruling, they are vulnerable to the courts.

Furthermore, when citizens choose to litigate their claims, the courts become a truster in their own respect – that is, in their relationship with the elected branches. This trust relationship arises out of the fact that, in contemporary constitutional democracies, the courts must rely on the elected branches to carry out their constitutional decisions.[55]

[53] On judicial discretion generally, see Ronald Dworkin, 'Judicial Discretion' (1963) 60 *The Journal of Philosophy* 624; Ronald M. Dworkin, 'The Model of Rules' (1967) 35 *The University of Chicago Law Review* 14; Ronald M. Dworkin, 'Social Rules and Legal Theory' (1972) 81 *The Yale Law Journal* 855; Kent Greenawalt, 'Discretion and Judicial Discretion: The Elusive Quest for the Fetters That Bind Judges' (1975) 75 *Columbia Law Review* 359.

[54] Dworkin, 'Judicial Discretion', 624.

[55] Mark Kesselman, Joel Krieger and William A. Joseph, *Introduction to Comparative Politics: Political Challenges and Changing Agendas* (Belmont, CA: Wadsworth, 2012), p. 337.

As I established in Chapter 2, in contemporary social democracies, the elected branches have control and discretion over social goods and services that citizens need. While the courts' rulings may seek to impact the elected branches' exercise of control and discretion, the ultimate decision remains that of the elected branches. For instance, a court may rule that a citizen, or a certain group of citizens, is entitled to a particular social good or service and accordingly order the elected branches to fund and/or deliver that good or service. Without the elected branches' ensuing decision to actually fund and/or deliver the good or service, however, the court's ruling is largely meaningless. For this reason, we may fairly say that the courts cannot be certain of how the elected branches will respond to their rulings. Lastly, the courts are vulnerable to the elected branches. This vulnerability chiefly assumes the form of institutional credibility: if the courts' rulings are not followed by the elected branches, it diminishes their credibility in the eyes of the elected branches and the public.[56] Also, to make matters worse, owing to such rulings, the judiciary may suffer repercussions from the elected branches, including a lack of cooperation in the future, a reduction in resources or impeachment.[57] The courts are, as Frank Cross has described, 'politically vulnerable institutions that have powerful reasons to be cautious in imposing restrictions on the other branches'.[58]

Further expanding on the relationships considered thus far, and rounding out our social rights network in this chapter, I will refer to the courts as E. Figure 3.5 incorporates the courts into the network, situating them, as I just noted, between citizens and the elected branches.

Before moving on from the construction of the social rights network (as part of my first claim) to my second claim, I would like to stress once again, in the interests of greater clarity, a point that I made earlier. The social rights network undoubtedly consists of relationships beyond those that I have identified and analysed in the above sections. The relevant relationships include not only relationships with new parties (i.e., other than the five parties that I have identified) but also new configurations of the five parties beyond those configurations that I have expressly identified. For instance, with respect to the relationship between the elected branches and alternative sources, we may conceive of a trust relationship

[56] Katharine G. Young, *Constituting Economic and Social Rights* (Oxford: Oxford University Press, 2012), p. 161.

[57] Frank B. Cross, 'The Error of Positive Rights' (2001) *UCLA Law Review* 857, 887–889.

[58] Ibid, 887–888.

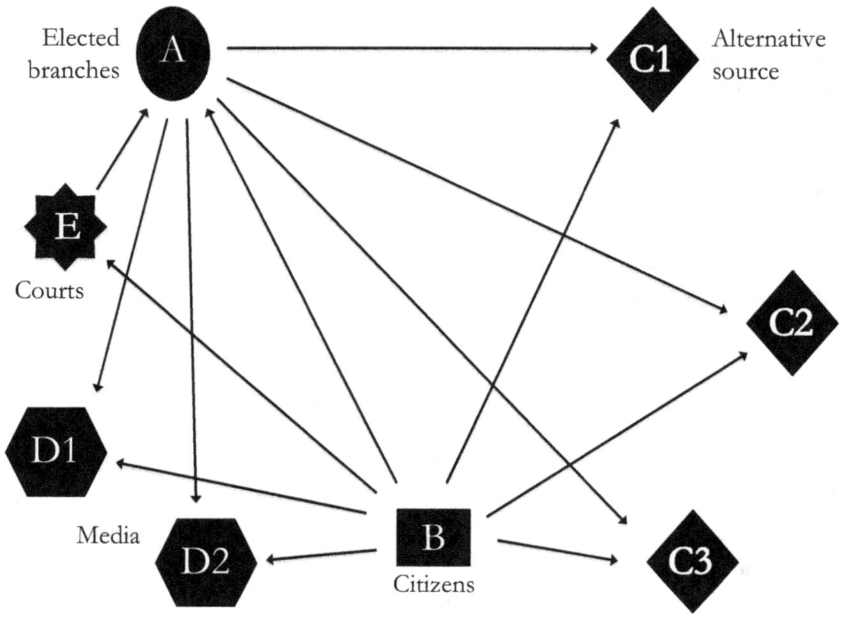

Figure 3.5 The trust relationships with the courts

operating in the reverse direction to that which I described in that section, where the alternative source is truster and the elected branches are trustee. Or in the case of the courts, we may speak of a trust relationship operating between the courts and the media. But as my aim here is not to provide an exhaustive analysis of the social rights network, I will not venture further to consider these parties or these relationships.

3.3.3 Trust in the Citizen–Government Relationship Depends on the Relationships in the Social Rights Network

This brings me to my second claim: that trust in the citizen–government relationship depends on the network of relationships in which it is embedded. This claim follows on from a straightforward application of the second fundamental feature of the network conception of trust to the citizen–government relationship. That is, if trust in a trust relationship depends on the network of relationships in which that relationship is embedded (as this feature of the network conception of trust posits), applying it to the citizen–government relationship means that trust in that relationship, as a trust relationship, depends on the network of relationships in which the relationship is embedded. And if we accept, based on the foregoing constructive analysis, that the network in which the citizen–government relationship is embedded is that which I have called the social rights network, then that means that trust in the citizen–government relationship depends on the relationships that constitute the social rights network. Or, to rephrase this claim using, again, more active language: we can expect the relationships in the social rights network to be able to impact trust in the citizen–government relationship – including, in the right circumstances, to foster trust.

As an example, let us consider two relationships in the social rights network: the citizen–government relationship, and the relationship between citizens and the media with respect to social rights (what I will call the 'citizen–media relationship'). An application of my claim here to these relationships suggests that we can expect the citizen–media relationship, as part of the social rights network, to be able to impact trust in the citizen–government relationship, including to foster trust in that relationship. This conclusion follows on from applying the network conception of trust to these relationships, together, of course, with my earlier construction of the social rights network.

At this time, I think that two points of clarification are warranted. First, the claim that I am making here is a theoretical one. It draws from the work of the many writers on trust who I identified at this chapter's outset as advocating a network conception of trust and it applies that work to the citizen–government relationship. In my view, these writers' work – taken together to form what I have called the network conception of trust – supports the claim that I am making. To be fair, however, if we wanted to say with greater certainty that a specific relationship in the social rights network does indeed impact trust in the citizen–government relationship, we should conduct an empirical investigation. In other words, we should measure trust in the citizen–government relationship as a variable of that other relationship. And as I pointed out in the first chapter of the book, such an investigation is beyond the book's scope. Granted, significant challenges would be in store for such an investigation, including difficulties with accurately measuring trust (as conceptualised) and controlling for the impact of a single relationship; however, I would be remiss if I did not draw attention to this relevant fact. In my example involving the citizen–government and citizen–media relationships, for instance, to say with greater certainty that the latter does impact trust in the former would require empirical evidence. That said, empirical studies have consistently shown that the media, through its relationship with citizens, can impact public trust in government (albeit not specifically in the social rights context).[59]

Secondly, it is also beyond the scope of this book to go further than the general claim that I am making by offering an analysis of how we can expect each trust relationship in the social rights network to be able to impact trust in the citizen–government relationship. Based on my reading of the above writers on trust, it is likely that different trust relationships would be expected to impact trust in the citizen–government relationship via different paths. In the above citizen–media example, Coleman's idea of 'the advisor' as an intermediary is a plausible path, especially given Coleman's identification of the media as an advisor to citizens in their relationship with government.[60] So, applying Coleman's idea specifically to the social rights context, we can say that where the media, through its conveyance of political information vis-à-vis social rights to citizens, portrays the elected branches in a positive light, the media advises citizens to trust the elected branches with respect to social rights. Assuming that citizens trust the media (which is obviously not a given, but I will assume it to be true for the present purpose), based on Coleman's argument, the media's advice to trust the elected branches – and so, citizens' relationship with the media – can be expected to foster citizens' trust in the elected branches with respect to social rights.

Given the variety of paths by which we can expect different trust relationships to impact one another, just as it would be impossible to analyse all the parties and relationships that constitute the social rights network, it would be equally impossible to analyse all the relevant paths. Fortunately, again, my aim is not to do so. It is, to repeat, to introduce the network conception of trust to social rights law for the specific purpose of my analysis in Chapter 4 on the proper role of the courts in enforcing constitutional social rights. I will therefore limit my analysis in this book to the path that is pertinent to this aim – that is, how the citizen–court relationship can be expected to foster trust in the citizen–government relationship. That path is considered in Chapter 4.

[59] As a representative sample, see (and the studies referenced therein) Aarts et al., 'Media, Political Trust', pp. 98–99; Bovens and Wille, 'Falling or Fluctuating', p. 59; Moy and Hussain, 'Media Influences', pp. 222–223.

[60] Coleman, *Foundations of Social Theory*, p. 194.

4

A Trust-Based Framework for Enforcing Social Rights?

In this chapter, I explain why political trust is not only of significance to social rights law (as I argued in Chapter 1) but should also provide the basis for a social rights enforcement framework to be used by the courts. In so explaining, I organise my discussion around three questions. First, 'why the courts'? Why do the courts warrant a special role in the social rights network developed in the previous chapter, making them the focus of this book? Secondly, 'how trust'? How can the courts use the concept of political trust as the basis for a social rights enforcement framework? And lastly, 'why trust'? Why should political trust provide the basis for an enforcement framework?

4.1 Why the Courts? Justifying a Special Role for the Courts in the Social Rights Network

In Chapter 3, I detailed the social rights network in which the citizen–government relationship is embedded; and the courts, I explained there, form part of that network. More than forming part of the network, however, the courts, we must recognise, occupy a special role in the network – that is, legally speaking. This special role follows on from a conclusion that I drew in Chapter 3 (and to some extent, in Chapter 1): that social rights are justiciable. Given social rights' justiciability, the courts, as constitutional guardians, have a constitutional obligation to enforce them. They are obliged, effectively, to oversee the citizen–government relationship and to ensure that the elected branches, in exercising their control over social goods and services, fulfil citizens' social rights.

The trust-based framework that I propose responds to this special role, offering the courts a legal framework that they can, and I claim should, use when fulfilling it. The remainder of this book will therefore be devoted to developing that framework. But before turning to the details of the framework, I will briefly substantiate my conclusion that social rights are justiciable – and in turn, justify the courts' special role in the social rights network. To do so, I will identify the key arguments on both sides of the justiciability debate, explaining how the side for justiciability prevailed and how the conversation regarding the judicial enforcement of social rights evolved to where it is now – focusing on how, rather than whether, the courts should enforce social rights. It is worth noting that the arguments in this debate remain relevant to the conversation in its current form. Thus, I also identify these arguments here to provide foundation for my subsequent analysis.

The arguments against justiciability can be divided into two categories: institutional legitimacy and institutional capacity.[1] The argument from legitimacy follows on from the well-known criticism made against the institution of judicial review more generally. This criticism, most-frequently associated with Jeremy Waldron, challenges judicial review as anti-democratic and so, illegitimate.[2] This is the case because it enables judges – who are unelected – to overrule the decisions and actions of democratically elected officials, thereby undermining the will of the majority. Alexander Bickel famously called this problem with judicial review the 'counter-majoritarian difficulty'.[3] Building on this criticism, the argument from legitimacy posits that the counter-majoritarian difficulty is all-the-more damning to judicial review where the decisions and actions being reviewed by the courts concern social rights. Why is this so? First, social rights have significant budgetary consequences. If the courts are allowed to adjudicate social rights matters, they are interfering with the drawing of the budget and in turn encroaching on one of the legislature's principal prerogatives.[4] Secondly, because resources are scarce, social rights are likely to conflict with one another, necessitating

[1] For example, see Lorne Sossin, *Boundaries of Judicial Review: The Law of Justiciability in Canada* (Toronto: Carswell, 1999), p. 233.

[2] See Jeremy Waldron, 'The Core of the Case against Judicial Review' (2006) 115 *The Yale Law Journal* 1346.

[3] Alexander M. Bickel, *The Least Dangerous Branch: The Supreme Court at the Bar of Politics*, 2nd ed. (New Haven, CT: Yale University Press, 1986), p. 16.

[4] For a summary of this argument (although not in support of it), see Cécile Fabre, 'Constitutionalising Social Rights' (1998) 6 *The Journal of Political Philosophy* 263, 280; Roberto Gargarella, 'Deliberative Democracy, Dialogic Justice and the Promise of Social and Economic Rights' in Helena Alviar Garcia, Karl Klare and Lucy A. Williams (eds.), *Social and Economic Rights in Theory and Practice: Critical Inquiries* (Abingdon: Routledge, 2015), p. 107.

the making of difficult choices which shape what society looks like.[5] For these reasons, it has been argued, the matters raised by social rights are better left to the elected, and politically accountable, branches of government; the courts, as unelected bodies, are said to lack legitimacy to interfere with or second-guess those branches' decisions or actions.

The argument from capacity arises out of Lon Fuller's idea of polycentricity.[6] According to Fuller, certain problems – which he described as 'polycentric' – are not suitable for adjudication. Polycentric problems are those characterised by the interconnection of several issues, and which affect a large number of individuals, yielding a complex web of interdependent relationships.[7] The issues are interconnected, and the relationships, interdependent, in the sense that when an action is taken to address one issue, that action reverberates through the web, producing a series of unpredictable consequences vis-à-vis the other issues. Fuller argued that polycentric problems do not lend themselves well to adjudication because of certain defining characteristics of the adjudicative process, namely: adjudication is binary in nature, with the two parties having diametrically opposed interests; the courts can only satisfy one party's interests; and despite being affected by judicial rulings, third parties have limited influence over the outcome of a case. Relying on Fuller, the argument from capacity suggests that social rights raise polycentric problems.[8] A governmental decision about whether to fund a health care treatment, for example, is a polycentric problem, it can be said, because it has budgetary implications for a range of social goods and services and because it affects all the people who depend on those goods and services. Put bluntly, since governmental budgets are finite, a decision to fund one treatment means less funds available for other treatments as well as other social goods and services. At the same time, but

[5] For a summary of this argument (although again not in support of it), see Fabre, 'Constitutionalising Social Rights', 281.

[6] Lon Fuller, 'The Forms and Limits of Adjudication' (1978–1979) 92 *Harvard Law Review* 353. For a good summary of Fuller's argument, see Jeff King, 'The Pervasiveness of Polycentricity' (2008) *Public Law* 101.

[7] Mark Elliott and Robert Thomas, *Public Law*, 2nd ed. (Oxford: Oxford University Press, 2014), p. 551.

[8] For a summary, see King, 'The Pervasiveness of Polycentricity', 107–108, citing Trevor R.S. Allan, *Constitutional Justice: A Liberal Theory of the Rule of Law* (Oxford: Oxford University Press, 2001), pp. 188–192; David Feldman, *Civil Liberties and Human Rights in England and Wales*, 2nd ed. (Oxford: Oxford University Press, 2002), pp. 229–230; Stanley de Smith, Harry Woolf and Jeffrey Jowell, *Judicial Review of Administrative Action*, 5th ed. (London: Sweet and Maxwell, 1995), pp. 311–312.

relatedly, the argument from capacity posits that the courts lack the expertise as well as the resources necessary to make social rights decisions. It has thus been argued that judges are not competent to tell the elected branches how to allocate resources as they have neither the training nor the information-gathering tools that are required to assess the suitability of such a resource allocation decision.[9]

Several commentators have forcefully countered these arguments, however. They have done so by questioning the assumptions on which the arguments from legitimacy and capacity are based. The argument from legitimacy, for example, assumes that members of the legislature (and by extension under a parliamentary system, the executive), having been elected, are representatives of the people and are accountable to them through the democratic process. This representativeness and accountability, so the argument from legitimacy goes, renders the elected branches more legitimate than the courts. Many constitutional scholars have challenged this assumption, especially as it pertains to low-income citizens. As I pointed out in Chapter 2, these scholars have emphasised that those with low income do not exert much political influence.[10] Governmental policy-making is heavily influenced by the wealthy through lobbying and interest groups. Low-income citizens, who often feel excluded from the political and democratic processes due to the wealthy's heavy influence, tend not to participate in them, thereby generating a negative feedback loop. Constitutional social rights adjudication, it has therefore been said, offers low-income citizens an alternative forum in which their interests may be better protected, and it introduces into the system another type of accountability from which low-income citizens may benefit: legal accountability.[11]

[9] For a summary (although again not in support of it), see Fabre, 'Constitutionalising Social Rights', 281.

[10] Sandra Fredman, *Human Rights Transformed: Positive Rights and Positive Duties* (Oxford: Oxford University Press, 2008), p. 34; Jeff King, *Judging Social Rights* (Cambridge: Cambridge University Press, 2012), pp. 157–169; Paul O'Connell, *Vindicating Socio-economic Rights: International Standards and Comparative Experiences* (Abingdon: Routledge, 2013), p. 5; Kim Lane Scheppele, 'A Realpolitik Defense of Social Rights' (2004) 82 *Texas Law Review* 1921, 1926–1927.

[11] Gargarella, 'Deliberative Democracy', pp. 107–108; Martha Jackman, 'Charter Review as a Health Care Accountability Mechanism in Canada' (2010) 18 *Health Law Journal* 1, 2; King, *Judging Social Rights*, p. 60; Colm O'Cinneide, 'Legal Accountability and Social Justice' in Nicholas Bamforth and Peter Leyland (eds.), *Accountability in the Contemporary Constitution* (Oxford: Oxford University Press, 2013), pp. 406–407;

Secondly, the argument from capacity assumes that the judiciary's competence vis-à-vis social rights matters is fixed, such that judges can acquire neither the skills nor the expertise necessary to competently decide such matters. Cécile Fabre, Virginia Mantouvalou and David Wiseman, among others, have questioned this assumption.[12] For these scholars, the argument from capacity underestimates the judiciary's ability to develop competence in this area. In Fabre's apt words, 'there is no reason why specialised judges could not be trained to acquire those skills, or could not seek advice from independent experts, as they actually already do'.[13] Wiseman has referred to the acquisition of such skills and knowledge by the judiciary as 'competence-building'.[14]

Finally, both arguments assume that judicial review will take on a 'strong form' with the effect that the courts, in enforcing social rights, will overrule the decisions and actions of the elected branches.[15] This assumption leads, in turn, to a further assumption: that social rights enforcement requires the courts to make the 'hapless choice' between what has been termed the 'two wrongs of enforcement' – judicial usurpation and judicial abdication.[16] By assuming strong-form judicial review, the arguments from legitimacy and capacity assume that the courts face a binary choice between usurping the policy-making role of the elected branches, and abdicating their judicial role as enforcer of constitutional rights. As with the other two counter-arguments, however, these assumptions are not well founded. There is an ever-growing trend among social rights scholars to advocate weaker forms of judicial review built on principles of inter-institutional dialogue and deliberative

Margot Young, 'Social Justice and the *Charter*: Comparison and Choice' (2013) 50 *Osgoode Hall Law Journal* 669, 670–671.

12 Fabre, 'Constitutionalising Social Rights', 281–282; Virginia Mantouvalou, 'In Support of Legalisation' in Conor Gearty and Virginia Mantouvalou (eds.), *Debating Social Rights* (Oxford: Hart, 2010), p. 117; David Wiseman, 'Competence Concerns in Charter Adjudication: Countering the Anti-Poverty Incompetence Argument' (2006) 51 *McGill Law Journal* 503.

13 Fabre, 'Constitutionalising Social Rights', 282.

14 Wiseman, 'Competence Concerns', 516.

15 For this terminology, see Mark Tushnet, *Weak Courts, Strong Rights: Judicial Review and Social Welfare Rights in Comparative Constitutional Law* (Princeton, NJ: Princeton University Press, 2007).

16 Katharine G. Young, *Constituting Economic and Social Rights* (Oxford: Oxford University Press, 2012), p. 34. See also Frank I. Michelman, 'The Constitution, Social Rights, and Liberal Political Justification' (2003) 1 *International Journal of Constitutional Law* 13, 16.

democracy.[17] These scholars have suggested that the courts can work with the elected branches, rather than be pitted against them, in their development of social policy. Under these weaker forms of judicial review, it is not necessary for the courts to choose between usurpation and abdication; instead, they may opt for a middle ground. As Matthias Klatt has rightly noted, 'usurpation and abdication do not represent a strict antagonism. Rather, they are a matter of degree. Both represent the two ends of the spectrum of different forms of judicial review'.[18]

This is not to say that the arguments from legitimacy and capacity are without merit. There is very good reason for us to be concerned about giving the courts too much power vis-à-vis social rights so as to usurp the elected branches' policy-making role. To use Colm O'Cinneide's words, 'it would be foolish to rely on legal controls to give effect to a "total" vision of social justice, i.e. a comprehensive system of resource distribution that satisfies a particular philosophical ideal of group justice'.[19] But the arguments from legitimacy and capacity, at the same time, do not warrant the conclusion that social rights are, or should be, non-justiciable. They suggest, rather, that 'caution is warranted' in our determination of how the courts should enforce social rights.[20]

Given these arguments, most jurists and politicians, as I have already noted, have come to accept social rights' justiciability. Following the height of the justiciability debate in the 1980s–1990s, most new democracies opted for the inclusion of express and justiciable constitutional social rights provisions. To repeat, more than 90 per cent of constitutions worldwide contain at least one express and justiciable social (or economic) rights provision.[21] In more established democracies (e.g., India,

[17] Rosalind Dixon, 'Creating Dialogue about Socioeconomic Rights: Strong-Form versus Weak-Form Judicial Review Revisited' (2007) 5 *International Journal of Constitutional Law* 391; Alana Klein, 'Judging as Nudging' (2008) 39 *Columbia Human Rights Law Review* 351; O'Connell, *Vindicating Socio-economic Rights*, pp. 194–196; Scheppele, 'A Realpolitik Defense', 1935; Young, *Constituting Economic and Social Rights*, 6.

[18] Matthias Klatt, 'Positive Rights: Who Decides? Judicial Review in Balance' (2015) 13 *International Journal of Constitutional Law* 354, 361. See also King, *Judging Social Rights*, p. 8.

[19] O'Cinneide, 'Legal Accountability', p. 401.

[20] Ibid, p. 401. See also King, *Judging Social Rights*, p. 8.

[21] Courtney Jung, Ran Hirschl and Evan Rosevear, 'Economic and Social Rights in National Constitutions' (2014) 62 *The American Journal of Comparative Law* 1043, 1053. Moreover, 70 per cent of constitutions include at least one social (or economic) right which is recognised in the constitution itself as justiciable (1053). See also Evan Rosevear, Ran Hirschl and Courtney Jung, 'Justiciable and Aspirational Economic and Social Rights

Germany and Israel) whose constitutions do not include express social rights provisions, courts have recognised implicit constitutional protection for these rights.[22] Thus, as O'Cinneide has summarised, 'it is clear that key constitutional actors in many states (including legislators, judges and academic commentators) are becoming more accepting of the possibility that judicial protection of social rights may be a worthwhile addition to the repertoire of modern constitutionalism'.[23] And because of this, as we know, recent years have witnessed a shift in the conversation from the issue of justiciability to judicial approaches for enforcing social rights.[24]

For these reasons, I think that it is fair to conclude, as I have in previous chapters, that social rights (at least as a general category) are justiciable. There may be readers who disagree with my conclusion in this regard; and for those readers, I can do no more than refer to the vast body of literature already cited. In recognition of the shift in the social rights enforcement conversation, however, and in an effort to continue moving the conversation forward, I start from the position that social rights are indeed justiciable. It is therefore not my intention in this book to contribute to the justiciability debate. I seek, rather, to contribute to the social rights enforcement conversation in its new form – that is, the question of how the courts should enforce social rights.[25] Following on

in National Constitutions' in Katharine G. Young (ed.), *The Future of Economic and Social Rights* (Cambridge: Cambridge University Press, 2019), pp. 37–65.

22 *Hartz IV*, 125 BVerfGE 172; *Hassan v. National Insurance Institute* [2012] HCJ 10662/04; *Olga Tellis and Others v. Bombay Municipal Corporation* [1985] 2 Supp SCR 51.

23 Colm O'Cinneide, 'The Problematic of Social Rights – Uniformity and Diversity in the Development of Social Rights Review' in Liora Lazarus, Christopher McCrudden and Nigel Bowles (eds.), *Reasoning Rights: Comparative Judicial Engagement* (Oxford: Hart, 2014), p. 310.

24 David Landau, 'The Reality of Social Rights Enforcement' (2012) 53 *Harvard International Law Journal* 189, 196; Malcolm Langford, 'The Justiciability of Social Rights: From Practice to Theory' in Malcolm Langford (ed.), *Social Rights Jurisprudence: Emerging Trends in International and Comparative Law* (Cambridge: Cambridge University Press, 2008), p. 29; Marius Pieterse, 'Coming to Terms with Judicial Enforcement of Socio-economic Rights' (2004) 20 *South African Journal on Human Rights* 383, 404–405; Anashri Pillay, 'Economic and Social Rights Adjudication: Developing Principles of Judicial Restraint in South Africa and the United Kingdom' (2013) *Public Law* 599, 599.

25 Richard Stacey, 'Dynamic Regulatory Constitutionalism: Taking Legislation Seriously in the Judicial Enforcement of Economic and Social Rights' (2017) 31 *Notre Dame Journal of Law, Ethics and Public Policy* 85, 85–86.

from this, I accept that the courts have a special role in the social rights network.

This said, I will make one point clear. I do not mean to suggest in this book that the courts are the ideal branch of government to realise citizens' social rights. For the reasons I have already outlined (i.e., the courts' limited legitimacy and capacity relative to the elected branches), those branches of government are, I think, much better positioned than the courts to realise citizens' social rights. At the same time, there may be other, and some may argue better, means for citizens to vindicate their social rights vis-à-vis the elected branches than via adjudication by the courts (e.g., via administrative tribunals or the ombudsmen system). However, in circumstances where social rights are constitutionalised, the courts, again, have a constitutional obligation to enforce those rights against the other branches of government. With these circumstances in mind, the trust-based framework that I propose is thus intended to offer a defensible role for the courts.

4.2 How Trust? Transforming Political Trust into a Tool for Social Rights Enforcement

Having substantiated social rights' justiciability, and the courts' special role in the social rights network, I will now discuss how the courts can use political trust as the basis for social rights enforcement – or put differently, how trust can be transformed into a tool for such enforcement.

4.2.1 What Is Trustworthiness?

I introduced the trust-based framework at the outset of this book by stating that under it, the courts aim to promote the trustworthiness of government actors, specifically vis-à-vis their delivery of social goods and services to the public. Given the foundation laid in Chapters 2 and 3, I can now be more specific in this regard: under the framework, the courts promote the trustworthiness of the *elected branches* with respect to *social rights*. But this leaves the question: what is trustworthiness?

The concept of trustworthiness is closely related to that of trust. As the term itself suggests, trustworthiness follows on from trust: it implies that a trustee in a trust relationship is worthy of the truster's trust in them. It therefore represents the likelihood – or probability – that the trustee will fulfil the truster's trust in them.[26] Hence, if trust is the set of expectations that I outlined in Chapter 2 (goodwill, competence and fiduciary responsibility), trustworthiness indicates that the trustee is likely to act in accordance with those expectations in exercising their control over the relevant good or service. Applying this idea to the citizen–government relationship – where trust means that citizens hold the expectations from Chapter 2 (that the elected branches will exercise goodwill towards citizens, will act competently and will fulfil their fiduciary responsibility to citizens) – trustworthiness means that the elected branches, in exercising their control over the social goods and services that citizens need, will likely act in accordance with those expectations.

A trustee's trustworthiness may stem from two sources.[27] These two sources follow on from my discussion of discretion and uncertainty in Chapter 2. First, a trustee may be trustworthy owing to their person or character. Put simply, the trustee's person or character make it such that acting with goodwill, competence and in fulfilment of their fiduciary responsibility is likely. If the truster trusts the trustee in these circumstances, the resultant trust is described, it will be recalled, as personal trust or primary trust. Secondly, and especially relevant to the trust-based framework, a trustee may be trustworthy owing to external constraints that have been imposed on them to restrict the discretion that the trustee exercises over the good or service. Here, rather than the trustee's person or character, it is the external constraints imposed on them which make it likely that the trustee will act with goodwill, competence and in

[26] See Paul C. Bauer, 'Clearing the Jungle: Conceptualising Trust and Trustworthiness' in Raquel Barradas de Freitas and Sergio Lo Iacono (eds.), *Trust Matters: Cross-Disciplinary Essays* (London: Bloomsbury, 2021), pp. 21–22. For this reason, some writers have even defined trust (rather than in terms of the expectations I have of goodwill, competence and fiduciary responsibility) in a circular manner in terms of the truster's expectations about the trustee's trustworthiness – that is, a truster may be said to trust the trustee if the truster expects trustworthiness from the trustee: for example, see Lawrence Becker, 'Trust as Noncognitive Security about Motives' (1996) 107 *Ethics* 43, 44.

[27] Orlando Patterson, 'Liberty against the Democratic State: On the Historical and Contemporary Sources of American Trust' in Mark E. Warren (ed.), *Democracy and Trust* (Cambridge: Cambridge University Press, 1999), pp. 151–207; Philip Pettit, 'Republican Theory and Political Trust' in Valerie Braithwaite and Margaret Levi (eds.), *Trust and Governance* (New York: Russell Sage Foundation, 1998); Jocelyn Pixley, 'Impersonal Trust in Global Mediating Organizations' (1999) 42 *Sociological Perspectives* 647; Susan P. Shapiro, 'The Social Control of Impersonal Trust' (1987) 93 *American Journal of Sociology* 623; Susan Shapiro, 'The Grammar of Trust' in Jocelyn Pixley (ed.), *New Perspectives on Emotions in Finance: The Sociology of Confidence, Fear and Betrayal* (Abingdon: Routledge, 2012).

fulfilment of their fiduciary responsibility. If the truster trusts the trustee in these circumstances, the resultant trust is impersonal trust or secondary trust. Applying these two sources of trustworthiness to the citizen–government relationship, the elected branches' trustworthiness with respect to social rights may therefore stem from the person or character of the personnel who staff those branches, or from various external constraints that have been imposed on the relevant personnel in their decision-making on behalf of those institutions.

4.2.2 Promoting the Elected Branches' Trustworthiness via Judicial Constraints

Adjudication by the courts, I propose, can serve as a source of the external constraints capable of promoting the elected branches' trustworthiness with respect to social rights. That is, the courts, in deciding social rights cases, can impose constraints on the elected branches to make them trustworthy. This conclusion finds support in the literature on trust.[28] Let us consider, for instance, an argument advanced by political philosopher Philip Pettit.[29] In his work, Pettit has applied the distinction between personal and impersonal trust to the political context – 'either of which', he has claimed, 'might pass as the trust of people in their government'.[30] To make his point, Pettit has employed the example of a traffic call centre, arguing that we may trust the call centre's personnel (to, e.g., provide accurate information) on two grounds. First, we may trust them because we believe 'that they are responsive to the reliance of individual people, or of the people as a whole, on their decisions'.[31] We trust the personnel, in this case, because of their person or character – that is, because, we think, they have the person or character to fulfil our trust in them. This is personal trust. Pettit has argued,

[28] Russell Hardin, 'Trustworthiness' (1996) 107 *Ethics* 26; Russell Hardin, *Trust and Trustworthiness* (New York: Russell Sage Foundation, 2004); Pettit, 'Republican Theory and Political Trust'; Shapiro, 'The Social Control of Impersonal Trust'. The effectiveness of such constraints on actually promoting trust has been challenged: for example, see Sim B. Sitkin and Nancy L. Roth, 'Explaining the Limited Effectiveness of Legalistic "Remedies" for Trust/Distrust' (1993) 4 *Organization Science* 367. Sitkin and Roth's claim of ineffectiveness, however, is a product, in large part, of their conceptualisation of trust.

[29] Pettit, 'Republican Theory and Political Trust'.

[30] Ibid, pp. 296–297.

[31] Ibid, p. 299.

however, that we may also trust the personnel based on our knowledge of institutional constraints that have been placed on them. As he has noted, our trust in the personnel, in this case, 'is not prompted by any beliefs about their person or character' but 'is grounded in the belief that the agents are so constrained by regulations that they are more or less bound to pass on the information available to them'.[32] We trust the personnel, therefore, because we 'believe that such employees are subject to fairly exacting scrutiny and sanctions and that they are unlikely to give inaccurate information'.[33] This is impersonal trust.

Sociologist Susan Shapiro has made a similar argument, though not in the political context.[34] According to Shapiro, specific actors (professional associations, regulatory watchdogs and certified public accountants, as will be recalled from Chapter 3) can increase the likelihood that a trustee in a trust relationship will fulfil the truster's trust in them, by imposing constraints or 'social-control measures' on the trustee. She has called these actors 'guardians of trust'. For Shapiro, these guardians offer the truster a basis to trust the trustee, albeit impersonally. Such trust, as she has explained, arises 'when social-control measures derived from social ties and direct contact between principal and agent are unavailable, when faceless and readily interchangeable individual or organizational agents exercise considerable delegated power and privilege on behalf of principals who can neither specify, scrutinize, evaluate, nor constrain their performance.'[35] Accordingly, the truster trusts the trustee owing to the social-control measures imposed on the trustee.

Based on my reading of their work, the essence of Pettit's and Shapiro's arguments is as follows. By imposing constraints on a trustee in a trust relationship, institutional actors – like those that regulate a traffic call centre, or professional associations, regulatory watchdogs and certified public accountants – can promote that trustee's trustworthiness.[36] They can make it more likely that the trustee will fulfil the truster's trust in them. And so, relying on this idea, I propose that the courts are such an institutional actor, capable of promoting trustworthiness – specifically the elected branches' trustworthiness in the citizen–government relationship. The courts, by imposing constraints on the

32 Ibid, p. 297.
33 Ibid.
34 Shapiro, 'The Social Control of Impersonal Trust'.
35 Ibid, 634.
36 Pettit, however, does not use the language of 'trustworthiness' but 'trust-responsiveness'.

elected branches vis-à-vis their exercise of control over the social goods and services that citizens need, can promote the latter's trustworthiness with respect to social rights. Or to use Shapiro's term, they can act as a guardian of trust in the citizen–government relationship.

4.2.3 What Is a Trustworthiness-Promoting Judicial Constraint?

We may ask: what form of constraint imposed by the courts will promote the elected branches' trustworthiness with respect to social rights? A trustworthiness-promoting judicial constraint is, at its simplest, one that makes it more likely that the elected branches, in exercising their control over social goods and services, will fulfil citizens' three constituent expectations of trust: that they will exercise goodwill, will act competently and will fulfil their fiduciary responsibility to citizens.

To do so, this form of judicial constraint, I suggest, must satisfy two key requirements. First, the courts must decide social rights cases broadly. They must set broad rules for the future that prospectively constrain the elected branches' discretion over social goods and services. Given that trust is a set of expectations (as I have defined it), and expectations are beliefs about future events, trust is necessarily prospective. It relates to the trustee's exercise of control over the good or service *in the future*. Accordingly, if trust in the citizen–government relationship is a set of expectations held by citizens regarding how the elected branches will, in the future, exercise their control over social goods and services, for a judicial constraint to promote the elected branches' trustworthiness – and so, increase the likelihood of their fulfilling citizens' trust – it must constrain the elected branches' future conduct. A broad judicial ruling, I submit, best achieves this result. Such a ruling offers the elected branches guidance regarding how they must, and so likely will, in future interactions with citizens, exercise their control over the relevant social goods and services.

To be clear, I am not suggesting that the courts make resource allocation decisions, telling the elected branches which social goods and services to provide. This brings me to the second requirement. The judicial constraint must target specifically the constituent expectations of trust (goodwill, competence and fiduciary responsibility), making one of their fulfilment by the elected branches more likely. As I noted in previous chapters, and will elaborate in the next part, these expectations focus on the procedure by which the elected branches exercise their control over social goods and services. A trustworthiness-promoting constraint is thus to be contrasted with a constraint directed at the social goods and services themselves (i.e., the outcome of the elected branches' decision-making). The constraint makes the elected branches, in their exercise of control over social goods and services, more likely to exercise goodwill, act competently or fulfil their fiduciary responsibility to citizens – and consequently, it follows, renders them more trustworthy.

Chapters 5–7 will detail, more precisely, what trustworthiness-promoting judicial constraints entail and how the courts can impose them on the elected branches. However, I will outline in this section, briefly, what the framework I propose involves. I provide this outline now because it is necessary to appreciate the justifications for the framework set out in the next part.

The proposed framework requires the courts to hold the elected branches to what I will refer to as a 'standard of trustworthiness'. This standard consists of two inter-related forms of judicial intervention in social rights cases. First, the courts use the three constituent expectations of trust to ex ante define the elected branches' obligations to citizens in exercising their control over social goods and services. The courts explicitly set out these obligations in their judgments – both generally and as they play out in particular areas of social welfare – so the elected branches know what their obligations are, and citizens know what their corresponding entitlements are.

Secondly, the courts hold the elected branches accountable where they fail to meet this trustworthiness standard. To explain what I mean by accountability, I will rely on what I consider to be a useful definition of the term offered by Barbara Cameron in her work on social welfare in Canada. Cameron has defined accountability as 'a relationship between parties whereby one party is answerable to the other for the performance of commitments or obligations that are evaluated against criteria or standards known to the parties, and sanctions are applied for failure to meet the commitments'.[37] Adapting Cameron's definition of

[37] Barbara Cameron, 'Accountability Regimes for Federal Social Transfers: An Exercise in Deconstruction and Reconstruction' in Peter Graefe, Julie M. Simmons and Linda Ann White (eds.), *Overpromising and Underperforming?: Understanding and Evaluating New Intergovernmental Accountability Regimes* (Toronto: University of Toronto Press, 2013), p. 260, cited in Martha Jackman, 'The Future of Health Care Accountability: A Human Rights Approach' (2016) 47 *Ottawa Law Review* 441, 443. For other, but similar, definitions of accountability, see Mark Bovens, 'Analysing and Assessing Accountability: A Conceptual Framework' (2007) 13 *European Law Journal* 447; Dawn Oliver, 'Accountability and the Foundations of British Democracy – the Public Interest

accountability for the purpose of the proposed trust-based framework, the elected branches, under this trustworthiness standard, are answerable to the courts (and to citizens through the courts) for their obligations pursuant to constitutional social rights. The courts are responsible for reviewing both the elected branches' social welfare legislation and executive action vis-à-vis social welfare. Next, the 'criteria or standards' against which that legislation and executive action are evaluated by the courts are derived from the three constituent expectations of trust. In other words, in enforcing constitutional social rights, what the courts do is enforce the elected branches' trustworthiness, enforcing, against the elected branches, the three constituent expectations of trust.[38] And where the elected branches have failed to satisfy trust's three constituent expectations, the courts censure and/or sanction them for that failure.

From a trustworthiness-promoting perspective, it is imperative that both forms of judicial intervention be present. That is, it is not sufficient for the courts to review social welfare legislation and executive action vis-à-vis social welfare without, in advance, expressly defining the elected branches' obligations to citizens. This is so for two inter-related reasons. For one, as Piotr Sztompka has pointed out, accountability 'enhances trustworthiness because it changes the truster's calculation of interests; it adds an extra incentive to be trustworthy – namely to avoid censure and punishment'.[39] We should therefore expect judicial accountability to render the elected branches more trustworthy because they have an incentive to act trustworthily (i.e., to avoid the courts' censure and punishment). However, if the elected branches are not made aware of what is expected of them in advance – and hence, that for which they will be censured or punished by the courts – they are not likely to change their behaviour accordingly. For another, an express judicial definition of the elected branches' obligations, provides citizens, and those who

and Public Service Principles' in Bamforth and Leyland, *Accountability in the Contemporary Constitution*. Carol Harlow has been critical of such definitions of accountability for being too retrospective, suggesting that accountability is also prospective: see Carol Harlow, 'Accountability and Constitutional Law' in Mark Bovens, Robert E. Goodin and Thomas Schillemans (eds.), *The Oxford Handbook of Public Accountability* (Oxford: Oxford University Press, 2014), p. 196. However, the first form of judicial intervention under the trustworthiness standard, I think, addresses Harlow's concern.

[38] Piotr Sztompka, *Trust: A Sociological Theory* (Cambridge: Cambridge University Press, 1999), p. 87.

[39] Ibid, pp. 87–88.

represent citizens, including special interest groups and non-governmental organisations, with the tools they need to hold the elected branches accountable via non-judicial means. Since litigation is time-consuming and expensive, to truly promote the elected branches' trustworthiness (i.e., increase the likelihood that the elected branches will act with goodwill, competence and in fulfilment of their fiduciary responsibility), accountability, with its censures and punishments, cannot be limited to the courts.

4.3 Why Trust? Justifying Political Trust as the Basis for Social Rights Enforcement

If we accept that political trust can be transformed into a tool for social rights enforcement, as I have just outlined, it still does not justify why it should be used as such. Why should political trust be at the centre of social rights enforcement, providing the basis for a legal framework? Granted, the concept of political trust has some intuitive appeal when it comes to social rights enforcement: it seems correct, on an intuitive level, that the courts, in fulfilling their role as enforcers of social rights, should be concerned with citizens' trust in government actors. After all, should citizens not be entitled to trust their government vis-à-vis the social goods and services that they need? And so, should the courts, in overseeing the citizen–government relationship, not be concerned with trust? Intuitive appeal aside, however, I will now present four principled reasons why political trust, I submit, should provide the basis for a social rights enforcement framework.

4.3.1 *An Instrumental Justification*

My first justification for why political trust should provide the basis for a social rights enforcement framework follows on from the instrumental value of such trust to contemporary democracies. We know that political trust encourages public cooperation, affecting the public's willingness to accept authority decisions, its feelings of obligation to obey laws and its performance evaluations of authority figures.[40] Making such trust

[40] Russell J. Dalton, *Democratic Challenges, Democratic Choices: The Erosion of Political Support in Advanced Industrial Democracies* (Oxford: Oxford University Press, 2004); Pippa Norris, 'Conclusion: The Growth of Critical Citizens and Its Consequences' in Pippa Norris (ed.), *Critical Citizens: Global Support for Democratic Government* (Oxford:

especially significant for social rights law, we also know that cooperation manifests itself as public willingness to pay taxes and support for social policies.

I submit that this link between political trust and public cooperation justifies the use of the former as the basis for a social rights enforcement framework. If we want to realise the value of political trust – which I suggest we should, given that a lack of public cooperation, it will be recalled, may endanger the ability of states to provide social goods and services to the public – social rights adjudication presents a means by which we can realise this value. Based on our application of the network conception of trust to the citizen–government relationship, we know that the relationships that constitute the social rights network can impact – including, in the right circumstances, foster – trust in the citizen–government relationship. We also know that included among these relationships is the citizen–court relationship that arises out of social rights adjudication. From these two points it follows that social rights adjudication, if structured along specific lines, can foster citizens' trust in the elected branches, at least with respect to social rights; and therefore, adjudication can realise the value of political trust – namely, public cooperation.

By promoting the elected branches' trustworthiness in the way that I set out earlier, the courts, via social rights adjudication, should be able to foster political trust. As Russell Hardin has recognised in his work, '[t]he best device for creating trust is to establish and support trustworthiness'.[41] Hardin has explained this relationship between trust and trustworthiness as follows. A truster's learning to trust a trustee depends on the success of the truster's trusting – that is, the truster will learn to trust the trustee if the former's trust in the latter proves to be well placed. And the success of the truster trusting depends in turn on the trustee's trustworthiness: if the trustee is trustworthy, the truster's trust in the trustee will likely prove to be well placed. Consequently, as Hardin has concluded, 'we can imagine that enhancing trustworthiness in general will increase levels of trust'.[42] In fact, this understanding of the relationship between trust and trustworthiness underlies the very idea of

Oxford University Press, 1999), pp. 257–272; Bo Rothstein, *Just Institutions Matter* (Cambridge: Cambridge University Press, 1998).

41 Hardin, 'Trustworthiness', 29.

42 Ibid, 32.

impersonal trust, including the corresponding arguments of both Pettit and Shapiro from earlier.

Nevertheless, even if we do not accept this understanding of the trust–trustworthiness relationship, there is good reason to conclude that the promotion of trustworthiness itself will generate the valuable ends of political trust. To repeat: the instrumental value of political trust stems from its effects on the public's willingness to accept authority decisions, feelings of obligation to obey laws and performance evaluations of authority figures. The research of Tom Tyler has established that, in actuality, it is not people's trust in authorities per se that is linked with these effects, but, more precisely, it is people's attributions of authority trustworthiness.[43] If people consider organisational authorities to be trustworthy (even though they may not trust those authorities), then they are more likely to accept the authorities' decisions, obey their laws and positively evaluate them. Hence, regardless of whether trustworthiness has value as a path to trust, or has value in itself, it is reasonable to expect that the courts' promotion of the elected branches' trustworthiness in social rights adjudication, in the way that I have set out, will generate the valuable ends of political trust.

In this respect, the trust-based framework that I propose for enforcing social rights aligns with the growing legal scholarship that advocates more relational approaches to law, including human rights law.[44] As Jennifer Nedelsky has said in her work in this area, 'people will do a better job of making all the difficult decisions involving rights if they focus on the kinds of relationships they actually want to foster, what the values at stake in that fostering are, and how different concepts and institutions will best contribute to that fostering'.[45] I am suggesting, therefore, that given the instrumental value of political trust, the type of citizen–government relationship that we should aim to foster is a trusting relationship, stemming from the elected branches'

43 Tom R. Tyler and Peter Degoey, 'Trust in Organizational Authorities: The Influence of Motive Attributions on Willingness to Accept Decisions' in Roderick M. Kramer and Tom R. Tyler (eds.), *Trust in Organizations: Frontiers of Theory and Research* (Thousand Oaks, CA: Sage Publications, 1996), p. 336.

44 See Jonathan Herring, *Law and the Relational Self* (Cambridge: Cambridge University Press, 2019); Robert Leckey, *Contextual Subjects: Family, State, and Relational Theory* (Toronto: University of Toronto Press, 2008); Jennifer Nedelsky, *Law's Relations: A Relational Theory of Self, Autonomy, and Law* (Cambridge: Cambridge University Press, 2011).

45 Nedelsky, *Law's Relations*, pp. 237–238.

trustworthiness with respect to social rights; and that the courts can, in their enforcement of social rights, contribute to this fostering by imposing the previously noted constraints on the elected branches.

To be fair, my justification here assumes that the elected branches will comply with the social rights judgments of the courts. It is, after all, the elected branches' compliance with those judgments, specifically the constraints imposed in those judgments, that makes them trustworthy (i.e., likely to act with goodwill, competence and in fulfilment of their fiduciary responsibility to citizens). Such compliance is not a given, of course, with governments often flouting judicial orders. But as we will see in Chapter 5, the trust-based framework, as part of the expectation of goodwill, responds to governmental intransigence, helping to address potential non-compliance.

4.3.2 A Theoretical Justification

My second justification is theoretical in character. It stems from the fiduciary nature of the citizen–government relationship. In Chapter 2, I built an argument, drawing on the work of public law scholars like Evan Fox-Decent and sociologist Bernard Barber, as to why the citizen–government relationship should be characterised as fiduciary. It was this characterisation that yielded the expectation of fiduciary responsibility as a constituent expectation of trust in the relationship.

In the private law context, fiduciary law scholars have argued, perhaps not so surprisingly, that the law regulating the relationship between fiduciaries and their principals should centre on the concept of trust.[46] Because fiduciary relationships have trust at their core, fiduciary law, it is said, 'regulates relationships that are based on reasonable trust'.[47] Accordingly, so the argument goes, it makes sense that fiduciary law should centre on trust. Matthew Harding, for instance, has claimed that given the centrality of trust to the fiduciary relationship, fiduciary law ought to be aimed at facilitating trusting relationships between fiduciaries and principals. As he has stated, 'a main purpose of fiduciary law [ought

[46] Tamar Frankel, 'Fiduciary Law' (1983) 71 *California Law Review* 795; Joshua Getzler, '"As If." Accountability and Counterfactual Trust' (2011) 91 *Boston University Law Review* 973; Matthew Harding, 'Trust and Fiduciary Law' (2013) 33 *Oxford Journal of Legal Studies* 81.

[47] Tamar Frankel, 'Fiduciary Law in the Twenty-First Century' (2011) 91 *Boston University Law Review* 1289, 1291.

to be] to enable such relationships to form, persist and deepen in ways that generate the instrumental and intrinsic value' of such relationships.[48] For Harding, fiduciary law can achieve this purpose by providing principals with 'guarantees that the conduct of the fiduciaries will be consistent with the requirements of trustworthiness'.[49] In other words, owing to fiduciary law, a principal in a fiduciary relationship can expect the fiduciary to act trustworthily and so, can trust the fiduciary with respect to the property or power in their relationship.

If we apply this reasoning to the social rights context, it follows that social rights enforcement should centre on political trust. Given that social rights enforcement is the means by which the courts oversee the citizen–government relationship, its governing law – that is, social rights law – regulates the citizen–government relationship. If we accept the above reasoning – that the law regulating fiduciary relationships should centre on trust – it follows that social rights law, as law that regulates the fiduciary citizen–government relationship, should centre on trust in that relationship. Social rights law should aim to facilitate trust between citizens and the elected branches with respect to social rights so as to, in Harding's words, 'generate the instrumental and intrinsic value' of trust in the citizen–government relationship. The trust-based framework that I propose does so: it increases the likelihood that the elected branches will act trustworthily with respect to social rights, just as Harding has advocated for fiduciary relationships more broadly.

Granted, I recognise the dangers of extending private law principles to a public law context, given their differences both in purpose and application.[50] I emphasise, however, that in characterising the citizen–government relationship as a fiduciary relationship, I do not adopt a 'literalist' approach to public fiduciary theorising.[51] I am therefore not

48 Harding, 'Trust and Fiduciary Law', 97.

49 Ibid, 95.

50 See Seth Davis, 'The False Promise of Fiduciary Government' (2014) 89 *Notre Dame Law Review* 1145, 1198–1206; Timothy Endicott, 'Equity and Administrative Behaviour: A Commentary' in P.G. Turner (ed.), *Equity and Administration* (Cambridge: Cambridge University Press, 2016), p. 375. For example, Timothy Endicott has noted that in the administrative law context, the role of the fiduciary is 'deeply different' from the role of administrative agencies in general and the role of judges in enforcing the fiduciary duties of trustees is different from their role in reviewing the lawfulness of administrative decision-making (p. 375).

51 Evan Fox-Decent, 'Challenges to Public Fiduciary Theory: An Assessment' in D. Gordon Smith and Andrew S. Gold (eds.), *Research Handbook on Fiduciary Law* (Cheltenham: Edward Elgar, 2018), pp. 379–400. The 'literalist' terminology has been used by Stephen

suggesting that the elected branches' duties to citizens are literally identical to those of a trustee in the private law context. And in arguing that social rights enforcement by courts should centre on political trust, I am not advocating transplantation of private law doctrine to public law. I am suggesting, rather, as Fox-Decent has appropriately phrased it, that 'the principles relevant to acting on behalf of another in private law might help illuminate' this public law context.[52] To be sure, we need to exercise 'caution when considering the application of fiduciary concepts to public law'; and fiduciary duties in a public law context like that of social rights, will likely assume a different form.[53] That said, I do think that this reasoning can be justifiably extended to the social rights context in light of the fact that the fiduciary political theory literature has, like the private law literature, recognised trust's centrality to fiduciary relationships. It will be recalled that in Fox-Decent's work, for example, trust is the basis for the state's authority over its subjects and its duty to them: their trust authorises the state to act on their behalf and in turn, the state must act on the basis of that trust. Given the public law literature's recognition of the central role played by trust in fiduciary relationships, I think that this reasoning is not misplaced in the social rights context.

At the same time, my justification in this section finds support in an argument made by Paul Finn. Finn, who may be included in the camp of fiduciary political theory scholars, has argued that we may fairly characterise government as a trust and in turn characterise government actors as trustees for the people.[54] To support his argument, Finn has advanced three propositions: (i) that sovereign power resides in the people; (ii) that where the public's power is entrusted to others for the purposes of civil governance, the relevant actors are trustees for the people; and (iii) that those 'entrusted with public power are accountable to the public for the exercise of their trust'.[55] As part of his argument, Finn has proposed that the people, in virtue of their sovereignty, are entitled to have certain expectations about the manner of their governing; and these expectations

R. Galoob and Ethan J. Leib, 'The Core of Fiduciary Political Theory' in Smith and Gold, *Research Handbook on Fiduciary Law*, pp. 401–417.

[52] Fox-Decent, 'Challenges to Public Fiduciary Theory', p. 382 (footnote 21).

[53] Ibid, p. 400.

[54] Paul Finn, 'Public Trust and Public Accountability' (1994) 3 *Griffith Law Review* 224; Paul Finn, 'A Sovereign People, A Public Trust' in P.D. Finn (ed.), *Essays on Law and Government, Volume 1: Principles and Values* (North Ryde: The Law Book Company, 1995), pp. 1–32.

[55] Finn, 'Public Trust and Public Accountability', pp. 227–228.

may ground corresponding duties on government actors. One key expectation is what Finn has called the 'integrity principle'. It necessitates that 'government is structured and practised in ways that invite and retain public trust in government itself'.[56] In other words, the people are entitled to expect that government actors, as trustees for the people, will exercise public power in a trustworthy manner; and government actors may have a corresponding duty to the people to exercise the power that has been entrusted to them trustworthily.[57] In light of Finn's work, there is precedent in the public law literature for the idea that political trust can and should be used as the basis for a government's obligations to its citizens. The trust-based framework that I propose in this book may thus be viewed as an extension of Finn's argument to the social rights context.

4.3.3 A Practical Justification

As a third justification, I suggest that political trust should provide the basis for a social rights enforcement framework because trust, as I conceptualised it in Chapters 2 and 3, fits well with social rights adjudication, including the many difficulties that this category of adjudication has been said to raise. In this section, I advance three sub-arguments: (i) because a constituent element of a trust relationship is discretion/uncertainty, trust responds to the prospectivity of social rights; (ii) focusing social rights enforcement on political trust, unlike much of the literature to date in this area, rightfully brings the beneficiaries of social goods and services (i.e., citizens) to the centre of social rights matters, shifting the emphasis from the bilateral relationship between the courts and the elected branches, to the triangular relationship among the courts, the elected branches and citizens; and (iii) the trust-based framework that I propose offers a good middle ground between the 'two wrongs' of social rights enforcement – judicial usurpation and judicial abdication.

56 Finn, 'A Sovereign People', p. 27.

57 In more recent work, Finn has suggested that 'we should be slow to embrace' such trust/fiduciary principles 'so as to channel and control official decision making' (including judicial review), in large part owing to the fact that, in Finn's view, they are unlikely to 'provide workable criteria upon which to found judicial review of official decision making': Paul Finn, 'Public Trusts, Public Fiduciaries' (2010) 38 *Federal Law Review* 335, 335–336. I disagree with Finn in this regard, however; I suggest that my conceptualisation of trust in this book does provide such workable criteria.

4.3.3.1 Trust Responds to the Prospectivity of Social Rights

Abram Chayes noted decades ago that traditional adjudication has a 'retrospective orientation': it focuses on the past conduct of the parties, it is concerned primarily with assessing the legal consequences of that past conduct, and the remedy granted by the courts derives logically from that conduct.[58] Chayes argued that this traditional idea of adjudication did not fit well with the then-emerging model of 'public law litigation' in the United States. That model (exemplified by cases involving school desegregation like *Brown v. Board of Education II*) was characterised by the courts reviewing the application of regulatory policy and creating or managing 'complex forms of ongoing relief' in the form of injunctions, with the effect of reforming public institutions.[59] Chayes claimed that the misfit between that model and the traditional idea of adjudication was attributable to the former's prospectivity – that is, its focus on the parties' future, rather than past, conduct.

Public law litigation, Chayes claimed, is prospective in three respects. First, in public law litigation a court's liability determination 'is not simply a pronouncement of the legal consequences of past events' (as it is for the traditional idea of adjudication) 'but to some extent a prediction of what is likely to be in the future'.[60] The courts must make educated guesses about whether future actions 'will materialize, in what circumstances, and with what consequences'.[61] Secondly, remediation in public law litigation is prospective in purpose. Whereas under the traditional idea of adjudication, relief seeks to 'compensate for past wrong', in public law litigation it 'seeks to adjust future behavior'.[62] Public law litigation achieves this purpose by making use of injunctive relief. Lastly, injunctive relief is itself prospective. Not only is it a significant constraint on the parties' future conduct, enforceable by contempt, but since it is continuing, the parties may return to the courts to enforce the order, or to modify it should the surrounding circumstances change.[63]

Social rights litigation (by which I mean litigation that involves the enforcement of *positive* social rights, the focus of this book) fits within

[58] Abram Chayes, 'The Role of the Judge in Public Law Litigation' (1976) 89 *Harvard Law Review* 1281, 1296.

[59] Ibid, 1284.

[60] Ibid, 1294.

[61] Ibid, 1296.

[62] Ibid, 1296, 1298.

[63] Ibid, 1292.

Chayes's broader category of public law litigation. Consistent with his characterisation of public law litigation, these cases usually involve the judicial review of policy and/or the application of that policy, they regularly ask the courts to create and manage complex injunctive relief (usually of an ongoing nature where the courts choose to exercise their supervisory jurisdiction over their orders), and they can result, if the courts choose to intervene to such an extent, in the reform of public institutions. Therefore, as is true for public law litigation more generally, I think it is fair to characterise social rights litigation as prospective.

This is not to say that social rights litigation does not also have a retrospective element. It does. For example, in reviewing the application of policy, the courts must examine past conduct (i.e., the circumstances in which the relevant policy was applied). However, as Chayes said of public law litigation, the courts do not simply pronounce on the legal consequences of that past conduct. They consider the policy's future application and often issue remedies that adjust future behaviour.

Social rights litigation is prospective, I claim, because the rights are themselves prospective. Social rights demand that the courts adopt a prospective orientation: they require the courts, in defining the substance of a social right and granting a remedy for the violation of that right, to consider, and to some extent predict, the elected branches' future conduct. This prospectivity is attributable, in large part, to three features of social rights: (i) their positiveness; (ii) their internal limitation based on available resources; and (iii) the fact that they are not immediately realisable.

First, the social rights on which this book focuses are positive in nature.[64] We may define a positive right as a claim to something like a good or service.[65] It may be contrasted with a negative right which is, rather, a right 'that something not be done, that some particular imposition be withheld'.[66] As Cécile Fabre has explained, there is therefore a 'duty distinction' between positive and negative rights: positive rights ground positive duties that require the state to do something, whereas

[64] I want to emphasise, however, that not all social rights are positive. Social rights can come in the form of negative rights rather than positive ones (recall from Chapter 1 the duties to respect and protect which may arise from social rights). Nor is positiveness unique to social rights. Positiveness is a feature often shared by social rights' counterparts – civil and political rights.

[65] Fabre, 'Constitutionalising Social Rights', 263.

[66] Charles Fried, *Right and Wrong* (Cambridge, MA: Harvard University Press, 1978), p. 110, cited in Fabre, 'Constitutionalising Social Rights', 263.

negative rights ground negative duties of non-interference.[67] From this it follows that the realisation of social rights, as positive rights, requires state 'action rather than inaction'.[68]

The positiveness of social rights demands that the courts adopt a prospective orientation, in a few respects. As Etienne Mureinik has pointed out, given their positiveness, there is more than one appropriate way in which a government may fulfil a social right. If a civil or political right 'is denied, the court knows, almost without thinking, that it must respond by quashing the denial. The right generates its own remedy, and the remedy is usually an annulment'.[69] Social rights, in contrast, 'can be delivered in many different ways, and it is always a matter of political and economic controversy which is the best'.[70] For this reason, coupled with the arguments from legitimacy and capacity, critics of the courts' involvement in social rights matters have highlighted the importance of leaving the elected branches with discretion, allowing them to arrive at an appropriate decision. In fact, even those in favour of the courts' involvement accept the importance of such discretion. In Albie Sachs's fitting words, governments have the 'right . . . to be stupid'; we must be 'cautious about constitutional principles that preempt any government forward planning, for they inhibit democratic governmental experimentation and public innovation'.[71] Hence, assuming the courts do not want to inhibit governmental experimentation and innovation, they must leave the elected branches with discretion. This demands a prospective orientation. It requires the courts to predict how the elected branches will exercise their discretion in the future, and to decide whether they should place restrictions on that exercise of discretion.

Additionally, owing to their positiveness, the courts cannot directly enforce social rights. The courts are dependent, rather, on the elected branches to implement any directive that they make.[72] Cass Sunstein has made the often-quoted observation that '[c]ourts lack the tools of a

[67] Fabre, 'Constitutionalising Social Rights', 263–264.

[68] Etienne Mureinik, 'Beyond a Charter of Luxuries: Economic Rights in the Constitution' (1992) 8 *South African Journal on Human Rights* 464, 467.

[69] Ibid, 467.

[70] Ibid, 467.

[71] Albie Sachs, 'Economic and Social Rights and the Right to Health: An Interdisciplinary Discussion Held at Harvard Law School in September, 1993' (Harvard Law School Human Rights Program, 1995), http://hrp.law.harvard.edu/wp-content/uploads/2013/08/EconomicandSocialRightsandtheRighttoHealth.pdf, accessed 10 January 2023, 24.

[72] Frank B. Cross, 'The Error of Positive Rights' (2001) 48 *UCLA Law Review* 857, 892.

bureaucracy. They cannot create government programs. They do not have systematic overview of government policy'.[73] In the absence of a decision on the part of government to implement it, a court's ruling on social rights may be nothing more than 'merely symbolic or supportive'.[74] Civil and political rights, as Mureinik has observed, are different in that they 'are typically enforced by judicial review of government action, resulting, if the action is found to conflict with the right, in a court order striking it down'.[75] Where the conflict arises out of a legislative omission or under-inclusion, a court may, alternatively, read into, or read down, the legislation. In either case, the issue is resolved, and the remedy implemented, immediately. With social rights, in contrast, because the courts are dependent on the elected branches for implementation, the issue cannot be resolved, or the remedy implemented, immediately: their resolution and implementation are necessarily pushed into the future. So, the courts must, once again, predict the elected branches' future conduct, including the likelihood of them implementing the rulings the courts have made.

Secondly, social rights are usually not absolute. The duty upon the state to fulfil social rights is frequently limited by available resources. As Fabre has stressed, '[p]ositive rights are inevitably asserted to scarce goods, and consequently scarcity implies a limit to the claim'.[76] Not to oversimplify the point, but the state cannot provide something that is beyond its physical and financial means. Given this limitation, social rights provisions frequently include qualifying language to this effect. Such qualification can be made either explicitly (e.g., sections 26(2) and 27(2) of the South African Constitution (the rights to housing and health, food, water and social security, respectively) which qualify the obligation on the state to achieve these rights to that which is 'within its available resources') or implicitly, through the use of vague terms like 'reasonable' or 'fair' to describe the obligation imposed on the state or the social goods and services at issue.[77]

[73] Cass R. Sunstein, 'Against Positive Rights' in Andràs Sajó (ed.), *Western Rights? Post-Communist Application* (The Hague: Kluwer Law International, 1996), p. 229, cited in Cross, 'The Error of Positive Rights', 891.

[74] Christopher E. Smith, *Courts and the Poor* (Belmont, CA: Wadsworth, 1991), p. 89, cited in Cross, 'The Error of Positive Rights', 891.

[75] Mureinik, 'Beyond a Charter', 467.

[76] Fabre, 'Constitutionalising Social Rights', 263.

[77] King, *Judging Social Rights*, pp. 103–104.

This qualification on social rights pushes courts towards a prospective orientation, again, for a few reasons. For one, available resources is an ambiguous concept.[78] It can be understood in two senses: one narrow and the other broad.[79] In its narrow sense, available resources refers to those resources that a ministry or department has been allotted and that it has chosen to allocate to the protection of the right. In its broad sense, in contrast, available resources refers to any resources that the state can assemble and put towards the protection of the right.[80] Scholars like Darrel Moellendorf and David Bilchitz have advocated the broad interpretation, arguing that the narrow sense 'would allow the government to avoid realizing conditional rights merely by virtue of its allocation of the budget',[81] and so, would 'ignore the special weight that should be attached to rights'.[82] However, even if the broad interpretation is accepted, it in turn is open to multiple interpretations depending on where we decide the state must look to assemble resources. As Bilchitz has pointed out, available resources may refer to resources that are owned by the state, resources that may be obtained through increased taxes, and broader still, resources from third parties like foreign loans.[83] This ambiguity of the available resources concept pushes the courts towards a prospective orientation, for one simple reason: the task of defining what resources are 'available' to the state is exactly the type of polycentric, budgetary decision that the courts should not be making. As critics of judicial involvement in social rights matters have explained, for the courts to make this sort of decision would encroach 'upon the jealously guarded "power of the purse"',[84] and under the broadest interpretation of the concept, interfere with the state's foreign relations. Given this, it is unlikely that the courts will resolve, explicitly and clearly, the ambiguity in the available resources qualification, preferring to leave it in

[78] David Bilchitz, *Poverty and Fundamental Rights: The Justification and Enforcement of Socio-economic Rights* (Oxford: Oxford University Press, 2007), pp. 227–229; Mark S. Kende, *Constitutional Rights in Two Worlds: South Africa and the United States* (Cambridge: Cambridge University Press, 2009), pp. 268–269; Darrel Moellendorf, 'Reasoning about Resources: *Soobramoney* and the Future of Socio-economic Rights Claims' (1998) 14 *South African Journal on Human Rights* 327, 330. Of note, terms such as 'fair' and 'reasonable' are equally ambiguous and therefore raise similar concerns.

[79] Moellendorf, 'Reasoning about Resources', 330.

[80] Ibid, 330.

[81] Ibid, 331. See also Bilchitz, *Poverty and Fundamental Rights*, pp. 228–229.

[82] Moellendorf, 'Reasoning about Resources', 331.

[83] Bilchitz, *Poverty and Fundamental Rights*, pp. 228–229.

[84] Cross, 'The Error of Positive Rights', 890.

the discretion of the elected branches. And as with the multiple ways open to governments to fulfil social rights, this demands that the courts adopt a prospective orientation. It requires the courts, yet again, to predict how the elected branches will exercise their discretion in the future and to consider possible constraints.

For another, available resources is a fluid concept. The availability of a resource depends on many factors, including whether it is physically available, the financial situation of the state, and under the broadest interpretation of the term, the health of the state's foreign relations. All these factors are subject to change over time. For example, the fluidity of the available resources concept and its dependence on the state's finances became especially apparent following the 2008 global financial and economic crisis. As Xenophon Contiades and Alkmene Fotiadou have highlighted in their work, '[d]ependent upon the economic contingencies and the inevitable fluctuations of economic growth, the content of social rights is by definition open-ended and ever-changing'.[85] Given this fluidity, the courts cannot provide fixed content to the concept of available resources. For them to do so would be artificial, leading to serious injustices should resources become more available in the future, and placing the elected branches in an impossible position should resources instead become less available (e.g., in an economic downturn or resource shortage). The elected branches thus require discretion, requiring the courts to, yet again, adopt a prospective orientation.

Lastly, characteristically speaking, social rights are not immediately realisable. Owing to resource constraints, it is generally understood that it would be unreasonable to expect the state to fully realise the social rights of all citizens immediately. As Cass Sunstein has said, '[n]o one thinks that every individual has an enforceable right to full protection of the interests at stake'.[86] The obligation on the state is therefore usually in the form of a duty to work towards the 'progressive realisation' of the right. Sections 26(2), 27(2) and 29(1)(b) (the right to further education) of the South African Constitution, for example, place an obligation on the state to 'take reasonable legislative and other measures ... to achieve the progressive realisation' of the right (and in the case of section 29(1)(b),

[85] Xenophon Contiades and Alkmene Fotiadou, 'Social Rights in the Age of Proportionality: Global Economic Crisis and Constitutional Litigation' (2012) 10 *International Journal of Constitutional Law* 660, 670–671.

[86] Cass R. Sunstein, 'Social and Economic Rights? Lessons from South Africa' (2000) 11 *Constitutional Forum* 123, 130.

to make 'further education . . . through reasonable measures . . . progressively available and accessible'). This does not mean that the state does not have any immediate obligations. The South African Constitutional Court, for instance, has recognised immediate obligations on the state under the afore-mentioned provisions: an obligation to take reasonable measures to secure the rights and, relatedly, an obligation to meaningfully engage with the relevant parties.[87] That said, the progressive realisation idea nevertheless presents a significant challenge for social rights adjudication. Despite the immediate obligations which are imposed on the state such as those identified earlier, progressive realisation means that the full realisation of social rights does not need to be, and so, likely will not be, realised immediately.[88] As Katharine Young has described, the effect of progressive realisation is to grant governments 'latitude to implement rights over time depending on the availability of necessary resources, rather than requiring them to guarantee rights immediately'.[89] The result of this latitude is to push the obligation on the state to fully realise social rights, and so, their full enforcement by the courts, into the future. In other words, the full realisation of social rights becomes a future obligation that the courts cannot – at least with traditional approaches to adjudication – enforce in the present.[90]

Given the three points above, we may ask: how does the trust-based framework respond to social rights' prospectivity? It responds, I suggest, because the concept of trust, from which the concept of trustworthiness follows on, is itself prospective. From Chapter 2 we know that not only does trust relate to future events, but it necessitates that the trustee has discretion in exercising their control over the good or service at issue, with the truster, in turn, being uncertain, at least to some extent. As I explained in that chapter, without such discretion and uncertainty, we do not have trust – and necessarily, we do not have trustworthiness. As a result, because trustworthiness represents the likelihood that the

[87] For example, see *Government of the Republic of South Africa and Others v. Grootboom and Others* [2000] ZACC 19; *Occupiers of 51 Olivia Road and Others v. City of Johannesburg and Others* [2008] ZACC 1.

[88] Bruce Porter, 'Rethinking Progressive Realization: How Should It Be Implemented in Canada?' (SRAC, 2015), www.socialrights.ca/documents/publications/Porter%20Progressive%20Implementation.pdf, accessed 10 January 2023, 3–4.

[89] Young, *Constituting Economic and Social Rights*, p. 71.

[90] Mitra Ebadolahi, 'Using Structural Interdicts and the South African Human Rights Commission to Achieve Judicial Enforcement of Economic and Social Rights in South Africa' (2008) 83 *New York University Law Review* 1565, 1567.

trustee will fulfil the truster's trust, a court, in applying the trustworthiness standard, must leave the elected branches with discretion in exercising their control over social goods and services. Otherwise, the courts would not be promoting the elected branches' trustworthiness. Hence, social rights' prospectivity, which necessitates that the elected branches have discretion in fulfilling those rights, does not prove problematic for the trust-based framework that I propose. Trust – and by extension, trustworthiness – actually requires discretion.

4.3.3.2 Trust Brings Citizens to the Centre of Social Rights Matters

Many social rights scholars have taken issue with the over-emphasis that the courts, in social rights cases, place on their relationship with the elected branches, and the relatively little weight that they give to citizens and their interests.[91] The courts, according to these scholars, are overly concerned with what we can call 'institutional' issues. This concern follows on from the arguments from legitimacy and capacity. While the focus of the social rights enforcement debate has moved on from justiciability to judicial approaches, its underlying arguments, by and large, have not. Commentators and litigants now employ those same arguments to advocate judicial restraint and deference to the elected branches in social rights adjudication. And so, not surprisingly, the courts, in adjudicating social rights matters, continue to strongly emphasise these institutional issues.[92]

Danie Brand, for instance, has argued that South African courts, due to their over-emphasis on and concern with institutional issues, have employed 'the strategy of deference, in a binary institutional relations mode – that is, by deferring decisions to the other branches of government'.[93] As he has explained, judicial deference is not neutral for

[91] Danie Brand, 'Judicial Deference and Democracy in Socio-economic Rights Cases in South Africa' (2011) 3 *Stellenbosch Law Review* 614, 630–631, citing Emilios A. Christodoulis, 'Paradoxes of Sovereignty and Representation' (2002) 1 *TSAR* 108; David Landau, 'A Dynamic Theory of Judicial Role' (2014) 55 *Boston College Law Review* 1501; Bruce Porter, 'Enforcing the Right to Reasonableness in Social Rights Litigation: The Canadian Experience' in Malcolm Langford, César Rodriguez-Garavito and Julieta Rossi (eds.), *Compliance with Socio-economic Rights Judgments: Making It Stick* (Cambridge: Cambridge University Press, 2017), pp. 201–254; Sachs, 'Economic and Social Rights', 14.

[92] Brand, 'Judicial Deference and Democracy', 616–620.

[93] Ibid, 620.

claimants in social rights cases; it constitutes, rather, a 'loss' for them. In Brand's words, 'when courts employ deference in [social] rights cases to deal with problems of institutional capacity, legitimacy, integrity, security or constitutional comity, they favour the point of view with respect to the issues in dispute of one of the parties to that dispute (the state) over another (the claimants)'.[94] Relying on the theoretical work of Emilios Christodoulis, Brand has therefore argued that instead of conceiving of social rights adjudication in binary terms of this sort, 'we should recognise that it occurs within a more complex triangular relationship' – among the courts, the elected branches and citizens.[95] Brand has suggested that the 'courts should move away from regarding the institutional problems they face in deciding [social] rights cases in binary, institutional relations terms' and instead 'should recognise that . . . they stand in relationship not only to the representative branches of government', but also to citizens.[96] Citizens and their interests, put simply, must be at the centre of social rights matters. Brand has thus proposed, based on his argument, that South African courts operationalise this 'shift of perspective' into 'their doctrine, techniques and reasoning' in social rights cases.[97]

Much in fulfilment of Brand's proposal, the trust-based framework that I propose brings citizens and their interests to the centre of social rights matters. First, owing to its roots in the network conception of trust, the framework necessarily conceptualises social rights adjudication as a triangular relationship among the courts, the elected branches and citizens. Recognising that the courts are in a relationship with citizens as well as the elected branches, it envisages the courts as using these two relationships to mediate the relationship that the two parties have with one another – in accordance with what Brand has suggested for South African courts. Also, by focusing on citizens' trust in the elected branches, citizens are necessarily a paramount consideration in the trust-based framework. While the relationship between the courts and the elected branches remains relevant under the trust-based framework,

94 Ibid, 620.

95 Ibid, 631.

96 Ibid, 631. See also Porter, 'Enforcing the Right to Reasonableness', p. 222 who has said: 'Under the traditional separation of powers doctrine, courts have the ultimate authority to interpret rights and to determine how they apply in a particular context. This interpretive role must be informed by a dialogue not only with governments, but also with rights holders'.

97 Brand, 'Judicial Deference and Democracy', 631.

including of course the issues of relative legitimacy and capacity (such that the courts should not usurp the elected branches' policy-making role), that relationship and its institutional issues do not, however, overshadow citizens' interests.

4.3.3.3 Trust Offers a Good Middle Ground for the 'Two Wrongs' of Enforcement

As I have noted, when enforcing social rights, there are two errors or wrongs that a court can make.[98] The first is judicial usurpation, which 'occurs when the judiciary interprets and applies [social] rights in such a manner that it assumes control of the political system ... crowding out ... the democratically elected branches'.[99] In doing so, the courts usurp the policy-making role of the elected branches. The second wrong, judicial abdication, 'occurs when the judiciary declines to protect constitutional rights', thereby abdicating its role as enforcer of constitutional rights.[100] A court abdicates its role where, for instance, it shows too much deference to the elected branches.[101]

Judicial usurpation and judicial abdication, however, it will be recalled, 'do not represent a strict antagonism: 'they are a matter of degree', and therefore courts can – and should – opt for a middle ground between these two extremes.[102] The trust-based framework that I propose offers the courts, I suggest, such a middle ground. It does so because of trust's procedural orientation.

We know that the three constituent expectations of trust (goodwill, competence and fiduciary responsibility) focus on the procedure by which a trustee, like the elected branches, exercises their control over the good or service at issue in the trust relationship. It thus follows that under the trust-based framework, which has the courts enforce these three expectations, the courts review, at least principally, the procedure by which the elected branches exercise their control over social goods and

98 Young, *Constituting Economic and Social Rights*, p. 134. See also Michelman, 'The Constitution, Social Rights', 16.

99 Young, *Constituting Economic and Social Rights*, p. 134. See also Klatt, 'Positive Rights', 361.

100 Young, *Constituting Economic and Social Rights*, p. 134.

101 Klatt, 'Positive Rights', 361.

102 Ibid, 361.

services rather than the outcome of that exercise of control.[103] Because of this, the courts, in their application of the trust-based framework, do not define the substance of social policy in a way that usurps the elected branches' policy-making role. But at the same time, they also do not abdicate their role: by ensuring that the procedure followed by the elected branches in developing and implementing social policy evinces goodwill, competence and fulfilment of their fiduciary responsibility to citizens, the courts, I submit, play a meaningful part in the realisation of citizens' social rights and, consequently, fulfil their role as enforcers of rights.

In this respect, the trust-based framework aligns with procedural approaches to social rights enforcement – either that are currently in use or have been proposed.[104] It also stands in contrast to approaches that focus on outcome, like the individualised enforcement model that dominates right-to-health adjudication in many Latin American countries.[105] In the latter model, the court interprets right-to-health provisions as protecting individually enforceable rights and, where it finds a violation, grants the claimant immediate, individualised relief in the form of the medical treatment sought. An extensively studied example is Brazil. Brazil's Federal Constitution guarantees the right to health in Article 196, declaring health a 'right of all and a duty of the

[103] As I explain in Chapter 5, I say 'principally' here because the respect for the right to equality sub-element of procedural fairness under the expectation of goodwill necessitates some substantive content.

[104] For example, see Sandra Liebenberg, *Socio-economic Rights: Adjudication under a Transformative Constitution* (Cape Town: Juta Law, 2010); Brian Ray, 'Engagement's Possibilities and Limits as a Socioeconomic Rights Remedy' (2010) 9 *Washington Global Studies Law Review* 399; Brian Ray, 'Proceduralisation's Triumph and Engagement's Promise in Socio-economic Rights Litigation' (2011) 27 *South African Journal on Human Rights* 107; Brian Ray, *Engaging with Social Rights: Procedure, Participation, and Democracy in South Africa's Second Wave* (Cambridge: Cambridge University Press, 2016).

[105] Landau, 'The Reality of Social Rights Enforcement', 199; David Landau, 'South African Social Rights Jurisprudence and the Global Cannon: A Revisionist View' in Rosalind Dixon and Theunis Roux (eds.), *Constitutional Triumphs, Constitutional Disappointments: A Critical Account of the 1996 South African Constitution's Local and International Influence* (Cambridge: Cambridge University Press, 2018), p. 410. It should be noted, however, that some Latin American countries (e.g., Colombia) have employed 'two-track remedial strategies' that 'combine more immediate relief for successful litigants with longer-term processes designed to achieve systemic reform for both the litigants and similar groups': Kent Roach, 'The Challenges of Crafting Remedies for Violations of Socio-economic Rights' in Langford, *Social Rights Jurisprudence*, p. 57. See also David Landau, 'Choosing between Simple and Complex Remedies in Socio-economic Rights Cases' (2019) 69 *University of Toronto Law Journal* 105.

State'. It provides that the right 'shall be guaranteed by means of social and economic policies aimed at reducing the risk of illness and other hazards and at the universal and equal access to actions and services for its promotion, protection and recovery'. In the late 1990s, the Supreme Federal Tribunal interpreted this right as 'an individual entitlement to the satisfaction of one's health needs with the most advanced treatment available, irrespective of costs'.[106] And following on from that interpretation, Brazilian courts have used the right to order their government to provide individuals with treatments for health conditions, including diabetes, HIV/AIDS, Parkinson's disease, hepatitis C, Alzheimer's disease and multiple sclerosis. So, the 'Brazilian model' for right-to-health adjudication is characterised 'by a prevalence of individualized claims demanding curative medical treatment (most often drugs) and by an extremely high success rate for the litigant'.[107]

The individualised enforcement model has received significant criticism to date.[108] This criticism has centred on the fact that aside from usurping the elected branches' policy-making role, the model's by-product, it has been argued and empirically shown, is to direct resources to higher-income groups who have the resources to litigate their social rights (rather than the poor or marginalised).[109] Because litigation, as we know, is both expensive and time-consuming, there is 'a natural tendency to skew litigation toward higher-income groups because they are more likely to have the resources to learn their rights and hire an effective lawyer', and they are in a position to wait for a judicial resolution.[110] Accordingly, the model effectively enables those in higher-income groups to 'queue-jump'.[111] In fact, the empirical work on the impact of social rights judgments in various jurisdictions supports this conclusion. Octàvio Ferraz's work on the right to health in Brazil, for instance, has

106 Octàvio Luiz Motta Ferraz, 'The Right to Health in the Courts of Brazil: Worsening Health Inequities?' (2009) 11 *Health and Human Rights* 33, 34.

107 Ibid, 34.

108 Bilchitz, *Poverty and Fundamental Rights*, p. 203; Adam Chilton and Mila Versteeg, 'Rights without Resources: The Impact of Constitutional Social Rights on Social Spending' (2017) 60 *Journal of Law and Economics* 713, 720; Ferraz, 'The Right to Health', 34.

109 Chilton and Versteeg, 'Rights without Resources', 720.

110 David Landau and Rosalind Dixon, 'Constitutional Non-transformation? Socioeconomic Rights beyond the Poor?' in Young, *The Future of Economic*, p. 115.

111 Kent Roach, 'Dialogic Remedies' (2019) 17 *International Journal of Constitutional Law* 860. See also Adam Chilton and Mila Versteeg, *How Constitutional Rights Matter* (Oxford: Oxford University Press, 2020), p. 200.

shown that litigation has 'by and large diverted an increasingly larger amount of the already severely limited health budget to health treatments of dubious effectiveness and priority (mostly expensive new medicines) to a minority of people who are capable to litigate'.[112] And because this contradicts an implicit assumption held by advocates of social rights – that the key beneficiaries of courts' social rights judgments will be the most poor and marginalised – the individualised model is viewed as a 'betrayal or capture of these rights'.[113]

Because of trust's procedural orientation, the trust-based framework, which focuses on the procedure by which the elected branches exercise their control over social goods and services, does not suffer from these issues. That said, procedural approaches to social rights enforcement have also been criticised. This criticism has been largely in response to the 'reasonableness review' standard adopted by the South African Constitutional Court in its interpretation and application of its constitution's social rights provisions – a standard that scholars have viewed as procedural in nature.[114] The principal concerns raised by scholars in this regard are that procedural approaches: (i) fail to set standards or lay down principles that can both guide future policy-making and aid courts in future social rights cases; and (ii) have limited practical effect in that they do little to protect vulnerable groups – and following on from this, they may discourage litigation.

These concerns are without doubt valid. However, I think that the trust-based framework, while principally procedural in nature, mitigates these two concerns to a significant degree. On the first concern, we know

[112] Octàvio Luiz Motta Ferraz, *Health as a Human Right: The Politics and Judicialisation of Health in Brazil* (Cambridge: Cambridge University Press, 2021), pp. 2–3.

[113] Landau and Dixon, 'Constitutional Non-transformation', 111, 113.

[114] David Bilchitz, 'Giving Socio-economic Rights Teeth: The Minimum Core and Its Importance' (2002) 119 *South African Law Journal* 484; Bilchitz, *Poverty and Fundamental Rights*, pp. 136–176; Danie Brand, 'The Proceduralisation of South African Socio-economic Rights Jurisprudence, or "What Are Socio-economic Rights For?"' in Henk Botha, Andre van der Walt and Johan van der Walt (eds.), *Rights and Democracy in a Transformative Constitution* (Stellenbosch: Sun Press, 2003), pp. 33–56; Marius Pieterse, 'Resuscitating Socio-economic Rights: Constitutional Entitlements to Health Care Services' (2006) 22 *South African Journal on Human Rights* 473; Marius Pieterse, 'Eating Socioeconomic Rights: The Usefulness of Rights Talk in Alleviating Social Hardship Revisited' (2007) 29 *Human Rights Quarterly* 796. There have also been more recent criticisms aimed at the 'proceduralisation' of social rights in terms of the Court's adoption of engagement as an enforcement tool in social rights cases: for example, see Kirsty McLean, 'Meaningful Engagement: One Step Forward or Two Back? Some Thoughts on *Joe Slovo*' (2010) 3 *Constitutional Court Review* 223.

that the trust-based framework requires the courts to use trust's three constituent expectations to define the elected branches' obligations to citizens. Given this requirement, the trust-based framework, unlike some procedural approaches, does set standards and lay down principles, both to guide future policy-making and to aid courts in future cases: those standards and principles ultimately stemming from the three constituent expectations of trust.

Additionally, I submit that the trust-based framework mitigates the second concern of procedural approaches having limited practical effect. In particular, by using trust's three constituent expectations to define the elected branches' obligations to citizens, the courts can promote what Brian Ray has termed the 'institutionalisation' of procedural remedies. Ray, in his work on social rights, has argued that engagement (a procedural remedy introduced by the Constitutional Court that obliges governments to engage meaningfully with affected communities on social welfare matters) 'can give poor people and their advocates an important enforcement tool'.[115] To do so, however, he has suggested, engagement must be institutionalised. For Ray, institutionalisation requires governments to adopt measures that 'ensure systematic implementation of engagement' such that they 'work to develop a more generalised capacity for engagement outside of specific projects'.[116] In parallel to Ray's argument vis-à-vis engagement, I suggest that the expectations of trust – if institutionalised in the elected branches' exercise of control over social goods and services – could do a lot to protect vulnerable groups.[117] They would promote government goodwill, competence and fulfilment of its fiduciary responsibility. And the trust-based framework would encourage the institutionalisation of these expectations because the courts would use the expectations to define the elected branches' obligations. The expectations would not only serve as an accountability measure, used by the courts on an ex-post basis to review decisions, but the elected branches would be expected to develop and implement social policy in compliance with those expectations, with failure to comply giving rise to court intervention. The trust-based framework would therefore promote the expectations' 'systematic implementation' in the elected branches' exercise of control over the social goods and services that citizens need.

115 Ray, 'Proceduralisation's Triumph', 117.
116 Ibid, 117.
117 I elaborate on such protection in the next three chapters of the book.

The middle ground offered by the trust-based framework – and its corresponding appeal for social rights enforcement – is most apparent when we consider the well-recognised tension in the administrative state between technocracy and democracy.[118] Given the increasing technological complexity of government-regulated areas (including the provision of social goods and services), the administrative state has necessarily come to rely on experts. As I explain in more detail in Chapter 6, contemporary administrative agencies are increasingly staffed by experts who are trained in everything from the medical sciences to urban planning. This administrative expertise has generated a tension, however. On the one hand, expertise provides a strong – and in fact, the central – rationale for the courts affording deference to administrative actors on matters of social policy. Owing to judges' lack of training in the relevant areas, courts are (generally speaking) in a comparatively disadvantaged position to resolve such matters.[119] There is therefore good reason to leave these matters to those actors with the relevant expertise. On the other hand, there exists a valid fear of 'regulation by experts'.[120] As many commentators have noted, experts suffer from a panoply of limitations that militate against deferring to them.[121] These limitations include not only the possibility that experts will not apply the expertise for which they are being relied on, but that expertise is itself not as objective as some would suggest it is, with experts being unduly influenced by the interests of well-organised businesses (so-called 'agency capture' or factionalism) as well as their own interests. Furthermore, because the decisions made by experts are often value-laden, with technical and political decisions overlapping, expertise should not usurp democratic values such as participation and transparency.[122] To adopt the appropriate words of

[118] Catherine Donnelly, 'Participation and Expertise: Judicial Attitudes in Comparative Perspective' in Susan Rose-Ackerman and Peter L. Lindseth (eds.), *Comparative Administrative Law* (Cheltenham: Edward Elgar, 2017), pp. 370–386; King, *Judging Social Rights*, p. 229; Martin Shapiro, '"Deliberative," "Independent" *Technocracy v. Democratic Politics*: Will the Globe Echo the E.U.?"' (2005) 58 *Law and Contemporary Problems* 341.

[119] King, *Judging Social Rights*, p. 248.

[120] Shapiro, '"Deliberative," "Independent"', 343.

[121] Paul Daly, *A Theory of Deference in Administrative Law: Basis, Application and Scope* (Cambridge: Cambridge University Press, 2012), pp. 85–88; King, *Judging Social Rights*, pp. 235–240; Harold J. Laski, *The Limitation of the Expert* (London: The Fabian Society, 1931).

[122] Shapiro, '"Deliberative," "Independent"'.

Susan Rose-Ackerman, '[a]nalysis, however competent, cannot eliminate deep disagreements over values'.[123]

The trust-based framework is responsive to this tension. As I elaborate in Chapter 6, through its constituent expectation of competence (which, it will be explained, translates into an expectation of evidence-based policy-making (EBPM)), the trust-based framework accords expertise the prominent role it deserves. It necessitates that governmental decisions with respect to social goods and services be based on the relevant evidence from the natural and social sciences. It does not, however, blindly defer to experts. First, the expectation of competence is defined by reference to the evidence on which the decision is based and not the expertise of the decision-maker. It therefore ensures that the expert applies the expertise for which they are relied on. Secondly, EBPM encompasses more than knowledge from scientific research, but includes what Brian Head has called 'practical implementation knowledge'.[124] The trust-based framework thus necessarily adopts a more holistic approach to expertise.[125] Lastly, under the trust-based framework, competence is not the end of the story. The other two expectations of trust (goodwill and fiduciary responsibility) allow a court, in enforcing social rights, to consider, as we will see, democratic values like participation and transparency, with which expertise is frequently in tension.

4.3.4 A Democratic Justification

My final justification for why political trust should provide the basis for a social rights enforcement framework relates to a traditional defence for constitutional review more broadly. Constitutional law scholars have long suggested that while the courts may be counter-majoritarian, they are not, at least not necessarily, anti-democratic.[126] Via constitutional

[123] Susan Rose-Ackerman, 'Regulation and Public Law in Comparative Perspective' (2010) 60 *University of Toronto Law Journal* 519, 528.

[124] Brian W. Head, 'Three Lenses of Evidence-Based Policy' (2008) 67 *The Australian Journal of Public Administration* 1. See Chapter 6 for elaboration on this point.

[125] J.A. Muir Gray, 'Evidence Based Policy Making' (2004) 329 *British Medical Journal* 988, 988.

[126] Broadly speaking, see Ronald Dworkin, *Freedom's Law: The Moral Reasoning of the American Constitution* (Oxford: Oxford University Press, 1996); John Hart Ely, *Democracy and Distrust: A Theory of Judicial Review* (Cambridge, MA: Harvard University Press, 1980); David Feldman, 'Democracy, the Rule of Law and Judicial Review' (1990) 19 *Federal Law Review* 1. For a summary of this defence (although not in support of it), see Richard Bellamy, *Political Constitutionalism: A Republican Defence*

review, the courts can, instead, support or enhance democracy, together with the values that underlie democracy.[127]

In the social rights context, commentators have relied on variations of this defence to carve out democratically defensible roles for the courts in enforcing social rights.[128] Rosalind Dixon, for example, has argued that the courts can remedy 'blockages' in the legislative process that produce omissions and delays in that process – what she has described as 'blind spots' and 'burdens of inertia'.[129] According to Dixon, because the resultant omissions and delays 'are not driven by resource constraints or supported by principled forms of justification', they have 'profound significance to the legitimacy of the constitutional system'.[130] By remedying the relevant blockages, the courts support democracy – specifically, they 'enhance the overall inclusiveness and responsiveness of a constitutional democracy'.[131] Sandra Fredman has likewise relied on this defence, but has granted the courts an even larger role than Dixon. She has argued specifically that the judicial enforcement of social rights is justified to the extent that it strengthens democracy.[132] As she has explained, 'a major role of [social] rights duties is to strengthen democracy'; hence, 'justiciability [of these rights] may be appropriate to the extent that it can be harnessed to the achievement of these aims'.[133] Fredman has identified three key values that, according to her, lie behind

of the Constitutionality of Democracy (Cambridge: Cambridge University Press, 2007); Richard Bellamy, 'The Democratic Qualities of Courts: A Critical Analysis of Three Arguments' (2013) 49 *Representation* 333, 335.

127 For some examples of this line of argument, see Ely, *Democracy and Distrust*; William N. Eskridge, Jr., 'Pluralism and Distrust: How Courts Can Support Democracy by Lowering the Stakes of Politics' (2005) 114 *The Yale Law Journal* 1279; Feldman, 'Democracy, the Rule of Law'; Peter W. Hogg, 'The *Charter* Revolution: Is It Undemocratic?' (2001) 12 *Constitutional Forum* 1; Patrick J. Monahan, 'Judicial Review and Democracy: A Theory of Judicial Review' (1987) 21 *UBC Law Review* 87.

128 Dixon, 'Creating Dialogue'; Fredman, *Human Rights Transformed*; Murray Wesson, 'Disagreement and the Constitutionalisation of Social Rights' (2012) 12 *Human Rights Law Review* 221.

129 Dixon, 'Creating Dialogue'.

130 Ibid, 403–405.

131 Ibid, 394.

132 Fredman, *Human Rights Transformed*, pp. 100–113. For similar reasoning (although in the broader public law context), see Feldman, 'Democracy, the Rule of Law'. As Feldman has summarised: 'Judicial review has a place in democratic constitutions, alongside political and bureaucratic processes, in advancing the values on which democratic society is based. So long as it pursues those values, judicial review is not undemocratic' (p. 30).

133 Fredman, *Human Rights Transformed*, p. 100.

the democratic ideal: accountability, participation and equality. She has therefore argued that to the extent that social rights enforcement can support these three values, it is justified.

The trust-based framework, I submit, is compatible with this defence for constitutional review – that is, the courts, in using the trust-based framework to enforce social rights, support or enhance democracy.[134] First, the framework supports or enhances democracy because political trust is itself supportive of, or 'good for', democracy. This conclusion follows on from the link between political trust and public cooperation. Owing to this link, which it will be recalled ties political trust to social stability, economic welfare and effective governance, many writers have argued that political trust is supportive of democracy as a form of government.[135] Mark Warren, for example, has developed a convincing argument. Warren has defined 'democracy' as 'the systems of institutions and associations that enable people to engage in collective self-government with respect to matters that affect their self-determination'.[136] When people trust 'they relinquish some control over their self-determination to the will of others'.[137] Given the link between trust and cooperation, however, this relinquishment of control, Warren has argued, comes with a significant benefit: people 'can dramatically increase their collective capabilities, since trust enables cooperative divisions of labour, and does so without the burdens of coercion or other costly means of organization'.[138] As a result of this, he has said, political trust may be viewed as supportive of or 'good for' democracy: owing to its power to increase people's collective capabilities, political trust

[134] I recognise that 'democracy' is open to interpretation (and thus, that whether the trust-based framework can be said to support democracy depends on one's definition of the term). For the purpose of this argument, I adopt the definition of 'democracy' advanced by Mark Warren that I set out in this section: Mark E. Warren, 'What Kinds of Trust Does a Democracy Need? Trust from the Perspective of Democratic Theory' in Sonja Zmerli and Tom W.G. van der Meer (eds.), *Handbook on Political Trust* (Cheltenham: Edward Elgar, 2017), p. 33.

[135] Bernard Barber, *The Logic and Limits of Trust* (New Brunswick, NJ: Rutgers University Press, 1983), p. 93; Joseph S. Nye, Jr., 'Introduction: The Decline of Confidence in Government' in Joseph S. Nye, Jr., Philip D. Zelikow and David C. King (eds.), *Why People Do Not Trust Government* (Cambridge, MA: Harvard University Press, 1997), pp. 4–5; Mark Warren, 'Trust and Democracy' in Eric M. Uslaner (ed.), *The Oxford Handbook of Social and Political Trust* (Oxford: Oxford University Press, 2018), pp. 75–94; Warren, 'What Kinds of Trust'.

[136] Warren, 'What Kinds of Trust', p. 33.

[137] Ibid, p. 33. For greater clarity, Warren is speaking of trust at a behavioural level.

[138] Ibid, p. 33.

'expands domains of collective self-rule', thereby supporting the very idea of democracy.[139]

Of course, political trust is not always good for democracy. For one, because trust 'can be deferential, naïve or misplaced', it can, and often does, support authoritarian politics.[140] Such politics are, for obvious reasons, not good for democracy. Owing to this, some writers have argued that rather than political trust, it is distrust or scepticism that is valuable to democracy because it 'keeps constituents alert, and therefore public officials responsive'.[141] As I said earlier, I do not dispute that argument. Its applicability, however, as I explain shortly, is limited to certain kinds of trust. For another, trust can be problematic for democracy because it provides 'the social glue for clans, ethnic and racial groups, and sectarian religious communities'; it holds 'together criminal conspiracies and corrupt exchanges'; and it 'is involved in "bad social capital": relationships of mutual social investment that have broader divisive or corrosive social effects' (e.g., organised crime).[142] All these consequences, I think we can reasonably conclude, are bad for democracy.

As Warren has explained, to be good for democracy (or 'democracy-supporting'), political trust must satisfy two conditions. It must, first of all, be 'warranted'. Put simply, government actors must be worthy of citizens' trust in them (i.e., trustworthy with respect to the good or service that is at issue in their trust relationship). By being trustworthy, government actors grant citizens the knowledge (or in Warren's terms, the 'warrant') that is necessary for them to make 'a good trust judgment'.[143] This condition, in my view, distinguishes those circumstances in which political trust is valuable to democracy from those where, rather, distrust or scepticism is valuable.[144] Where a government has shown itself to be untrustworthy, it is without doubt that citizens should not blindly trust their government; they should be sceptical.[145] But

[139] Warren, 'Trust and Democracy', p. 75. See also Warren, 'What Kinds of Trust', p. 33.

[140] Warren, 'What Kinds of Trust', p. 35.

[141] Karen S. Cook, Russell Hardin and Margaret Levi, *Cooperation without Trust?* (New York: Russell Sage Foundation, 2005), p. 165.

[142] Warren, 'Trust and Democracy', p. 82.

[143] Ibid, p. 81.

[144] See Chiara Destri, 'Democratic Politics and the Circles of Trust' in Barradas de Freitas and Lo Iacono, *Trust Matters*, p. 102.

[145] As Onora O'Neill has put it, 'it is foolish to assume that we should always, or indeed generally, seek to "restore trust" or to "build more trust". Where we have to deal with

distrust or scepticism of an unwarranted nature (i.e., where government has not shown itself to be untrustworthy) is not valuable to democracy.[146] Secondly, to be good for democracy, Warren has claimed, the trust in question must be justifiable to those affected by the relevant trusting relationship. So, trust is only consistent with democracy if those who are affected by a trusting relationship find, or would find, the relationship acceptable. For instance, corrupt relationships, crime organisations, and ethnic and religious factions are built on trusting relationships, and the trust in those relationships is usually warranted, but that trust is not democracy-supporting because the relationship has a negative impact on others who, if they were aware of the reasons supporting the trusting relationship, would not approve of it. We may thus say that a trusting relationship is 'democratically legitimate just to the extent that it could be justified to those affected by its externalities'.[147]

The trust promoted by the trust-based framework satisfies both these conditions. First, because the framework focuses on the elected branches' trustworthiness, rather than some other means of promoting citizens' trust, the trust expected to result from its application is warranted. Citizens, via social rights adjudication, are given the knowledge or 'warrant' they need to make 'a good trust judgment' vis-à-vis the elected branches with respect to social rights.[148] Next, as Warren has noted, the second condition maps roughly onto a distinction drawn in the trust literature between 'generalised' trust (i.e., trust in people generally) and 'particularised' trust (i.e., trust between particular individuals), with the condition usually met where the relevant trust is of a more general nature (i.e., citizens' trust in government generally) as opposed to a more particular nature (i.e., particular citizens' trust in particular government actors).[149] Trust of the latter, particularised nature supports, instead, the

untrustworthy persons or institutions it would be a bad idea to aim for more trust': Onora O'Neill, 'Accountable Institutions, Trustworthy Cultures' (2017) 9 *Hague Journal on the Rule of Law* 401, 406.

146 Warren, 'What Kinds of Trust', p. 35. See also Pamela S. Karlan, 'Foreword: Democracy and Disdain' (2011) 126 *Harvard Law Review* 1.

147 Warren, 'Trust and Democracy', p. 81.

148 In this regard, the trust-based framework responds to a call that Warren has made that '[i]nstitutions that make warrants available for good trust decisions should be a key consideration in the design and reform of democratic institutions': Warren, 'What Kinds of Trust', p. 36.

149 Warren, 'Trust and Democracy', p. 82; Warren, 'What Kinds of Trust', p. 35. That said, particularised trust can, in some very limited cases, be democracy-supporting.

corrupt relationships, crime organisations, and ethnic and religious factions that are bad for democracy. In contrast to these, the trust-based framework promotes trust in the citizen–government relationship of a more general nature. To be fair, some citizens will likely be negatively impacted by a trusting citizen–government relationship, seeing as not all citizens will be satisfied with the outcome of governmental decision-making. However, because the trust-based framework is rooted in criteria that are aimed at promoting a general form of citizens' trust in the elected branches with respect to social rights – that is, goodwill, competence and the fulfilment of fiduciary responsibility – rather than that of a more particular nature, the resulting trusting relationship cannot be considered unacceptable. We can publicly justify the trusting relationship to those citizens who are negatively affected by it. For these reasons, I submit that the trust-based framework promotes the kind of trust that is good for democracy, or is 'democracy-supporting', and following on from this, the framework itself can be said to support democracy.

Furthermore, there is another reason, I contend, why the trust-based framework supports democracy. It relates to a more specific defence for constitutional review. It has been argued by scholars that one of the ways in which constitutional review supports or enhances democracy is by protecting the rights of minorities from the so-called 'tyranny of the majority'. The courts, given their isolation from the electoral process and their independence from government interference, are said to be in a better position to protect minority groups. Constitutional review is therefore 'justified as a counter-weight to potentially myopic, prejudiced, careless and occasionally tyrannous majorities and the democratically elected politicians who feel obliged to respond to their demands'.[150] The trust-based framework, I submit, is compatible with this more specific defence – that is, the courts, by applying the trust-based framework in their enforcement of social rights, would be expected to protect the rights of minorities. This conclusion follows on from the expectations by which I have conceptualised trust in the citizen–government relationship, and which the courts would accordingly enforce in applying the trust-based framework in social rights cases. I elaborate on this protection of minority rights in the next three chapters of the book.

150 Bellamy, 'The Democratic Qualities', 334. See also Ely, *Democracy and Distrust*; Feldman, 'Democracy, the Rule of Law'.

4.4 A Point of Clarification: The Relevance of Constitutional Text

The argument that I make in this chapter – and indeed, this book – is based on an assumption about social rights, specifically about the form that constitutional social rights provisions take. I assume that these provisions are formulated with vague language that qualifies the right and in turn affords the elected branches significant discretion. Such vague language includes, as I have identified earlier, the use of terms like 'reasonable' or 'fair' to describe the state's obligation to citizens, the limitation of that obligation to that which is within the state's 'available resources' and the adoption of the 'progressive realisation' idea to defer the right's full realisation into the future.

I make this assumption because it is what we characteristically see in constitutions globally.[151] That said, constitutional social rights provisions are sometimes formulated in more definite terms that afford the elected branches less discretion. Section 29(1)(a) of the South African Constitution offers an example. It provides that '[e]veryone has the right . . . to a basic education, including adult basic education'; but unlike the other social rights provisions in the Constitution, including section 26 (the right to housing), section 27 (the rights to health, food, water and social security) and section 29(1)(b) (the right to further education), section 29(1)(a) does not include qualifying language. For instance, section 29(1)(b), in guaranteeing everyone 'the right . . . to further education', qualifies the right, indicating that 'the state, through reasonable measures, must make [the right] progressively available and accessible'. Given this difference in constitutional text, South African courts have adopted a different approach for enforcing section 29(1)(a) than they have for the Constitution's other social rights provisions.[152] They have identified that in section 29(1)(a) '[t]here is no internal limitation requiring that the right be "progressively realised" within "available resources" subject to "reasonable legislative measures"'; and thus, the courts have said, the right to basic education is 'immediately realisable'.[153] It may

[151] For support of this assumption, see King, *Judging Social Rights*, pp. 100–106; Anders Molander, *Discretion in the Welfare State: Social Rights and Professional Judgment* (Abingdon: Routledge, 2016), p. 49.

[152] See *Governing Body of the Juma Musjid Primary School and Others v. Essay N.O. and Others* [2011] ZACC 13 ('*Juma Musjid*'); *Minister of Basic Education and Others v. Basic Education for All and Others* [2015] ZASCA 198 ('*BEFA*'). For a summary, see Faranaaz Veriava, 'The Limpopo Textbook Litigation: A Case Study into the Possibilities of a Transformative Constitution' (2016) 32 *South African Journal on Human Rights* 321.

[153] See *Juma Musjid*, para. 37; *BEFA*, para. 36.

only be limited under the Constitution's general limitations provision 'in terms of a law of general application that is "reasonable and justifiable in an open and democratic society based on human dignity, equality and freedom"'.[154]

In circumstances where a social right is expressed in such definite terms, thereby affording the elected branches much less discretion in their exercise of control over social goods and services, the trust-based framework that I propose must be adapted. In particular, the courts must, in their enforcement of the social right, respect the express terms of the constitution which may necessitate a more substantive approach from them. This is what the South African courts have done with section 29(1)(a). Departing from the 'reasonableness review' standard that they have adopted for other social rights provisions, they have recognised that the right to basic education, given the earlier interpretation, includes proper buildings, textbooks, desks, chairs and teachers, and have ordered the government to provide these items to students.[155] Therefore, the trust-based framework proposed in this book is intended for those characteristic circumstances where the elected branches are afforded significant discretion – either because the constitutional text is vague, or because the relevant social right is not expressly guaranteed in the constitution, instead being read in by the court. Outside these circumstances, while I maintain that trust should nevertheless be an objective for social rights enforcement, the courts must adopt a slightly different approach.

[154] *Juma Musjid*, para. 37; *BEFA*, para. 36.

[155] See Sandra Fredman, *Comparative Human Rights* (Oxford: Oxford University Press, 2018), pp. 393–395, citing *BEFA* and *Madzozo and Others v. Minister of Basic Education and Others* [2014] ZAECMHC 5. For more on the 'reasonableness review' standard, see Chapters 5–7.

5

The Expectation of Goodwill

In this chapter, I address the first constituent expectation of trust in the citizen–government relationship: goodwill. For citizens to trust their elected branches with respect to social rights means, put simply, that they expect the elected branches to show them goodwill in their exercise of control over social goods and services. But what does this mean in more concrete terms? That is the focus of this chapter. I will first detail what this expectation of goodwill entails from the elected branches in such concrete terms, and then, following on from my discussion in Chapter 4 of judicial enforcement, I will turn to the question of how the courts can enforce the expectation.

5.1 The Expectation of Goodwill: Two Sub-expectations

Based on my reading of the literature on trust, I suggest that applied to the citizen–government relationship, the expectation of goodwill translates into a pair of inter-related sub-expectations from the elected branches: first, an expectation of procedural fairness; and secondly, what I will describe as an 'expectation of good intentions'. I will consider each sub-expectation in turn.

5.1.1 Sub-expectation 1: An Expectation of Procedural Fairness

The first sub-expectation of goodwill in the citizen–government relationship is an expectation that in exercising their control over social goods and services, the elected branches will adopt fair procedures. It is a cornerstone of democratic theory that 'procedural propriety builds confidence in authorities and institutions'.[1] Empirical research has also consistently demonstrated a link between citizens' perceptions of

[1] Marcia Grimes, 'Procedural Fairness and Political Trust' in Sonja Zmerli and Tom van der Meer (eds.), *Handbook on Political Trust* (Cheltenham: Edward Elgar, 2017), p. 256.

procedural fairness and their trust in government actors across a range of settings and types of issues.[2] Accordingly, it makes sense to include procedural fairness in our overall definition of trust. More specifically tied to goodwill, however, Joel Brockner and Phyllis Siegel have explained that '[t]he fairness of procedures says a lot about whether the [trusted] party's "heart is in the right place." Fair procedures signify that a trusted party [like the elected branches] "means well," that is, the party appears to want to live up to its commitments'.[3] Thus, the adoption of fair procedures by the elected branches in their exercise of control over social goods and services, manifests, I submit, their goodwill towards citizens. And it follows, based on my discussion in Chapter 4, that for the elected branches to be trustworthy means that they 'have procedures for making and implementing policy that meet prevailing standards of fairness'.[4]

It is not possible in this relatively brief chapter to offer an exhaustive definition of 'fair procedures' – either generally or in the specific context of social rights. Scholars across various disciplines have long debated the parameters of procedural fairness. What I will do instead is provide some elaboration of the notion for the specific purpose of explaining my proposed trust-based framework for social rights enforcement. To start off, it should be noted that because I have defined trust in the citizen–government relationship as a set of expectations that are held by citizens, and the expectation of goodwill is an expectation held by citizens, the 'fairness' of the relevant procedures should be judged from the perspective of citizens. In other words, fairness is defined by what citizens would reasonably be expected to consider fair vis-à-vis the elected branches and social goods and services. Next, in debating the parameters of procedural fairness, scholars have identified a lengthy list of elements which they say, supported by empirical studies, contribute to people's assessments of procedural fairness.[5] Unable to consider all such elements, I will focus

[2] Marcia Grimes, 'Organizing Consent: The Role of Procedural Fairness in Political Trust and Compliance' (2006) 45 *European Journal of Political Research* 285; Tom R. Tyler, *Why People Obey the Law* (Princeton, NJ: Princeton University Press, 1990).

[3] Joel Brockner and Phyllis Siegel, 'Understanding the Interaction between Procedural and Distributive Justice: The Role of Trust' in Roderick M. Kramer and Tom R. Tyler (eds.), *Trust in Organizations: Frontiers of Theory and Research* (Thousand Oaks, CA: Sage Publications, 1996), p. 407.

[4] Margaret Levi, 'A State of Trust' in Valerie Braithwaite and Margaret Levi (eds.), *Trust and Governance* (New York: Russell Sage Foundation, 1998), p. 88.

[5] Tom R. Tyler, 'Social Justice: Outcome and Procedure' (2000) 35 *International Journal of Psychology* 117, 121.

on three in particular. I do so for two reasons. First, procedural fairness elements carry different weight depending on context.[6] While I cannot, in this chapter, exhaustively define fair procedures in the social rights context (and so, consider every element of procedural fairness in it), the three elements that I describe carry, in my view (and the social rights literature supports this), particular weight in the social rights context. Secondly, there appears to be a consensus in the literature on trust that at a minimum, procedural fairness includes the three elements that follow. Accordingly, on any account of trust, these three elements would, I propose, be included.

The first of these elements is transparency: for citizens to perceive the process by which the elected branches exercise their control over social goods and services as fair, it must be transparent.[7] A transparent process enables citizens to see how the elected branches are exercising their control over social goods and services and to know whether, in that process, the actors who staff those branches are indeed exercising goodwill (not to mention acting in accordance with the other two constituent expectations of trust). Linking transparency directly to citizen trust, Karen Cook, Russell Hardin and Margaret Levi have noted that because '[p]ower is often correlated with lack of transparency and secrecy', 'opening up the decisionmaking processes of powerful actors to public scrutiny . . . may increase the extent to which those in power are viewed as reliable'.[8] In the social rights context, such transparency is especially important because the 'welfare state presents itself to the public as an extraordinar[ily] complex, diversified and unintelligible institutional arrangement'.[9] A transparent process signals to citizens that the elected

6 Gerald S. Leventhal, 'What Should Be Done with Equity Theory? New Approaches to the Study of Fairness in Social Relationships' in Kenneth J. Gergen, Martin S. Greenberg and Richard H. Willis (eds.), *Social Exchange: Advances in Theory and Research* (St. Louis, MO: Plenus Press, 1980), p. 39.

7 Grimes, 'Procedural Fairness'; Margaret Levi, Audrey Sacks and Tom Tyler, 'Conceptualizing Legitimacy, Measuring Legitimating Beliefs' (2009) 53 *American Behavioral Scientist* 354, 360; Tom R. Tyler, 'Procedural Justice and the Rule of Law: Fostering Legitimacy in Alternative Dispute Resolution' (2011) *Journal of Dispute Resolution* 1, 5 (Tyler includes transparency under the overarching procedural fairness element of 'neutrality').

8 Karen S. Cook, Russell Hardin and Margaret Levi, *Cooperation without Trust?* (New York: Russell Sage Foundation, 2005), pp. 56–57.

9 Karl Hinrichs, 'Social Insurances and the Culture of Solidarity: The Moral Infrastructure of Interpersonal Redistributions – with Special Reference to the German Health Care System' (Centre for Social Policy Research, University of Bremen, 1997), cited in Eva-Maria Trüdinger and Uwe Bollow, 'Evaluations of Welfare State Reforms in Germany:

branches have nothing to hide in this complex arrangement. Transparency thus gives citizens good reason to expect goodwill to be exercised by the elected branches (as well as again, the other two expectations of trust). This is because if the elected branches fail to meet citizens' expectations in this regard, their failure will be on display for all to see.[10] And relatedly, if a citizen wants to challenge a governmental decision in this area, a transparent process equips the citizen with the information that they need to do so, holding the elected branches accountable. As Mark Warren has said, 'trust thrives when institutions are structured so as to respond to communication', granting access to information and providing the relevant 'institutional means for challenging authorities, institutions, and trusted individuals'.[11]

That said, the relationship between transparency and trust is a complex one. As some have cautioned, in certain circumstances, transparency can be bad for trust.[12] Transparency 'brings to light the shortcomings of the political system',[13] exposing 'aspects of political institutions and the policy process of which citizens disapprove.'[14] Additionally, in our 'increasingly complex information-based society, the provision of more information and increased transparency may even obscure public

Political Trust Makes a (Big) Difference' in Sonja Zmerli and Marc Hooghe (eds.), *Political Trust: Why Context Matters* (Colchester: ECPR Press, 2011), p. 191. See also Colm O'Cinneide, 'Legal Accountability and Social Justice' in Nicholas Bamforth and Peter Leyland (eds.), *Accountability in the Contemporary Constitution* (Oxford: Oxford University Press, 2013), pp. 404–405.

10 In fact, Pierre Rosanvallon has suggested that transparency has 'replace[d] the exercise of responsibility as the end of politics. Instead of seeking to achieve political *objectives*, people seek certain physical and moral *qualities*. Disillusioned citizens want to eliminate anything that stands in the way of total transparency': Pierre Rosanvallon, *Counter-Democracy: Politics in an Age of Distrust* (Cambridge: Cambridge University Press, 2008), pp. 258–259.

11 Mark E. Warren, 'Democratic Theory and Trust' in Mark E. Warren (ed.), *Democracy and Trust* (Cambridge: Cambridge University Press, 1999), p. 338.

12 See Jenny de Fine Licht, 'The Janus Face of Transparency: Balancing Openness and Secrecy in Democratic Decision-Making' in Dorota Mokrosinska (ed.), *Transparency and Secrecy in European Democracies: Contested Trade-Offs* (Abingdon: Routledge, 2020), pp. 17–35; Stephan Grimmelikhuijsen, 'Linking Transparency, Knowledge and Citizen Trust in Government: An Experiment' (2012) 78 *International Review of Administrative Sciences* 50.

13 Tom W.G. van der Meer, 'Political Trust and the "Crisis of Democracy"' in *Oxford Research Encyclopedia of Politics* (Oxford: Oxford University Press, 2017), p. 14. See also Onora O'Neill, *A Question of Trust* (Cambridge: Cambridge University Press, 2002), p. 68.

14 Grimes, 'Procedural Fairness', p. 265.

understanding and undermine trust through information overload'.[15] For these reasons, if one of our aims in adopting a trust-based framework for social rights enforcement is to foster citizens' trust in the elected branches with respect to social rights (as I argued in Chapter 4), we must recognise the complexity of the relationship between trust and transparency, and be alert to the types of transparency that are likely to foster such trust – as well as those that are not. For example, based on the literature on trust and transparency, complete openness to the point of information overload will not foster citizens' trust in the elected branches. In fact, empirical work has shown that contrary to what we may expect, providing more information to people tends to lead to lower trust.[16] It is therefore not about providing as much information as possible to citizens. Rather, it is about providing sufficient information to citizens so that they can assess whether the elected branches are exercising goodwill (and acting in accordance with the other two expectations of trust) when exercising their control over social goods and services. As Cook, Hardin and Levi have explained the point, those in power can increase the probability of them being seen as trustworthy if they adopt 'a decisionmaking process that is transparent enough to those dependent on them to reveal that their actions are in the best interest of those over whom they have power'.[17]

The second element of procedural fairness which is of considerable importance in the social rights context is participation: for citizens to judge the elected branches' process for exercising their control over social goods and services as fair, it must be participatory.[18] To use the fitting words of Margaret Levi: 'If a group perceives that its voice is

[15] Cook et al., *Cooperation without Trust*, pp. 56–57. See also Haridimos Tsoukas, 'The Tyranny of Light: The Temptations and the Paradoxes of the Information Society' (1997) 29 *Futures* 827.

[16] Jenny de Fine Licht, 'Do We Really Want to Know? The Potentially Negative Effect of Transparency in Decision Making on Perceived Legitimacy' (2011) 34 *Scandinavian Political Studies* 183; Jenny de Fine Licht, 'Transparency Actually: How Transparency Affects Public Perceptions of Political Decision-Making' (2014) 6 *European Political Science Review* 309.

[17] Cook et al., *Cooperation without Trust*, pp. 56–57. See also Claus Offe, 'How Can We Trust Our Fellow Citizens?' in Warren, *Democracy and Trust*, p. 54.

[18] Participation's significance to perceptions of fairness and, in turn, to trust is well-established in the procedural fairness literature: Leventhal, 'What Should Be Done'; Margaret Levi, *Consent, Dissent and Patriotism* (Cambridge: Cambridge University Press, 1997).

systematically ignored, it will not accept the policy-making process as fair'.[19] The relevance of participation to procedural fairness is owed, in large part, to the fact that participation renders the process more representative. Gerald Leventhal, in his influential work on procedural fairness in allocative procedures, has identified 'representativeness' as a key criterion which such procedures must satisfy to be perceived as fair.[20] As Leventhal has explained, for a perceiver to judge an allocative process as fair, 'all phases of the allocative process must reflect the basic concerns, values, and outlooks of important subgroups in the population of individuals affected by the allocative process'.[21] This criterion of representativeness intertwines with the element of participation where the perceiver (the person determining the fairness of the procedure) is one of the individuals affected by the allocative process: in Leventhal's words, his participation in the process makes it 'fairer because it gives greater representation to a very important individual, namely, himself'.[22] In the social rights context, participation is especially important because, for the reasons I outlined in earlier chapters, it is questionable whether low-income citizens and their interests are truly represented via the political and democratic processes. Their participation thus makes such representation more likely.

The significance of participation to perceptions of procedural fairness is supported by empirical studies. For example, based on an extensive body of studies conducted by him as well as others, Tom Tyler has concluded that people feel more fairly treated if they are given opportunities 'to participate in the resolution of their problems or conflicts by presenting their suggestions about what should be done'.[23] He has referred to such opportunities for participation as 'process control or voice'. That said, and of particular note, Tyler has found in his work that participation in the process does not need to amount to control over the outcome of the process. People value the simple opportunity to share their views with decision-makers even if those views have little to no influence on the ultimate decisions that are being made.[24] In fact, when it comes to political disputes, Tyler has found that not only do people not

[19] Levi, *Consent, Dissent and Patriotism*, pp. 23–24.
[20] Leventhal, 'What Should Be Done'.
[21] Ibid, pp. 43–44.
[22] Ibid, p. 44.
[23] Tyler, 'Social Justice', 121.
[24] Ibid, 121–122.

need control over outcomes, but they also do not want it: people expect political authorities to make those decisions for them.[25]

As with transparency, however, it has been argued and empirically demonstrated that voice alone is insufficient for a decision-making process to be perceived as fair.[26] In addition to having a voice, people also need to feel that their views were sincerely considered by the decision-makers in making their decisions – that is, that their voice was indeed heard by the relevant decision-makers.[27] To quote Tyler, for participation to lead to 'the evaluation of procedures as fairer', people 'must trust that the authority sincerely considered their argument, even if they were then rejected'.[28]

Accordingly, based on this theoretical and empirical research, I suggest that for citizens to perceive the process by which the elected branches exercise their control over social goods and services as fair, citizens must be able to participate in that process. If a governmental decision has particular impact on a specific group of citizens, procedural fairness requires that the group be able to express its views to the relevant government actor and that the latter, in turn, sincerely consider those views in the process of making its decision. The relevant government actor does not need to allow those views to dictate its ultimate decision; but it must sincerely consider them.

The final element of procedural fairness that I will note here is respect for citizens' rights: for citizens to perceive the process by which the elected branches exercise their control over social goods and services as fair, their rights must be respected in that process.[29] For Tyler, this element falls under a larger fairness element that he has called 'treatment with dignity and respect'.[30] Tyler has found that people judge a procedure as fairer when they are treated with dignity and respect in that procedure – and such treatment includes both 'common respect and

25 Ibid.

26 See John R. Hibbing and Elizabeth Theiss-Morse, 'The Means Is the End' in John R. Hibbing and Elizabeth Theiss-Morse (eds.), *What Is It about Government that Americans Dislike?* (Cambridge: Cambridge University Press, 2001), pp. 246–247; Stacy Ulbig, 'Voice Is Not Enough: The Importance of Influence in Political Trust and Policy Assessments' (2008) *The Public Opinion Quarterly* 523.

27 Tyler, 'Social Justice', 122. See also Ulbig, 'Voice Is Not Enough'.

28 Tyler, 'Social Justice', 122.

29 Levi et al., 'Conceptualizing Legitimacy', 460; Tyler, 'Social Justice', 122.

30 Tyler, 'Social Justice', 122.

courtesy' and 'respect for peoples' rights'.[31] In Tyler's words, '[p]eople value having respect shown for their rights and for their status within society. They are very concerned that, in the process of dealing with authorities, their dignity as people and as members of society is recognized and acknowledged'.[32]

Respect for citizens' rights, as Tyler has identified, encompasses both human rights and legal process rights (e.g., standing to bring a legal case).[33] Therefore, procedural fairness requires that the elected branches respect all these rights when exercising their control over social goods and services. I would like to emphasise, however, one human right of critical importance here: the right to equality. I single out this right for a few reasons. First, most constitutions globally, and the vast majority of those adopted since 2010, explicitly protect the right to equality.[34] Hence, in most constitutions that protect social rights, those rights will arise alongside the right to equality; and the courts will often be asked to enforce both simultaneously. Secondly, as many scholars have noted, the right to equality is closely connected with social rights.[35] The relationship between social rights and equality is a complex one that is not within this

31 Tyler, 'Procedural Justice', 6.

32 Tyler, 'Social Justice', 122.

33 Tyler, 'Procedural Justice', 6.

34 Jody Heymann, Aleta Sprague and Amy Raub, *Advancing Equality: How Constitutional Rights Can Make a Difference Worldwide* (Oakland: University of California Press, 2020), p. 251. See also Kate O'Regan and Nick Friedman, 'Equality' in Tom Ginsburg and Rosalind Dixon (eds.), *Comparative Constitutional Law* (Cheltenham: Edward Elgar, 2011), p. 473, who note that the 'right to equality is found in nearly all modern democratic constitutions'.

35 See Gwen Brodsky and Shelagh Day, 'Beyond the Social and Economic Rights Debate: Substantive Equality Speaks to Poverty' (2002) 14 *Canadian Journal of Women and the Law* 184; Sandra Fredman, 'Redistribution and Recognition: Reconciling Inequalities' (2007) 23 *South African Journal on Human Rights* 214; Sandra Fredman, *Human Rights Transformed: Positive Rights and Positive Duties* (Oxford: Oxford University Press, 2008); Sarah Ganty, 'Poverty as Misrecognition: What Role for Antidiscrimination Law in Europe?' (2021) 21 *Human Rights Law Review* 962; Sandra Liebenberg, 'The Value of Human Dignity in Interpreting Socio-economic Rights' (2005) 21 *South African Journal on Human Rights* 1; Sandra Liebenberg, *Socio-economic Rights: Adjudication under a Transformative Constitution* (Cape Town: Juta Law, 2010); Sandra Liebenberg and Beth Goldblatt, 'The Interrelationship between Equality and Socio-economic Rights under South Africa's Transformative Constitution' (2007) 23 *South African Journal on Human Rights* 335; Murray Wesson, 'Equality and Social Rights: An Exploration in Light of the South African Constitution' (2007) *Public Law* 748; Murray Wesson, 'Discrimination Law and Social Rights: InterSections and Possibilities' (2007) 13 *Juridica International* 74; David Wiseman, 'The Past and Future of Constitutional Law and Social Justice: Majestic or Substantive Equality?' (2015) 71 *The Supreme Court Law*

book's scope. That said, we should recognise that poverty intersects with various recognised grounds of discrimination in constitutional and human rights law, including race and sex.[36] Poverty 'is socially and legislatively created': therefore, for the groups that are predominantly affected by poverty (e.g., women, people of colour, people with disabilities, the young and the old), 'it is a result of discrimination'.[37] At the same time, 'poverty intensifies the effects of sexist, racist, and other discriminatory social practices.'[38] Consequently, as Colm O'Cinneide has identified, 'inadequate protection for social rights or cuts to existing levels of protection may overlap with other forms of discriminatory or exclusionary treatment in a way that imposes particular disadvantages on specific groups.'[39] And while this book cannot fully examine this intersectionality, in recognition of poverty's intersection with other grounds of discrimination, including race and sex, I think that it is imperative that we include in our analysis of the elected branches' respect for citizens' rights, and more broadly our consideration of the judicial enforcement of social rights, the right to equality.

What does it mean for the elected branches to respect citizens' right to equality? This is undoubtedly a complex question. Under a formal approach to equality, it means that the elected branches will, in exercising their control over social goods and services, treat all citizens alike. However, the equality literature makes clear that the formal approach suffers from several problems, including its failure to address deeply entrenched patterns of social disadvantage and its perverse capability of disallowing governmental measures aimed at promoting equality.[40] For this reason, I contend that respect for citizens' right to equality cannot reasonably be interpreted as the protection of formal equality. Rather, in line with the dominant view in the equality literature, and the position

Review 563. These scholars have adopted different perspectives, however, on the precise nature of the relationship between these sets of rights.

36 See Shreya Atrey, 'The Intersectional Case of Poverty in Discrimination Law' (2018) 18 *Human Rights Law Review* 411; Shreya Atrey, *Intersectional Discrimination* (Oxford: Oxford University Press, 2019); Rosalind Dixon and Julie Suk, 'Liberal Constitutionalism and Economic Inequality' (2018) 85 *The University of Chicago Law Review* 369, 381.

37 Brodsky and Day, 'Beyond the Social and Economic', 187.

38 Ibid, 187.

39 Colm O'Cinneide, 'The Potential and Pitfalls of Intersectionality in the Context of Social Rights Adjudication' in Shreya Atrey and Peter Dunne (eds.), *Intersectionality and Human Rights Law* (Oxford: Hart, 2020), p. 69.

40 Fredman, 'Redistribution and Recognition', 216; Wesson, 'Equality and Social Rights', 751.

adopted by some national courts, I submit that equality denotes substantive equality.[41] Thus, for the elected branches to respect citizens' right to equality in their exercise of control over social goods and services, they must exercise that control in furtherance of substantive equality.

Unlike formal equality (which focuses on, and seeks to eliminate, differential treatment in law), substantive equality focuses on 'patterns of group-based disadvantage' that give rise to structural inequality.[42] It recognises that 'equality cannot be achieved by adopting a merely negative or "hands-off" approach', accepting the need for positive governmental measures which address that group's disadvantaged position.[43] Substantive equality 'transcends formal equality at the point where it demands differential legal treatment in order to ameliorate and overcome inequalities'.[44]

While there is much agreement in the equality literature in favour of a substantive (rather than formal) approach to equality, there is disagreement as to the overarching objectives of such an approach: that is, commentators agree that equality demands positive governmental measures but disagree over what is to be equalised in introducing such positive measures.[45] Sandra Fredman, in her influential work in the area, has argued that substantive equality 'resists capture by a single principle'.[46] According to her, substantive equality is, rather, a multi-dimensional concept.[47] And drawing on the strengths of various principles in the substantive equality discourse, Fredman has identified four objectives for the concept: (i) to promote respect for the equal dignity and worth of all (including to redress stigma, stereotyping, humiliation and violence); (ii)

[41] As examples of cases supporting a substantive equality approach, see *R v. Kapp* [2008] 2 SCR 483 (Canada); *National Coalition for Gay and Lesbian Equality and Another v. Minister of Justice and Others* [1998] ZACC 15 (South Africa).

[42] Liebenberg and Goldblatt, 'The Interrelationship Between', 342–343.

[43] Brodsky and Day, 'Beyond the Social and Economic', 206; Wiseman, 'The Past and Future', 564.

[44] Wiseman, 'The Past and Future', 564.

[45] See Catherine Albertyn, Sandra Fredman and Judy Fudge, 'Introduction: Substantive Equality, Social Rights and Women: A Comparative Perspective' (2007) 23 *South African Journal on Human Rights* 209, 209. Two of the best-known objectives in this regard are equality of opportunity and equality of results: see Sandra Fredman, 'Providing Equality: Substantive Equality and the Positive Duty to Provide' (2005) 21 *South African Journal on Human Rights* 163, 167.

[46] Sandra Fredman, 'Substantive Equality Revisited' (2016) 14 *International Journal of Constitutional Law* 712, 713.

[47] Fredman, 'Redistribution and Recognition', 225–227. See also Fredman, *Human Rights Transformed*, p. 179.

to accommodate, affirm and celebrate identity within a community; (iii) to break the cycle of disadvantage that is associated with out-group membership; and (iv) to facilitate full participation in society. For Fredman, these objectives – or dimensions – interact and have synergies with one another; and we therefore can, and should, consider how the dimensions might be used to buttress one another.

I agree with Fredman's conceptualisation. It recognises the complexity of inequality, locating the right to equality, as she has noted, in its 'social context, responsive to those who are disadvantaged, demeaned, excluded, or ignored'.[48] So, adopting Fredman's multi-dimensional conceptualisation for the purpose of conceptualising trust in the citizen–government relationship, I contend that for the elected branches to exercise their control over social goods and services in furtherance of substantive equality, they must strive to implement measures that achieve the four objectives outlined by Fredman.[49] And given the procedural fairness requirement that citizens' rights (including the right to equality) be respected, such striving is required for the process by which the elected branches exercise their control over the goods and services to be judged as fair.

To be clear, my choice to adopt a substantive conception of equality presents a complication for the trust-based framework that I propose. It complicates, in particular, the argument that I advanced in Chapter 4 that given the framework's focus on the procedure by which the elected branches make their decisions (as opposed to outcome), it strikes a good middle ground between the two wrongs of judicial usurpation and judicial abdication. Given my choice here, the framework is not fully procedural. A substantive conception of equality necessarily involves a consideration of outcome. It is for this reason that I said in Chapter 4 that under a trust-based framework, the courts *principally* review the procedure by which the elected branches exercise their control over social goods and services. I used 'principally' to recognise the substantive conception of equality encompassed by the framework. That said, a distinction can – and, I think, should – be drawn between, on the one hand, what equality signifies within the right and, on the other, how the

[48] Fredman, 'Substantive Equality Revisited', 713.

[49] I say 'strive' because, as Sandra Liebenberg and Beth Goldblatt have recognised, substantive equality 'contains a forward looking vision of a society where people are provided with the resources and the opportunities to develop, participate and flourish as human beings': Liebenberg and Goldblatt, 'The Interrelationship Between', 342–343.

courts should enforce the right.[50] As Fredman has noted, human rights have roles and functions beyond the courts.[51] I submit that the courts can, in enforcing the right to equality, further substantive equality while not usurping the elected branches' policy-making role; and thereby they can still strike a good middle ground between the two wrongs of enforcement. I will explain this point in greater detail later when I address the expectation's enforcement by the courts.

5.1.2 *Sub-expectation 2: An Expectation of Good Intentions*

This brings me to the second sub-expectation. I submit that in the citizen–government relationship, the expectation of goodwill encompasses, in addition to an expectation of procedural fairness, what I will call an 'expectation of good intentions'. As John Dunn has said, in the political context, trust must include an 'expectation of benign intentions' from government actors.[52] Applied to the citizen–government relationship, trust thus includes an expectation of good intentions from those who staff the elected branches in exercising their control over social goods and services.

The expectation of good intentions is not an expectation that those who staff the elected branches *have* good intentions towards citizens. It is, rather, an expectation that they will *manifest* good intentions towards citizens, acting in a way that would be expected of government actors who have such intentions towards citizens. Accordingly, in including an expectation of good intentions in the broader expectation of goodwill, I am not adopting a motivation-based account of trust. Under a motivation-based account, trust includes an expectation that

[50] Fredman, *Human Rights Transformed*, p. 182; Matthias Klatt, 'Positive Rights: Who Decides? Judicial Review in Balance' (2015) 13 *International Journal of Constitutional Law* 354, 356.

[51] Such roles and functions include 'an expressive and educational role, signalling the values a society stands for, regardless of the method for their enforcement' as well as a 'proactive function, guiding political and executive decision-making so that legislation, policy, and administration are formulated to meet human rights demands': Fredman, *Human Rights Transformed*, pp. 32–33.

[52] John Dunn, 'Trust and Political Agency' in Diego Gambetta (ed.), *Trust: Making and Breaking Cooperative Relations* (Oxford: Basil Blackwell, 1988), pp. 74, 89–90. Some scholars have also spoken of the 'motives' of political actors: Tom R. Tyler, 'Trust and Law Abidingness: A Proactive Model of Social Regulation' (2001) 81 *Boston University Law Review* 361.

the trustee has good motivations for behaving the way they do towards the truster.[53] Such accounts, however, are problematic for a few reasons. First, because they necessitate that the trustee has specific motivations towards the truster, they limit trust to, or at least make it difficult to extend trust beyond, personal relationships. As a result, they leave little room for trust to arise in a relatively impersonal relationship like the citizen–government relationship. Secondly, motivation-based accounts reject, or call into question, the possibility of impersonal or secondary trust as a form of trust. If trust requires the trustee to have good motivations for acting the way they do, can trust be the result of external constraints that have been imposed on the trustee (as impersonal or secondary trust suggests)? It does not appear so. These accounts of trust therefore undermine the arguments of writers like Pettit and Shapiro that we can foster trust through the imposition of constraints – which, it will be recalled, is pivotal to the trust-based framework that I propose.

To explain what the expectation of good intentions means more concretely, I will draw on the well-known typology of reasons outlined by Kent Roach and Geoff Budlender as to why governments fail to comply with constitutional standards vis-à-vis social rights matters.[54] Roach and Budlender (relying on a typology that was originally developed by Chris Hansen in another context) have set out three such reasons: inattentiveness, incompetence and intransigence on the part of government. Inattentiveness refers to those circumstances in which government actors make unintentional oversights, or, as is more common, they fail to appreciate the nature of their constitutional obligations to citizens.[55] Incompetence captures those cases of government non-compliance that are due to incapacity or, as Roach and Budlender state, the product of 'decades of neglect, inadequate budgets and inadequate

[53] See Annette Baier, 'Trust and Antitrust' (1985) 96, *Ethics* 231, 234–235; Annette Baier, 'What Is Trust?' in David Archard et al. (eds.), *Reading Onora O'Neill* (Abingdon: Routledge, 2013), p. 175; Daniel Weinstock, 'Building Trust in Divided Societies' (1999) 7 *The Journal of Political Philosophy* 287, 293; Daniel Weinstock, 'Trust in Institutions' in Archard et al., *Reading Onora O'Neill*, pp. 201–202.

[54] Kent Roach and Geoff Budlender, 'Mandatory Relief and Supervisory Jurisdiction: When Is It Appropriate, Just and Equitable?' (2005) 5 *South African Law Journal* 325. Roach and Budlender's typology was adapted from a typology set out in the following work: Chris Hansen, 'Inattentive, Intransigent and Incompetent' in Randall S. Humm et al. (eds.), *Child, Parent and State* (Philadelphia, PA: Temple University Press, 1994), pp. 224, 232.

[55] Roach and Budlender, 'Mandatory Relief and Supervisory Jurisdiction', 346.

training of public officials'.[56] I will address incompetence in Chapter 6. Lastly, intransigence covers those situations in which government actors understand their constitutional obligations to citizens and have the capacity to meet them, yet they refuse to do so.[57] The expectation of good intentions, I submit, is an expectation that those who staff the elected branches will not act – to use this terminology – 'intransigently' in exercising their control over social goods and services. So, where the relevant staff understand their constitutional obligations to citizens vis-à-vis social rights and can meet those obligations – yet choose not to, as intransigence denotes – they fail to manifest good intentions towards citizens.

In referring to intransigence, to be consistent with the rest of the trust-based framework, I mean specifically the elected branches' intransigence vis-à-vis the constituent expectations of trust. Intransigence thus refers to the elected branches' refusal to fulfil either the expectation of goodwill (i.e., by refusing to satisfy the elements of transparency, participation and equality) or the other two expectations of trust: competence and fiduciary responsibility (which I detail in Chapters 6 and 7). Therefore, where those who staff the elected branches are aware of their obligations to fulfil the above expectations (with the courts, under the trust-based framework, expressly defining these obligations in their social rights judgments) and are in a position to do so, yet refuse to fulfil them, they behave intransigently and in turn fail to fulfil this expectation of good intentions.

5.2 Enforcing the Expectation of Goodwill

Having detailed the expectation of goodwill's two sub-expectations in the previous part, I will now turn to the question of how the courts in social rights cases can enforce this expectation.

5.2.1 Requiring a Fair Decision-Making Procedure

Given that the first sub-expectation of goodwill is that the elected branches exercise a fair procedure when exercising their control over social goods and services, to enforce this expectation, the courts must

[56] Ibid, 349.

[57] Aoife Nolan, *Children's Socio-economic Rights, Democracy and the Courts* (London: Bloomsbury, 2011), p. 210.

require the elected branches to follow a fair procedure when they exercise their control in this regard. This includes the three elements of procedural fairness from earlier.

5.2.1.1 Transparency

Following on from the procedural fairness element of transparency, to enforce the expectation of goodwill, the courts should require that the elected branches follow a transparent decision-making process when they exercise their control over social goods and services. In this respect, the framework that I propose aligns with what others have advocated regarding transparency's importance as a democratic value and how the courts can enhance it via social rights enforcement.[58] Sandra Liebenberg, for example, justifying a 'transformative approach to the adjudication of socio-economic rights' in South Africa, has noted as one of the benefits of such an approach its potential to enhance 'the transparency and accountability of social policy-making by requiring the State and private actors to justify their decisions in the light of the purposes of socio-economic rights.'[59] Likewise, Martha Jackman, who has advocated the use of section 7 in the Canadian *Charter of Rights and Freedoms* as a mechanism for holding public actors accountable for their health care decisions (especially those that affect access to care), has stressed that courts, in reviewing government action under section 7, can question whether such decision-making is, among other things, transparent.[60]

However, given the social science research from earlier indicating that transparency to the point of information overload is bad for trust, it is not advisable that the courts demand complete openness from the elected branches. Rather, the courts should require the elected branches to provide citizens with sufficient information about their decision-making

[58] See Fredman, *Human Rights Transformed*; Martha Jackman, 'Charter Review as a Health Care Accountability Mechanism in Canada' (2010) 18 *Health Law Journal* 1; Jeff King, *Judging Social Rights* (Cambridge: Cambridge University Press, 2012); Liebenberg, *Socio-economic Rights*; O'Cinneide, 'Legal Accountability and Social Justice'.

[59] Liebenberg, *Socio-economic Rights*, p. 65.

[60] Jackman, 'Charter Review', 21. Section 7 provides: 'Everyone has the right to life, liberty and security of the person and the right not to be deprived thereof except in accordance with the principles of fundamental justice'. As I explain later, Canadian courts have not, to date, recognised positive social rights in their Constitution. And various scholars, including Jackman, have advocated such recognition under section 7 and section 15 (the right to equality).

process for those citizens to both: (i) know whether the elected branches are acting with goodwill (as well as, again, in accordance with the other two expectations of trust); and (ii) be able to challenge that process where the elected branches fail to meet the expectations. In this way, the courts' requirement for government transparency serves as an important precondition to the courts' enforcement of both the other elements of goodwill and the other expectations of trust: by obliging the elected branches to act transparently, the courts equip citizens with the information they need to ensure the elected branches' decision-making processes are participatory and respectful of citizens' right to equality; and also that they are fulfilling citizens' expectations of competence and fiduciary responsibility.

To illustrate what this looks like in practice, I will use examples from social rights cases in various jurisdictions. A good, and well-known, example is the South African Constitutional Court's 'reasonableness review' standard which incorporates a requirement of transparency. Under this standard, first set out in the *Grootboom* decision, the state must 'devise and implement a coherent, co-ordinated programme' in the relevant area of social welfare (in the case of *Grootboom*, public housing) and the court, in enforcing the Constitution's social rights (in *Grootboom*, the right to housing under section 26), subjects the relevant programme to a standard of reasonableness.[61] In first setting out this standard, Yacoob J., writing for the court, outlined a series of relatively vague considerations that, he said, speak to the reasonableness of a programme. He noted that: (i) the programme must be 'comprehensive and coordinated'; (ii) it must be 'balanced and flexible'; (iii) 'appropriate financial and human resources' must be made available for the programme; (iv) it must 'make appropriate provision for . . . short, medium and long term needs'; (v) it must be 'reasonably implemented'; and (vi) it must cater to '[t]hose whose needs are the most urgent'.[62]

[61] *Government of the Republic of South Africa and Others v. Grootboom and Others* [2000] ZACC 19, paras. 95, 41 ('*Grootboom*').

[62] Given the vagueness of these considerations, social rights scholars were, as I noted in Chapter 3, critical of reasonableness review: see David Bilchitz, *Poverty and Fundamental Rights: The Justification and Enforcement of Socio-economic Rights* (Oxford: Oxford University Press, 2007), p. 176; Dennis Davis, 'Adjudicating the Socio-economic Rights in the South African Constitution: Towards "Deference Lite"?' (2006) 22 *South African Journal on Human Rights* 301, 312; William Forbath, 'Cultural Transformation, Deep Institutional Reform, and ESR Practice: South Africa's Treatment Action Campaign' in Lucie E. White and Jeremy Perelman (eds.), *Stones of Hope: How African Activists*

In later decisions, however, the court has taken steps to make reasonableness review slightly more concrete – and this has included a requirement of transparency. In *Treatment Action Campaign* ('*TAC*'), for instance, addressing the right to health in section 27 of the Constitution, the court added that a reasonable social welfare programme must be transparent such that 'its contents must be made known appropriately' to all concerned.[63] It concluded that the public health programme at issue there, which restricted the availability of the antiretroviral drug nevirapine to limited research and training sites in South Africa, was unreasonable, at least in part, because of the government's lack of transparency with respect to it. The court stressed that remedying the 'HIV/AIDS challenge facing the country' required 'proper communication, especially by government'; and in concluding that there had been a violation of the right to health vis-à-vis the government's nevirapine programme, it found no evidence of communication of this standard.[64]

Another example is the German Constitutional Court's recognition and interpretation of the right to a subsistence minimum which, the court has held, requires a transparent legislative decision-making process. Unlike the South African Constitution, the German Basic Law does not expressly protect social rights. In the *Hartz IV* case, however, the court recognised the 'fundamental right to the guarantee of a subsistence minimum'. It derived this right from the declaration of human dignity in Article 1(1) together with the principle of the social welfare state in Article 20(1). The court held that everyone has an enforceable and subjective right (*subjecktives Recht*) to the 'material prerequisites which are indispensable for his or her physical existence and for a minimum of participation in social, cultural and political life'.[65] This, the court concluded, requires the legislature to pass legislation that ensures a subsistence minimum to all individuals.[66]

Reclaim Human Rights to Challenge Global Poverty (Stanford, CA: Stanford University Press, 2010), p. 67.

63 *Minister of Health and Others v. Treatment Action Campaign and Others* [2002] ZACC 15, para. 123 ('*TAC*').

64 Ibid, para. 123.

65 125 BVerfGE 172 (headnote 1) ('*Hartz IV*').

66 See ibid, paras. 136–137. See also Susan Rose-Ackerman, Stefanie Egidy and James Fowkes, *Due Process of Lawmaking: The United States, South Africa, Germany, and the European Union* (Cambridge: Cambridge University Press, 2014), p. 179.

The legislation at issue in the *Hartz IV* case was the 'Hartz IV Act' which determined standard social benefits for adults and children according to a statistical model. While the court held that the legislation was unconstitutional primarily on the basis that the legislature did not undertake a statistical investigation to determine the relevant level of social benefits (a point I will consider in detail when I discuss the expectation of competence in Chapter 6), it did, however, also recognise, as part of the right to a subsistence minimum, an obligation on the legislature to be transparent in its decision-making process (together with an obligation of consistency). In fact, as Susan Rose-Ackerman, Stefanie Egidy and James Fowkes have noted in their research, '[t]-ransparency was a key aspect of *Hartz IV*'.[67] Whereas prior to *Hartz IV* legislative transparency 'was seen as good constitutional practice', the court's decision, they have explained, 'appears to transform this practice into an enforceable constitutional duty'.[68] And though the court afforded the legislature discretion – specifically in choosing which statistical models to use to calculate benefits – it held that the legislature must exercise its discretion transparently (and consistently). It said that 'to facilitate constitutional review' of legislation, 'there is an obligation for the legislature to disclose the methods and calculations used to determine the subsistence minimum in the legislative procedure'.[69] If the legislature 'fails to do so adequately', the court noted, 'the ascertainment of the subsistence minimum is already no longer' compliant with the Basic Law.[70]

One final illustration is the UK Supreme Court's decision in *Nzolameso*, where the court demanded greater transparency from local authorities in their decision-making about temporary accommodation provision to homeless residents.[71] The UK, unlike the other jurisdictions considered in this book, does not have a codified constitution. It therefore does not have constitutional social rights – at least not in the traditional sense.[72] Nonetheless, UK courts have taken steps to

[67] Rose-Ackerman et al., *Due Process of Lawmaking*, p. 183.

[68] Ibid, p. 183.

[69] *Hartz IV*, para. 144.

[70] Ibid, para. 144.

[71] *Nzolameso v. City of Westminster* [2015] UKSC 22 ('*Nzolameso*').

[72] The UK does, however, have a constitution which comprises the common law, parliamentary legislation, the royal prerogative and constitutional conventions. And UK courts have used public law to protect social welfare. See Stefano Civitarese Matteucci and Simon Halliday, 'Social Rights, the Welfare State and European Austerity' in Stefano

protect citizens' social welfare, drawing on their body of public law – steps which, I contend, courts in jurisdictions with constitutional social rights could likewise take, or at least parallel. Hence, despite the UK's unique constitutional arrangement, UK cases, in my view, offer a helpful source to illustrate the workings of a trust-based social rights enforcement framework.

The claimant and her children lived in Westminster in a privately rented house paid for with housing benefits. With the introduction of a benefit cap, however, the house became unaffordable for the claimant, rendering her and her children homeless. Under legislation, local authorities like Westminster have a duty to provide accommodation in their own area (that is, 'in borough') 'so far as reasonably practicable'.[73] Claiming a shortage of accommodation in Westminster, Westminster City Council instead offered the claimant a house 'out of borough' (approximately 1 hour and 15 minutes from Westminster). On an application for judicial review, the Supreme Court held that in doing so, Westminster had acted unlawfully. Of note, Lady Hale, who wrote the court's judgment, issued guidance for local authorities to be applied by them when making temporary accommodation decisions with the aim of making this public decision-making process more transparent. She specifically stated that 'each local authority should have, and keep up to date, a policy for procuring sufficient units of temporary accommodation to meet the anticipated demand during the coming year.[74] That policy, Lady Hale explained, should reflect the local authority's statutory obligations and should be approved by the democratically accountable members of the council. She also noted that 'each local authority should have, and keep up to date, a policy for allocating those units to individual homeless households'.[75] Where the council anticipates a shortfall of 'in borough' units, the policy should explain 'the factors which would be taken into account in offering households those units', 'the factors which would be taken into account in offering units close to home' and where a shortage exists, 'the factors which would make it suitable to accommodate a household further away'.[76] And further promoting transparency in the

Civitarese Matteucci and Simon Halliday (eds.), *Social Rights in Europe in an Age of Austerity* (Abingdon: Routledge, 2017), p. 9.

[73] Housing Act 1996, s. 208(1).

[74] *Nzolameso*, para. 39.

[75] Ibid, para. 39.

[76] Ibid, para. 39.

process, both policies, Lady Hale said in her judgment, 'should be made publicly available'.[77]

5.2.1.2 Participation

Next, following on from the participation element of procedural fairness, the courts, in enforcing the expectation of goodwill, should also require that citizens be included in the elected branches' decision-making vis-à-vis social goods and services. This means, put simply, that the courts should demand that citizens' voice is heard by the elected branches when they exercise their control over social goods and services. And given the link between participation and representativeness, they should be especially attentive to whether, and the extent to which, the elected branches have engaged or discussed the relevant decision with those citizens who are particularly impacted by it.

A good example of such a requirement in practice again comes from South Africa. In developing its reasonableness review standard, the Constitutional Court has incorporated, in addition to transparency, an element of participation. It has done so specifically via the remedy of 'meaningful engagement'. In the *Olivia Road* case, for instance, occupiers of two buildings in the inner city of Johannesburg challenged an order granted by a lower court authorising the City of Johannesburg to evict the occupiers on the basis that those buildings were unsafe and unhealthy.[78] As part of its resolution of the case, the court issued an order 'aimed at ensuring that the City and the occupiers engaged with each other meaningfully on certain issues', including on the issue of how to make 'the buildings as safe and as conducive to health as is reasonably practicable'.[79] The court therefore required that the building's occupiers be given an opportunity to participate in the City's decision-making process around eviction, as well as the safety and health of the buildings.

While meaningful engagement was the remedy ordered by the court (rather than its ultimate holding in the case), it should be noted that the court rooted the requirement to meaningfully engage in the government's overarching obligation to take 'reasonable measures'. Yacoob J., writing for the court, specifically explained that the City's duty to engage was 'squarely grounded in section 26(2) of the Constitution' (which reads

[77] Ibid, para. 39.

[78] *Occupiers of 51 Olivia Road and Others v. City of Johannesburg and Others* [2008] ZACC 1 ('*Olivia Road*').

[79] Ibid, para. 5.

that the 'state must take reasonable legislative and other measures, within its available resources, to achieve the progressive realisation of' the right to housing).[80] The court therefore connected the meaningful engagement remedy to its reasonableness review standard,[81] with the *Olivia Road* judgment's ultimate effect being, as Anashri Pillay has summarised, to include as a 'factor for a court to consider in evaluating the reasonableness of government action' the question of meaningful engagement.[82] In doing so, the court's remedy, in line with what I said in Chapter 4 for a trustworthiness standard, had a prospective effect. Not only did the court hold the City of Johannesburg accountable for its failure to engage with the occupiers in that case, but, in rooting the requirement to engage in the state's obligation to take reasonable measures under section 26, it constrained state actors' discretion with respect to future decisions about social goods and services. Accordingly, it made it more likely that the South African government, in its future interactions with citizens, would engage with them.

It is noteworthy that in enforcing the expectation of goodwill's participation element, the court also enforced its transparency element. Specifically, the court required the government, as part of its obligation to meaningfully engage, to develop and maintain a public record of each engagement, so as to enable courts to later review the engagement process. The court stressed that 'secrecy is counter-productive to the process of engagement' and so, explained that 'the provision of a complete and accurate account of the process of engagement including at least the reasonable efforts of the municipality with that process would ordinarily be essential'.[83] This is noteworthy as it illustrates my earlier point: that a court's enforcement of the transparency element is a precondition to enforcing goodwill's other elements, including participation (not to mention trust's other expectations). The court in *Olivia Road* explicitly recognised this link. As it emphasised, by requiring a transparent engagement process, the courts are empowered to review '[w]hether

80 Ibid, para. 17.

81 Brian Ray, *Engaging with Social Rights: Procedure, Participation, and Democracy in South Africa's Second Wave* (Cambridge: Cambridge University Press, 2016), p. 116.

82 Anashri Pillay, 'Towards Effective Social and Economic Rights Adjudication: The Role of Meaningful Engagement' (2012) 10 *International Journal of Constitutional Law* 732, 745. See also Sandra Liebenberg, 'The Participatory Democratic Turn in South Africa's Social Rights Jurisprudence' in Katherine G. Young (ed.), *The Future of Economic and Social Rights* (Cambridge: Cambridge University Press, 2019), p. 198.

83 *Olivia Road*, para. 21.

there had been meaningful engagement between a city and the resident about to be rendered homeless'.[84]

In its subsequent cases, the South African court has continued to apply this doctrine of meaningful engagement, thereby requiring citizens' participation in the government's decisions vis-à-vis social goods and services (especially housing). In the *Joe Slovo* case, for instance, some 20,000 residents of a settlement near Cape Town known as the Joe Slovo settlement area were evicted as part of a large-scale housing project along the N2 highway.[85] This 'N2 Gateway' project was part of the 'Breaking New Ground' policy, adopted in 2004 as a new framework for housing delivery, partially in response to the court's judgment in *Grootboom*.[86] Because the effect of the evictions was not to render the residents homeless (they were instead relocated to temporary housing relatively far from the city centre), the court was, in this case, 'dealing with challenges to the adequacy, wisdom, and execution of legislative and executive decisions over how best to fulfill the right to housing'.[87] The residents asserted that they had been promised by the state that 70 per cent of the houses built in the settlement would be allocated to them as subsidised low-rental accommodation. These promises, however, it was alleged by the residents, were broken.

In assessing the reasonableness of the state's actions under section 26 of the Constitution, the court again considered whether the state had meaningfully engaged with the residents. In doing so, Sachs J., clarifying the purpose of meaningful engagement, explained that it was inadequate for state officials to simply 'pass on information about decisions already taken'; they were obliged, rather, to 'involve the residents as partners in the process of decision-making itself'.[88] And rooting this requirement in the overarching reasonableness review standard (as in *Olivia Road*), he emphasised that 'meaningful engagement between the authorities and those who may become homeless as a result of government activity, is vital to the reasonableness of the government activity'.[89] Applied to the facts, the court ultimately held that the state in this case had meaningfully engaged with the residents. But to deal with matters going forward, it

[84] Ibid, para. 22. See also Ray, *Engaging with Social Rights*, p. 125.

[85] *Residents of Joe Slovo Community v. Thubelisha Homes and Others* [2009] ZACC 16 ('*Joe Slovo*').

[86] Ray, *Engaging with Social Rights*, p. 119.

[87] Ibid, p. 121.

[88] *Joe Slovo*, para. 378.

[89] Ibid, para. 378.

issued a detailed order and agenda requiring the state to engage further over the timing and details of the evictions process.

The Colombian Constitutional Court's jurisprudence on the right to health has likewise emphasised citizens' participation in governmental decision-making in this area. Like many Latin American countries, the Colombian court has often adopted an individualised model in enforcing its constitution's right to health.[90] It has used, in particular, the 'tutela' – a device entitling a person to bring action before any judge 'for the immediate protection of his fundamental rights when that person fears they may be violated by the action or omission of any public authority'.[91] And claimants have successfully brought forth tutelas in court to demand medical treatments from their government. At the same time, however, and important for present purposes, the court has issued structural remedies that require regulatory authorities to take steps to rectify some of 'the major problems in the system that were driving the individual litigation'.[92] Such structural remedies are relevant here because in line with what I have said about the South African court's use of meaningful engagement, they have prospective effect. They constrain state actors' discretion with respect to future decisions about social goods and services, increasing the likelihood that what is ordered by the court (e.g., engagement) will form part of future citizen–government interactions.

An example is the court's *T-760* judgment. In response to an escalating and unmanageable number of tutelas brought to enforce the right to health, the court collected 22 tutelas to illustrate the systemic problems in Colombia's health care system.[93] In its structural remedy, the court called for a restructuring of the country's benefit plans (the contributory plan called Plan Obligatorio de Salud, or POS; and the subsidised plan called Plan Obligatorio de Salud Subsidiado, or POSS). Increasing the

[90] See David Landau, 'The Reality of Social Rights Enforcement' (2012) 53 *Harvard International Law Journal* 189, 199; David Landau, 'South African Social Rights Jurisprudence and the Global Cannon: A Revisionist View' in Rosalind Dixon and Theunis Roux (eds.), *Constitutional Triumphs, Constitutional Disappointments: A Critical Account of the 1996 South African Constitution's Local and International Influence* (Cambridge: Cambridge University Press, 2018), p. 410.

[91] Constitution of Colombia, cited in Landau, 'The Reality of Social Rights Enforcement', 205 (footnote 67).

[92] David Landau, 'Choosing between Simple and Complex Remedies in Socio-economic Rights Cases' (2019) 69 *University of Toronto Law Journal* 105, 109. See also Kent Roach, 'Dialogic Remedies' (2019) 17 *International Journal of Constitutional Law* 860, 877.

[93] Alicia Ely Yamin and Oscar Parra-Vera, 'How Do Courts Set Health Policy? The Case of the Colombian Constitutional Court' (2009) 6 *PLoS Medicine* 147, 148.

likelihood of citizen participation, it ordered an updating of the benefits to be included in both plans immediately, and on an annual basis after that, via a process that included 'direct and effective participation of the medical community and the users of the health system'.[94] The court thus required the government to engage with those citizens who were most impacted by decisions regarding the relevant health care plans. Furthermore, much like in *Olivia Road*, the court demanded greater transparency from the government in its determinations of benefits, simultaneously enforcing the transparency element of the expectation of goodwill.[95]

In respect of this element of participation, the trust-based framework that I propose aligns, once again, with the work of many scholars who have recognised the value of participation to social rights enforcement and have incorporated it into their proposed frameworks.[96] That said, I want to highlight a few points that clarify my position on participation in such enforcement, considering my discussion of trust in earlier chapters. First, because participation, as an element of procedural fairness, does not require that the views of citizens dictate the ultimate decision made, a choice by the elected branches to not follow citizens' views should not be sufficient for a court to find a violation of a social right. The courts should demand, rather, that the elected branches are sincerely considering citizens' views in their decision-making process, even if they do not ultimately follow those views. This approach aligns with what the South African Constitutional Court has said in its engagement jurisprudence. In *Joe Slovo*, for instance, in finding meaningful engagement had been satisfied, Ngcobo J. stressed that 'the process of engagement does not require the parties to agree on every issue. What is required is good faith and reasonableness on both sides and the willingness to listen and

[94] Corte Constitutional de Colombia (2008) Sala Segunda de Revisión, *T-760*, cited in Yamin and Parra-Vera, 'How Do Courts Set Health Policy?', 148.

[95] Yamin and Parra-Vera, 'How Do Courts Set Health Policy?', 148.

[96] See Natalia Angel-Cabo and Domingo Lovera Parmo, 'Latin American Social Constitutionalism: Courts and Popular Participation' in Helena Alviar Garcia, Karl Klare and Lucy A. Williams (eds.), *Social and Economic Rights in Theory and Practice: Critical Inquiries* (Abingdon: Routledge, 2015), pp. 85–104; Lilian Chenwi, 'Democratizing the Socio-economic Rights-Enforcement Process' in Garcia et al., *Social and Economic Rights*; Fredman, *Human Rights Transformed*; Roberto Gargarella, 'Deliberative Democracy, Dialogic Justice and the Promise of Social and Economic Rights' in Garcia et al., *Social and Economic Rights*, pp. 178–196; Jackman, 'Charter Review'; Liebenberg, *Socio-economic Rights*; O'Cinneide, 'Legal Accountability'; Pillay, 'Towards Effective'; Ray, *Engaging with Social Rights*.

understand the concerns of the other side.'[97] He explained that while the government's decision must 'be informed by the concerns raised by residents during the process of engagement', '[u]ltimately, the decision lies with the government'.[98]

A second point is that, as I noted in Chapter 4, to promote government trustworthiness, the courts must further the institutionalisation of participation. They must, put simply, seek to ensure that citizen participation becomes part of the decision-making process. This is why I stressed earlier the prospective effect of the South African and Colombian courts' remedies – this prospective effect furthers the remedy's institutionalisation. To be fair, there has been debate about whether meaningful engagement has been institutionalised in South Africa. Liebenberg, for example, has been critical of the South African court's engagement jurisprudence. In her view, meaningful engagement has been used 'purely as a dispute resolution mechanism' rather than 'to resolve the broader systemic issue pertaining to housing for the urban poor'.[99] Owing to its use in this way, meaningful engagement, Liebenberg has suggested, has not been institutionalised. She has acknowledged, however, that engagement may 'evolve in this direction over time' thereby contributing 'to a deepening of citizen participation in rights-based development in South Africa'.[100] Ray, in contrast, has taken a more optimistic perspective, claiming that engagement has, in fact, been institutionalised. First, Ray has stressed that the court, as I noted earlier, has connected meaningful engagement to reasonableness review.[101] And in doing so, it has, he has argued, furthered engagement's institutionalisation. Secondly, the court in *Olivia Road* made clear that engagement cannot be 'ad hoc'.[102] As Ray has noted, 'anytime a municipality begins a planning process like the regeneration plan, it is required to consider the effects of that process and build engagement into it from the beginning'.[103] 'The government', based on

[97] *Joe Slovo*, para. 244.

[98] Ibid, para. 244. See Sandra Liebenberg, 'Participatory Justice in Social Rights Adjudication' (2018) 18 *Human Rights Law Review* 623, 641.

[99] Sandra Liebenberg, 'Participatory Approaches to Socio-economic Rights Adjudication: Tentative Lessons from South African Evictions Law' (2014) 32 *Nordic Journal of Human Rights* 312, 328.

[100] Ibid, 328.

[101] Ray, *Engaging with Social Rights*, p. 116.

[102] *Olivia Road*, para. 19.

[103] Ray, *Engaging with Social Rights*, p. 117.

the court's judgment, thus 'has an obligation to use [its] resources to engage well before litigation is even a possibility'.[104]

Lastly, but related to my second point, the objective of the trust-based framework with respect to participation is what Ray has termed 'political engagement' rather than 'litigation engagement'.[105] As he has explained, with political engagement, participation or engagement is extended 'beyond a litigation aspect' and is 'turn[ed] into an administrative requirement'.[106] Under the trust-based framework, political engagement is our objective because it follows on from the institutionalisation of participation. For the courts to promote the trustworthiness of the elected branches with respect to social rights, they must, I repeat, further the institutionalisation of participation. When participation is institutionalised, the resulting participation is political. In *Olivia Road*, for instance, the court demanded this form of participation, somewhat ambiguously though.[107] It held that 'the process of engagement should take place before litigation commences unless it is not possible, or reasonable to do so because of urgency or some other compelling reason'.[108] And in *Joe Slovo*, Sachs J. confirmed this, noting that the government's engagements were lacking as they did not 'involve the residents as partners in the process of decision-making'.[109]

5.2.1.3 Equality

Procedural fairness, as I remarked earlier, also requires that the elected branches, in exercising their control over social goods and services, respect citizens' rights. This necessarily includes, we know, the right to equality. Accordingly, as part of its enforcement of trust's expectation of goodwill, the courts should enforce the right to equality. What does it mean for the courts to do so?

To be clear, it is not my objective here to exhaustively consider what the right to equality entails. My objective is more modest than that: it is to consider the right to equality as it specifically pertains to the judicial enforcement of social rights. Therefore, my consideration of the right to equality is restricted in two inter-related respects. First, I am only

[104] Ibid, p. 117.
[105] Brian Ray, 'Engagement's Possibilities and Limits as a Socioeconomic Rights Remedy' (2010) 9 *Washington University Global Studies Law Review* 399, 417–418.
[106] Ibid, 417–418.
[107] Ibid, 418–419.
[108] *Olivia Road*, para. 30.
[109] *Joe Slovo*, para. 378.

concerned with equality vis-à-vis the elected branches' exercise of control over social goods and services. The right to equality will, of course, extend beyond this narrow field to broader legislative and administrative acts. But my focus is on what it means for the elected branches to act in furtherance of substantive equality when they make allocation decisions regarding social rights-related goods and services. Secondly, it will be recalled that there is a distinction to be drawn between what equality signifies, on the one hand, and how the courts should enforce the right to equality, on the other. The right to equality extends beyond adjudication. It reflects more than 'legal entitlements, the meaning of which is to be determined by the courts' but requires 'all of the institutions of the state . . . to recognize substantive equality as entailing positive duties.'[110] This distinction is central to understanding how, I propose, courts can and should enforce the right to equality when enforcing the expectation of goodwill. Consequently, my discussion of the right to equality here is restricted, institutionally, to the courts – that is, the courts' role in enforcing the right against the other branches of government.

Recognising the above distinction, Sandra Fredman has suggested that the courts, given their legitimacy and capacity limitations, should occupy a catalytic or 'supervisory' role in enforcing the right to equality vis-à-vis the state's positive obligations.[111] As she has clarified, 'the existence of a right [like the right to equality] does not mean that the court needs to make primary decisions about the allocation of resources'.[112] For her, the courts, rather than detract from democracy (which would be the case if they made primary decisions about resource allocation), can and should enhance democracy by requiring decision-makers to justify their decisions in light of the principle of equality.[113] They should insist on 'reasoned justification' from government decision-makers for distributive decisions that burden or exclude disadvantaged groups, requiring them to show that their choice of eligibility criteria satisfies the four previously described objectives of substantive equality, such that their choice in this regard 'not only redresses disadvantage, but also promotes respect and dignity, accommodates diverse identities, and facilitates participation or

[110] Albertyn et al., 'Introduction', 212–213.
[111] Fredman, *Human Rights Transformed*, p. 182.
[112] Fredman, 'Providing Equality', 182.
[113] Fredman, 'Redistribution and Recognition', 230.

counters social exclusion'.[114] Where decision-makers fail to so satisfy, they 'should be required to justify the breach' via a proportionality analysis with the burden of proof falling on the decision-maker.[115]

I agree with Fredman's advocated approach. Not only does it recognise the complexity of inequality, but it acknowledges the limited legitimacy and capacity of the courts in making resource allocation decisions. It thus neither strips equality of substance (in the way that a formal conception of equality does) nor does it yield judicial usurpation of the elected branches' policy-making role.

As an illustration of an approach that aligns, at least substantially, with that advocated by Fredman, let us consider the South African Constitutional Court's decision in *Khosa*.[116] At issue in the case was legislation that excluded permanent residents from child benefits and old age pensions. Under section 27(1)(c) of the South African Constitution, 'everyone' is guaranteed 'the right to have access to ... social security'. In addition, section 9 of the Constitution protects the right to equality. The claimants, who were Mozambican citizens, relied on both provisions to argue that their exclusion from the child benefits and old age pensions scheme was unconstitutional.

The court agreed. And in so concluding, it applied its reasonableness review standard in a way that reflects at least three of the above-identified objectives of substantive equality.[117] First, the court found that the eligibility criteria under the legislation did not redress disadvantage. Consistent with past jurisprudence, it recognised that permanent residents were a vulnerable group worthy of constitutional protection.[118] Secondly, with respect to the claimants' respect and dignity, the court concluded that the 'intentional, statutorily sanctioned unequal treatment of part of the South African community' in this case had 'a strong stigmatizing effect'.[119] Mokgoro J., in his judgment for the court, reasoned that because permanent residents and citizens alike contributed to the welfare system through the payment of taxes, the former's exclusion from the scheme created 'the impression that permanent residents

[114] Fredman, 'Providing Equality', 164, 182; Fredman, 'Redistribution and Recognition', 230. See also Fredman, *Human Rights Transformed*, p. 182.

[115] Fredman, 'Redistribution and Recognition', 230.

[116] *Khosa and Others v. Minister of Social Development and Others* [2004] ZACC 11 ('*Khosa*').

[117] Fredman, *Human Rights Transformed*, p. 183.

[118] *Khosa*, para. 74.

[119] Ibid, para. 74.

are in some way inferior to citizens and less worthy of social assistance'.[120] Thirdly, in relation to the fourth objective of participation, the court found that in effect the scheme undermined permanent residents' participation: it relegated them 'to the margins of society' and deprived them 'of what may be essential to enable them to enjoy other rights vested in them under the Constitution'.[121] Therefore, the exclusion of permanent residents from the scheme, the court held, was 'discriminatory and unfair', contrary to section 9.

Aside from its appeal in balancing the complexity of inequality and the two wrongs of social rights enforcement, Fredman's approach to enforcing the right to equality also fits well with the trust-based framework that I propose. This is so, I suggest, because it is consistent with other components of the framework. For example, consistent with the expectation of competence (to be discussed in Chapter 6), Fredman's approach demands evidence-based decision-making from government actors. As she has said, state criteria for social welfare programmes are often based on 'stereotypical assumptions and unwarranted generalisations' that can 'further structural inequalities'.[122] These assumptions or generalisations include that women are dependent on male breadwinners and that relationships are heterosexual in nature. Fredman has advocated, in response to this, that as part of requiring government decision-makers to provide a reasoned justification for distributive decisions that burden or exclude disadvantaged groups, the courts should require 'the state to provide evidence to back up its decisions'.[123] They should demand that decisions regarding resource allocation be 'based on proper evidence rather than generalisations or assumptions which are at high risk of incorporating damaging stereotypes or worsening the lot [of] the disadvantaged'.[124] This aligns with what the courts do, under the framework that I propose, when enforcing trust's expectation of competence. As I explain in the next chapter, the expectation of competence is an expectation that the elected branches, in exercising their control over social goods and services, will make decisions based on the best available evidence. That is, they will exercise their control over the relevant goods

[120] Ibid, para. 74.
[121] Ibid, para. 77.
[122] Fredman, 'Providing Equality', 171. See also Fredman, *Human Rights Transformed*, p. 182.
[123] Fredman, 'Providing Equality', 182.
[124] Ibid, 182.

and services in accordance with the principles of evidence-based decision-making. As a result, in enforcing the expectation, the courts should require the elected branches to base their decisions on such evidence. Consequently, where a resource allocation decision raises the equality concerns that I have noted above, the two approaches – the trust-based framework's approach to enforcing the expectation of competence and Fredman's approach to enforcing the right to equality – align, producing the same outcome.

A helpful illustration of this point is the Canadian Supreme Court's decision in *Gosselin*.[125] Before turning to the case, I should note that unlike many of the constitutions considered in this book, the Canadian Constitution does not expressly protect social rights.[126] And Canadian courts have been reluctant to read social rights into more general provisions, including the right to life (under section 7 of the Canadian *Charter of Rights and Freedoms* (the '*Charter*')) and the right to equality (under section 15 of the *Charter*). Nonetheless, *Gosselin* offers an illustration of how the courts can, and I claim should, enforce the right to equality to guard against the elected branches' use of assumptions or generalisations in exercising their control over social goods and services.

The case involved a social assistance scheme that was created by the government of the province of Québec in 1984. The scheme drew a distinction between those 30 years of age and over, and those under 30. Pursuant to the scheme, the base amount of welfare payable to those under 30 was roughly one third the base amount payable to those 30 and over. This distinction was drawn by the government in an apparent 'effort to encourage young people to get job training and join the labour force'.[127] In pursuit of this objective, those under 30 were required to participate in a designated work activity or education programme if they wanted to receive an amount comparable to that received by those 30 and over. Of central importance, the Québec government based the distinction drawn between the two age groups in the scheme on an assumption or generalisation that welfare recipients who were under 30 had better

125 *Gosselin v. Québec (Attorney General)*, 2002 SCC 84 ('*Gosselin*').

126 Martha Jackman and Bruce Porter, 'Socio-economic Rights under the Canadian Charter' in Malcolm Langford (ed.), *Social Rights Jurisprudence: Emerging Trends in International and Comparative Law* (Cambridge: Cambridge University Press, 2009), p. 209. As Jackman and Porter explain, '[t]he closest the Charter comes to recognising a socio-economic right is the section 23 right to publicly funded minority language education at the primary and secondary levels, "where numbers warrant".'

127 *Gosselin*, paras. 2, 41.

labour force prospects than their older counterparts. Louise Gosselin, a welfare recipient under 30 who battled with mental health issues, challenged the scheme as a violation of, among other things, section 15 of the *Charter* (the equality provision) on the basis that it discriminated against her based on age.

The majority of the Supreme Court adopted an approach that does not align with that advocated by Fredman. Despite evidence adduced which demonstrated that young people, in fact, struggle to find employment, the majority upheld the scheme's constitutionality, finding the government's assumption in this respect to be 'informed' and that it was entitled to proceed on such 'informed general assumptions', provided they were 'not based on arbitrary and demeaning stereotypes'.[128] McLachlin CJ., writing for the majority, concluded that young adults as a class did 'not seem especially vulnerable or undervalued' and the 'idea that younger people may have an easier time finding employment than older people' was, according to her, 'not such a stereotype'.[129] Furthermore, in contrast to Fredman's advocated approach, the majority did not require the government to justify its assumptions in this regard with evidence. On the contrary, the Chief Justice stated that imposing a duty on the legislator 'to verify all its assumptions empirically' was too high a standard.[130] The government's programme, the majority therefore held, 'was calibrated to address the particular needs and circumstances of young adults requiring social assistance'.[131]

The dissenting judges took a different approach, testing the Québec government's claims against what Martha Jackman has called the 'reality checks' provided by Gosselin's evidence.[132] Their approach thus aligns with that advocated by Fredman. In particular, the dissenting judges tested the veracity of the assumption that those under 30 have better labour force prospects than those 30 and over. Bastarache J., for instance, found that from the record it was clear 'that it was not, in fact, easier for persons under 30 to get jobs as opposed to their elders', with the unemployment rate in 1982 being higher among young people.[133]

128 Ibid, para. 56.
129 Ibid, paras. 33, 56.
130 Ibid, para. 56.
131 Ibid, para. 70.
132 Martha Jackman, 'Reality Checks: Presuming Innocence and Proving Guilt in *Charter* Welfare Cases' in Margot Young et al. (eds.), *Poverty: Rights, Social Citizenship, and Legal Activism* (Vancouver: UBC Press, 2007), p. 33.
133 *Gosselin*, para. 235.

He observed that as a percentage of the total population on social assistance, 'those under 30 years of age rose from 3 percent in 1975 to 12 percent in 1983'.[134] On this basis, he concluded that the distinction drawn in the scheme between those under 30 and those 30 and over 'was not grounded in fact' but 'based on old assumptions regarding the employability of young people'.[135] LeBel J. likewise found the government's assumption to be unfounded. Drawing on expert studies, he noted 'the extreme sensitivity of the youth unemployment rate to general conditions in the economy'.[136] Both judges also found the distinction to not be respectful of young welfare recipients' dignity. LeBel J. reasoned that the distinction 'perpetuated the stereotypical view that a majority of young social assistance recipients choose to freeload off society permanently and have no desire to get out of that comfortable situation' – that is, they are 'happy being dependent on the state, even though they are better able to make a go of things than their elders during periods of economic slowdown.'[137] So, in line with Fredman's approach, the dissenting judges demanded from the Québec government 'an explanation of the decision' to differentiate between these two age groups of welfare recipients which was 'based on evidence rather than generalisations'.[138] And this, as we will see in Chapter 6, aligns with how the courts are to enforce the expectation of competence.

Incorporating Fredman's approach to enforcing the right to equality into the trust-based framework, I suggest that the courts, in enforcing the expectation of goodwill, should enforce the right to equality in the way that Fredman has advocated in her work. That is, they should demand from the elected branches a reasoned justification for distributive decisions that burden or exclude disadvantaged groups. By doing so, the courts send a clear message to the elected branches that they must have a reasoned justification for their choice of eligibility criteria, requiring the elected branches to reflect upon how their decisions satisfy the four substantive equality objectives. This promotes an expectation in citizens that the elected branches will respect their right to equality.

At the same time, the courts, to indeed further substantive equality, must not prohibit social welfare programmes that are aimed at

[134] Ibid, para. 235.
[135] Ibid, para. 235.
[136] Ibid, para. 409.
[137] Ibid, para. 407.
[138] Fredman, 'Providing Equality', 190.

benefitting disadvantaged groups. Affirmative action, on a substantive view of equality, 'is not a breach of or even an exception to equality'; on the contrary, 'it is a means to achieve equality'.[139] And social rights can be relied on, and in fact have been in various jurisdictions, to challenge programmes of this sort. The right to education, for example, has been relied on to challenge preferential education policies that benefit students from disadvantaged backgrounds. When presented with such challenges, the courts, to further substantive equality, must be supportive of the programmes. As Fredman has said in the context of gender, 'to adopt a symmetrical approach, whereby unequal treatment of men is regarded as morally identical to discrimination against women, is to empty the equality principle of real social meaning.'[140] The same can be said for programmes that support other disadvantaged groups.

This does not mean, however, that there should be no judicial scrutiny of these affirmative action programmes. The courts 'should still require governments to demonstrate that the aim of the measure is indeed to further substantive equality and to justify their choice of means'.[141] In parallel to what I said earlier with respect to decisions that burden or exclude disadvantaged groups, the elected branches must evidence that their chosen measures are not based on stereotypical assumptions or unwarranted generalisations. The Kenyan High Court's decision in *John Kabui Mwai* offers an illustration of this sort of judicial scrutiny.[142] In the case, private school pupils challenged a governmental policy that limited the number of spaces in public schools made available to pupils from private schools. They challenged the policy, in significant part and as I identified above, on the basis of the right to education in Article 53(1)(b) of the Kenyan Constitution that guarantees '[e]very child . . . the right . . . to free and compulsory basic education'.

In furtherance of substantive equality, the Kenyan court dismissed the challenge. Like other constitutions, including that of South Africa, the Kenyan Constitution has been recognised by the High Court as a transformative document.[143] Significant for present purposes, the focus, in a

139 Sandra Fredman, *Discrimination Law* (Oxford: Oxford University Press, 2011), p. 259.

140 Ibid, p. 235.

141 Ibid, p. 273.

142 *John Kabui Mwai and Others v. Kenya National Examination Council and Others* [2011] eKLR ('*John Kabui Mwai*').

143 See Eric Kibet and Charles Fombad, 'Transformative Constitutionalism and the Adjudication of Constitutional Rights in Africa' (2017) 17 *African Human Rights Law Journal* 340.

transformative constitution, 'is on substantive equality and substantive justice'.[144] Former South African Deputy Chief Justice, Dikgang Moseneke once said that '[c]entral to [South Africa's constitutional] transformation is the achievement of equality', 'the primary purpose of [which] is to intervene in unjust, uneven and impermissible power and resource distributions, in order to restore substantive equality'.[145] In line with this idea, the Kenyan court stressed in the case that its constitution's 'transformative agenda looks beyond merely guaranteeing abstract equality', encompassing a commitment to substantive equality 'to transform Kenya from a society based on socio-economic deprivation to one based on equal and equitable distribution of resources'.[146]

Given its transformative nature, the court interpreted and applied the Constitution, including the right to education in Article 53(1)(b), in accordance with the principles of substantive equality, holding that the government's policy did not violate the Constitution. In particular, it considered the right to education in light of the relative vulnerability of public school and private school pupils, noting that public schools were traditionally characterised by 'overcrowded classes, shortage of teachers, inadequate infrastructure and diminished parental support as a result of viewing education as free', which compromised the quality in these schools.[147] '[I]f merit was the only criteria for admission into national schools', the court said, 'candidates from private school would take most of the . . . places available'.[148] It therefore concluded that the Minister of Education here had 'sought to temper merit with equity', realising 'that the previous policy, based on merit alone, had occasioned unfairness and prejudice to the candidates from public schools'.[149]

[144] Ibid, 353. See also Cathi Albertyn and Beth Goldblatt, 'Facing the Challenge of Transformation: Difficulties in the Development of an Indigenous Jurisprudence of Equality' (1998) 14 *South African Journal on Human Rights* 248, 250; Pius Langa, 'Transformative Constitutionalism' (2006) 17 *Stellenbosch Law Review* 351, 352; Dikgang Moseneke, 'The Fourth Bram Fischer Memorial Lecture: Transformative Adjudication' (2002) 18 *South African Journal on Human Rights* 309, 315; Marius Pieterse, 'What Do We Mean When We Talk about Transformative Constitutionalism?' (2005) 20 *SAPR/PL* 155, 159.

[145] Moseneke, 'The Fourth Bram Fischer Memorial Lecture', 316.

[146] *John Kabui Mwai*, 6.

[147] Ibid, 11.

[148] Ibid.

[149] Ibid.

5.2.2 *Responding to Government Intransigence*

To enforce the second sub-expectation of goodwill – what I have called the expectation of good intentions – the courts must be responsive to intransigence, as I defined it earlier, from the elected branches. Enforcing this sub-expectation, especially in a way that promotes the trustworthiness of the elected branches vis-à-vis social goods and services, is tricky because of the delicate balance between discretion and external constraints necessary for impersonal trust. It will be recalled from Chapter 2 that trust requires discretion. A trustee must exercise discretion in their exercise of control over the relevant goods and services for trust to arise in the trustee's relationship with the truster. Thus, while we can impose external constraints on the elected branches to promote their trustworthiness, increasing the likelihood of them fulfilling citizens' expectations of goodwill, competence and fiduciary responsibility, those constraints cannot remove their discretion entirely. This necessitates that the courts leave the elected branches with sufficient discretion to allow trust to arise in the citizen–government relationship, while, at the same time, respond to their intransigence (if any).

Relevant to this balance, John Braithwaite, in his work on trust, has advocated organising government institutions around what he has called 'regulatory pyramids'.[150] The fundamental idea is that contemporary societies should enculturate trust in government actors by structuring distrust deeply into our institutions. By doing so, according to Braithwaite, we institutionalise distrust. Such institutionalisation of distrust has a long history in liberal political thought.[151] Braithwaite's approach, however, is more specific than the general notion that citizens should be wary of government actors. The regulatory pyramid assumes that motives underlying abuses of governmental power are varied, including incompetence and sometimes intransigence.[152] Given this, in a regulatory pyramid, we '[t]rust first, and thereby get the efficiency benefits of trust in most cases, but motivate trust as obligation by signaling very clearly a preparedness to escalate intervention to progressively less trusting interventions when trust is abused.'[153] In other words,

[150] John Braithwaite, 'Institutionalizing Distrust, Enculturating Trust', in Valerie Braithwaite and Margaret Levi (eds.), *Trust and Governance* (New York: Russell Sage Foundation, 1999), pp. 343–375.

[151] For a summary, see Russell Hardin, 'Liberal Distrust' (2002) 10 *European Review* 73.

[152] Braithwaite, 'Institutionalizing Distrust', p. 352.

[153] Ibid, p. 352.

while we start off by manifesting our trust in government actors, we simultaneously put them on guard, alerting them to the fact that we can, and are prepared to, resort to distrustful behaviours. And if they abuse our trust, we turn to these sorts of distrustful behaviour, escalating our response.

Applying this idea of regulatory pyramids to social rights enforcement, the courts, I submit, should start social rights cases from a position of trust. That is, they should assume good faith from the elected branches, at least initially, expecting them to fulfil the relevant expectations when they exercise their control over social goods and services. Such an assumption may be well founded. According to Jeff King, for example, the principle of inter-institutional collaboration, under which it is accepted that the three branches of government will seek in good faith to do their respective work and cooperate with one another, is not 'naïve optimism': as he has explained, '[a]ll *good* welfare states were built by legislatures, run by administrators, sustained by political consensus, and respected by the courts'.[154] This is not a given, however. John Dunn has stressed instead that '[p]olitics is not on the whole good for the character; and it is unlikely that there really are sound reasons for viewing the intentions of most of those who have devoted decades to it with unreserved trust'.[155] In any event, as Braithwaite has suggested, a judicial assumption of good faith from the elected branches is imperative to enculturate trust in the citizen–government relationship.

This means that the courts should refrain from employing as an initial response what we can consider less trusting judicial interventions. These include structural interdicts (or supervisory jurisdiction), the involvement of third parties (e.g., human rights bodies or anti-corruption agencies) and sanctions like contempt orders. Structural interdicts and the involvement of third parties are less trusting judicial interventions because they significantly reduce, and may eliminate, discretion from the citizen–government relationship – at least with respect to the matter at issue in the case before the court. The court, or the third party, supervises the elected branches, showing that the court has little to no expectation that the elected branches will fulfil the expectations of goodwill, competence and fiduciary responsibility. And in turn, this is not likely to instil much trust in citizens vis-à-vis the elected branches' exercise of control over social goods and services more broadly. Also, sanctions like

[154] King, *Judging Social Rights*, p. 310.

[155] Dunn, 'Trust and Political Agency', pp. 89–90.

contempt orders are, of course, less trusting because they are an ex post punitive consequence that responds to the elected branches' intransigence. When a court orders a sanction, it is far beyond the point of assuming that a government actor will comply with its obligations, and the sanction sends a signal to citizens that the relevant actor is not to be trusted.

Although these judicial interventions are less trusting of the elected branches, the courts, in line with Braithwaite's suggestion, should be prepared to escalate to them should the elected branches manifest intransigence. And they should indicate such preparedness in their judgments, to alert the elected branches that any intransigence will be met with interventions of this sort.

The South African Constitutional Court, in recent years, has adopted an approach that aligns with this.[156] The *AllPay* and *Black Sash* litigation is a good example. Historically, the South African Constitutional Court has manifested trust in its government, even where it may not have been warranted. For instance, in the *TAC* case, the court refused to issue a structural interdict, commenting that the government had 'always respected and executed orders of' the court giving the court 'no reason to believe' that it would not do so in the case.[157] In the *AllPay* and *Black Sash* litigation, however, we see the court escalating – in response to government intransigence in the case and likely, recent egregious government lapses outside the social rights context (e.g., former President Jacob Zuma's corrupt practices) that have left the courts 'frustrated [or] emboldened'.[158]

I describe the litigation in detail in Chapter 7 in relation to the expectation of fiduciary responsibility. In brief, it involved a procurement contract for the payment of government-funded social grants awarded by the South African Social Security Agency (SASSA) to an electronic

[156] See Katharine G. Young, 'The New Managerialism: Courts, Positive Duties, and Economic and Social Rights' in Vicki Jackson and Yasmin Dawood (eds.), *Constitutionalism and a Right to Effective Government* (Cambridge: Cambridge University Press, 2022), pp. 135–150.

[157] *TAC*, para. 129. As David Bilchitz has pointed out, owing to the government's handling of the HIV epidemic up to that point, this seemed 'like a strikingly bad moment to express good faith in the government's ability to deliver nevirapine expeditiously': 'Towards a Reasonable Approach to the Minimum Core: Laying the Foundations for Future Socio-economic Rights Jurisprudence' (2003) 19 *South African Journal on Human Rights* 1, 23–24.

[158] Young, 'The New Managerialism', p. 5.

payments firm called Cash Paymaster Services (CPS). Owing to several irregularities in the tender process, the court declared the tender constitutionally invalid. Recognising its limitations in terms of relative institutional legitimacy and competence, however, the court suspended its declaration of invalidity to afford SASSA the opportunity to award a new tender following a proper procurement process, or to take over the payment of social grants itself when the CPS contract came to an end in March 2017.[159] Despite offering SASSA this choice, the court, in response to some intransigence from SASSA – noting that SASSA had adopted 'an unhelpful and almost obstructionist stance' – constrained SASSA's discretion vis-à-vis any new tender process.[160] In particular, the court specified the term of the new procurement contract to be 5 years (whereas the term would ordinarily be within the powers of the executive), and it ordered SASSA to report back, either on the tender process or on whether (and if so, when) it would be in a position to take on the social grant payments itself.[161]

In fulfilment of the court's order, SASSA reported back that it had decided to take over the payments itself, and that it would be ready to do so by March 2017 (when the CPS contract would come to an end). On SASSA's assurance, the court accordingly discharged its supervisory jurisdiction. SASSA, however, was fully aware that it would not be able to meet the March 2017 deadline; yet neither it nor the Minister of Social Development took any steps to inform the court of this.[162] So, in March 2017, when the matter was brought back before the court, there was no option but to rely on CPS to continue to make the social grant payments for the foreseeable future.

The court, as a result, ordered SASSA and CPS to 'continue to fulfil their respective constitutional obligations in the payment of social grants for a period of 12 months as an extension of the current contract'.[163] It also ordered that its 'earlier declaration of invalidity of that contract [would] be further extended, as well as the suspension of that declaration

[159] *AllPay Consolidated Investment (Pty) and Others v. Chief Executive Officer, South African Social Security Agency and Others (no. 2)* [2014] ZACC 12, para. 40 ('*AllPay (Remedy)*').

[160] Ibid, para. 75.

[161] Ibid, para. 44.

[162] *Black Sash Trust v. Minister of Social Development and Others (Freedom under Law NPC Intervening)* [2017] ZACC 8, para. 6 ('*Black Sash I*').

[163] Ibid, para. 6.

of invalidity'.[164] But this time, in response to SASSA's and the Minister's further intransigence, the court escalated to less trusting interventions. For it, the 'inference that [the Minister] did not act in good faith' in withholding from it the fact that SASSA would be unable to meet the March 2017 deadline was 'irresistible' and there needed to be consequences, the court reasoned, 'if it is not to happen again'.[165] First, it ordered more extensive supervision. The Minister and SASSA were required to file reports with the court every three months, setting out how they planned to ensure the social grant payments after the expiry of the 12-month period, the steps they had taken in this regard, what further steps they planned to take and when each step would be taken.[166] Secondly, on the advice of Corruption Watch, it appointed the Auditor General as an independent monitor vis-à-vis its order. Thirdly, the court took the additional step of joining the Minister, in her personal capacity, as a party to the proceedings,[167] ordering her to pay 20 per cent of the claimants' costs.[168]

The South African court's approach evinces an escalation in response to government intransigence. Contrary to the trust it had historically shown its government, the court employed progressively less trusting interventions, starting with constraints on the new tender process, and then escalating to more extensive supervision, involvement of the Auditor General and a costs order against the Minister of Social Development personally. The court's approach thus aligns with Braithwaite's idea of a regulatory pyramid. Whereas the court, in its earlier case law, started from a position of trust, when the government (in this case, SASSA and the Minister of Development) responded with intransigence, the court turned to less trusting interventions.

Arguably, the court could have done more to signal to SASSA and the Minister of Development its preparedness to escalate – that is, the court could have warned them that further intransigence would not be tolerated, doing work to promote their trustworthiness. However, in its *AllPay (Remedy)* judgment, where the court ordered SASSA to either run a new tender process or take up the payments itself, Froneman J., writing for

[164] Ibid, para. 50.

[165] *Black Sash Trust v. Minister of Social Development and Others (Freedom under Law NPC Intervening)* [2018] ZACC 36, paras. 12, 13 ('*Black Sash III*').

[166] *Black Sash I*, para. 76.

[167] *Black Sash Trust v. Minister of Social Development and Others (Freedom under Law NPC Intervening)* [2017] ZACC 20, para. 24 ('*Black Sash II*').

[168] *Black Sash III*, para. 18.

the court, did convey cautionary words, highlighting that SASSA's 'unhelpful and almost obstructionist stance' had to 'be deprecated, particularly in view of the important role it plays as guardian of the right to social security and as controller of beneficiaries' access to social assistance'.[169] And in his subsequent *Black Sash I* judgment, Froneman J. referred back to these cautionary words, noting 'not much has changed, except that this time around the Minister may have contributed to the continued recalcitrance'.[170] Hence, I suggest that the court, in its judgments, did enough to signal its preparedness to escalate.

To be fair, it may be argued that judicial escalation of the sort observed in the *AllPay* and *Black Sash* litigation will have the effect of diminishing trust in the elected branches, contrary to what I advocated in Chapter 4. This is most likely true. This is because judicial interventions like those used by the South African court either eliminate governmental discretion (making trust no longer necessary) or punish government actors (sending a signal to citizens that they are not to be trusted). But the elected branches, by this point, have, proven themselves unworthy of trust. So, trustworthiness and trust, I submit, can no longer be a primary consideration in the relationship. What is of the utmost importance is encouraging the elected branches to comply with the courts' rulings. These judicial interventions, it is reasonable to conclude, aid in getting government actors to comply in immediate cases, while also setting a precedent that encourages the elected branches, in future interactions both with citizens and with the courts, to comply with their obligations.

169 *AllPay (Remedy)*, para. 75.
170 *Black Sash I*, para. 57.

6

The Expectation of Competence

In this chapter, I address the second constituent expectation of trust in the citizen–government relationship: competence. Relative to that of goodwill, the expectation of competence usually receives significantly less attention when the concept of trust is discussed. This is especially the case in the context of political relationships like the citizen–government relationship. As John Dunn has pointed out, 'modern political theory . . . gives inadequate weight to the human importance of practical skill in politics'.[1] This bias in the literature towards the expectation of goodwill should not be taken, however, as a reason to disregard the expectation of competence. In fact, Dunn has argued that while both 'trust in the good intentions' of political actors (i.e., the expectation of goodwill) and 'trust in their practical capacities' are vital to modern democracies, if we must make a choice, 'it is wiser in most circumstances . . . to opt for trust in practical capacity'.[2]

It will be recalled from Chapter 2 that the expectation of competence means that citizens expect the elected branches, in their exercise of control over social goods and services, to act competently. But this, of course, raises the question: what does it mean for the elected branches to act 'competently'? This chapter answers that question. In parallel to Chapter 5, it starts by addressing what the expectation of competence entails from the elected branches, before turning to how the courts, in social rights cases, can enforce the expectation against the elected branches.

6.1 The Expectation of Competence: An Expectation of Evidence-Based Policy-Making

So, what defines 'competence' from the elected branches in the citizen–government relationship? Or more specifically, how do they exercise

[1] John Dunn, 'Trust and Political Agency' in Diego Gambetta (ed.), *Trust: Making and Breaking Cooperative Relations* (Oxford: Basil Blackwell, 1988), pp. 74, 89–90.

[2] Ibid, pp. 89–90.

their control over social goods and services 'competently'? To start, we must recognise that competence can be understood from different perspectives – that is, what is competent to one may not be to another. In parallel to how I defined procedural fairness in Chapter 5, I submit that competence should be judged from the perspective of citizens. After all, the expectation of competence is an expectation held by citizens. Therefore, as in Chapter 5, it should be defined by what citizens would reasonably be expected to consider competent vis-à-vis the elected branches' exercise of control over social goods and services.

I emphasise here the word 'reasonably' because it is important to highlight that some citizens may have unreasonable understandings of what it means for a government actor to act competently. Recent literature, for instance, has suggested that we are currently witnessing the 'death of expertise', with the public showing hostility towards expert knowledge.[3] In the UK, as an example, it was famously said by one politician that the public has 'had enough of experts'.[4] It appears that this politician's conclusion is untrue.[5] But even if it were, such rejection of expert knowledge by citizens, I claim, is not reasonable. Experts 'provide an apparently indispensable bridge between complex and uncertain bodies of knowledge and publics who seek guidance on how to act on such knowledge'.[6] And as I argue in a moment, expert knowledge forms a significant part of what citizens would reasonably expect from competent government actors.

In Chapter 5, to define a 'fair' procedure under the expectation of goodwill, I drew on research examining public assessments of procedural fairness vis-à-vis public trust in government actors. I specifically highlighted three elements of fairness: transparency, participation and respect for citizens' rights. With the expectation of competence, however, there is

[3] See Tom Nichols, *The Death of Expertise: The Campaign against Established Knowledge and Why It Matters* (Oxford: Oxford University Press, 2017), p. 20.

[4] See Henry Mance, 'Britain Has Had Enough of Experts, Says Gove' *Financial Times* (3 June 2016), www.ft.com/content/3be49734-29cb-11e6-83e4-abc22d5d108c, accessed 18 January 2023.

[5] Katharine Dommett and Warren Pearce, 'What Do We Know about Public Attitudes towards Experts? Reviewing Survey Data in the United Kingdom and European Union' (2019) 28 *Public Understanding of Science* 669. See also Ipsos, 'Doctors Become the World's Most Trusted Profession' (12 October 2021) <www.ipsos.com/en/global-trust worthiness-index-2021> accessed 18 January 2023.

[6] Dommett and Pearce, 'What Do We Know about Public Attitudes towards Experts?', 669, citing Sheila Jasanoff, *Designs on Nature: Science and Democracy in Europe and the United States* (Princeton, NJ: Princeton University Press, 2005), p. 267.

very limited scholarship (at least to my knowledge) of public assessments of government competence vis-à-vis such trust. Put simply, we do not have the same understanding of what competence means to citizens as we do regarding what a fair procedure means to them. Hence, I propose that to define competence from the elected branches in the citizen–government relationship, we must, relying on relevant literature, approximate what citizens would reasonably expect from competent government actors.

To so approximate, we can start by considering the public law literature. For example, Elizabeth Fisher and Sidney Shapiro, in their book on administrative competence, have defined competence in the administrative law context as referring to an administrative actor having both 'legitimate authority' and 'the necessary capacity to accomplish its mission'.[7] Susan Rose-Ackerman, in her work on public accountability, has defined competence from government actors as encompassing 'both the use of experts' and the 'existence of hard-working, well-trained civil servants who do not take bribes, embezzle funds, or create conflicts of interest.'[8] While these public law definitions of competence are reasonable, they are far too broad for this book's purpose. Given that I am defining competence here for the specific purpose of understanding trust and trustworthiness in the citizen–government relationship, I suggest that it is more appropriate to define competence in line with how it is understood in the literature on trust (which will be recalled from Chapter 2). In that literature, competence is defined narrowly. It refers to a trustee, like the elected branches, exercising the requisite *technical* competence (i.e., the knowledge and skills required vis-à-vis the good or service that is at issue in the relevant trust relationship).[9] For this reason, the term 'competence' is often used interchangeably with 'ability' and 'capacity'.

[7] Elizabeth Fisher and Sidney A. Shapiro, *Administrative Competence: Reimagining Administrative Law* (Cambridge: Cambridge University Press, 2020), p. 15.

[8] Susan Rose-Ackerman, 'Regulation and Public Law in Comparative Perspective' (2010) 60 *University of Toronto Law Journal* 519, 523.

[9] See, for example, Bernard Barber, *The Logic and Limits of Trust* (New Brunswick, NJ: Rutgers University Press, 1983), p. 14 (referring to 'technically competent role performance'); T.K. Das and Bing-Sheng Teng, 'The Risk-Based View of Trust: A Conceptual Framework' (2004) 19 *Journal of Business and Psychology* 85, 102–103 (describing competence as the trustee having 'the necessary skills and abilities to carry out certain actions and achieve desired results'). See also Frank Cross's discussion of trust in the legal context, describing competence as 'trust[ing] the person's abilities to accomplish the task at issue': Frank B. Cross, 'Law and Trust' (2005) 93 *Georgetown Law Journal* 1457, 1463.

This narrow understanding of competence also makes sense in the context of trust as a whole. The expectation of competence should supplement the other two expectations of trust (goodwill and fiduciary responsibility). If competence were defined broadly, like those employed by the legal scholars above, the expectation of competence would supplant the expectations of goodwill and fiduciary responsibility – at least in part. For example, Rose-Ackerman's definition of competence (which includes an element of non-corruption with its reference to bribes and embezzlement) overlaps with the expectation of fiduciary responsibility as I define it in Chapter 7. Therefore, adopting it here would render the expectation of fiduciary responsibility redundant.

For these reasons, I define competence in the citizen–government relationship as the elected branches – or more accurately, those who staff the elected branches – exercising the requisite knowledge and skills vis-à-vis the social goods and services that are at issue in the relationship. To be clear, in parallel to what I indicated earlier with respect to the expectation of good intentions, the expectation of competence is an expectation that the trustee will *act* competently or will *exercise* competence. It is not an expectation that the trustee *has* the requisite competence. So, applied to the citizen–government relationship, the expectation of competence is an expectation that the elected branches' staff will exercise the requisite knowledge and skills when they exercise their control over social goods and services – not that they have the knowledge and skills. In some trust relationships, this may be a distinction without a difference. But in the citizen–government relationship, the distinction is important for at least two reasons. First, there will be circumstances in which the elected branches' staff indeed have the requisite knowledge and skills, but do not exercise them. For example, as I explain in more detail later, while administrative decision-makers are usually experts in relevant areas, they may not act in accordance with their expertise. Secondly, while the elected branches' staff may not have the requisite knowledge and skills themselves, they can draw on outside expertise to inform their decision-making. In such circumstances, the staff exercises the requisite knowledge and skills without having them per se.

With that matter clarified, what are the requisite knowledge and skills vis-à-vis the relevant social goods and services? Put another way, what knowledge and skills must the elected branches' staff exercise when exercising their control over social goods and services? To answer this question, I propose we turn to scholarship on the established idea of evidence-based policy-making (EBPM). As a starting point, it is imperative that we recognise the prominence of EBPM as an approach to policy-making. Although EBPM does have a small number of critics (usually related to what constitutes 'evidence' and how we should 'base' policy on that evidence), it is generally accepted by scholars and practitioners alike.[10] In fact, 'few researchers or policymakers would publicly disagree that evidence-based policy ... is a goal for both academe and government'.[11] For instance, the OECD has noted that '[e]vidence has a critical role to play in improving the quality, responsiveness and accessibility of public services', representing 'a critical part of good governance'.[12] Many countries, in fact, acknowledging EBPM's value, have established formal governmental and non-governmental agencies to increase the use of evidence in policy-making.[13] Given this widespread acceptance of EBPM as an approach to policy-making, it is appropriate, I suggest, to use EBPM as a basis for approximating what citizens would be expected to reasonably consider competent vis-à-vis the elected branches' exercise of control over social goods and services. And consequently, I submit that for citizens to reasonably consider the elected branches' staff competent in this area, the staff should exercise their control in accordance with EBPM.

The central idea of EBPM is that government actors, in developing and implementing public policies and programmes, should base those policies and programmes on relevant evidence.[14] Conventionally, 'the

[10] See Karen Bogenschneider and Thomas J. Corbett, *Evidence-Based Policymaking: Insights from Policy-Minded Researchers and Research-Minded Policymakers* (Abingdon: Routledge, 2010); Huw T.O. Davies, Sandra M. Nutley and Peter C. Smith (eds.), *What Works? Evidence-Based Policy and Practice in Public Services* (Bristol: Bristol University Press, 2000); Ian Goldman and Mine Pabari, *Using Evidence in Policy and Practice: Lessons from Africa* (Abingdon: Routledge, 2020); Benjamin Hawkins and Justin Parkhurst, 'The "Good Governance" of Evidence in Health Policy' (2016) 12 *Evidence & Policy* 575.

[11] Kathryn Oliver, Theo Lorenc and Simon Innvaer, 'New Directions in Evidence-Based Policy Research: A Critical Analysis of the Literature' (2014) 12 *Health Research Policy and Systems* 34.

[12] OECD, *Building Capacity for Evidence-Informed Policy-Making: Lessons from Country Experiences* (OECD Publishing, 2020), 13.

[13] See Justin Parkhurst, *The Politics of Evidence: From Evidence-Based Policy to the Good Governance of Evidence* (Abingdon: Routledge, 2017), p. 16.

[14] See Paul Cairney, *The Politics of Evidence-Based Policy Making* (London: Palgrave MacMillan, 2016); J.A. Muir Gray, 'Evidence Based Policy Making' (2004) 329 *British Medical Journal* 988; Hawkins and Parkhurst, 'The "Good Governance"'; Brian W. Head, 'Three Lenses of Evidence-Based Policy' (2008) 67 *The Australian Journal of Public Administration* 1; Brian W. Head, 'Reconsidering Evidence-Based Policy: Key Issues and Challenges' (2010) 29 *Policy and Society* 77.

"evidence" base seen as the foundation for evidence-based policy is the knowledge generated by applied research, whether undertaken inside or outside of government agencies'.[15] In other words, the EBPM 'movement has particularly championed *scientific evidence* (arising from research) as the form best suited to inform policymaking'.[16] EBPM therefore demands that government actors use the best available research from the natural and social sciences to better understand and improve public policies and programmes. And so, applied to the citizen–government relationship, EBPM requires the elected branches' staff to employ the best available scientific research when they exercise their control over social goods and services.

Aside from EBPM's overall prominence as an approach to policy-making, the use of the best scientific research is, I submit, an appropriate approximation of what citizens would expect from the elected branches' staff to reasonably consider their exercise of control over social goods and services competent. When exercising their control in this regard, the elected branches' staff make decisions – including which social goods and services to fund and deliver to citizens, how much money to invest in social programmes, and which citizens will be covered by those programmes – all to serve certain policy ends. Scientific research, by offering insights into which policy initiatives are the most effective to achieve those ends, is of fundamental value. The use of the best scientific research thus seems an appropriate indication of competent decision-making.

However, as the policy studies literature has recognised, under EBPM, scientific research is not, or at least should not be, determinative of policy decisions: in J.A. Muir Gray's words, with EBPM, 'decisions are *based* on evidence and not *made by* evidence'.[17] First, scientific evidence is not necessarily of equal quality and validity, and scientists themselves disagree on the relative quality and validity of different methods.[18] Government actors, in relying on scientific research, must consider 'the source of a given piece of evidence, including potential conflicts of interest by its producers which may affect its credibility', and be guided by 'established standards of systematic, rigorous, and internally valid

[15] Head, 'Three Lenses of Evidence-Based Policy', 4.

[16] Parkhurst, *The Politics of Evidence*, p. 16.

[17] Gray, 'Evidence Based Policy', 988 (emphasis added).

[18] Head, 'Reconsidering Evidence-Based Policy', 82.

review of evidence'.[19] Secondly, allowing evidence to determine policy 'risks leading to an over-reliance on data and metrics that are disconnected from the everyday experience of workers and citizens whose needs and interests cannot always be measured or managed'.[20] Thirdly, alternative policy choices may each be supported by valid, relevant research.[21] Put simply, scientific research may not point decision-makers in one direction. And from this it follows that while 'empirical evidence can inform ... the contests between competing interests, values and ideas which lie at the heart of' the policy-making process, it cannot settle them.[22]

For these reasons, the language of 'evidence-based' policy has, in much of the literature, given way to 'evidence-informed' policy.[23] As Benjamin Hawkins and Justin Parkhurst have pointed out, the language of evidence-informed policy implies that policy should be made '*in light of* relevant evidence on the issues at stake' while permitting 'recognition of the political nature of the decision-making process in which there are competing political priorities, often with their own evidence bases'.[24] That said, it is my view that we can maintain the language of EBPM if we understand the term 'based' in a more nuanced manner. What is key is to recognise that knowledge from scientific research must be synthesised with other forms of knowledge.[25] Brian Head has usefully categorised these other forms of knowledge into what he has called 'political knowledge' and 'practical implementation knowledge'. 'Political knowledge' – a form of knowledge which comes into play during the development stage for public policies and programmes – refers to the 'know-how, analysis and judgment of political actors'.[26] It is a vast and varied form of knowledge, including everything from persuasion and advocacy

[19] Hawkins and Parkhurst, 'The "Good Governance"', 581–582.

[20] Adrian Pabst, 'Rethinking Evidence-Based Policy' (2021) 255(1) *National Institute Economic Review* 85, 88. See also Jerry Z. Muller, *The Tyranny of Metrics* (Princeton, NJ: Princeton University Press, 2019).

[21] Hawkins and Parkhurst, 'The "Good Governance"', 578.

[22] Ibid, 576.

[23] Ibid, 580; Brian W. Head, 'Toward More "Evidence-Informed" Policy Making?' (2016) 76 *Public Administration Review* 472, 473.

[24] Hawkins and Parkhurst, 'The "Good Governance"', 580. See also Benjamin Hawkins and Arturo Alvarez Rosete, 'Judicialization and Health Policy in Colombia: The Implications for Evidence-Informed Policymaking' (2019) 47 *Policy Studies Journal* 953, 955.

[25] Ittai Bar-Siman-Tov, 'The Dual Meaning of Evidence-Based Judicial Review of Legislation' (2016) 4 *The Theory and Practice of Legislation* 107, 110.

[26] Head, 'Three Lenses of Evidence-Based Policy', 5.

skills as well as the ability to build coalitions of support, to the capacity to negotiate trade-offs and compromises. 'Practical implementation knowledge' – which comes into play during the policy and programme implementation stage – is knowledge relating to the management of social programmes. It encapsulates what one needs to know in order to 'wrestle with everyday problems of program implementation and client service'.[27] Stemming from 'the "practical wisdom" of professionals in their "communities of practice"', this form of knowledge ultimately assumes the form of government actors adopting a 'best practice'.[28]

These two forms of knowledge – together with the knowledge derived from scientific research – form the knowledge or 'evidence' bases that constitute EBPM. As Head has explained:

> There is not one evidence-base but several bases. These disparate bodies of knowledge become multiple sets of evidence that inform and influence policy rather than determine it. The three lenses of policy-relevant knowledge comprise three perspectives on useful and useable information. Each of these types has its distinctive protocols of knowledge, of expertise, of strategy, and what counts as 'evidence', albeit it is also clear that there are ongoing internal debates on such matters within each knowledge area.[29]

The synthesis of these three forms of knowledge is, again, I submit, an appropriate approximation of what citizens would expect from the elected branches' staff to reasonably consider their exercise of control over social goods and services competent. Although citizens, to reasonably consider the staff's decision-making competent, would expect their decisions to be informed by the best scientific research, they would not expect those decisions to be dictated by that research. There are other relevant factors that must be taken into account, including the availability of financial and other resources, and the large variety of interests that must be balanced in making any political decision. Citizens would therefore, I suggest, expect the staff to also exercise the other forms of knowledge identified by Head: they would expect political actors (e.g., members of the legislature, ministers) to exercise 'political knowledge' in carrying out their responsibilities vis-à-vis social goods and services (i.e., preparing, developing and promulgating primary legislation, as well as preparing and approving the budget), and administrative decision-

[27] Ibid, 7.
[28] Ibid, 7.
[29] Ibid, 4.

makers to exercise 'practical implementation knowledge' when administering social programmes.

6.2 Enforcing the Expectation of Competence

6.2.1 Incorporating EBPM into Social Rights Enforcement

I turn now to how the courts can enforce the expectation of competence. Because the expectation of competence, I have argued, is an expectation that the elected branches' staff will exercise their control over social goods and services in accordance with EBPM, it follows that to enforce the expectation, the courts should incorporate EBPM into their enforcement of social rights. More specifically, they should require the relevant staff to make their decisions in line with EBPM.

I will explain in a moment what the above demands from the courts. But first, I note that my argument in this respect, once again, accords with some existing social rights literature.[30] Donna Greschner, for instance, in her work on the adjudication of claims about health care policies under the Canadian *Charter of Rights and Freedoms* (the '*Charter*'), has argued that in adjudicating these types of claims, Canadian courts should 'adopt approaches that will encourage EBDM [evidence-based decision-making] throughout the health care system.'[31] In other words, 'judicial review of health care decisions should use standards that promote EBDM'.[32] This is particularly so, according to Greschner, for claims that challenge the range of health care services to be publicly provided. She has argued that implementing EBDM in health care policy 'should be an uncontroversial goal because of its superiority to other methods of decision-making'.[33] In particular, it can 'reveal biases built into previously unquestioned assumptions and unexamined policies, and also correct and contextualise popular beliefs about health care

[30] See Donna Greschner, '*Charter* Challenges and Evidence-Based Decision-Making in the Health Care System: Towards a Symbiotic Relationship' in Colleen M. Flood (ed.), *Just Medicare: What's In, What's Out, How We Decide* (Toronto: University of Toronto Press, 2006); Donna Greschner and Steven Lewis, '*Auton* and Evidence-Based Decision-Making: Medicare in the Courts' (2003) 82 *The Canadian Bar Review* 501; Martha Jackman, 'Charter Review as a Health Care Accountability Mechanism in Canada' (2010) 18 *Health Law Journal* 1. For a related discussion in the public policy literature, see Hawkins and Rosete, 'Judicialization and Health Policy'.

[31] Greschner, '*Charter* Challenges', p. 42.

[32] Ibid, p. 53.

[33] Ibid, p. 49.

treatments'; it thereby serves 'as a bulwark against decisions that are unduly influenced by extraneous factors (such as political pressures, including interest group lobbying), which detract from the fairness and equity of a health care system'.[34]

To illustrate her advocated approach, Greschner has employed the Canadian Supreme Court's decision in *Auton*.[35] At issue in *Auton* was the province of British Columbia's refusal to fund, as part of its public health care plan, ABA/IBI therapy (a then-recent and emergent therapy) for preschool-aged children with autism. The claimants, parents of children with autism, challenged the British Columbia government's failure to fund the therapy on the basis that it unjustifiably discriminated against them, contrary to section 15 of the *Charter*. The case was decided on a technical point of law. Section 15, the *Charter*'s equality provision, states that '[e]very individual is equal before and under the law and has the right to the equal benefit of the law without discrimination', including discrimination based on 'physical disability'. To succeed under section 15, the claimants were accordingly required to show that they failed to receive a benefit that the law provided.[36] The relevant federal and provincial legislation, however, did not promise funding for all medically required treatment. They conferred, rather, core funding for services delivered by medical practitioners as well as, at a province's discretion, funding for non-core services. And because ABA/IBI therapy was a non-core service which the British Columbia government, in exercising its discretion, had decided not to fund, the court concluded that the therapy was not a benefit provided by law.[37] Consequently, it held that the claim did not come within section 15.

The court could have ended its analysis there as this disposed of the action. However, it chose to consider whether the claimants would have succeeded, if they had established that the therapy was a benefit provided by law. Greschner has argued that in this analysis, the court promoted EBDM. Under section 15, the claimants were also required to show that they were denied a benefit that an appropriate comparator group was receiving. The claimants argued that the appropriate comparator group was either non-disabled children and their parents, or adults with mental

[34] Ibid, p. 50. See also Greschner and Lewis, '*Auton* and Evidence-Based', 531–532.

[35] *Auton (Guardian ad litem of) v. British Columbia (Attorney General)*, 2004 SCC 78 ('*Auton*').

[36] Ibid, para. 27.

[37] Ibid, paras. 27–47.

illness; but the court disagreed, finding the proposed comparator groups to be overly broad since 'the recent and emergent nature of ABA/IBI therapy' was left 'out of the equation'.[38] Instead, the court reasoned, the appropriate comparator was 'a non-disabled person or a person suffering a disability other than a mental disability (here autism) seeking or receiving funding for a non-core therapy important for his or her present and future health, *which is emergent and only recently becoming recognized as medically required*'.[39] Because the claimants had not adduced any evidence before the court that another group had been receiving, as part of British Columbia's public health care plan, a non-core therapy that was 'emergent and only recently becoming recognized as medically required', a finding of discrimination against the claimants could therefore not be sustained.[40]

Greschner has argued that in this section 15 analysis, the court 'furthered the methods and values of EBDM'.[41] In particular, its analysis of comparator groups, she has noted, 'showed sensitivity to the dynamic nature of health treatments and the role of evidence in evaluating and implementing them.' Ultimately, Greschner has explained, the court 'recognized that until sufficient evidence is available about emergent treatments, governments can be cautious about funding them'.[42] And building her argument in support of courts promoting EBDM in their adjudication of health policy claims, she has stressed that this 'cautious approach' from the court 'has considerable merit'.[43] For her, '[e]very patient has an interest in a safe and sustainable health care system' and the court's approach serves both ends: safety because 'continued testing and experimentation may uncover dangers with experimental therapies', and sustainability by enabling governments to restrict their limited funds to cover treatments supported by sufficient evidence.[44]

Martha Jackman has made a parallel argument to that of Greschner. She has argued that Canadian courts, in reviewing *Charter*-based claims, can do more to hold governments accountable to patients and the public in their health care decision-making. *Charter*-based adjudication, for Jackman, can thus serve as a (better) health care 'accountability

38 Ibid, para. 56.
39 Ibid, para. 55 (emphasis added).
40 Ibid, paras. 48–62.
41 Greschner, '*Charter* Challenges', p. 50.
42 Ibid, pp. 51–52.
43 Ibid, p. 52.
44 Ibid, p. 52.

mechanism'. As part of this mechanism, she has noted, the courts can promote EBPM. Specifically, they can use the evidence presented by the parties to 'verify a government's claims that cost savings decisions are rational and evidence based – as opposed to merely reactive, speculative, or the product of stereotypes and systemic patterns of neglect in relation to the health interests and needs of disadvantaged groups'.[45]

In support of her argument, Jackman has used the Canadian Supreme Court's decision in *Eldridge*.[46] Similar to *Auton*, at issue before the court in *Eldridge* was British Columbia's refusal to fund a health care service – but this time, it was sign language interpretation services for deaf patients. The claimants once again challenged this decision under section 15 of the *Charter*. After the court concluded that the decision constituted a prima facie violation of section 15, it turned to whether the limitation of section 15 was justified under section 1 of the *Charter*. Section 1 permits 'reasonable limits' to *Charter* rights, provided they are 'prescribed by law' and 'can be demonstrably justified in a free and democratic society'. The British Columbia government justified their decision not to fund sign language interpretation services based on a concern that it would open doors to non-official language speakers to demand interpretation services. They argued that if they were compelled to provide interpreters for deaf patients, they would need to do the same for non-official language speakers, 'thereby increasing the expense of the program dramatically and placing severe strain on the fiscal sustainability of the health care system'.[47]

The government's argument, however, was 'in no way evidence-based'.[48] Illustrating Jackman's point that *Charter*-based adjudication can serve as an 'accountability mechanism' in the health care context, the court rejected the government's argument as 'purely speculative'.[49] It highlighted that the government had 'presented no evidence as to the potential scope or cost of an oral language medical interpretation program'.[50] And it reasoned that it was 'possible that the nature and extent of any reasonable accommodation required for hearing persons under [section] 1 would differ from that required for deaf persons'.[51] So, in

45 Jackman, 'Charter Review', 21.
46 *Eldridge v. British Columbia (Attorney General)* [1997] 3 SCR 624 ('*Eldridge*').
47 Ibid, para. 88.
48 Jackman, 'Charter Review', 22.
49 *Eldridge*, para. 89.
50 Ibid, para. 89.
51 Ibid, para. 89.

effect, the court in *Eldridge* required the government to justify, as evidence based, the limits it imposes on access to health care services.

I agree substantially with Greschner's and Jackman's arguments. However, my argument here departs from theirs in a few respects. First, I am advocating the incorporation of EBPM into social rights enforcement. While Greschner's and Jackman's arguments arise in the health care context, their arguments, and the cases to which they refer, do not involve social rights per se. This is because, as I noted in Chapter 5, the Canadian Constitution does not expressly protect social rights, nor have Canadian courts to date interpreted more general constitutional provisions as protecting such rights. Both *Auton* and *Eldridge* were therefore decided under section 15 as a violation of the right to equality, not as a violation of social rights. Thus, while I am advocating, in line with Greschner's and Jackman's arguments, that the courts promote EBPM from the elected branches' staff, I am doing so specifically in the context of the judicial enforcement of social rights.

Secondly, but relatedly, I think that Greschner's and Jackman's arguments can be extended beyond the health care context to include public policies and programmes pertaining to other social goods and services. While EBPM has its roots in the health care context (i.e., from evidence-based medicine),[52] it has since been advocated in, and applied to, other areas of policy-making.[53] Hence, my argument is that, as Greschner and Jackman have argued for health care, the courts can incorporate EBPM into their review of the elected branches' decisions regarding various social goods and services (i.e., pertaining to education, housing and social security, as well as health care). In this respect, my argument finds parallels with the work of Alberto Alemanno.[54] He has argued that across a range of policy areas, courts globally are moving towards the

52 Greschner, '*Charter* Challenges', p. 45.

53 See Philip Davies, 'What Is Evidence-Based Education?' (1999) 47 *British Journal of Educational Studies* 108; Joe Doherty, 'Housing: Linking Theory and Practice' in Davies, Nutley and Smith, *What Works?*; Robert E. Slavin, 'How Evidence-Based Reform Will Transform Research and Practice in Education' (2020) 55 *Educational Psychologist* 21; Robert Walker, 'Welfare Policy: Tendering for Evidence' in Davies, Nutley and Smith, *What Works?*; United Nations Economic Commission for Europe, 'Guidelines on Evidence-Based Policies and Decision-Making for Sustainable Housing and Urban Development' (2020), https://unece.org/DAM/hlm/documents/Publications/2020_Guidelines_on_evidence-based_policies.pdf, accessed 19 January 2023.

54 Alberto Alemanno, 'The Emergence of the Evidence-Based Judicial Reflex: A Response to Bar-Siman-Tov's Semiprocedural Review' (2013) 1 *The Theory and Practice of Legislation* 327.

imposition of evidence-based requirements on policy-makers which demand that they 'inter alia consult ... experts, conduct studies and collect evidence'.[55] Importantly, this move towards 'a more evidence-based approach to judicial review' is, for him, a welcome development in global jurisprudence, 'capable of promoting a broader culture of proof, evidence and rationality in policymaking'.[56] Like Alemanno, I advocate the incorporation of EBPM into judicial review across several policy areas.

Thirdly, Greschner's and Jackman's arguments (as well as Alemanno's) are rooted in principles of fairness, equity and equality. They contend that the incorporation of EBPM into judicial review is beneficial because it promotes these fundamental values. I do not disagree with them per se. That said, the basis of my argument here is the concept of trust – and more specifically the expectation of competence that partially constitutes trust in the citizen–government relationship. I have claimed in Chapter 4 that the role of the courts in social rights enforcement is to promote the trustworthiness of the elected branches with respect to social rights. Because an element of that trustworthiness is an expectation that the elected branches will exercise their control over social goods and services competently – which, I have argued, translates into an expectation that the elected branches will act in accordance with EBPM – I am suggesting that the courts, to promote the elected branches' trustworthiness, should require the elected branches to act in line with EBPM. In doing so, they make it more likely that the elected branches will act in accordance with EBPM, and more likely that they will fulfil citizens' expectation of competence.

6.2.2 How Can the Courts Incorporate EBPM into Social Rights Enforcement?

To answer this question, I will start by addressing two preliminary points. The first is that although EBPM encompasses the three forms of knowledge that I identified earlier (knowledge from scientific research, political knowledge and practical implementation knowledge), it is only the first and last – knowledge from scientific research and practical implementation knowledge – that, I suggest, courts should directly enforce through social rights enforcement. Whereas I have recognised

55 Ibid, 333.
56 Ibid, 338.

that citizens expect political actors to exercise political knowledge to reasonably consider them competent vis-à-vis social goods and services, the courts are not in a position to enforce this knowledge against political actors. As Head has explained, political knowledge is 'diffuse, highly fluid, and heavily contested owing to its partisan and adversarial context'.[57] It is effectively knowledge about how to advocate one's position, including how to consider and adjust one's strategies, how to determine priorities, how to undertake persuasion, how to communicate key messages and how to negotiate trade-offs and compromises. There is no objective basis on which a court could assess, in their adjudication of social rights, either what political knowledge demands or whether it has in fact been exercised.

I say that the courts should not 'directly' enforce political knowledge because they can still, I propose, indirectly do so. The courts can indirectly enforce political knowledge by enforcing the expectation of goodwill, particularly in terms of the elements of transparency and participation discussed in Chapter 5. By enforcing these elements, the courts make it more likely that the elected branches will make their decisions in a transparent and participatory way; and the transparency and participation that follow from this can help subject political actors to political accountability.

Secondly, we must reconcile the courts' enforcement of the two remaining knowledge forms, with established principles of administrative law. It is received wisdom that administrative decision-makers possess specialised knowledge that the courts (at least traditionally) do not.[58] This specialised knowledge serves as one, if not the primary, justification for the courts to show deference to these decision-makers' decisions when they review them. Administrative decision-makers possess, in particular, explicit knowledge and tacit knowledge.[59] Explicit knowledge refers to knowledge that follows from formal training. Because what is being regulated by governments 'is technologically complex and rapidly changing', administrative decision-makers are required to 'have high

[57] Head, 'Three Lenses of Evidence-Based Policy', 5.

[58] Paul Daly, *A Theory of Deference in Administrative Law: Basis, Application and Scope* (Cambridge: Cambridge University Press, 2012), pp. 72–73; Jeffrey Jowell, 'Judicial Deference: Servility, Civility or Institutional Capacity?' (2003) *Public Law* 592, 598; Jeff King, *Judging Social Rights* (Cambridge: Cambridge University Press, 2012), pp. 211–213, 218–219.

[59] Fisher and Shapiro, *Administrative Competence*, p. 50. See also Daly, *A Theory of Deference*, pp. 75–76.

technical skills themselves'.[60] Accordingly, experts with formal training are usually appointed into the relevant positions.[61] Tacit knowledge results from experience and engagement with specific communities and situations. It is developed over time, following from repeated exposure 'to a particular area and the legal, factual and policy issues that most often arise there'.[62]

Owing to their knowledge in this respect, administrative decision-makers' decisions are entitled to deference.[63] Hence, given this general rule of deference, we may ask: how can the courts enforce the expectation of competence – specifically the knowledge from scientific research and practical implementation knowledge that are the evidence bases of EBPM? Should the courts not defer to these decision-makers' decisions because of their expertise? Put bluntly, no. There is an important exception to the above general rule: administrative decision-makers' decisions are not entitled to deference where there has been a 'failure of expertise'.[64] Deference is not warranted where these decision-makers have not applied their expertise to the problem at hand, or where the government's position runs contrary to established scientific evidence.[65] Enforcing the expectation of competence against administrative decision-makers involves the courts, as I explain shortly, holding administrative decision-makers accountable for such failures of expertise. It has the courts require that these decision-makers apply their knowledge and act in line with established scientific evidence when making the relevant decisions – which is effectively what it means for a decision-maker to exercise the knowledge from scientific research and practical implementation knowledge that constitute EBPM. Such enforcement thus, I say, aligns with the principles of administrative law.

With those preliminary points addressed, I will consider next what incorporation of EBPM into social rights enforcement entails. For this,

60 Martin Shapiro, '"Deliberative," "Independent" *Technocracy v. Democratic Politics*: While the Globe Echo the E.U.?' (2005) 58 *Law and Contemporary Problems* 341, 342–343.

61 Daly, *A Theory of Deference*, p. 75; King, *Judging Social Rights*, p. 213.

62 Daly, *A Theory of Deference*, p. 76. See also Fisher and Shapiro, *Administrative Competence*, p. 50.

63 As for political or legislative decision-makers, they are much less likely than their administrative counterparts to possess specialised knowledge – either of the explicit or tacit form. Their claim to expertise is therefore more tenuous. They are better seen as 'a repository of knowledge about constituent preferences' rather than as 'a source of knowledge about general states of affairs': King, *Judging Social Rights*, p. 221.

64 Ibid, pp. 235, 240.

65 Ibid, pp. 235, 240.

I think we can glean insight from recent trends in judicial review globally. As I mentioned earlier, Alberto Alemanno (alongside some other legal scholars) has argued that courts across the globe are moving towards the imposition of evidence-based requirements on policy-makers.[66] This judicial trend has been described as 'evidence-based judicial review' (EBJR).[67] Its fundamental idea is 'that courts should ensure that the constitutional claims of the parties and the court's constitutional analysis have a sound evidentiary and empirical basis'.[68] Through EBJR, courts seek to avoid two common pitfalls of judicial review. They aim to not afford 'automatic and unquestioning deference to the parties' claims', which, as we saw earlier in the *Eldridge* case, may be based on unsubstantiated speculations or so-called 'junk science'.[69] And at the same time, courts seek to not substitute the parties' claims 'with their own unfounded conjectures', which include 'common-sense assumptions, intuitions and anecdotal evidence'.[70] To incorporate EBPM into their enforcement of social rights, it is my contention here that the courts engage in EBJR when reviewing the elected branches' decisions vis-à-vis social goods and services.

That said, as Ittai Bar-Siman-Tov has argued, EBJR has two versions.[71] In the first, courts themselves engage in an evidence-based decision-making process, analysing scientific evidence to assess whether policy-makers' decisions are evidence based. Courts, therefore, in this version of EBJR, review the *substance* of policy-makers' decisions, specifically for whether they are evidence based. In the second version, rather than engage in an evidence-based decision-making process themselves, courts require evidence from policy-makers that the relevant decision-making process was evidence based. For example, in determining the constitutionality of legislation, the court, under this second version, would 'look for evidence in the legislative record (or the statute itself) that the legislature followed an evidence-based decision-making process in

66 Alemanno, 'The Emergence of the Evidence-Based'. Contrary to what I have proposed for social rights enforcement, however, this trend has emerged more from 'judicial practice, through incremental, case-by-case development, than through explicit and fully-theorized judicial pronouncement in landmark cases', described as 'reflexive' by Alemanno: Bar-Siman-Tov, 'The Dual Meaning', 108–109.

67 Bar-Siman-Tov, 'The Dual Meaning', 108–109.

68 Ibid, 111.

69 Ibid, 111–112.

70 Ibid, 111–112.

71 Ibid, 112.

enacting the law'.[72] Consequently, the courts' review under this version is more procedural in nature, with the court examining the *procedure* that was followed by the policy-maker in arriving at the relevant decision.[73]

To incorporate EBPM into social rights enforcement, the courts can, in principle, use either version of EBJR. They can themselves engage in an evidence-based decision-making process and analyse the relevant evidence to assess whether the elected branches' decision (i.e., social welfare legislation or social programme) is evidence based, or, alternatively, they can demand that the elected branches provide evidence showing that their decision-making process was evidence based. I submit, however, that the courts should adopt the latter, more procedural approach.

This is for a few reasons. The first stems from the arguments from legitimacy and capacity identified in Chapter 4. As I explained there, there is good reason for us to exercise caution in our determination of how the courts should enforce social rights. We do not want to grant the courts too much power in a way that usurps the elected branches' policy-making role. It is for this reason that the trust-based framework, I argued in that chapter, is appropriate for social rights enforcement: given the procedural orientation of trust as a concept, the trust-based framework offers a good middle ground between judicial usurpation and judicial abdication. It is worth noting, in addition to the general arguments from legitimacy and capacity, that the elected branches are in a significantly better position, relative to the courts, to analyse evidence. For administrative decision-makers, this conclusion follows on from their specialised explicit and tacit knowledge, that the courts traditionally do not possess. Legislative decision-makers, granted, do not usually have such specialised knowledge. However, they do 'amass and rely upon evidence provided by other sources'.[74] And critically, they 'have institutional structures and decision-making processes that facilitate broad empirical investigation', with legislative committees having the ability to 'gather evidence, call witnesses, and initiate studies, all with the assistance of scientifically trained staff'.[75] The courts, in contrast, 'generally lack internal

[72] Ibid, 112–113.

[73] Bar-Siman-Tov has described such review as 'semiprocedural': Ittai Bar-Siman-Tov, 'Semiprocedural Judicial Review' (2012) 6 *Legisprudence* 271.

[74] King, *Judging Social Rights*, p. 221.

[75] Paul Yowell, 'Empirical Research in Rights-Based Judicial Review of Legislation' in Katja Ziegler and Peter Huber (eds.), *Current Problems in the Protection of Human Rights: Perspectives from Germany and the UK* (Oxford: Hart, 2013), pp. 167–168.

fact-finding resources'.[76] While judges 'may have law clerks and access to library staff' to assist them, they usually do not have relevant scientific training.[77] I therefore submit, in parallel to my argument regarding the trust-based framework overall, that a more procedural approach to incorporating EBPM into social rights enforcement offers a good middle ground between the two wrongs of judicial usurpation and judicial abdication. It allows the courts to confirm that the relevant decision of the elected branches is evidence based without undertaking a full analysis of the evidence themselves, the latter of which would amount to judicial usurpation. As Alemanno has argued, courts should 'be assisted by robust and comprehensible analyses enabling them to effectively discharge their duty of review'; they should not, however, 'replace policy-makers in the evaluation of complex socio-economic evaluations'.[78]

Additionally, a more procedural approach to EBJR, I contend, is more likely to promote the elected branches' trustworthiness; and in this regard, it fits much better with the trust-based framework overall. By focusing on the elected branches' decision-making process, the courts can scrutinise that process and can lay out what is required of the elected branches to fulfil citizens' expectation of competence. This, we can expect, will increase the likelihood that those who staff the elected branches, in future decisions, will engage in EBPM and, in turn, fulfil citizens' expectation of competence. If the courts were to instead engage in an evidence-based process themselves, although they ensure that the decision before them is, in actuality, evidence based, their judgment is less likely to change the future behaviour of those who staff the elected branches. Put simply, we can expect a substantive approach in this regard to have less prospective effect.

So, I suggest that to incorporate EBPM into social rights enforcement, and enforce the expectation of competence, the courts should review the elected branches' decision-making process vis-à-vis their exercise of control over social goods and services, requiring them to prove, in a given case, that their process was evidence based. For administrative decision-makers, this involves holding them accountable for their 'failures of expertise'. Assuming that these decision-makers have specialised knowledge (which administrative law usually does), the courts should demand evidence that that knowledge was applied to the relevant

[76] Ibid, p. 168.

[77] Ibid.

[78] Alemanno, 'The Emergence of the Evidence-Based', 338–339.

decision and that the decision-makers acted in line with established scientific evidence when making it. And for legislative decision-makers, the courts should examine the legislative record and statute to ensure that the decision-makers followed an evidence-based process in their enactment of the relevant legislation.

6.2.3 *Illustrations*

To expand on the above idea, and thus help explain what my proposed approach to incorporating EBPM into social rights enforcement entails, I will now consider, as I did for the expectation of goodwill in Chapter 5, a few examples from social rights cases in various jurisdictions.

Some of the best illustrations of EBJR of this sort, especially with respect to the judicial review of social welfare legislation, come from the German Constitutional Court. In fact, as Klaus Meßerschmidt has identified, the German court 'has gained an international reputation as a frontrunner of empirical review', particularly because it 'sometimes scrutinizes the quality of the information underlying a statute'.[79] In the *Hartz IV* case, for instance, which I discussed briefly in Chapter 5, the German court did precisely this.[80] The case, it will be recalled, dealt with the 'Hartz IV Act' which amended the German Code of Social Law, reforming the systems of social benefits that are available to unemployed and other needy people. Under the Act, the standard benefit available to those living in a joint household (as opposed to single adults) was reduced, calculated as a percentage of the standard benefit that was available to single adults.[81] For example, spouses, under the Act, were entitled to a standard benefit of 90 per cent of that of a single adult; children under 14 were entitled to 60 per cent; and children over 14 were entitled to 80 per cent.

[79] Klaus Meßerschmidt, 'Evidence-Based Review of Legislation in Germany' (2016) 4 *The Theory and Practice of Legislation* 209, 218, citing Susan Rose-Ackerman, Stefanie Egidy and James Fowkes, *Due Process of Lawmaking: The United States, South Africa, Germany, and the European Union* (Cambridge: Cambridge University Press, 2014), p. 19.

[80] 125 BVerfGE 172 ('*Hartz IV*').

[81] For a good summary of the case and its factual background, see Stefanie Egidy, 'Casenote – The Fundamental Right to the Guarantee of a Subsistence Minimum in the *Hartz IV* Decision of the German Federal Constitutional Court' (2011) 12 *German Law Journal* 1961; Claudia Bittner, 'Casenote – Human Dignity as a Matter of Legislative Consistency in an Ideal World: The Fundamental Right to Guarantee a Subsistence Minimum in the German Federal Constitutional Court's Judgment of 9 February 2010' (2011) 12 *German Law Journal* 1941.

The provisions that set out these benefits were referred to the German Constitutional Court. To repeat from Chapter 5, the Basic Law does not expressly protect social rights, but the Court recognised in this case the 'fundamental right to the guarantee of a subsistence minimum', derived from the Basic Law's declaration of human dignity and its principle of the social welfare state. And important for present purposes, its enforcement of this right incorporated EBPM. The court held that while the right to the guarantee of a subsistence minimum 'cannot provide any quantifiable requirements' (so as to point the courts to a specific quantity of social benefits), it does require 'a review of the basis and of the method of the assessment of benefits in terms of whether they do justice to the goal of the fundamental right'.[82] Specifically, the court stated, 'the assessment of the benefits must be clearly justifiable on the basis of reliable figures and plausible methods of calculation'.[83] The court therefore imposed an obligation on the legislature to ensure that its assessment of social benefits is evidence based, and it recognised a corresponding power of judicial review for the courts to confirm that the legislature fulfils its obligation in this respect.

Much in line with what I have proposed in this chapter, the court adopted what we can interpret as a more procedural approach to EBJR.[84] It explained that the legislature ultimately has discretion to choose a statistical model for calculating benefits, with the role of the court being to examine 'whether within [the legislature's] margin of appreciation it had selected a calculation procedure that is fundamentally suited to an assessment of the subsistence minimum', 'whether, in essence, it had completely and correctly ascertained the necessary facts', and 'whether it kept within the bounds of what is justifiable in all calculation steps with a comprehensible set of figures within this selected procedure and its structural principles'.[85] Also, as I pointed out in Chapter 5 with respect to the expectation of goodwill, the court stressed that to facilitate its review in this regard, the legislature must be transparent, as well as consistent, in its decision-making process.

Applying the above reasoning to the Hartz IV Act, the court declared the relevant provisions unconstitutional. It found that the legislature, in calculating the standard benefits available under these provisions, had

[82] *Hartz IV*, para. 142.
[83] Ibid, para. 142.
[84] For further support of this conclusion, see Bar-Siman-Tov, 'The Dual Meaning'.
[85] *Hartz IV*, para. 143.

relied on, rather than empirical research, what it referred to as '"random" estimates'.[86] For example, in certain divisions (e.g., clothing and shoes, furnishings, communication, and leisure, entertainment and culture), the legislature had made deductions for specific goods and services (e.g., camping furniture and works of art) even though it had no evidence of whether the lowest quintile of households actually spent money on these goods and services.[87] The court concluded that in doing so, the legislature had 'made a "random" estimate of a share of expenditure allegedly not serving to secure the subsistence minimum, and [had] deducted it, without an adequate basis in fact'.[88] The court similarly found that the legislature's calculation of children's standard benefits as a percentage of single adults lacked empirical basis. It observed that '[c]hildren are not small adults' and accordingly, their needs vis-à-vis a subsistence minimum that complies with human dignity 'must be orientated in line with child development phases and towards what is necessary for the development of a child's personality'.[89] The court found that the legislature had 'omitted to carry out any investigation of this', with the calculated deduction of 40 per cent ultimately being 'set freely with no empirical and methodical basis'.[90]

In the subsequent *Asylum Seekers Benefits* case, the German Constitutional Court followed a parallel approach.[91] This time the legislation at issue was the Asylum Seekers Benefits Act which provides for social benefits available to asylum seekers and certain other foreign nationals. The benefits provided for under the Act had not been updated since 1993 (when the legislation was introduced) and following on from this, were considerably lower than those available to other needy people under the Hartz IV Act. The German court, relying on the fundamental right to the guarantee of a subsistence minimum, likewise declared the challenged provisions unconstitutional. Adopting the EBJR approach that it laid out in the *Hartz IV* case, the court explained that the benefits provided for under the Act must be 'justifiable, based on reliable data and plausible methods of calculation'.[92] While the court again recognised that the legislature had discretion to choose a method for calculating benefits,

[86] Ibid, paras. 171, 175.
[87] Ibid, para. 175.
[88] Ibid, para. 175.
[89] Ibid, para. 191.
[90] Ibid, para. 191.
[91] 132 BVerfGE 134 ('*Asylum Seekers Benefits*').
[92] Ibid, para. 79.

it stressed that '[i]f different methods are applied to different specific groups of individuals', as it was here, it must 'be justifiable by facts'.[93] And of particular relevance to the legislation in this case, it noted that the legislature was obligated 'to update amounts of benefits . . . in light of the actual costs of living, to cover the actual need'.[94]

The court found that the relevant provisions of the Asylum Seekers Benefits Act did not satisfy these requirements.[95] As I have already identified, the benefits had not been updated since 1993, even though the cost of living in Germany had risen by more than 30 per cent since then.[96] Also, the court found that the amount of benefits under the Act were 'not based on reliable data' – neither when it was introduced in 1993 nor at the time of the case in 2012. Based on its examination of the relevant legislative materials, it concluded that the legislature had instead 'used a mere estimate of costs at the time' which did not meet the requirements under the Basic Law.[97] The Act was also based on a set of presumptions that those covered by it only stay in Germany for a short period of time and that this short period of residence justified a limited amount of benefits. However, neither presumption, the court explained, had an 'adequately reliable basis'.[98]

Another illustration of EBJR along these lines is the South African Constitutional Court's *TAC* judgment.[99] It will be recalled that at issue in the case was a public health programme that restricted the availability of the antiretroviral drug nevirapine to limited research and training sites in South Africa. Nevirapine was used specifically to reduce the transmission of HIV from mothers to children during pregnancy. The HIV/AIDS activist organisation, the Treatment Action Campaign ('TAC'), together with other members of civil society, challenged the government's programme – specifically its restricting the availability of nevirapine to the relevant research and training sites – as a violation of, principally, sections 27 and 28(1)(c) of the South African Constitution. Section 27 (1) guarantees 'the right to have access to . . . health care services' and section 27(2) obliges the state to 'take reasonable legislative and other

93 Ibid, para. 71.
94 Ibid, para. 79.
95 Ibid, para. 80.
96 Ibid, paras. 82–83.
97 Ibid, paras. 90–91.
98 Ibid, para. 92.
99 *Minister of Health and Others v. Treatment Action Campaign and Others* [2002] ZACC 15 ('*TAC*').

measures, within its available resources, to achieve the progressive realisation' of that right. As the government's programme necessarily affected the babies of pregnant women living with HIV, it also engaged section 28(1)(c) which guarantees every child 'the right ... to basic nutrition, shelter, basic health care services and social services'. The TAC sought a declaration that the programme was unconstitutional under both provisions. It also requested that the government be ordered to make nevirapine available to pregnant women living with HIV who gave birth in public health facilities (as well as their new-born babies) and that the government both plan and implement in a reasonable manner an effective national programme for the prevention of mother-to-children transmission of HIV.[100]

The South African government justified its programme – again, specifically its decision to confine nevirapine's administration to limited research and training sites – on several grounds, including concerns about the drug's efficacy and safety. The court, however, rejected these arguments; and in doing so, incorporated EBPM into its enforcement of sections 27 and 28(1)(c). With respect to the drug's efficacy, the government argued that it was necessary to administer the drug as part of a 'full package', which included milk substitutes because HIV was transmitted from mother to child through breastmilk; so, if the infants were not given milk substitutes, the benefits of nevirapine would have been negated. For this reason, nevirapine could only be administered, it was argued, at the relevant sites where the 'full package' could be provided. The court found, however, based on its review of the evidence, that this argument was not supported by the data on which the government relied. It concluded that 'the wealth of scientific material produced by both sides makes plain that sero-conversion of HIV takes place in some, but not all, cases and that nevirapine thus remains to some extent efficacious in combating mother-to-child transmission even if the mother breastfeeds her baby'.[101] Likewise, regarding the drug's safety, the court found that there was no evidence to support the government's concerns. It explained that '[a]ccording to the [then-] current medical consensus, there [was] no reason to fear any harm from this particular administration of nevirapine'.[102] It highlighted that the drug's use was 'recommended without qualification for this purpose by the World Health

[100] Ibid, paras. 294–295.
[101] Ibid, para. 58.
[102] Ibid, para. 60.

Organization' and that there was 'cogent South African endorsement of the safety of nevirapine', including by the Medicines Control Council.[103]

The jurisprudence of UK courts regarding the rationing of medical treatment in the National Health Service (NHS) offers another illustration of the sort of procedural EBJR that I propose.[104] As Daniel Wang has documented, UK courts, relying on various grounds of judicial review, have scrutinised NHS rationing decisions, both for procedural fairness (illustrating the expectation of goodwill from Chapter 5) and for the evidence used to make those decisions (illustrating the expectation of competence here).[105] The *A, D and G* case illustrates the latter.[106] In the case, the Court of Appeal challenged a local health authority's refusal to fund gender reassignment surgery on the basis that the authority's scientific assessment had not engaged with existing evidence that the surgery was an effective treatment for gender identity dysphoria. Under the National Health Service Act 1977 (in combination with relevant regulations), the local health authority had a duty to provide 'to such extent as [it] considers necessary to meet all reasonable requirements . . . such . . . services as are required for the diagnosis and treatment of illness'. Until 1995, the authority had funded gender reassignment surgery where a local consultant psychiatrist recommended it as necessary. But in 1995, the authority adopted a policy that allocated a low priority for public funding of procedures that it considered clinically ineffective – and gender reassignment surgery, which was classified as falling in the lowest 10 per cent under the policy in terms of effectiveness/priority, would not be funded 'except in cases of overriding clinical need'.

The Court of Appeal quashed the health authority's decision not to fund the surgery, along with the policy on which it was based, and remitted the matter to the authority for reconsideration. Both Lord Justice Auld and Lord Justice Buxton, in their respective judgments, incorporated EBPM along the lines of a more procedural approach to EBJR. Lord Justice Auld reasoned that while it was not the judiciary's

[103] Ibid, paras. 60–61.

[104] To repeat from Chapter 5, owing to the various steps that UK courts have taken to protect social welfare (steps that courts in jurisdictions with constitutional social rights could also take or parallel), I think that UK cases offer a good source to illustrate the workings of a trust-based social rights enforcement framework.

[105] Daniel Wei L. Wang, 'From Wednesbury Unreasonableness to Accountability for Reasonableness' (2017) 76 *Cambridge Law Journal* 642.

[106] *R v. North West Lancashire Health Authority, ex parte A, D and G* [1999] EWCA Civ 2022, [2000] 1 WLR 977 ('*A, D and G*').

place 'to express opinions as to the likelihood of the effectiveness of medical treatment' (which would represent a more substantive approach to EBJR), the health authority's refusal to engage with the evidence, and its follow-on conclusion that there was no effective treatment for gender identity dysphoria, made a 'nonsense' of its policy not to fund low-priority treatments 'except in cases of overriding clinical need'.[107] The policy, he said, effectively amounted to 'the operation of a "blanket policy" against funding treatment for the condition [gender identity dysphoria] because it [the health authority] does not believe in such treatment'.[108] In his concurring judgment, Lord Justice Buxton similarly explained that where there is 'a strong and respectable body of medical opinion' that considers a treatment to be effective and suitable (as was the case with gender reassignment surgery), it is 'not open to a rational health authority simply to determine that a procedure has no proven clinical benefit while giving no indication of why it considers that that is so'.[109] Consequently, Lord Justice Buxton concluded, the health authority's refusal to engage with this medical evidence rendered its rationing decision irrational.

It is worth noting that the UK's case law in this area has had an impact on decision-making in the NHS; and in this respect, it supports my claim that the courts, via the incorporation of EBPM into their enforcement of social rights, can increase the likelihood of the elected branches making their relevant decisions in line with EBPM and, in turn, fulfilling citizens' expectation of competence. Wang has explained that UK courts, through their rulings, have 'established a continuous policy dialogue with decision-makers in the NHS that [has] contributed to [making] rationing explicit "about why and how"'.[110] Health authorities have become increasingly aware that their rationing decisions are more visible and are more likely to be scrutinised – inside and outside the courtroom.[111] The courts have also made clear what these health authorities need to do to comply with the law: their decisions must be, among other things, based on a 'rigorous assessment of the evidence'.[112] And this has led, Wang has noted, to EBPM initiatives in the NHS, including 'greater

[107] Ibid, 993, citing *R v. Cambridge Health Authority* [1995] EWCA Civ 49, [1995] WLR 898, 905.
[108] Ibid, 994.
[109] Ibid, 997–998.
[110] Wang, 'From Wednesbury Unreasonableness', 658.
[111] Ibid, 660–661.
[112] Ibid, 661–662.

involvement of external advisors, the establishment of scientific committees to provide better scientific evidence, and attempts to apply an explicit priority-setting framework with clear and standardized criteria against which services and treatments [can] be assessed.'[113] Therefore, ultimately, UK courts' rulings in this area have promoted the adoption of EBPM by NHS staff in their rationing decisions which, based on my definition of the expectation of competence from earlier in the chapter, has promoted that staff's fulfilment of citizens' expectation of competence.

One final illustration of EBJR of this sort (although less pronounced than in the other examples so far) comes from the Latvian Constitutional Court. In its *Disbursement Law* judgment, the court reviewed a new statute (the 'Disbursement Law') that introduced cuts to old age and service pensions in the period from 2009 to 2012.[114] The cuts were a response to the rapidly declining economy of Latvia in 2009 given the financial crisis.[115] The Law was challenged as a violation of, among other provisions, Article 109 of the Latvian Constitution that guarantees everyone 'the right to social security in old age, for work disability, for unemployment and in other cases as provided by law', with restriction of the right permissible if that restriction is established by law, is justified by a legitimate end and conforms to the principle of proportionality.[116]

The court found the Disbursement Law to be unconstitutional. It held, first, that the Law restricted the right to social security and, secondly, that while the relevant cuts were established by law (the Disbursement Law) and were justified by a legitimate end (to secure the sustainability of Latvia's social insurance system), they did not conform to the principle of proportionality.[117] Accordingly, the restriction of the right was not permissible. The court said that the elected branches had failed specifically to carry out an objective and balanced analysis regarding both 'the consequences of the adoption of the impugned provisions' as well as 'other, less restrictive means' that they could have implemented to attain

[113] Ibid, 661.

[114] Case No. 2009-43-01 ('*Disbursement Law*').

[115] Ineta Ziemele, Alla Spale and Laila Jurcēna, 'The Constitutional Court of the Republic of Latvia' in Armin von Bogdandy, Peter M. Huber and Christoph Grabenwarter (eds.), *The Max Planck Handbooks in European Public Law*, Vol. 3 (Oxford: Oxford University Press, 2020), p. 519.

[116] *Disbursement Law*, para. 26.

[117] Sandra Liebenberg, 'Participatory Justice in Social Rights Adjudication' (2018) 18 *Human Rights Law Review* 623, 647.

the end sought.[118] And important for present purposes, the court relied on several factors – many of which speak to the how evidence based the Disbursement Law was – to reach this conclusion. The court highlighted, for example, that 'no consultations with experts' had taken place (based on its review of an annotation of a draft of the Law).[119] It also noted that whereas propositions alternative to the adoption of the impugned provisions, including reducing the expenditures of ministries and increasing the mandatory social insurance contribution rate, had been 'uttered', they had not been 'reviewed' by the legislature (based on its review of the transcripts of the debates concerning the Law).[120] In parallel to the German court in the *Hartz IV* case, the Latvian court therefore examined the legislative record to assess the extent to which the Disbursement Law (specifically the relevant cuts) were evidence based. And its lacking in this respect was a key factor in the court's conclusion on proportionality.

To sum up, I have presented the above cases to illustrate how the courts can enforce the expectation of competence under the trust-based framework. In each case, the courts have incorporated EBPM into their enforcement of social rights, adopting a procedural approach to incorporation: they have confirmed that the relevant government actors followed an evidence-based decision-making process, rather than undertaking a full evidence-based analysis themselves.

[118] *Disbursement Law*, para. 30.2.2.
[119] Ibid, para. 30.2.2.
[120] Ibid, para. 30.2.2.

7

The Expectation of Fiduciary Responsibility

In Chapters 2 and 4, I sought to make out a case for why the citizen–government relationship is accurately characterised as a fiduciary relationship. It will be recalled that characterising the citizen–government relationship as such means, based on the work of sociologist Bernard Barber, that trust in that relationship encompasses, in addition to expectations of goodwill and competence, an expectation of fiduciary responsibility. In this chapter, I elaborate on this expectation of fiduciary responsibility. In line with Chapters 5 and 6, I detail what the expectation of fiduciary responsibility entails vis-à-vis the elected branches of government and their exercise of control over social goods and services, and following this, I address how the courts can enforce it in their social rights cases.

7.1 Defining the Scope of the Expectation of Fiduciary Responsibility

From Chapter 2, we know that in the citizen–government relationship, the expectation of fiduciary responsibility is, at least generally, an expectation that the elected branches will fulfil their fiduciary obligation to citizens vis-à-vis social goods and services. But what is the content of this obligation?

Because the expectation of fiduciary responsibility stems from Barber's work, the starting point to answer this question should be his understanding of a fiduciary's obligation to the truster or beneficiary. For Barber, it will be recalled from Chapter 2, the obligation of the fiduciary under this expectation is 'to demonstrate a special concern for others' interests above their own'.[1] This obligation follows on from the fiduciary's expertise which hinders the truster's/beneficiary's ability to

[1] Bernard Barber, *The Logic and Limits of Trust* (New Brunswick, NJ: Rutgers University Press, 1983), p. 14.

monitor the truster's/beneficiary's technical competence (for the purpose of the expectation of competence). The fiduciary's expertise affords them power that they can abuse in exercising it. So, in Barber's words, '[t]rust of this kind [fiduciary responsibility] ... is a social mechanism that makes possible the effective and just use of the power that knowledge and position give and forestalls abuses of that power'.[2] The fiduciary, therefore, according to Barber, has a moral obligation not to abuse the power that their expertise affords them, by furthering their interests over the interests of their beneficiary.

To expand on this understanding for the purpose of applying it to the citizen–government relationship, we can also draw on the legal literature – both on fiduciary political theory and private fiduciary law. This literature is relevant, I contend, because whereas I am referring to the idea of fiduciary responsibility in a sociological sense, as arising out of Barber's work, I do so for the purpose of developing a legal framework for social rights enforcement. Because the legal literature has examined the idea of fiduciary responsibility for legal purposes, including its enforcement by the courts, it is, I submit, a valuable source to consider when defining this expectation in the citizen–government relationship. That said, I repeat that in drawing on the private law literature, I do not adopt a 'literalist' approach, but rather use it to help illuminate this public law context.[3]

In the legal literature, writers disagree on the precise nature of a fiduciary's obligation to their beneficiary. Writers fall along a spectrum regarding the breadth of the obligation. On one end, fiduciary relationships are said to give rise to various duties on the part of the fiduciary, including a duty of loyalty, a duty of care, a duty of good faith and a duty to act for proper purposes.[4] As I noted in Chapter 4, the aim of fiduciary law, it has frequently been argued, is to promote the fiduciary's trustworthiness and in turn to promote trust in the fiduciary relationship. The fiduciary obligation, under this broader understanding, is thus 'defined by whatever rules are required in order to maintain the integrity of the particular relationship'.[5] And so, if we adopt this sort of broader

[2] Ibid, pp. 15–16.

[3] Evan Fox-Decent, 'Challenges to Public Fiduciary Theory: An Assessment' in D. Gordon Smith and Andrew S. Gold (eds.), *Research Handbook on Fiduciary Law* (Cheltenham: Edward Elgar, 2018).

[4] See P.D. Finn, *Fiduciary Obligations* (North Ryde: The Law Book Company, 1977).

[5] Robert Flannigan, 'The Fiduciary Obligation' (1989) 9 *Oxford Journal of Legal Studies* 285, 310–311.

understanding of the fiduciary's obligation to their beneficiary, the expectation of fiduciary responsibility in the citizen–government relationship is an expectation that the elected branches, in exercising their control over social goods and services, will fulfil this collection of duties – that is, whatever duties are required from the elected branches to promote their trustworthiness.

On the other end of the spectrum, legal writers have argued that while these various duties may be owed by a fiduciary to their beneficiary, they are not all 'fiduciary' in nature. According to these writers, there is a distinction to be drawn between 'the duties that fiduciaries owe but which are not owed by non-fiduciaries' and the 'duties that can be owed by fiduciaries and non-fiduciaries alike'.[6] The former set of duties are called 'peculiarly' or 'uniquely' fiduciary, because non-fiduciaries do not owe them.[7] Specifically, it is the duty of loyalty that is said to be peculiarly or uniquely fiduciary.[8] I will elaborate on the duty of loyalty shortly. But for now, it suffices to say that if we adopt a narrower understanding of the fiduciary obligation, the expectation of fiduciary responsibility in the citizen–government relationship is an expectation that the elected branches, in exercising their control over social goods and services, will fulfil their duty of loyalty to citizens.

For my purpose, I define the fiduciary obligation, and therefore the expectation of fiduciary responsibility in the citizen–government relationship, in the latter, narrower terms. But in doing so, I should highlight, I do not take a position on the above debate. I define the fiduciary obligation in this way for reasons specific to the argument I advance in this book. First, as I have said, I am referring to fiduciary responsibility in a sociological sense, arising out of Barber's work. Barber's understanding of fiduciary responsibility, as I discuss shortly, aligns far more closely with the narrower definition from the legal literature, than it does with the broader definition.

[6] Matthew Conaglen, 'The Nature and Function of Fiduciary Loyalty' (2005) 121 *Law Quarterly Review* 452, 455.

[7] Ibid, 456–457. See also Matthew Conaglen, *Fiduciary Loyalty: Protecting the Due Performance of Non-Fiduciary Duties* (Oxford: Hart, 2010); R.C. Nolan, 'Controlling Fiduciary Power' (2009) 68 *Cambridge Law Journal* 293, 315.

[8] Conaglen, 'The Nature and Function', 459–460; Andrew S. Gold, 'Purposive Loyalty' (2017) 74 *Washington and Lee Law Review* 881, 884; Paul B. Miller, 'Justifying Fiduciary Duties' (2013) 58 *McGill Law Journal* 969, 977; Nolan, 'Controlling Fiduciary Power', 312, 315.

Secondly, defining the fiduciary obligation in narrower terms makes sense in the context of the trust-based framework overall. The framework that I am developing represents a collection of duties on the elected branches that promote their trustworthiness vis-à-vis social goods and services. The duties beyond the duty of loyalty that are included in the broader understanding of fiduciary responsibility, are thus redundant in the framework, captured already by the other two expectations of trust outlined in Chapters 5 and 6 (goodwill and competence). For example, the fiduciary duty of care, which necessitates that the fiduciary exercise a requisite degree of technical competence when fulfilling their fiduciary obligation to the beneficiary, is, I suggest, captured by trust's expectation of competence. Similarly, the duties of good faith and proper purposes, which require, among other things, transparency and adequate consideration of the beneficiary's wishes, are captured by trust's expectation of goodwill. The expectation of fiduciary responsibility, accordingly, covers what remains and uniquely applies to fiduciary relationships. After all, as I explained in Chapter 2, the expectation of fiduciary responsibility does not apply to all trust relationships, but only to those trust relationships that are accurately characterised as fiduciary.

Finally, though there is disagreement among legal writers on whether the duties of care, good faith and proper purposes are properly included in the scope of the fiduciary obligation, there is broad agreement that the duty of loyalty is fundamental to the fiduciary relationship and the fiduciary's obligation to their beneficiary.[9] As Paul Miller has explained, '[w]hatever else fiduciary law might require of fiduciaries, it undeniably demands that they act faithfully toward beneficiaries. The duty of loyalty applies to all fiduciaries regardless of differences among the mandates under which they act'.[10] In this way, the duty of loyalty represents the 'core' of the fiduciary's obligation.[11] This conclusion likewise applies to fiduciary relationships that arise in the public law context.[12]

Given this definition of the fiduciary obligation as a duty of loyalty, we may next ask: what does the duty of loyalty require of the elected

[9] Miller, 'Justifying Fiduciary Duties', 976. See also Andrew S. Gold, 'The Loyalties of Fiduciary Law' in Andrew S. Gold and Paul B. Miller (eds.), *Philosophical Foundations of Fiduciary Law* (Oxford: Oxford University Press, 2014), p. 176.

[10] Miller, 'Justifying Fiduciary Duties', 976–977.

[11] Ibid, 976–977. See also Gold, 'The Loyalties of Fiduciary', p. 176.

[12] Stephen R. Galoob and Ethan J. Leib, 'The Core of Fiduciary Political Theory' in D.G. Smith and Andrew S. Gold (eds.), *Research Handbook on Fiduciary Law* (Cheltenham: Edward Elgar, 2018), p. 402.

branches in the citizen–government relationship?[13] To answer this, we must give content to the duty of loyalty. However, legal writers, as was the case with the fiduciary obligation more broadly, disagree on what precisely the duty of loyalty requires, ranging from very narrow understandings to very broad or expansive ones.[14] To define the duty of loyalty in the context of the citizen–government relationship, I will again use Evan Fox-Decent's influential account as a starting point.[15] In defining the duty of loyalty in the relationship between the state and its subjects, Fox-Decent has argued that the 'fundamental fiduciary obligation is not loyalty *per se*, but rather a duty to act exclusively in accordance with the other-regarding purposes for which fiduciary power is held or conferred.'[16] Therefore, for Fox-Decent, the duty of loyalty is a duty on the fiduciary to maintain an 'other-regarding posture' when they exercise their powers.[17]

Fox-Decent has extrapolated from this fundamental duty broader duties of reasonableness and fairness.[18] For my purpose, however, I will adopt a more restricted understanding of what this duty to maintain an other-regarding posture means for a public authority. This is not because I disagree with Fox-Decent per se but because my purpose in drawing on fiduciary principles is different than his. Whereas his objective is largely to justify these broader duties on public authorities, mine is to understand what it means for the elected branches to fulfil citizens' trust-based expectation of fiduciary responsibility.[19] Given this difference in purpose, the duties of reasonableness and fairness that Fox-Decent has extrapolated from the duty to maintain an other-regarding posture – much like the duties beyond loyalty in the broader understanding of fiduciary

[13] As Andrew Gold has noted, '[f]iduciary loyalty has different content and scope across fiduciary relationships, reflecting the characteristic features of each fiduciary relationship type': Andrew S. Gold, 'The Fiduciary Duty of Loyalty' in Evan J. Criddle, Paul B. Miller and Robert H. Sitkoff (eds.), *The Oxford Handbook of Fiduciary Law* (Oxford: Oxford University Press, 2019), p. 386.

[14] See Lindsay Breach, '*Fiducia* in Public Law' (2017) 48 *Victoria University of Wellington Review* 413, 436; Gold, 'The Loyalties of Fiduciary'; Paul B. Miller, 'Dimensions of Fiduciary Loyalty' in Smith and Gold, *Research Handbook on Fiduciary*.

[15] Evan Fox-Decent, *Sovereignty's Promise: The State as Fiduciary* (Oxford: Oxford University Press, 2011).

[16] Ibid, p. 167.

[17] Laura S. Underkuffler, 'Fiduciary Theory: The Missing Piece for Positive Rights' in Smith and Gold, *Research Handbook on Fiduciary*, p. 111.

[18] Fox-Decent, *Sovereignty's Promise*.

[19] Ibid, p. 26.

responsibility – are redundant in the framework, captured by the other two expectations of trust.

Applied to the citizen–government relationship, I propose that in this relationship the elected branches' duty of loyalty to citizens is a duty to maintain an other-regarding posture when exercising their control over social goods and services. It obliges the elected branches to exercise that control, and the power that follows on from it, exclusively in the interests of citizens. They must not exercise that control and power in furtherance of their own personal interests. This approach to the duty of loyalty not only aligns with Fox-Decent's influential account in the public law context, but also accords with Barber's understanding of fiduciary responsibility. As we know, according to Barber, the fiduciary's obligation to their beneficiary is 'to demonstrate a special concern for others' interests above their own'.[20] By maintaining an other-regarding posture, exercising their control and power exclusively in citizens' interests, the elected branches, I suggest, do precisely that: they demonstrate 'a special concern' for citizens' interests 'above their own'.

With that broad conclusion drawn, two points of clarification are warranted. First, I am not claiming here that the elected branches of government per se have personal interests. Rather, I am claiming that the actors who staff the elected branches have such interests. As I noted in Chapter 2, when making political decisions, it is in bureaucrats' interests to maximise budgets and power, and in politicians' interests to maximise votes.[21] Aside from such professional interests, however, these actors may additionally have interests that are even more personal in nature. They may have pecuniary interests (e.g., having a financial stake in a relevant political decision) or non-pecuniary interests (e.g., having a personal relationship with a relevant stakeholder). It is thus possible for those who staff the elected branches to exercise their control over social goods and services in furtherance of these personal interests. The expectation of fiduciary responsibility is an expectation that these actors will not exercise their control, and corresponding power, in this way.[22]

[20] Barber, *The Logic and Limits*, p. 14.

[21] Margaret Levi, 'A State of Trust' in Valerie Braithwaite and Margaret Levi (eds.), *Trust and Governance* (New York: Russell Sage Foundation, 1998), p. 95.

[22] My understanding of fiduciary responsibility and its duty of loyalty is in line with the 'no conflict' and 'no profit' rules from the legal literature which are often considered the core of the duty of loyalty: see Gold, 'The Fiduciary Duty of Loyalty', pp. 385, 387; Galoob and Leib, 'The Core of Fiduciary Political Theory', pp. 403–404; Matthew Harding, 'Fiduciary Relationships, Fiduciary Law, and Trust' in Smith and Gold, *Research Handbook on*

Secondly, in more traditional, private law fiduciary relationships, the fiduciary usually has one beneficiary (or a discrete class of beneficiaries) whose interests they must pursue. Some legal writers have thus included in their definition of the duty of loyalty a prohibition on 'the fiduciary from acting under conflicting mandates'.[23] In a political relationship like the citizen–government relationship, however, the fiduciary (e.g., the elected branches) has multiple beneficiaries (e.g., different citizens) whose interests are bound to conflict with one another, at least in some cases.[24] The fiduciary must therefore pursue and balance multiple, often competing, interests. This makes a prohibition on public authorities from acting under conflicting mandates 'impossible to meet'.[25]

Owing to such conflicts of interest, there will inevitably be circumstances in which the interests of an elected branches' staff member align with the interests of one subset of citizens while conflicting with those of another. For instance, as we know, the interests of poor and marginalised citizens – specifically, their interests in a strong welfare state that regulates commerce and involves redistributive tax spending – usually run contrary to the interests of the wealthy.[26] And because the wealthy often have significant political power, with politicians having an interest in being re-elected, the interests of politicians will, we can expect, align with those of the wealthy and conflict with those of the poor and marginalised. In these cases of conflict, the expectation of fiduciary responsibility, I submit, is an expectation that the elected branches' staff members will not, as a means of furthering their personal interests, unfairly discount or disregard the interests of any subset of citizens with which those personal interests conflict (e.g., those of the poor and marginalised). That said, a staff member's decision to further one subset of citizens' interests over

Fiduciary, pp. 61–62, 64. And in the public law literature, my understanding of the fiduciary's obligation finds parallels in the work of Robert Flannigan who has defined the fiduciary duty in terms of 'opportunism': see Robert Flannigan, 'Fiduciary Control of Political Corruption' (2002) 26 *Advocates' Quarterly* 252; Robert Flannigan, 'Contesting Public Service Fiduciary Accountability' (2016) 36 *University of Queensland Law Journal* 7; Robert Flannigan, 'Fiduciary Accountability for Public Service Opportunism' (2018) *Public Law* 241. See also Robert Natelson's understanding of loyalty as 'the fiduciary's obligation to subordinate his own interests to the welfare of the beneficiaries': Robert G. Natelson, 'The Constitution and the Public Trust' (2004) 52 *Buffalo Law Review* 1078, 1089.

[23] See Miller, 'Justifying Fiduciary Duties', 977.

[24] Breach, '*Fiducia* in Public Law', 439–440; Fox-Decent, *Sovereignty's Promise*, p. 34.

[25] Gold, 'The Loyalties of Fiduciary', pp. 182–183.

[26] Jeff King, *Judging Social Rights* (Cambridge: Cambridge University Press, 2012), p. 157.

those of another will not per se breach their fiduciary obligation to the latter. Decisions of this sort are an inevitable part of political decision-making.[27] Decision-makers must have discretion to set priorities. Accordingly, the expectation of fiduciary responsibility cannot be an expectation that one set of interests will always be furthered over another set. It is, rather, an expectation that the elected branches' staff will seriously consider the interests of all citizens, even though they may not necessarily agree with, or ultimately act to further, some of those interests. We can thus describe the fiduciary duty of loyalty, as Laura Underkuffler has, as a duty on the elected branches' staff to 'engage in a serious reckoning' with citizens' interests – both collective and individual.[28]

7.2 Fiduciary Responsibility as Non-corruption

Given the above definition, the expectation of fiduciary responsibility, I claim, can be distilled into an expectation that the elected branches' staff, in exercising their control over social goods and services, will not engage in corruption. It is, put very simply, an expectation of non-corruption.

This may seem like an overly narrow position to take, and a low bar for fiduciary responsibility. I do not think that this is true, however, if we keep two things in mind. First, we must remember that the expectation of fiduciary responsibility is one of three expectations that constitute trust. The expectations of goodwill and competence, as I have already highlighted, cover aspects of the citizen–government relationship that we may associate with the elected branches' obligations as fiduciary to citizens. Thus, the expectation of fiduciary responsibility does not need to be as all-encompassing as one might expect. Secondly, we can define corruption in broad terms. It is important to recognise that corruption 'is a complex and varied phenomenon' that 'eludes easy definition'.[29] While public corruption (i.e., corruption by public authorities) is conventionally defined as 'the abuse of public office for private gain', writers have

[27] Flannigan, 'Contesting Public Service Fiduciary Accountability', 21.

[28] Laura S. Underkuffler, 'Property, Sovereignty, and the Public Trust' (2017) 18 *Theoretical Inquiries in Law* 329, 346.

[29] Charles M. Fombad, 'Corruption and the Crisis of Constitutionalism in Africa' in Charles M. Fombad and Nico Steyler (eds.), *Corruption and Constitutionalism in Africa* (Oxford: Oxford University Press, 2020), p. 17; Dan Hough, *Corruption, Anti-corruption and Governance* (London: Palgrave MacMillan, 2013), pp. 2–3.

expanded on this conventional definition, describing corruption in terms that closely align, albeit inversely, with the above understanding of fiduciary responsibility.[30] For instance, John Warburton has defined corruption as 'the actions of government officials, whether elected or appointed, who use power, in the form of the authority vested in them on behalf of "the public", to promote their own interests over that of the public'.[31] As he has said, government officials, whose 'duty is to promote the interest of the public', have conferred on them owing to their position, 'authority and control over government-allocated resources'.[32] When they use that authority and control to serve their own interests, according to Warburton, they engage in corruption.[33] It will be recalled from Chapter 2 that the elected branches hold power over citizens owing to the control and discretion that they exercise vis-à-vis the social goods and services that citizens need. Where the elected branches' staff use that power to further their personal interests, they – under this definition – engage in corruption. At the same time, corruption, under this definition, is the antithesis of the staff's fiduciary obligation to citizens – that is, to refrain from exercising their control over social goods and services in furtherance of their personal interests. Consequently, if we adopt a broad definition of corruption like that proposed by Warburton, the expectation of fiduciary responsibility can, I submit, be accurately viewed as an expectation that the elected branches' staff will not engage in corruption.

We can find support for the idea that the expectation of fiduciary responsibility is one of non-corruption in the work of Barber himself. Applying the expectation to political relationships, Barber equated public corruption with untrustworthiness – specifically in terms of, or as a breach of, the expectation of fiduciary responsibility. He explained that in a democracy, 'political elites may be incompetent, corrupt, or untrustworthy in both respects'.[34] Because incompetence (the first aspect of

[30] Sung Hui Kim, 'Fiduciary Law and Corruption' in Criddle, Miller and Sitkoff, *The Oxford Handbook*, p. 814.

[31] John Warburton, 'Corruption as a Social Process: From Dyads to Networks' in Peter Larmour and Nick Wolanin (eds.), *Corruption and Anti-corruption* (Canberra: Australian National University Press, 2013), p. 224. See also Sung Hui Kim's work which expands upon the idea of 'private gain', using the more expansive term 'self-regarding gain': Kim, 'Fiduciary Law and Corruption', p. 817.

[32] John Warburton, 'Corruption, Power and the Public Interest' (1998) 17 *Business & Professional Ethics Journal* 79, 82.

[33] Ibid, 84.

[34] Barber, *The Logic and Limits*, p. 93.

political untrustworthiness identified by Barber) is a breach of the expectation of competence, it stands to reason that for Barber, corruption (the second aspect identified) was a breach of the other expectation of trust that he discussed in his work – fiduciary responsibility.[35]

Moreover, empirical research offers us good reason to factor corruption into our definition of trust and, in turn, our trust-based framework. Researchers have consistently established a link between citizens' perceptions of public corruption and their trust in government actors.[36] So, if one of our aims in adopting a trust-based framework is to promote citizens' trust in the elected branches (as I said in Chapter 4), then given this link, corruption should be part of the framework.

Public corruption, of course, assumes various forms.[37] A corrupt practice from those who staff the elected branches vis-à-vis their exercise of control over social goods and services includes 'bribery, embezzlement, patronage, nepotism and cronyism, influence-peddling, kickbacks, electoral fraud, and unholy alliances'.[38] It also occurs at different levels, ranging from 'grand' corruption, occurring at a 'high or prominent institutional level . . . where policies and rules are formulated' to so-called 'petty' corruption, occurring as 'small-scale, everyday corruption that takes place at the implementation end of policy formulation'.[39] No matter the form that this public corruption assumes, contrary to the fiduciary responsibility owed to citizens, as I have detailed it, the personal interests of one or more individuals who staff the elected branches are furthered.

[35] Additionally, Sung Hui Kim has argued that the 'no conflict' and 'no profit' rules – that are arguably the core of the fiduciary duty of loyalty and in line with my understanding of fiduciary responsibility in the citizen–government relationship – reflect an 'anti-corruption norm': Kim, 'Fiduciary Law and Corruption'. See also Sung Hui Kim, 'Fiduciary Law's Anti-corruption Norm' in Smith and Gold, *Research Handbook on Fiduciary*.

[36] See Christopher J. Anderson and Yuliya V. Tverdova, 'Corruption, Political Allegiances, and Attitudes toward Government in Contemporary Democracies' (2003) 47 *American Journal of Political Science* 91; Eric C.C. Chang and Yun-Han Chu, 'Corruption and Trust: Exceptionalism in Asian Democracies?' (2006) 68 *The Journal of Politics* 269; Michell A. Seligson, 'The Impact of Corruption on Regime Legitimacy: A Comparative Study of Four Latin American Countries' (2002) 64 *The Journal of Politics* 408.

[37] Fombad, 'Corruption and the Crisis', p. 17.

[38] Ibid, p. 17.

[39] Ibid, pp. 17–18. See also Patricia J. Garcia, 'Corruption in Global Health: The Open Secret' (2019) 394 *The Lancet* 2119, 2120; Sharifah Sekalala, Haleema Masud and Rebekah Thomas Bosco, 'Human Rights Mechanisms for Anti-corruption, Transparency and Accountability: Enabling the Right to Health' (2020) 13 *Global Health Action* 1, 1.

At the same time, citizens' interests are harmed – albeit, again, in different ways. First, government officials may divert public resources away from the social goods and services that are the subject of social rights towards other public ends that further their own interests. For example, 'bribe-seeking government officials may channel government spending away from the promotion of education and health, towards expenditures . . . such as unnecessary projects or military equipment.'[40] Or even worse, these officials may divert those funds into their own pockets. Citizens' interests are harmed, of course, because less funds are available for the state-delivered social programmes that grant citizens access to the social goods and services that they need.[41] In these instances, as Anne Peters has correctly described, 'the financing of the standard of living of high-level public officials is given priority over the realization of social human rights'.[42]

In other cases, while government officials may invest funds into social programmes, they may, in furtherance of their own interests, use those funds in an inefficient manner. In particular, the provision of social goods and services to citizens usually generates 'large public contracts which . . . create opportunities for corruption'.[43] Through the public procurement tender process, so-called 'tenderpreneurs' can make large sums of money from national, provincial or municipal contracts.[44] Problematically, these tenderpreneurs frequently pay bribes to win these contracts or have close associations with high-ranking government

[40] Cecily Rose, 'The Limitations of a Human Rights Approach to Corruption' (2016) 65 *International and Comparative Law Quarterly* 405, 433.

[41] Caroline Omari Lichuma, 'Economic Wrongs and Social Rights: Analyzing the Impact of Systemic Corruption on Realization of Economic and Social Rights in Kenya and the Potential Redress Offered by the Optional Protocol to the International Covenant on Economic, Social and Cultural Rights' (2018) 5 *Transnational Law Review* 63, 80.

[42] Anne Peters, 'Corruption as a Violation of International Human Rights' (2018) 29 *European Journal of International Law* 1251, 1263.

[43] International Council on Human Rights Policy, *Corruption and Human Rights: Making the Connection* (2009), https://assets.publishing.service.gov.uk/media/57a08b6540f0b64974000b10/humanrights-corruption.pdf, accessed 20 January 2023, 45. See also Zaid Al-Ali and Michael Dafel, 'Egyptian Constitutional Reform and the Fight against Corruption' (2013), www.constitutionaltransitions.org/wp-content/uploads/2017/05/1_Al-Ali_Dafel_Egypt_Corruption.pdf, accessed 20 January 2023, 7; Susan Rose-Ackerman, *Corruption and Government: Causes, Consequences, and Reform* (Cambridge: Cambridge University Press, 2010), p. 93.

[44] Fombad, 'Corruption and the Crisis', p. 27. See also John C. Mubangizi and Prenisha Sewpersadh, 'A Human Rights-Based Approach to Combating Public Procurement Corruption in Africa' (2017) 10 *African Journal of Legal Studies* 66.

officials, thereby biasing the tender process and leading governments to award contracts to bids that are less competitive and less beneficial to their citizens.[45] The companies that are awarded the contracts are often 'paid inflated amounts and lack the requisite experience, expertise, and equipment to deliver quality of services'.[46] As well, it is very often the case that the contracts awarded to these companies, in the end, go unfulfilled.[47]

An example is the 'Limpopo Textbook Crisis' in South Africa. In 2010, the Department of Education for the province of Limpopo awarded a contract to a company called EduSolutions for the procurement of delivery of learner-teacher support materials, including textbooks.[48] Several allegations of corruption were made.[49] They included: that in awarding the tender, the procedures set out in the applicable statute (the Public Management Finance Act) were not followed; that members of the Bid Adjudication Committee were unduly influenced; and that when attempts were made by the Committee to cancel the award, senior officials overrode the attempts.[50] Also, there was speculation in the media that EduSolutions had been favoured because of its close links with government officials, including the Director General.[51] This contract was not in the interests of South Africans. For instance, the contract, which was worth 343 million South African Rand, was almost triple the budget for the 2011–2012 academic year. And even with the inflated amount paid to EduSolutions, there were significant shortfalls in the delivery of textbooks to schools.[52]

Corruption in the public procurement tender process was especially pronounced during the COVID-19 pandemic. Corruption and

[45] In certain jurisdictions (e.g., some African countries), public procurement for social goods and services are not managed through tender processes at all: Fombad, 'Corruption and the Crisis', p. 27.

[46] Ibid, p. 28.

[47] Ibid, p. 28.

[48] For a good summary, see Faranaaz Veriava, 'The Limpopo Textbook Litigation: A Case Study into the Possibilities of a Transformative Constitution' (2016) 32 *South African Journal on Human Rights* 321.

[49] Section 27, 'The 2012 Limpopo Textbook Crisis: A Study in Rights-Based Advocacy, the Raising of Rights Consciousness and Governance' (September 2013), www.section27.org.za/wp-content/uploads/2013/10/The-2012-Limpopo-Textbook-Crisis1.pdf, accessed 20 January 2023, 32.

[50] Ibid, 32.

[51] Ibid, 32.

[52] Ibid, 11. See also Veriava, 'The Limpopo Textbook Litigation', 325.

emergencies like the pandemic 'feed off each other, creating a vicious cycle of mismanagement and deeper crisis.'[53] In early 2020, for example, the UK Government awarded contracts for personal protective equipment (PPE) to various companies in response to COVID-19. Many of these contracts, however, were highly suspect. A study by Transparency International UK found that 65 contracts, worth GBP 2.9 billion, merited further investigation.[54] And 24 of them, worth GBP 1.6 billion, 'went to those with known political connections to the party of government in Westminster'.[55] Additionally, in a recent application for judicial review, the process adopted by the Government in awarding many of these contracts was challenged as unlawful.[56] For instance, whereas most suppliers were directed to make offers through an online survey, the Government also operated a high priority lane (or 'VIP Lane') with a dedicated priority email address that was reserved for referrals from Members of Parliament, ministers and senior officials.[57] Because the VIP Lane team had more resources, and so was able to respond to offers on the same day that they arrived (in contrast to the team that handled the offers through the online survey), suppliers in the VIP Lane received earlier consideration.[58] This, Mrs. Justice O'Farrell concluded in her judgment, 'was a material advantage in obtaining the award of a contract given the urgency of the procurement' in light of global health conditions and the race for securing PPE.[59] Again, these contracts were against the interests of most people in the UK. Many of the masks and other PPE supplied under the contracts, for example, were not suitable for use in the UK National Health Service (NHS), wasting valuable public resources.[60]

[53] Jon Vrushi and Roberto Martínez B. Kukutschka, 'Why Fighting Corruption Matters in Times of COVID-19, Corruption Perceptions Index 2020: Research Analysis' (28 January 2021) Transparency International, www.transparency.org/en/news/cpi-2020-research-analysis-why-fighting-corruption-matters-in-times-of-covid-19, accessed 21 January 2023.

[54] Transparency International, 'Track and Trace: Identifying Corruption Risks in UK Public Procurement for the COVID-19 Pandemic' (2021), www.transparency.org.uk/sites/default/files/pdf/publications/Track%20and%20Trace%20-%20Transparency%20International%20UK.pdf, accessed 21 January 2023, 5.

[55] Ibid.

[56] *R (on the application of Good Law Project Ltd. and EveryDoctor) v. Secretary of State for Health and Social Care* [2022] EWHC 46 (TCC) ('*Good Law Project 2*').

[57] Ibid, paras. 58, 372–373.

[58] Ibid, paras. 395, 397.

[59] Ibid, para. 397.

[60] Ibid, paras. 115, 138, 486. Similar allegations have been made in other jurisdictions, including Kenya: see Emmanuel Igunza, 'Coronavirus Corruption in Kenya: Officials and

Citizens' interests may also be harmed in a more indirect manner. A prime example is the reduction of foreign investment and aid. Corruption 'creates unpredictability for investors and acts like a random tax'.[61] Charles Fombad has made this argument in the context of corruption in Africa. As he has put it, 'corruption makes doing business an inefficient and costly undertaking; it also makes legal outcomes unpredictable. This combination of factors means that investing in Africa is a very risky proposition.'[62] At the same time, it makes other jurisdictions rethink their foreign aid. For instance, the health and education sectors in Kenya have long been marred by public corruption.[63] In 2012, it was revealed that millions of shillings in medical claims had been paid by the National Hospital Insurance Fund to 'phantom' hospitals.[64] Owing to these corrupt practices, the US government in 2017 suspended USD 21 million in direct aid to Kenya's Ministry of Health. In justifying their action, the US Embassy released a statement indicating that they had taken 'this step because of ongoing concern about reports of corruption and weak accounting procedures at the Ministry'.[65] Likewise, the free primary education programme in Kenya has seen the misappropriation and embezzlement of its funds.[66] Owing to large-scale theft by high-ranking public officials, with such officials diverting funds intended for schools to private bank accounts, donors including the UK Government have demanded refunds of their contributions.[67] Such reductions in foreign investment and aid harm citizens' interests because they constrain the resources available to the state to provide citizens the social

Businesspeople Targeted' (24 September 2020) *BBC*, www.bbc.co.uk/news/world-africa-54278417, accessed 21 January 2023.

61 Rose, 'The Limitations of a Human Rights', 434.

62 Fombad, 'Corruption and the Crisis', pp. 28–29.

63 Lichuma, 'Economic Wrongs and Social Rights'.

64 James Macharia, 'Kenya Minister Urged to Resign over Medical Scam' (8 May 2012) *Reuters*, www.reuters.com/article/ozatp-kenya-corruption-20120508-idAFJOE84709Z20120508, accessed 21 January 2023.

65 Katharine Houreld, 'U.S. Suspends Aid to Kenyan Health Ministry over Corruption Concerns' (9 May 2017), *Reuters*, www.reuters.com/article/us-kenya-health-corruption-idUSKBN1851RY, accessed 21 January 2023.

66 Lichuma, 'Economic Wrongs and Social Rights', 81. Further, a 2015 report by the Ethics and Anti-corruption Commission revealed massive fraud in the procurement of school supplies.

67 Katy Migiro, 'Donors Want Their Money Back in Kenyan Education Scam' (11 June 2011) *Thomson Reuters Foundation News*, https://news.trust.org/item/20110617115200-fytp5, accessed 21 January 2023.

goods and services that they need. They cut off a pool of funds that would otherwise be available, limiting the state to domestic funds.

Another way in which citizens' interests may be indirectly harmed is 'the "brain drain" that occurs from corrupt societies because of endemic corruption'.[68] Studies have found a correlation between higher levels of corruption and increased motivation for migration.[69] This correlation has been documented in many parts of the world, including Eastern Europe, Latin America, the Middle East and Africa.[70] Migration is especially likely for the highly skilled workers who are necessary for a state to offer its citizens quality social goods and services, like physicians, nurses and teachers.[71] Where 'corruption and nepotism are perceived to undermine meritocracy, it is a plausible reaction to turn towards opportunities elsewhere, especially among the highly-skilled.'[72] Compounding this effect, public corruption can also affect tax rates 'which may in turn push those affected to leave the country in search of more favourable economic conditions'.[73]

Even when public corruption is 'petty', it can have a significant detrimental impact on citizens' interests. In the context of global health, for example, Patricia Garcia, the former Minister of Health of Peru, has noted that 'individual acts of corruption at the level of the day-to-day interactions of patients with health services and providers can look small in scale, but they represent millions of negative interactions and have an enormous and damaging effect on our efforts to improve health.'[74] One common form of petty corruption that harms citizens' interests is informal payments demanded by service providers, including physicians, nurses and teachers, for their services.[75] With this form of corruption, 'citizens are subjected to paying bribes . . . in order to access that which is lawfully their right, for example, access to public healthcare and public

[68] Bo Rothstein and Aiysha Varraich, *Making Sense of Corruption* (Oxford: Oxford University Press, 2017), p. 61.

[69] For a summary, see Transparency International, 'Literature Review: Corruption as a Driver of Migration' (22 December 2015), https://knowledgehub.transparency.org/assets/uploads/helpdesk/Literature_review_corruption_and_migrations.pdf, accessed 21 January 2023.

[70] Ibid.

[71] Ibid. See also Arusha Cooray and Friedrich Schneider, 'Does Corruption Promote Emigration? An Empirical Examination' (2016) 29 *Journal of Population Economics* 293.

[72] Transparency International, 'Literature Review', 2.

[73] Ibid, 4.

[74] Garcia, 'Corruption in Global Health', 2121.

[75] Transparency International, 'Literature Review', 5.

education.'[76] This form of corruption represents to some extent a knock-on effect of the other forms of corruption owing to the relevant personnel not being paid or being underpaid for their services.[77] Such demands for informal payments are especially prevalent in the education sector as teachers, principals and admission officers usually have considerable autonomy and discretion.[78] The demands can take many forms, including bribes to ensure access to education or allow transition to higher levels of education, the sale of academic credentials and so-called 'shadow education' where teachers demand that their students take private lessons as a condition for passing an exam.[79] Petty corruption of this form is also common in the health sector. Health care workers may charge patients more than official prices and pocket the difference, refer patients to their private practice or deliberately damage equipment in the public sector to force patients to pay for private services.[80] Again, the COVID-19 pandemic exacerbated these problems.[81] Moreover, because these corrupt practices are systemic, they have 'become normalised in society and are considered to be just the way things work'.[82] As a result, the practices can prevent or delay patients, especially low-income patients, from seeking the medical assistance that they need.

Another form of petty corruption that harms citizens' interests is 'absenteeism' from relevant staff. It refers to situations where 'public employees choose to engage in private pursuits during their working hours, either pursuing private business interests or enjoying unauthorised leisure time at public expense'.[83] In the health sector, absence rates vary widely across countries with rates as high as 35 per cent in

[76] Rothstein and Varraich, *Making Sense of Corruption*, p. 61.

[77] Kolawole Olaniyan, *Corruption and Human Rights Law in Africa* (Oxford: Hart, 2014), p. 255.

[78] Ibid, 61. See also Mihaylo Milovanovitch, 'Fighting Corruption in Education: A Call for Sector Integrity Standards' (2013) 5 *World Bank Law Review* 367, 368.

[79] Milovanovitch, 'Fighting Corruption in Education', 379, 375.

[80] Garcia, 'Corruption in Global Health', 2121.

[81] Dunja Mijatović, 'Corruption Undermines Human Rights and the Rule of Law' (19 January 2021) Council of Europe, www.coe.int/en/web/commissioner/-/corruption-undermines-human-rights-and-the-rule-of-law, accessed 21 January 2023.

[82] Garcia, 'Corruption in Global Health', 2121.

[83] Transparency International, 'The Ignored Pandemic: How Corruption in Healthcare Service Delivery Threatens Universal Health Coverage' (March 2019), www.transparency.org.uk/publications/ignored-pandemic, accessed 21 January 2023. For a discussion of absenteeism in education, see Milovanovitch, 'Fighting Corruption in Education'.

Bangladesh, 40 per cent in India and Peru,[84] and 48 per cent in Uganda.[85] Such high rates have adversely affected both the quantity and quality of health care services.[86] In Uganda, for instance, high absenteeism among physicians has been associated with delays in the provision of care, and adverse patient outcomes for new mothers and neonates.[87]

7.3 Enforcing the Expectation of Fiduciary Responsibility

Because the expectation of fiduciary responsibility is an expectation of non-corruption, enforcing the expectation requires the courts, in social rights cases, to curb corruption from those who staff the elected branches – specifically in the staff's exercise of control over social goods and services.

I will detail in a moment steps that the courts can take in this regard. First, however, I note that with respect to this expectation, the trust-based framework aligns with a growing literature recognising a link between corruption and human rights.[88] This literature claims that '[t]o overlook corruption in human rights work is to . . . ignore many of the dynamics and processes that are at the root of human rights violations'.[89] Corruption is viewed as a 'pandemic' that has detrimental effects on human rights, especially social rights.[90] Courts in various jurisdictions have also recognised this corruption-human rights link. The South African Constitutional Court, for instance, has noted that '[e]ndemic corruption threatens the injunction that government must be accountable, responsive and open', it being 'incontestable that corruption

[84] Angela N. Kisakye et al., 'Regulatory Mechanisms for Absenteeism in the Health Sector: A Systemic Review of Strategies and Their Implementation' (2016) 8 *Journal of Healthcare Leadership* 81.

[85] Raymond Tweheyo et al., '"Nobody Is after You; It Is Your Initiative to Start Work": A Qualitative Study of Health Workforce Absenteeism in Rural Uganda' (2017) 2 *BMJ Global Health* 1, 1, cited in Transparency International, 'Literature Review', 6.

[86] Transparency International, 'Literature Review', 7.

[87] Louise Ackers, Elena Ioannou and James Ackers-Johnson, 'The Impact of Delays on Maternal and Neonatal Outcomes in Ugandan Public Health Facilities: The Role of Absenteeism' (2016) 31 *Health Policy and Planning* 1152.

[88] See Peters, 'Corruption as a Violation'; C. Raj Kumar, *Corruption and Human Rights in India: Comparative Perspectives on Transparency and Good Governance* (Oxford: Oxford University Press, 2011).

[89] Marten Koch Andersen, 'Why Corruption Matters in Human Rights' (2018) 10 *Journal of Human Rights Practice* 179, 185.

[90] See Peters, 'Corruption as a Violation', 1252.

undermines the rights in the [South African] Bill of Rights, and imperils democracy'.[91] The Indian Supreme Court has likewise highlighted that '[c]orruption ... undermines human rights, indirectly violating them'.[92]

In light of this link, legal writers have advocated a 'human rights-based' approach to corruption.[93] They have advanced arguments grounded in, among other things: suggestions that corruption undermines the rule of law; that corruption violates international human rights treaties (e.g., the International Covenant on Economic, Social and Cultural Rights); and that human rights law has benefits over criminal law in addressing corruption (including that a human-rights-based approach 'creates a type of social, political, and moral response that is not generated by crime',[94] focuses on victims as opposed to individual perpetrators, 'empowers' victims, as well as civil society and domestic judges, and shifts attention away from repression towards prevention).[95]

I do not adopt a human-rights-based approach to corruption per se. This is not because I disagree with this work but because my consideration of public corruption has different roots. I argue that because corruption from the elected branches' staff breaches their expectation of fiduciary responsibility to citizens – which breaches citizens' trust in them – the courts, in enforcing social rights, should aim to curb corruption from this staff in their exercise of control over social goods and services. By doing so, the courts increase the likelihood that the elected branches will fulfil citizens' trust in them, thereby promoting their trustworthiness. At the same time, I do not mean to suggest that the courts' enforcement of social rights is, or should be, the primary means of tackling public corruption. As a complex problem, corruption necessitates a multi-pronged strategy to combat it.[96] This consists of a legal framework that draws on multiple areas of law, including criminal law,

91 *Glenister v. President of the Republic of South Africa and Others* [2011] ZACC 6, paras. 176–177.

92 *State of Maharashtra through CBI, Anti Corruption Branch, Mumbat v. Balakrishna Dattatrya Kumbhar* [2012] 9 SCR 601, para. 14. See also *Vineet Narain and Others v. Union of India and Another*, (1998) 1 SCC 226: 'It cannot be doubted that there is a *serious human rights aspect* involved in such a proceeding because the prevailing corruption in public life, if permitted to continue unchecked, has ultimately the deleterious effect of eroding the Indian polity'.

93 Peters, 'Corruption as a Violation', 1252. In some cases, scholars have advocated a right to a 'corruption-free' society: see Kumar, *Corruption and Human Rights.*

94 Kumar, *Corruption and Human Rights*, p. 43.

95 Peters, 'Corruption as a Violation', 1276–1277.

96 Kumar, *Corruption and Human Rights*, p. 172.

administrative law and professional codes of conduct.[97] I am accordingly advocating that the courts' enforcement of social rights is one part of this multi-pronged strategy, particularly when the corruption at issue concerns the social goods and services that citizens need.

So, what does it mean for the courts, in social rights cases, to curb corruption from the elected branches' staff? As Fombad has said, 'no constitutional design, however comprehensive and entrenched, could eliminate corruption'.[98] We cannot therefore expect the courts to eliminate altogether corrupt practices from the elected branches staff in exercising their control over social goods and services. What they can do, however, is 'reduce its incidence'.[99] That is, they can decrease the likelihood that the relevant personnel, in fulfilling their roles, will engage in corrupt practices.

And how do the courts do this? For starters, their enforcement of the expectations of goodwill and competence should help reduce the incidence of corruption. For example, it is well recognised that a 'crucial element in the fight against corruption is piercing the veil of secrecy around the financial dealings of politicians and officials'.[100] As some have colourfully noted, 'sunlight is the best of disinfectants'.[101] For this reason, enforcing the expectation of goodwill, with its constituent element of transparency (as I detailed in Chapter 5), should contribute to the courts' curbing of public corruption. With the transparency that follows from this enforcement, corrupt acts are more likely to come to the surface and become subject to political and legal accountability.

One example is the recent judicial review application brought by a not-for-profit campaign organisation, the Good Law Project, in relation to

[97] Jonathan Klaaren, 'Social Grant Payments and Regulatory Responses to Corruption in South Africa' in Fombad and Steyler, *Corruption and Constitutionalism*, p. 106.

[98] Fombad, 'Corruption and the Crisis', p. 39.

[99] Ibid, p. 39.

[100] Nico Steyler, 'Towards Understanding and Combating the Crime of Corruption in Africa' in Fombad and Steyler, *Corruption and Constitutionalism*, p. 490. See also Fombad, 'Corruption and the Crisis', p. 41. For relevant discussion in the Latin American context, see Benjamin N. Gedan and Santiago Canton, 'Radical Transparency: The Last Hope for Fighting Corruption in Latin America' (1 April 2022), https://gjia.georgetown.edu/2022/04/01/radical-transparency-the-last-hope-for-fighting-corruption-in-latin-america%EF%BF%BC/, accessed 8 April 2023.

[101] Robert D. Anderson, Alison Jones and William E. Kovacic, 'Preventing Corruption, Supplier Collusion, and the Corrosion of Civic Trust: A Procompetitive Program to Improve the Effectiveness and Legitimacy of Public Procurement' (2019) 26 *George Mason Law Review* 1233, 1236.

the UK Government's procurement of COVID-19 PPE.[102] In this case, which arose out of the procurement contracts described earlier, the UK High Court held that the Government had acted unlawfully in failing to comply with its Transparency Policy vis-à-vis the contracts it had awarded. The court said that the Government had failed specifically to publish the contracts, thereby rendering them not publicly available. In his judgment, Mr. Justice Chamberlain noted that because the Secretary of State had 'spent vast quantities of public money on pandemic-related procurement during 2020', the public 'was entitled to see who this money was going to, what it was being spent on and how the relevant contracts were awarded'.[103] He stressed that transparency was important 'so that oversight bodies such as the [National Audit Office], as well as Parliament and the public, could scrutinise and ask questions about this expenditure',[104] reasoning that transparency 'builds public trust and public confidence in public services', because without it, people 'start to harbour suspicions of improper conduct'.[105]

Transparency is especially important in the area of public procurement. The OECD, for instance, has identified transparency as central to combatting corruption in the public procurement process.[106] Transparency 'not only promotes accountability and ensures access to information' but it 'serves an important role in levelling the playing field for businesses and allowing small and medium enterprises to participate on a more equal footing'.[107] In fact, recent empirical work has shown that 'horizontal transparency' (i.e., transparency that offers information primarily to the parties who are involved in the bidding process), is especially valuable to preventing corruption.[108]

While enforcing the expectations of goodwill and competence should help to combat corruption (along the lines that I have just described), there are additional steps that the courts can take to reduce the incidence

[102] *R (on the application of Good Law Project Ltd.) v. Secretary of State for Health and Social Care* [2021] EWHC 346 (Admin) ('*Good Law Project 1*').

[103] Ibid, para. 40.

[104] Ibid, para. 40.

[105] Ibid, para. 40.

[106] Organisation for Economic Co-operation and Development (OECD), 'Preventing Corruption in Public Procurement' (2016), www.oecd.org/gov/ethics/Corruption-Public-Procurement-Brochure.pdf, accessed 21 January 2023, 15.

[107] Ibid, 15.

[108] Monika Bauhr et al., 'Lights on the Shadows of Public Procurement: Transparency as an Antidote to Corruption' (2020) 33 *Governance* 495.

of corruption, and in turn enforce the expectation of fiduciary responsibility. These steps should have as their main objective to make corruption 'too risky and unrewarding an endeavour in which to engage'.[109] Because without 'fear of penalty or sanctions, there is nothing to deter [those who wield power from] fraudulently enriching themselves'.[110] Whether a government actor engages in corruption depends on both the motivational forces or incentives that they have to so engage, and the inhibitory forces that are at play: where the motivational forces or incentives are high and the inhibitory forces are low, corruption is likely.[111]

In the rest of this chapter, I consider a few steps that the courts can take in social rights cases to augment the inhibitory forces at play in the citizen–government relationship. Before I do so, two points are worth noting. First, owing to their secretive nature, many forms of corruption are difficult to unearth. And in those instances where they are unearthed, they are difficult to prove. Citizens usually do not have access to the information necessary to substantiate an allegation of corruption, leaving the courts poorly placed to make 'definitive factual findings in relation to corruption, a crime of the shadows and hard to prove at the best of times'.[112] In addition, because corruption is a criminal offence with heavy sanctions attached to it, courts are generally reluctant to make findings of corruption without a criminal trial. Therefore, in most social rights cases, despite allegations of corruption being made, courts do not make a finding of public corruption.

Secondly, a growing number of constitutions globally, particularly those introduced in the last decade, include express anti-corruption provisions.[113] At the beginning of 2021, 74 countries had some form of express anti-corruption provision.[114] These provisions are in addition to

[109] Fombad, 'Corruption and the Crisis', p. 39.

[110] Migai Akech, 'Abuse of Power and Corruption in Kenya: Will the New Constitution Enhance Government Accountability' (2011) 18 *Indiana Journal of Global Legal Studies* 341, 343, citing N.G. Egbue, 'Africa: Cultural Dimensions of Corruption and Possibilities for Change' (2006) 12 *Journal of Social Sciences* 83, 84.

[111] Warburton, 'Corruption, Power and the Public', 230.

[112] Max Du Plessis and Andreas Coutsoudis, 'Considering Corruption through the AllPay Lens: On the Limits of Judicial Review, Strengthening Accountability, and the Long Arm of the Law' (2016) 133 *South African Law Journal* 755, 787.

[113] Kunain Rahman, 'Anti-corruption Measures in Constitutions' (2021) Transparency International, https://knowledgehub.transparency.org/helpdesk/anti-corruption-measures-in-constitutions, accessed 21 January 2023.

[114] Ibid, 5.

provisions that implicitly support anti-corruption efforts like those that uphold the rule of law, protect the separation of powers, guarantee an independent judiciary and require transparency in various decision-making processes. Among other things, the express provisions establish mechanisms that ensure the integrity and accountability of public officials, form institutions whose responsibility it is to monitor and investigate corruption, and make acting with integrity a fundamental duty of all citizens.[115] An example is the Constitution of Uganda which includes as one of its national objectives that '[a]ll lawful measures shall be taken to expose, combat and eradicate corruption and abuse or misuse of power by those holding political and other public offices'.[116]

Provisions of this sort have two consequences that are relevant to my analysis in this book. The first is that although courts have traditionally not made findings of public corruption in social rights cases – and may, in fact, be reluctant to address corruption at all in this type of case – the above constitutional provisions, that expressly tackle corruption, help to reinforce the courts in their enforcement of the expectation of fiduciary responsibility. In particular, the courts can use the provisions to bolster their justifications for taking the steps outlined in the following sections.

The second consequence relates to the judiciary's trustworthiness. I noted at the outset of this book that my analysis assumes, to some extent, that citizens can, and do, trust the courts. This, I think, is not an unreasonable assumption in light of the research that establishes the judiciary as the most trusted branch of the state. That said, the trustworthiness of the courts is not a given. And if judicial trustworthiness is an issue, as I have said, we must find ways to address this problem (rather than conclude that social rights are non-justiciable). Relevant to judicial trustworthiness, corruption is often prevalent in the judiciary itself.[117] So, the inclusion of anti-corruption provisions in a constitution (e.g., provisions that form institutions responsible for monitoring and investigating corruption) may, in addition to reinforcing the courts in their enforcement of this expectation, help combat corruption in the courts themselves and promote their trustworthiness.

[115] Ibid, 4–5.

[116] Constitution of Uganda, Objective XXVI.

[117] See Siri Gloppen, 'Courts, Corruption and Judicial Independence' in Tina Søreide and Aled Williams (eds.), *Corruption, Grabbing and Development* (Cheltenham: Edward Elgar, 2013).

7.3.1 *Greater Probing into the State's Financial Resources*

One key step that the courts can take to reduce the incidence of corruption in the elected branches' exercise of control over social goods and services is to undertake a more probing examination of the state's financial resources. This step is especially important where government actors rely upon a lack of resources as a defence for their failure to provide citizens with a social good or service. A characteristic feature of social rights provisions, it will be recalled, is their internal limitation based on available resources. The state, I repeat, cannot provide something beyond its physical and financial means. However, this internal limitation has the potential to serve as a protective shield for various forms of public corruption. For example, it enables government actors who have diverted funds away from social goods and services – either into their own pockets or into unnecessary projects for their own benefit – to claim that they do not have the resources available to provide citizens with a relevant social good or service. In the health sector, for instance, it is estimated that 10–25 per cent of global spending on health services is lost directly through corruption, amounting to hundreds of billions of US dollars per year.[118] Owing to the risk of corruption, it is therefore crucial that the courts not take government actors simply at their word.[119]

In some jurisdictions, the courts are expressly authorised under their constitution to engage in an examination of this sort. Article 20(5a) of the Kenyan Constitution, for example, provides that in applying its social rights under Article 43, 'if the State claims that it does not have the resources to implement the right', the courts shall be guided by the principle that 'it is the responsibility of the State to show that the resources are not available'. This provision, as some have suggested, empowers the courts to clamp down on public corruption.[120] 'For if the state has to prove that the resources are not available to it, then this

[118] Garcia, 'Corruption in Global Health', 2120. Transparency International cites a lower, but still concerning, statistic of 7 per cent: Transparency International, 'Literature Review', 2.

[119] On the relevance of government budgets to corruption, see Office of the United Nations High Commissioner for Human Rights, 'Realizing Human Rights through Government Budgets' (2017), www.ohchr.org/sites/default/files/Documents/Publications/RealizingHRThroughGovernmentBudgets.pdf, accessed 21 January 2023.

[120] Annika Engelbert and Markus Kaltenborn, 'Corruption and Social Rights Accountability' (2019) Institute of Development Research and Development Policy Working Paper No. 213, www.econstor.eu/handle/10419/202093, accessed 21 January 2023, 18.

obligation probably also includes that the state must justify *why* it lacks these resources'.[121] And the courts, in their social rights judgments, can, among other things, urge government actors to enforce their anti-corruption policy (if any), remind them of their obligation to remedy deficiencies in the policy and suggest options as to how they can prevent the state from losing financial resources owing to structural deficiencies. Thus, the courts can use such provisions to probe, curbing corruption from the elected branches' staff.

However, even where such express constitutional language is not present, courts in various jurisdictions have still probed into the state's resources where a lack of resources has been used by government actors as a defence. Accordingly, I suggest that the courts can, regardless of whether they have express language on which to rely, engage in this kind of probing. An example is the South African Constitutional Court's judgment in *Blue Moonlight.*[122] The issue in the case was whether the City of Johannesburg was obliged to make temporary housing available for individuals rendered homeless after being evicted by private landowners for unlawfully occupying their land. As I noted in earlier chapters, the South African Constitution protects social rights predominantly under sections 26–29. The evictees anchored their case in section 26 which provides that '[e]veryone has the right to have access to adequate housing' and requires the state to 'take reasonable legislative and other measures, within its available resources, to achieve the progressive realisation of [the] right'. The City argued that it was not obliged to provide accommodation in these circumstances. But in the alternative (i.e., should it have such an obligation), it said that it was not able to do so because it lacked the resources.[123] The court disagreed with the City on both counts. Despite the South African Constitution not containing an express provision placing the responsibility on the state to substantiate a lack of resources claim, the court still engaged in a careful review of the budget evidence and concluded that insufficient information was provided by the City to support its lack of resources argument.[124] Although

[121] Ibid, 18.

[122] *City of Johannesburg Metropolitan Municipality v. Blue Moonlight Properties 39 (Pty) Ltd. and Others* [2011] ZACC 33 ('*Blue Moonlight*').

[123] Ibid, para. 72.

[124] Sandra Liebenberg, 'Direct Constitutional Protection of Economic, Social and Cultural Rights in South Africa' in Danwood Mzikenge Chirwa and Lilian Chenwi (eds.), *The Protection of Economic, Social and Cultural Rights in Africa: International, Regional and National Perspectives* (Cambridge: Cambridge University Press, 2016), pp. 318–319.

the record showed that the City had been operating in a financial surplus for the previous year, the City submitted that it was not obligated to go beyond its available budgeted resources, arguing that '[r]esources not budgeted for are not available'.[125] The court rejected this line of reasoning. It stated that its 'determination of the reasonableness of measures within available resources [under section 26] cannot be restricted by budgetary and other decisions that may well have resulted from a mistaken understanding of constitutional or statutory obligations'.[126] The court explained that 'it is not good enough for the City to state that it has not budgeted for something, if it should indeed have planned and budgeted for it in the fulfilment of its obligations'.[127] Consequently, the court upheld the lower court's finding that the City had failed to show that it was incapable of meeting the needs of the evictees.[128]

Though *Blue Moonlight* did not involve allegations of corruption, the court's judgment – empowering the courts to probe into state resources vis-à-vis its realisation of social rights – is an important precedent that can aid, and in fact has aided, South African courts in curbing corruption. The court ultimately recognised 'an implicit duty on government to budget effectively'.[129] This duty impedes government actors from hiding any corrupt practices in which they may be involved behind bald assertions that they lack the resources to provide citizens with a social good or service.

As an illustration, let us consider the Supreme Court of Appeal's judgment in *Basic Education for All*.[130] The case arose out of the Limpopo Textbook Crisis. Given the shortfalls in the delivery of textbooks to schools – against the backdrop of corruption allegations – the High Court, on an application brought by the public interest law centre Section 27, terminated the contract between the Limpopo Department of Education ('LDoE') and EduSolutions on the basis that it was irregular.[131] It also declared the LDoE's failure to provide textbooks to schools a violation of the right to basic education, ordering the LDoE to provide

125 *Blue Moonlight*, para. 72.

126 Ibid, para. 74.

127 Ibid, para. 74.

128 Ibid, para. 75.

129 Veriava, 'The Limpopo Textbook Litigation', 340.

130 *Minister of Basic Education and Others v. Basic Education for All and Others* [2015] ZASCA 198 ('*Basic Education for All*').

131 Veriava, 'The Limpopo Textbook Litigation', 325.

textbooks to the relevant grades 'on an urgent basis'.[132] On appeal, the Department of Basic Education ('DBE') justified its failure to deliver textbooks based on budgetary constraints. It stated that while it required 768 million South African Rand (ZAR), only ZAR 480 million had been made available to the LDoE by the National Treasury.[133] It also argued that for the court to order the provision of textbooks in the face of budgetary constraints would violate the separation of powers. The Supreme Court of Appeal wholly rejected the DBE's line of reasoning. In parallel with the Constitutional Court's approach in *Blue Moonlight*, the court examined the state's resources and found that the 'DBE's reliance on budgetary constraints and its complaint that the order granted by the court below violated the doctrine of the separation of powers [was] fallacious and appear[ed] contrived'.[134] Recognising an implicit duty to budget effectively, it held that 'the DBE's management plan was inadequate and its logistical ability woeful', noting 'that there [was] no single statement anywhere in the affidavits filed on [behalf of the DBE] to the effect that it would be unable to procure the funds necessary to meet the shortfall either at provincial or national level'.[135] The court therefore concluded that 'the reliance by the DBE on budgetary constraints [could] rightly be discounted'.[136]

The Constitutional Court of Uganda has followed a similar approach to that of South Africa. In the *Centre for Health, Human Rights and Development* case, for instance, the court examined the state's financial resources in enforcing its constitutional right to health.[137] Unlike the South African and Kenyan Constitutions, in Uganda's Constitution, social rights, including the right to health, are protected primarily as national objectives and directive principles of state policy.[138] The rights are thus not directly justiciable. Objective XIV requires the state 'to fulfill

[132] *Section 27 and Others v. Minister of Education and Another* [2012] 3 All SA 579 (GNP), para. 43.
[133] *Basic Education for All*, para. 29.
[134] Ibid, para. 43.
[135] Ibid, para. 43.
[136] Ibid, para. 43.
[137] *Centre for Health, Human Rights and Development and Others v. Attorney General*, Constitutional Petition No. 16 of 2011 ('*Centre for Health, Human Rights and Development*').
[138] Christopher Mbazira, 'Uganda's Hybrid Constitutional Protection of Economic, Social and Cultural Rights' in Chirwa and Chenwi, *The Protection of Economic*, pp. 448, 454. The one exception is the right to education that is guaranteed under Article 30 of the Bill of Rights: p. 451.

the fundamental rights of all Ugandans to social and economic development'. In particular, the state must ensure 'that all developmental efforts are directed at ensuring maximum social and cultural well-being of the people' and that 'all Ugandans enjoy rights and opportunities and access to', among other things, health services. Objective XX further requires the state to 'take all practical measures to ensure the provision of basic medical services to the population'. In its jurisprudence, the Constitutional Court has held that while not directly justiciable, when read together with Article 8A of the Constitution (which states that 'Uganda shall be governed based on principles of national interest and common good enshrined in the national objectives and directive principles of state policy'), these rights oblige 'the government to provide health and basic medical services to the people of Uganda'.[139] Like South Africa, there is also no express language in the Constitution that empowers the courts to examine the state's resources. At most, Objective V(i) provides that the 'State shall guarantee and respect institutions which are charged by the State with responsibility for protecting human rights by providing them with adequate resources to function effectively.'

The case involved a constitutional challenge to certain actions and omissions of the Ugandan Government and its staff in their provision of maternal health services in public hospitals. The impugned acts and omissions, which allegedly led to the death of two women (Sylvia Nalubowa and Jennifer Anguko) and their new-borns during childbirth, included not providing basic indispensable maternal health facilities, an inadequate number of staff to provide maternal health services and an inadequate budget allocated to the maternal health sector.[140] There were also allegations of corruption – in particular, absenteeism and bribes by hospital staff members. Anguko was not attended to by a medical professional when she started bleeding, left instead in the care of family who were not medically trained and thus not in a position to attend to her health care needs. The doctor on duty was delayed for several hours, and as a result, Anguko and her child died.[141] Nalubowa bled to death because the doctor on duty delayed coming into the hospital when her family did not pay the bribe demanded.[142] In defending its challenged

[139] *Centre for Health, Human Rights and Development*, 18.

[140] Ibid, 2.

[141] Ibid, 31.

[142] Ibid, 19, 31.

acts and omissions, the Government argued, among other things, that it lacked the necessary resources. The court, however, was not persuaded by this argument, holding that the Government's failure to provide basic maternal health care services in public hospitals constituted a violation of the right to health (among other rights). And in so holding, it carefully probed the state's financial resources.

While the court accepted that 'financial resources are a constraint to the provision of adequate maternal health care services in Uganda', it stressed that the Government could not ignore 'the constitutional obligation of the state to provide these services to uphold the rights of women and fulfill their reproductive rights and needs'.[143] The court decided that in particular, the Government had failed to 'annually at the time of budgeting prioritize funding to the Maternal Health Sector and disburse all the budgeted amounts to the specific centres'.[144] For instance, it pointed to the fact that only 2.1 per cent of Uganda's GDP was spent on health care and that of the amount allocated to the health sector in the 2015–2016 fiscal year, only 93 per cent was actually spent.[145] The court reasoned that the remaining 7 per cent in the budget could have significantly contributed to improvement in maternal care and that '[t]he shortfall denied the health care sector an opportunity to provide basic maternal health care services', including, of particular note, emergency obstetric care services.[146] The court also explained that limited resources 'should not be used as a blanket excuse and defense for failure to provide basic services to save life because provision of some of these services do not require money'.[147] For example, this was the case in respect of Nalubowa, the Court noting: '[c]orruption killed Nalubowa and not lack of resources'.[148]

Of course, although examining the state's financial resources is a valuable step that the courts can take to reduce the incidence of public corruption, there are limitations on how far the courts can, and should be able to, go. Owing to their limited legitimacy and capacity relative to the elected branches, it is not the role of the courts to second-guess the elected branches' allocation of resources. For them to do so would be

[143] Ibid, 55.
[144] Ibid, 55.
[145] Ibid, 49–50.
[146] Ibid, 50.
[147] Ibid, 19.
[148] Ibid, 19.

judicial usurpation. Constitutions and the courts often recognise this limitation. For example, though the Kenyan Constitution grants the courts the powers that I described earlier, article 20(5c) of the Constitution limits those powers. It specifically prohibits a court from 'interfer[ing] with a decision by a State organ concerning the allocation of available resources, solely on the basis that it would have reached a different conclusion.' As always, the courts must strike a delicate balance between judicial usurpation and judicial abdication.

7.3.2 Strictly Enforcing Public Procurement Law

Another step that the courts can take to reduce the incidence of corruption in the elected branches' exercise of control over social goods and services is to enforce public procurement law in a strict fashion. The public procurement tender process, it will be recalled, is a key avenue for public corruption, including in the provision of social goods and services.[149] For example, the OECD has recognised that because of 'the financial interests at stake', the 'complexity of the process, the close interaction between public officials and businesses, and the multitude of stakeholders' involved in it, public procurement is 'one of the government activities most vulnerable to corruption'.[150]

Public procurement law often has as its central objective 'to ensure that government contractors are able to get the best value for public money that the market can deliver'.[151] By strictly enforcing public procurement law, specifically the legal requirements of the procurement tender process, the courts can increase the likelihood that those who staff the elected branches will accept bids that are the most competitive and beneficial to citizens, as opposed to those bids that for any number of reasons (e.g., bribery, kickbacks, nepotism, cronyism) are in the best interests of the relevant staff. This, in turn, increases the integrity of the procurement system which should help to 'create a civic sense that government institutions are dedicated to improving citizens' lives'.[152]

149 See Anderson et al., 'Preventing Corruption'; Alison Jones, 'Combatting Corruption and Collusion in UK Public Procurement: Proposals for Post-Brexit Reform' (2021) 84 *Modern Law Review* 667, 668, 670–672.

150 OECD, 'Preventing Corruption in Public Procurement', 6.

151 Jones, 'Combatting Corruption', 668.

152 Anderson et al., 'Preventing Corruption', 1235.

A good illustration of this step in practice is the South African Constitutional Court's 'merits' judgment in the *AllPay* litigation.[153] Briefly discussed in Chapter 5, the litigation involved 'the largest [procurement] contract in South African history'.[154] In 2011, the South African Social Security Agency (SASSA) awarded a ZAR 10-billion tender to an electronic payments firm called Cash Paymaster Services (CPS). The relevant contract was to administer the nationwide payment of government-funded social grants to over 15 million beneficiaries over a five-year period. An unsuccessful tenderer, AllPay, brought a review application to set aside the tender award, alleging several irregularities in the procurement process. These irregularities related to alleged non-compliance with requirements that SASSA itself had set for the tender. More specifically, they pertained to, among other things, the composition of the Bid Evaluation Committee, SASSA's investigation and confirmation of tenderers' Black Economic Empowerment credentials, and certain amendments that were made to the bid requirements.[155] As with the Limpopo Crisis, there were many allegations of corruption made by the media and civil society organisations regarding SASSA's contract with CPS.[156] In fact, CPS's parent company, Net1 UEPS Technologies, was investigated by the US Department of Justice and Federal Bureau of Investigation for allegedly making corrupt payments to South African government officials in connection with the contract.[157] And the non-profit organisation Corruption Watch participated in the litigation as amicus curiae.

The lower court adopted a relatively lax approach to enforcing public procurement law. It noted that 'a fair process does not demand perfection and [that] not every flaw is fatal', concluding that '[i]t would be gravely prejudicial to the public interest if the law was to invalidate public

[153] *AllPay Consolidated Investment Holdings (Pty) Ltd. and Others v. Chief Executive Officer of the South African Social Security Agency and Others* [2013] ZACC 42 ('*AllPay (Merits)*').

[154] Klaaren, 'Social Grant Payments', p. 90.

[155] *AllPay (Merits)*, para. 20.

[156] Klaaren, 'Social Grant Payments', pp. 92–102.

[157] 'South Africa's Net1 falls on news of US Justice Department probe' (4 December 2012) *Reuters*, www.reuters.com/article/us-net1ueps-investigation-idUKBRE8B30QS20121204, accessed 22 February 2023; 'Net1 under FBI investigation for corruption in SA' (4 December 2012) *BusinessTech*, https://businesstech.co.za/news/it-services/27861/net-1-under-fbi-investigation-for-corruption-in-sa/, accessed 22 February 2023.

contracts for inconsequential irregularities'.[158] Accordingly, it found that there were no unlawful irregularities in this case. The Constitutional Court disagreed, setting aside the lower court's order and declaring the tender constitutionally invalid. In line with the trend noted earlier, the court did not make a finding of corruption, concluding, rather, that SASSA's conduct was only a procedural irregularity. However, it did stress the importance of complying with procedural formalities to combatting public corruption. It recognised specifically that 'deviations from fair process may themselves all too often be symptoms of corruption or malfeasance in the process' and that insisting on compliance with formalities guards 'against a process skewed by corrupt influences'.[159]

The UK High Court's judgment in the *Good Law Project 1* case previously discussed also illustrates this step. The Transparency Policy with which the Government had failed to comply was a requirement of UK public procurement law. Under the then-Transparency Policy, it was 'advised that contracts [be] published with the award notice within 20 days' following the award of the contract or, where applicable, the end of a standstill period.[160] The Government had not done so. In finding the Government's omission unlawful, Mr. Justice Chamberlain highlighted not only the importance of transparency, but also how critical it is that Government follow published policy. He held, citing precedent, that 'the Secretary of State had a common law duty to comply with the Transparency Policy absent good reason to depart from it'.[161] The publication of contract documents, he explained, was 'part of the Government's "policy commitments" which reflected 'an important element of the Government's [overall] commitment to transparency'.[162]

The strict enforcement of public procurement law like that seen from the South African Constitutional Court in *AllPay* and the UK High Court in *Good Law Project 1* should help to reduce incidences of public

158 *AllPay Consolidated Investment Holdings (Pty) Ltd. and Others v. Chief Executive Officer of the South African Social Security Agency and Others* [2013] ZASCA 29, para. 21.

159 Ibid, para. 27.

160 Crown Commercial Service, 'Publication of Central Government Tenders and Contracts: Central Government Transparency Guidance Note' (November 2017), section 9.1, https://assets.publishing.service.gov.uk/government/uploads/system/uploads/attachment_data/file/996108/Withdrawn_Guidance_Publication_of_New_Central_Government_Tender_documents__and_Contracts_2017__1___1_.pdf, accessed 22 February 2023. Note that the publication was withdrawn on 24 June 2021.

161 *Good Law Project 1*, para. 132.

162 Ibid, para. 131.

corruption. It ensures that the tender process fulfils the objectives of public procurement law, including securing the most competitive bid, and demonstrates to government actors and tenderers that the courts will intervene to so secure. While the courts 'may never know [in actuality] what, if any, malfeasance they have thwarted, the possibility of such malfeasance within and its corroding influence on public procurement is nevertheless significantly checked'.[163]

7.3.3 Holding Non-state Actors Accountable to the Public

A third step that the courts can take to reduce the incidence of corruption in the elected branches' exercise of control over social goods and services is to hold non-state actors accountable to the public. As Susan Rose-Ackerman has stated, '[c]orruption describes a relationship between the state and the private sector'.[164] For example, in the case of corruption in public procurement, the private companies that are awarded the relevant contracts (in exchange for bribes or kickbacks) are key players in the corruption. When the courts hold these non-state actors accountable to the public, corrupt practices become more risky and less rewarding for these actors to participate in and thus, should in turn reduce the opportunities for corruption available to government actors.

The South African Constitutional Court's 'remedy' judgment in the *AllPay* litigation illustrates this step in practice. Specifically, the court took the significant step of recognising CPS as an 'organ of state'.[165] While the court, in its 'merits' judgment, declared CPS's tender constitutionally invalid, it suspended its declaration of invalidity, reserving the question of what would be a just and equitable remedy, and directed the parties to file additional factual and legal submissions on this question. CPS argued that if the existing contract with SASSA were declared invalid, it, as a non-state actor, had no obligations towards the beneficiaries of the social grant payments. This would mean that in the interim (between dissolution of the contract and the appointment of another service provider), CPS would not be obliged to provide the beneficiaries

[163] Du Plessis and Coutsoudis, 'Considering Corruption', 787.

[164] Rose-Ackerman, *Corruption and Government*, p. 275. See also Warburton, 'Corruption, Power and the Public', 82.

[165] *AllPay Consolidated Investment Holdings (Pty) Ltd. and Others v. Chief Executive Officer of the South African Social Security Agency and Others* [2014] ZACC 12 ('*AllPay (Remedy)*').

with their payments, leaving millions of vulnerable South Africans without the funds that they needed to survive. In rejecting CPS's argument, the court held that for the purpose of the procurement contract, CPS was an 'organ of state' within the meaning of section 239 of the Constitution.[166] It found that CPS, in administering the social grant system, 'exercise[d] a public power and perform[ed] a public function'.[167] According to the court, it played 'a unique and central role as the gatekeeper of the right to social security and effectively control[led] beneficiaries' access to social assistance'. The court thus concluded that CPS had 'obligations that extend[ed] beyond the merely contractual'.[168] These included constitutional obligations under sections 27(1)(c) (guaranteeing everyone the fundamental right to 'have access to social security, including, if they are unable to support themselves and their dependents, appropriate social assistance') and 27(2) (requiring the state to 'take reasonable legislative and other measures, within its available resources, to achieve the progressive realisation of this right').[169] The court explained that '[w]hen [CPS] concluded the contract for the rendering of public services, it . . . became accountable to the people of South Africa in relation to the public power it acquired and the public function it perform[ed]'.[170]

The court's conclusion that CPS was an 'organ of state' had three key implications.[171] First, it meant that CPS could not 'simply walk away' from the contract.[172] CPS had an obligation to 'ensure that a workable payment system' for social grant payments remained in place until a new system was operational.[173] Secondly, although CPS, the court explained, should not suffer a loss from its continued obligations, it also had 'no

166 Section 239 of the Constitution defines an 'organ of state' as '(a) any department of state or administration in the national, provincial or local sphere of government; or (b) any other functionary or institution – (i) exercising a power or performing a function in terms of the Constitution or a provincial constitution; or (ii) exercising a public power or performing a public function in terms of any legislation, but does not include a court or a judicial officer.'

167 *AllPay (Remedy)*, para. 54.

168 Ibid, para. 49.

169 Ibid, para. 54.

170 Ibid, para. 59.

171 David Bilchitz, *Fundamental Rights and the Legal Obligations of Business* (Cambridge: Cambridge University Press, 2021), p. 168.

172 *AllPay (Remedy)*, para. 67.

173 Ibid, paras. 63–64, 66.

right to benefit from an unlawful contract'.[174] And lastly, any benefit that CPS derived from the contract was not 'beyond public scrutiny', meaning that it had to disclose financial information regarding the contract. In particular, CPS had to show when the break-even point had arrived (or would arrive) as well as when it started to turn a profit.[175]

Importantly, the court's recognition of CPS as an 'organ of state' has the potential to reduce the incidence of corruption in South Africa. It sends a message to successful tenderers that where they perform a public function, they are accountable to the public: they have obligations to the public and they can neither benefit from unlawful practices nor hide those practices behind the confidentiality that they are normally afforded as private actors. Put simply, the judgment serves as a 'warning to those who would wish to profit on the back of an unlawful tender process', making 'any successful tenderer, even if innocent, wary of involving itself in an improper tender'.[176]

That said, there must be limitations on the extent of a private company's accountability to the public. Excessive accountability may deter legitimate tenderers from bidding on public procurement contracts, reducing the competitiveness of the tender pool and in turn harming the interests of citizens. In *AllPay*, for instance, the Constitutional Court stressed that recognising CPS as an 'organ of state' for the purpose of the procurement contract did not mean that 'its entire commercial operation suddenly becomes open to public scrutiny'.[177] It clarified that the 'commercial part dependent on, or derived from, the performance of public functions is subject to public scrutiny, both in its operational and financial aspects'.[178] The courts must therefore show a level of restraint and not overextend the accountability of non-state actors to the public.

7.3.4 *Involving Specialised Anti-corruption Agencies*

To reduce the incidence of corruption in the elected branches' exercise of control over social goods and services, the courts can also take the step of involving specialised agencies that have as part of their mandate the prevention of corruption. Examples of these agencies include institutions

174 Ibid, para. 67.
175 Ibid, para. 67.
176 Du Plessis and Coutsoudis, 'Considering Corruption', 770, 771.
177 *AllPay (Remedy)*, para. 59.
178 Ibid, para. 59.

of a general nature that are present in many jurisdictions globally (e.g., the Ombudsman, the Auditor General, the Public Service Commission and Audit Courts), as well as more specialised agencies that are specific to particular jurisdictions (e.g., the Independent Corrupt Practices and Other Related Offences Commission in Nigeria, and Kenya's Anti-Corruption Commission).[179]

The South African Constitutional Court took this step in the *Black Sash* litigation. This litigation followed the *AllPay* litigation discussed above. In its 'remedy' judgment, the court suspended its declaration of invalidity specifically on the premise that SASSA would either award a new five-year tender after a proper procurement process or would itself take over the payment of social grants when the suspended contract with CPS came to an end in March 2017.[180] The court thus ordered SASSA to report back on progress regarding the new tender process and its outcome. SASSA reported back that it had decided to itself take over the payment of social grants and that it would be able to meet the deadline of March 2017. And the court discharged its supervisory order on accepting this assurance. This assurance, however, 'turned out to be without foundation'.[181] From April 2016, SASSA was aware that it would not be able to meet the deadline of March 2017; nonetheless, neither SASSA nor the Minister of Social Development took any steps to inform the court.[182] Therefore, when the matter came before the court in March 2017, there was no choice but to rely on CPS to continue to make the social grant payments for the foreseeable future. Accordingly, the court concluded that 'SASSA and CPS should continue to fulfil their respective constitutional obligations in the payment of social grants for a period of 12 months as an extension of the current contract', and that its 'earlier declaration of invalidity of that contract [would] be further extended, as well as the suspension of that declaration of invalidity'.[183]

To monitor their performance, the court ordered the Minister and SASSA (it will be recalled from Chapter 5) to 'file reports on affidavit with the Court every three months' – specifically 'setting out how they [planned] to ensure the payment of social grants after the expiry of the

179 Fombad, 'Corruption and the Crisis', pp. 31–32.

180 *Black Sash Trust v. Minister of Social Development and Others (Freedom under Law NPC Intervening)* [2017] ZACC 8, para. 3 ('*Black Sash I*').

181 Ibid, para. 5.

182 Ibid, para. 6.

183 Ibid, para. 50.

12-month period, what steps they [had] taken in this regard, what further steps they [would] take, and when they [would] take each future step'.[184] In addition to these reports, the court decided, on the suggestion of the non-profit organisation Corruption Watch, to also appoint the Auditor General as an independent monitor. Citing section 188(2)(b) of the Constitution, the court noted that 'the Auditor-General may audit and report on the accounts, financial statements and financial management of any institution that is authorised in terms of any law to receive money for a public purpose' and found that CPS was 'such an institution in the present circumstances.'[185] Hence, the court included the Auditor General in its overseeing the process of fulfilling its order – and making social grant payments – making any corrupt practices in that process, less likely.

7.3.5 Imposing Financial Sanctions on Government Actors

One final step that the courts can take to reduce the incidence of corruption in the elected branches' exercise of control over social goods and services is one that I mentioned, in brief, in Chapter 5: imposing financial sanctions on government actors, including costs orders against the officials personally, as well as punitive damages. By imposing such sanctions on these actors, the courts make corrupt practices riskier to engage in, again augmenting the relevant inhibitory forces.

The South African Constitutional Court's approach in the *Black Sash* litigation illustrates this. In that litigation (it will be recalled from Chapter 5), the court ordered the Minister of Social Development personally to pay 20 per cent of the costs of the claimants.[186] Granted, this costs order was most likely a response to the recalcitrance of the Minister, rather than the allegations of corruption that were lurking in the background of the case. However, a court could, I suggest, link such a costs

[184] Ibid, para. 76.

[185] Ibid, para. 69. See also the Ugandan Constitutional Court's judgment in *Centre for Health, Human Rights and Development*, 58, where the Court ordered, in addition to other remedies (including damages, full training of all staff who provide maternal health care services, and prioritisation and provision of sufficient funds in the following financial year for maternal health care), that the Government 'compile and submit to Parliament with a copy to [the] Court a full audit report on the status of [m]aternal health in Uganda' at the end of the following two financial years.

[186] *Black Sash Trust v. Minister of Social Development and Others (Freedom under Law NPC Intervening)* [2018] ZACC 36, para. 18 ('*Black Sash III*').

order (or other relevant sanction) directly to the alleged corrupt practices committed.

The Ugandan Constitutional Court, for instance, followed such an approach in the *Centre for Health, Human Rights and Development* case. As I explained earlier, allegations of corruption were made in the case, specifically against hospital staff members relating to absenteeism and demands for bribes. Citing affidavit evidence, the court held that 'the ministry of health had failed to manage absenteeism in the health sector' – with absenteeism being termed by the Inspectorate of Government in a 2014 report as '"quiet corruption" or corruption stemming from behaviors that may be hard to observe and track'.[187] The court stressed that '[a]bsenteeism leads to delays in care, high rates of emergency surgery, unnecessary referrals and a multitude of other negative health outcomes'.[188] It noted that while the Government had identified workforce improvement goals, they 'were limited and lacked enforcement mechanisms to enable significant improvements in absenteeism or to any meaningful performance accountability in the sector'.[189] With respect to health workers' unprofessionalism, including their demands for bribes, it found that whereas these actions 'were not condoned by Government', there was also no 'constant supervision at the public health facilities and management structures'.[190] The court thus said that the 'extension and evaluation' of the Government's policies and programmes needed to be done 'to a larger extent'.[191]

In response to these acts of corruption, the court ordered the Government to pay exemplary or punitive damages.[192] These damages were in addition to the general damages that it awarded 'for the psychological torture, violation of the rights to life, health and cruel and degrading treatment of [Anguko's and Nalubowa's] loved ones'.[193] The court held that the relevant acts (i.e., leaving Anguko and Nalubowa 'to bleed to death without effort to save their lives' as well as Anguko's unborn child) 'justif[ied] an award of exemplary damages.'[194] And in

187 Ibid, 32.
188 Ibid.
189 Ibid.
190 Ibid, 32–33.
191 Ibid, 33.
192 Ibid, 56.
193 Ibid, 58.
194 Ibid.

ordering these damages, it highlighted that the damages were 'aimed at curbing the repeat of the offending act'.[195]

Financial sanctions of this sort against government actors are an important tool to reduce the incidence of corruption because they signal to those who staff the elected branches that above and beyond what would otherwise be ordered for constitutional violations, corrupt practices will attract additional sanctions, including against officials personally. This should make such practices less appealing to staff, reducing, as I have said, their occurrence.

[195] Ibid.

8

Conclusion

I conclude by returning to the problem identified at the outset of this book. With the global rise of constitutionalised and justiciable social rights, and the corresponding proliferation of social rights litigation, courts require guidance on how to enforce these rights. In so enforcing, the courts must avoid, as we know, two wrongs. As guardians of the constitution, they have a constitutional obligation to enforce these constitutional rights. They cannot, as they may have done in the past, show complete deference to the elected branches and steer clear of social policy matters. However, owing to their limited legitimacy and capacity, the courts must, at the same time, exercise caution, ensuring that they do not usurp the policy-making role that rightfully belongs to those branches.

My principal objective in this book has been to use the concept of political trust – and the literature on this concept – to develop a new framework that courts can use to enforce social rights. Under this framework, the courts enforce the three constituent expectations of trust: goodwill, competence and fiduciary responsibility. In doing so, the courts: (i) demand that the elected branches, in exercising their control over social goods and services, follow fair procedures, while addressing government intransigence (the expectation of goodwill, Chapter 5); (ii) require the elected branches' decisions to be evidence based (the expectation of competence, Chapter 6); and (iii) through a variety of measures, aim to curb corrupt practices from those who staff the elected branches (the expectation of fiduciary responsibility, Chapter 7).

This trust-based framework addresses the drawbacks of existing frameworks. Because the concept of trust focuses on procedure – that is, the manner in which a trustee, like the elected branches, exercises control over a good or service – a trust-based framework for social rights enforcement militates towards procedural review. The courts, in employing the framework, review the procedure by which the elected branches make resource allocation decisions, rather than the outcome of those decisions. The trust-based framework thus does not share the separation-of-powers and equity problems of frameworks that instead focus on outcome. Simultaneously, the trust-based framework mitigates the problems of other procedural approaches to enforcement. Using the constituent expectations of trust as the basis for a legal standard – the trustworthiness standard – it offers courts and policy-makers concrete guidance that they can follow. And by institutionalising the procedural remedies discussed, it can do a lot to protect vulnerable groups.

The trust-based framework is also justifiable on the four grounds I have outlined. Instrumentally, based on the network conception of trust and the literature on trustworthiness, we can expect it to foster trust in the citizen–government relationship and to realise the valuable ends of such trust, including public tax compliance and support for social policies. Theoretically, given the fiduciary nature of the citizen–government relationship, social rights law, as the law that regulates that relationship, should centre on trust, a conclusion supported by both the private fiduciary law and public fiduciary theory scholarship. Practically, the concept of trust fits well with social rights adjudication, responding to the prospectivity of social rights, placing citizens at the centre of social rights enforcement, and offering a good middle ground between judicial abdication and judicial usurpation. And democratically, owing to the trust-cooperation link and the type of trust that it promotes, the trust-based framework, it can fairly be said, supports democracy.

It may appear to some readers that basing a social rights enforcement framework on the concept of trust poses a danger. In particular, if the trust-based framework enables us to foster citizens' trust in the elected branches, as I have suggested, and to realise the public cooperation that follows from that trust, including support for social policies, there is a danger that citizens will support regressive social policies – even where such policies are not absolutely necessary. This may, in turn, lead to the erosion of the welfare state. For this reason, we must be cautious in our embrace of trust as a tool for social rights enforcement. However, the proposed trust-based framework – by focusing on the concept of trustworthiness, rather than that of trust alone – does introduce a degree of caution. It demands that governments, in exercising their control over social goods and services, including the introduction of regressive social policies, act in a trustworthy manner. As such, it creates conditions that foster citizens' trust in the elected branches with respect to social rights, rather than seek to increase such trust without any foundation for it.

Consequently, any trust which citizens hold in governments with respect to social rights as a result, including vis-à-vis regressive policies, will not be blind or indiscriminate – but, rather, warranted. It is for this reason, I have noted, the trust-based framework may be said to support democracy. Also, because the protection of social rights does not, and should not, stop at the courts, the other means by which social rights are protected and realised – which will not centre on political trust – can help mitigate any dangers the concept may present, including any potential it has to erode social welfare.

Before bringing this book to a close, I want to say something about the implications of the trust-based framework. Specifically, we may ask: why is the framework limited to the enforcement of social rights? What about other rights, including civil and political rights? While such other rights are undoubtedly beyond the scope of this book, I flag that the trust-based framework, in my view, is not limited per se to social rights enforcement. It can also be applied to the judicial enforcement of other rights. And therefore, this book and its framework have a broad currency. However, before the framework can be applied to other rights, appropriate modifications must be made. First, as I noted in Chapter 2, trust is a context-specific concept. In that chapter, I put forward a workable notion of the concept of trust which is useable in the social rights context. This includes my characterisation of the citizen–government relationship as a fiduciary relationship. Consequently, to apply the framework to other rights, our understanding of trust must be adapted to the relevant context. Secondly, my justification of a trust-based framework is, in many respects, specific to social rights enforcement. This is especially the case in my theoretical and practical justifications. In another context, the justifications that I have advanced may not hold or may carry different weight. Lastly, given the context-specificity of trust, the specifics of the framework, including how the courts enforce the expectations of trust, must be adapted. For example, in discussing procedural fairness in Chapter 5, I focused on the elements of transparency, participation and equality because they have particular relevance for social rights. In another context, the judicial enforcement of trust's expectations may assume a different form. Accordingly, while I recognise that the trust-based framework can be applied to other human rights contexts, I leave it to readers to adapt the framework, if considered relevant and helpful, to those other areas.

The trust-based framework, however, has been proposed in this book with the intention of assisting courts globally in enforcing social rights. Rooted in political trust, as understood in the scholarship on the concept, the framework is undoubtedly a novel one. That said, as I have demonstrated, the trust-based framework incorporates into social rights enforcement requirements that social rights scholars have advocated and with which courts should be familiar. Hence, the framework, in my view, strikes the ideal balance between innovation and pragmatism.

BIBLIOGRAPHY

Books

Allan, T.R.S., *Constitutional Justice: A Liberal Theory of the Rule of Law* (Oxford: Oxford University Press, 2001).

Atrey, S., *Intersectional Discrimination* (Oxford: Oxford University Press, 2019).

Baier, A., *Moral Prejudices: Essays on Ethics* (Cambridge, MA: Harvard University Press, 1995).

Barber, B., *The Logic and Limits of Trust* (New Brunswick, NJ: Rutgers University Press, 1983).

Bellamy, R., *Political Constitutionalism: A Republican Defence of the Constitutionality of Democracy* (Cambridge: Cambridge University Press, 2007).

Bickel, A.M., *The Least Dangerous Branch: The Supreme Court at the Bar of Politics*, 2nd ed. (New Haven, CT: Yale University Press, 1986).

Bilchitz, D., *Fundamental Rights and the Legal Obligations of Business* (Cambridge: Cambridge University Press, 2021).

Poverty and Fundamental Rights: The Justification and Enforcement of Socio-economic Rights (Oxford: Oxford University Press, 2007).

Bogenschneider, K. and T.J. Corbett, *Evidence-Based Policymaking: Insights from Policy-Minded Researchers and Research-Minded Policymakers* (Abingdon: Routledge, 2010).

Boswell, C., *Manufacturing Political Trust: Targets and Performance Measurement in Public Policy* (Cambridge: Cambridge University Press, 2018).

Cairney, P., *The Politics of Evidence-Based Policy Making* (London: Palgrave MacMillan, 2016).

Chilton, A. and M. Versteeg, *How Constitutional Rights Matter* (Oxford: Oxford University Press, 2020).

Coleman, J., *Foundations of Social Theory* (Cambridge, MA: Harvard University Press, 1994).

Conaglen, M., *Fiduciary Loyalty: Protecting the Due Performance of Non-Fiduciary Duties* (Oxford: Hart, 2010).

Cook, K.S., R. Hardin and M. Levi, *Cooperation without Trust?* (New York: Russell Sage Foundation, 2005).

Dalton, R.J., *Democratic Challenges, Democratic Choices: The Erosion of Political Support in Advanced Industrial Democracies* (Oxford: Oxford University Press, 2004).

Daly, P., *A Theory of Deference in Administrative Law: Basis, Application and Scope* (Cambridge: Cambridge University Press, 2012).

Davies, H.T.O., S.M. Nutley and P.C. Smith (eds.), *What Works? Evidence-Based Policy and Practice in Public Services* (Bristol: Bristol University Press, 2000).

Davis, K.C., *Discretionary Justice: A Preliminary Inquiry* (Baton Rouge: Louisiana State University Press, 1969).

De Smith, S., H. Woolf and J. Jowell, *Judicial Review of Administrative Action*, 5th ed. (London: Sweet and Maxwell, 1995).

Dworkin, R., *Freedom's Law: The Moral Reasoning of the American Constitution* (Oxford: Oxford University Press, 1996).

Elliott, M. and R. Thomas, *Public Law*, 2nd ed. (Oxford: Oxford University Press, 2014).

Ely, J.H., *Democracy and Distrust: A Theory of Judicial Review* (Cambridge, MA: Harvard University Press, 1980).

Fabre, C., *Social Rights under the Constitution: Government and the Decent Life* (Oxford: Oxford University Press, 2003).

Feldman, D., *Civil Liberties and Human Rights in England and Wales*, 2nd ed. (Oxford: Oxford University Press, 2002).

Ferraz, O.L.M., *Health as a Human Right: The Politics and Judicialisation of Health in Brazil* (Cambridge: Cambridge University Press, 2021).

Finn, P.D., *Fiduciary Obligations* (North Ryde: The Law Book Company, 1977).

Fisher, E. and S.A. Shapiro, *Administrative Competence: Reimagining Administrative Law* (Cambridge: Cambridge University Press, 2020).

Fox-Decent, E., *Sovereignty's Promise: The State as Fiduciary* (Oxford: Oxford University Press, 2011).

Fredman, S., *Human Rights Transformed: Positive Rights and Positive Duties* (Oxford: Oxford University Press, 2008).

Discrimination Law (Oxford: Oxford University Press, 2011).

Comparative Human Rights (Oxford: Oxford University Press, 2018).

Fried, C., *Right and Wrong* (Cambridge, MA: Harvard University Press, 1978).

Galligan, D.J., *Discretionary Power: A Legal Study of Official Discretion* (Oxford: Clarendon Press, 1986).

Gibson, J.L. and G.A. Caldeira, *Citizens, Courts, and Confirmations* (Princeton, NJ: Princeton University Press, 2009).

Goldman, I. and M. Pabari, *Using Evidence in Policy and Practice: Lessons from Africa* (Abingdon: Routledge, 2020).

Goldsmith, S. and W.D. Eggers, *Governing by Network: The New Shape of the Public Sector* (Washington, DC: Brookings Institution Press, 2004).

Goodin, R.E., *Reasons for Welfare: The Political Theory of the Welfare State* (Princeton, NJ: Princeton University Press, 1988).

Govier, T., *Social Trust and Human Communities* (Kingston, ON: McGill-Queen's University Press, 1997).

Gunther, R. and A. Mughan, *Democracy and the Media: A Comparative Perspective* (Cambridge: Cambridge University Press, 2000).

Hardin, R., *Trust and Trustworthiness* (New York: Russell Sage Foundation, 2002).

Herring, J., *Law and the Relational Self* (Cambridge: Cambridge University Press, 2019).

Hetherington, M.J., *Why Trust Matters: Declining Political Trust and the Demise of American Liberalism* (Princeton, NJ: Princeton University Press, 2005).

Heymann, J., A. Sprague and A. Raub, *Advancing Equality: How Constitutional Rights Can Make a Difference Worldwide* (Oakland: University of California Press, 2020).

Hibbing, J.R. and E. Theiss-Morse, *Stealth Democracy: Americans' Beliefs about How Government Should Work* (Cambridge: Cambridge University Press, 2002).

Hough, D., *Corruption, Anti-corruption and Governance* (London: Palgrave MacMillan, 2013).

Jasanoff, S., *Designs on Nature: Science and Democracy in Europe and the United States* (Princeton, NJ: Princeton University Press, 2005).

Kende, M.S., *Constitutional Rights in Two Worlds: South Africa and the United States* (Cambridge: Cambridge University Press, 2009).

Kesselman, M., J. Krieger and W.A. Joseph, *Introduction to Comparative Politics: Political Challenges and Changing Agendas* (Belmont, CA: Wadsworth, 2012).

King, J., *Judging Social Rights* (Cambridge: Cambridge University Press, 2012).

Kontler, L. and M. Somos (eds.), *Trust and Happiness in the History of European Political Thought* (Leiden: Brill, 2017).

Kumar, C.R., *Corruption and Human Rights in India: Comparative Perspectives on Transparency and Good Governance* (Oxford: Oxford University Press, 2011).

Langford, M., C. Rodriguez-Garavito and J. Rossi (eds.), *Social Rights Judgments and the Politics of Compliance: Making It Stick* (Cambridge: Cambridge University Press, 2017).

Laski, H.J., *The Limitation of the Expert* (London: The Fabian Society, 1931).

Leckey, R., *Contextual Subjects: Family, State, and Relational Theory* (Toronto: University of Toronto Press, 2008).

Levi, M., *Consent, Dissent and Patriotism* (Cambridge: Cambridge University Press, 1997).

Liebenberg, S., *Socio-economic Rights: Adjudication under a Transformative Constitution* (Cape Town: Juta Law, 2010).

Luhmann, N., *Trust and Power: Two Works* (Chichester: Wiley, 1979).

Miller, P.B. and M. Harding (eds.), *Fiduciaries and Trust: Ethics, Politics, Economics and Law* (Cambridge: Cambridge University Press, 2020).

Molander, A., *Discretion in the Welfare State: Social Rights and Professional Judgment* (Abingdon: Routledge, 2016).

Müller, J., *Mechanisms of Trust: News Media in Democratic and Authoritarian Regimes* (Frankfurt: Campus, 2013).

Muller, J.Z., *The Tyranny of Metrics* (Princeton, NJ: Princeton University Press, 2019).

Murphy, C., *A Moral Theory of Political Reconciliation* (Cambridge: Cambridge University Press, 2012).

Nedelsky, J., *Law's Relations: A Relational Theory of Self, Autonomy, and Law* (Cambridge: Cambridge University Press, 2011).

Nichols, T., *The Death of Expertise: The Campaign against Established Knowledge and Why It Matters* (Oxford: Oxford University Press, 2017).

Nolan, A., *Children's Socio-economic Rights, Democracy and the Courts* (London: Bloomsbury, 2011).

OECD, *Building Capacity for Evidence-Informed Policy-Making: Lessons from Country Experiences* (Paris: OECD Publishing, 2020).

O'Connell, P., *Vindicating Socio-economic Rights: International Standards and Comparative Experiences* (Abingdon: Routledge, 2013).

Olaniyan, K., *Corruption and Human Rights Law in Africa* (Oxford: Hart, 2014).

O'Neill, O., *A Question of Trust* (Cambridge: Cambridge University Press, 2002).

Parkhurst, J., *The Politics of Evidence: From Evidence-Based Policy to the Good Governance of Evidence* (Abingdon: Routledge, 2017).

Ray, B., *Engaging with Social Rights: Procedure, Participation, and Democracy in South Africa's Second Wave* (Cambridge: Cambridge University Press, 2016).

Rosanvallon, P., *Counter-Democracy: Politics in an Age of Distrust* (Cambridge: Cambridge University Press, 2008).

Rose-Ackerman, S., *Corruption and Government: Causes, Consequences, and Reform* (Cambridge: Cambridge University Press, 2010).

Rose-Ackerman, S., S. Egidy and J. Fowkes, *Due Process of Lawmaking: The United States, South Africa, Germany, and the European Union* (Cambridge: Cambridge University Press, 2014).

Rothstein, B., *Just Institutions Matter* (Cambridge: Cambridge University Press, 1998).

Rothstein, B. and A. Varraich, *Making Sense of Corruption* (Oxford: Oxford University Press, 2017).

Shue, H., *Basic Rights, Subsistence, Affluence, and U.S. Foreign Policy* (Princeton, NJ: Princeton University Press, 1980).

Smith, C.E., *Courts and the Poor* (Belmont, CA: Wadsworth, 1991).

Sossin, L., *Boundaries of Judicial Review: The Law of Justiciability in Canada* (Toronto: Carswell, 1999).

Steinmo, S., *Taxation and Democracy: Swedish, British and American Approaches to Financing the Modern State* (New Haven, CT: Yale University Press, 1993).

Steinmo, S.H. (ed.), *The Leap of Faith: The Fiscal Foundations of Successful Government in Europe and America* (Oxford: Oxford University Press, 2018).

Sztompka, P., *Trust: A Sociological Theory* (Cambridge: Cambridge University Press, 1999).

Tilly, C., *Democracy* (Cambridge: Cambridge University Press, 2007).

Tushnet, M., *Weak Courts, Strong Rights: Judicial Review and Social Welfare Rights in Comparative Constitutional Law* (Princeton, NJ: Princeton University Press, 2008).

Tyler, T.R., *Why People Obey the Law* (New Haven, CT: Yale University Press, 1990).

Tyler, T.R. and Y.J. Huo, *Trust in the Law: Encouraging Public Cooperation with the Police and Courts* (New York: Russell Sage Foundation, 2002).

Walker, M.U., *Moral Understandings: A Feminist Study in Ethics* (Oxford: Oxford University Press, 2008).

Young, K.G., *Constituting Economic and Social Rights* (Oxford: Oxford University Press, 2012).

Book Chapters

Aarts, K., A. Fladmoe and J. Stromback, 'Media, Political Trust, and Political Knowledge' in T. Aalberg and J. Curran (eds.), *How Media Inform Democracy: A Comparative Approach* (Abingdon: Routledge, 2012).

Aasen, H.S. et al., 'Juridification and Social Citizenship: International Law, Democracy and Professional Discretion' in H.S. Aasen et al. (eds.), *Juridification and Social Citizenship in the Welfare State* (Cheltenham: Edward Elgar, 2014).

Angel-Cabo, N. and D.L. Parmo, 'Latin American Social Constitutionalism: Courts and Popular Participation' in H.A. Garcia, K. Klare and L.A. Williams (eds.), *Social and Economic Rights in Theory and Practice: Critical Inquiries* (Abingdon: Routledge, 2015).

Baier, A., 'What Is Trust?' in D. Archard et al. (eds.), *Reading Onora O'Neill* (Abingdon: Routledge, 2013).

Bauer, P.C., 'Clearing the Jungle: Conceptualising Trust and Trustworthiness' in R. Barradas de Freitas and S. Lo Iacono (eds.), *Trust Matters: Cross-Disciplinary Essays* (London: Bloomsbury, 2021).

Bovens, M. and A. Wille, 'Falling or Fluctuating Trust Levels? The Case of the Netherlands' in S. Zmerli and M. Hooghe (eds.), *Political Trust: Why Context Matters* (Colchester: ECPR Press, 2011).

Braithwaite, J., 'Institutionalizing Distrust, Enculturating Trust' in V. Braithwaite and M. Levi (eds.), *Trust and Governance* (New York: Russell Sage Foundation, 1999).

Brand, D., 'The Proceduralisation of South African Socio-economic Rights Jurisprudence, or "What Are Socio-economic Rights For?"' in H. Botha, A.J. van der Walt and J.C. van der Walt (eds.), *Rights and Democracy: In a Transformative Constitution* (Stellenbosch: Sun Press, 2003).

Brinks, D.M. and V. Gauri, 'A New Policy Landscape: Legalizing Social and Economic Rights in the Developing World' in V. Gauri and D.M. Brinks (eds.), *Courting Social Justice: Judicial Enforcement of Social and Economic Rights in the Developing World* (Cambridge: Cambridge University Press, 2010).

Brockner, J. and P. Siegel, 'Understanding the Interaction between Procedural and Distributive Justice: The Role of Trust' in R.M. Kramer and T.R. Tyler (eds.), *Trust in Organizations: Frontiers of Theory and Research* (Thousand Oaks, CA: Sage Publications, 1996).

Cameron, B., 'Accountability Regimes for Federal Social Transfers: An Exercise in Deconstruction and Reconstruction' in P. Graefe, J.M. Simmons and L.A. White (eds.), *Overpowering and Underperforming?: Understanding and Evaluating New Intergovernmental Accountability Regimes* (Toronto: University of Toronto Press, 2013).

Chan, H.F., M.W. Supriyadi and B. Torgler, 'Trust and Tax Morale' in E.M. Uslaner (ed.), *The Oxford Handbook of Social and Political Trust* (Oxford: Oxford University Press, 2018).

Chenwi, L., 'Democratizing the Socio-economic Rights-Enforcement Process' in H.A. Garcia, K. Klare and L.A. Williams (eds.), *Social and Economic Rights in Theory and Practice: Critical Inquiries* (Abingdon: Routledge, 2015).

Connelly, J., 'Conclusion: Remaining the Welfare State?' in J. Connelly and J. Hayward (eds.), *The Withering of the Welfare State: Regression* (London: Palgrave Macmillan, 2012).

Cook, K.S., 'Trust in Society' in K.S. Cook (ed.), *Trust in Society* (New York: Russell Sage Foundation, 2003).

Cook, K.S. and A. Gerbasi, 'Trust' in P. Hedstrom and P.S. Bearman (eds.), *The Oxford Handbook of Analytical Sociology* (Oxford: Oxford University Press, 2009).

Cook, K.S. and R. Hardin, 'Norms of Cooperativeness and Networks of Trust' in M. Hechter and K.D. Opp (eds.), *Social Norms* (New York: Russell Sage Foundation, 2001).

Cook, K.S. et al., 'Social Exchange Theory' in J. DeLamater and A. Ward (eds.), *Handbook of Social Psychology* (New York: Springer, 2013).

Dasgupta, P., 'Trust as a Commodity' in D. Gambetta (ed.), *Trust: Making and Breaking Cooperative Relations* (Oxford: Basil Blackwell, 1988).

De Fine Licht, J., 'The Janus Face of Transparency: Balancing Openness and Secrecy in Democratic Decision-Making' in D. Mokrosinksa (ed.), *Transparency and Secrecy in European Democracies: Contested Trade-Offs* (Abingdon: Routledge, 2000).

Destri, C., 'Democratic Politics and the Circles of Trust' in R. Barradas de Freitas and S. Lo Iacono (eds.), *Trust Matters: Cross-Disciplinary Essays* (London: Bloomsbury, 2021).

Dodds, S., 'Dependence, Care, and Vulnerability' in C. MacKenzie, W. Rogers and S. Dodds (eds.), *Vulnerability: New Essays in Ethics and Feminist Philosophy* (Oxford: Oxford University Press, 2013).

Doherty, J., 'Housing: Linking Theory and Practice' in H.T.O. Davies, S.M. Nutley and P.C. Smith (eds.), *What Works? Evidence-Based Policy and Practice in Public Services* (Bristol: Bristol University Press, 2000).

Donnelly, C., 'Participation and Expertise: Judicial Attitudes in Comparative Perspective' in S. Rose-Ackerman and P.L. Lindseth (eds.), *Comparative Administrative Law* (Cheltenham: Edward Elgar, 2010).

Dunn, J., 'Trust and Political Agency' in D. Gambetta (ed.), *Trust: Making and Breaking Cooperative Relations* (Oxford: Basil Blackwell, 1988).

Endicott, T., 'Equity and Administrative Behaviour: A Commentary' in P.G. Turner (ed.), *Equity and Administration* (Cambridge: Cambridge University Press, 2016).

Farrell, H., 'Institutions and Midlevel Explanations of Trust' in K.S. Cook, M. Levi and R. Hardin (eds.), *Whom Can We Trust? How Groups, Networks, and Institutions Make Trust Possible* (New York: Russell Sage Foundation, 2009).

Finn, P., 'A Sovereign People, A Public Trust' in P.D. Finn (ed.), *Essays on Law and Government, Volume 1: Principles and Values* (North Ryde: The Law Book Company, 1995).

Fombad, C.M., 'Corruption and the Crisis of Constitutionalism in Africa' in C.M. Fombad and N. Steyler (eds.), *Corruption and Constitutionalism in Africa* (Oxford: Oxford University Press, 2020).

Forbath, W., 'Cultural Transformation, Deep Institutional Reform, and ESR Practice: South Africa's Treatment Action Campaign' in L.E. White and J. Perelman (eds.), *Stones of Hope: How African Activists Reclaim Human Rights to Challenge Global Poverty* (Stanford, CA: Stanford University Press, 2010).

Fox-Decent, E., 'Challenges to Public Fiduciary Theory: An Assessment' in D.G. Smith and A.S. Gold (eds.), *Research Handbook on Fiduciary Law* (Cheltenham: Edward Elgar, 2018).

Galoob, S.R. and E.J. Leib, 'The Core of Fiduciary Political Theory' in D.G. Smith and A.S. Gold (eds.), *Research Handbook on Fiduciary Law* (Cheltenham: Edward Elgar, 2018).

Gambetta, D., 'Can We Trust Trust?' in D. Gambetta (ed.), *Trust: Making and Breaking Cooperative Relations* (Oxford: Basil Blackwell, 1988).

Gargarella, R., 'Deliberative Democracy, Dialogic Justice and the Promise of Social and Economic Rights' in H.A. Garcia, K. Klare and L.A. Williams (eds.), *Social and Economic Rights in Theory and Practice: Critical Inquiries* (Abingdon: Routledge, 2015).

Gauri, V. and D.M. Brinks, 'Introduction: The Elements of Legalization and the Triangular Shape of Social and Economic Rights' in V. Gauri and D.M. Brinks (eds.), *Courting Social Justice: Judicial Enforcement of Social and Economic Rights in the Developing World* (Cambridge: Cambridge University Press, 2010).

Gearty, C., 'Against Judicial Enforcement' in C. Gearty and V. Mantouvalou (eds.), *Debating Social Rights* (Oxford: Hart, 2010).

Gloppen, S., 'Courts, Corruption and Judicial Independence' in T. Søreide and A. Williams (eds.), *Corruption, Grabbing and Development* (Cheltenham: Edward Elgar, 2013).

Gold, A.S., 'The Loyalties of Fiduciary Law' in A.S. Gold and P.B. Miller (eds.), *Philosophical Foundations of Fiduciary Law* (Oxford: Oxford University Press, 2014).

'The Fiduciary Duty of Loyalty' in E.J. Criddle, P.B. Miller and R.H. Sitkoff (eds.), *The Oxford Handbook of Fiduciary Law* (Oxford: Oxford University Press, 2019).

Greschner, D., '*Charter* Challenges and Evidence-Based Decision-Making in the Health Care System: Towards a Symbiotic Relationship' in C.M. Flood (ed.), *Just Medicare: What's In, What's Out, How We Decide* (Toronto: University of Toronto Press, 2006).

Grimes, M., 'Procedural Fairness and Political Trust' in S. Zmerli and T. van der Meer (eds.), *Handbook on Political Trust* (Cheltenham: Edward Elgar, 2017).

Gross, A., 'The Right to Health in Israel between Solidarity and Neoliberalism' in C.M. Flood and A. Gross (eds.), *The Right to Health at the Public/Private Divide* (Cambridge: Cambridge University Press, 2014).

Hansen, C., 'Inattentive, Intransigent and Incompetent' in R.S. Humm et al. (eds.), *Child, Parent and State* (Philadelphia, PA: Temple University Press, 1994).

Hardin, R., 'Conceptions and Explanations of Trust' in K.S. Cook (ed.), *Trust in Society* (New York: Russell Sage Foundation, 2001).

'Trust in Government' in V. Braithwaite and M. Levi (eds.), *Trust and Governance* (New York: Russell Sage Foundation, 2003).

Harding, M., 'Fiduciary Relationships, Fiduciary Law, and Trust' in D.G. Smith and A.S. Gold (eds.), *Research Handbook on Fiduciary Law* (Cheltenham: Edward Elgar, 2018).

Harlow, C., 'Accountability and Constitutional Law' in M. Bovens, R.E. Goodin and T. Schillemans (eds.), *The Oxford Handbook of Public Accountability* (Oxford: Oxford University Press, 2014).

Harré, R., 'Trust and Its Surrogates' in M.E. Warren (ed.), *Democracy and Trust* (Cambridge: Cambridge University Press, 1999).

Hibbing, J.R. and E. Theiss-Morse, 'The Means Is the End' in J.R. Hibbing and E. Theiss-Morse (eds.), *What Is It about Government that Americans Dislike?* (Cambridge: Cambridge University Press, 2001).

Heimer, C.A., 'Solving the Problem of Trust' in K.S. Cook (ed.), *Trust in Society* (New York: Russell Sage Foundation, 2001).

Jackman, M., 'Reality Checks: Presuming Innocence and Proving Guilt in *Charter* Welfare Cases' in M. Young et al. (eds.), *Poverty: Rights, Social Citizenship, and Legal Activism* (Vancouver: UBC Press, 2007).

Jackman, M. and B. Porter, 'Socio-economic Rights under the Canadian Charter' in M. Langford (ed.), *Social Rights Jurisprudence: Emerging Trends in International and Comparative Law* (Cambridge: Cambridge University Press, 2008).

Kim, S.H., 'Fiduciary Law's Anti-corruption Norm' in D.G. Smith and A.S. Gold (eds.), *Research Handbook on Fiduciary Law* (Cheltenham: Edward Elgar, 2018).

'Fiduciary Law and Corruption' in E.J. Criddle, P.B. Miller and R.H. Sitkoff (eds.), *The Oxford Handbook of Fiduciary Law* (Oxford: Oxford University Press, 2019).

Klaaren, J., 'Social Grant Payments and Regulatory Responses to Corruption in South Africa' in C.M. Fombad and N. Steyler (eds.), *Corruption and Constitutionalism in Africa* (Oxford: Oxford University Press, 2020).

Kumlin, S., 'Overloaded or Undermined? European Welfare States in the Face of Performance Dissatisfaction' in S. Svallfors (ed.), *The Political Sociology of the Welfare State: Institutions, Social Cleavages, and Orientations* (Stanford, CA: Stanford University Press, 2007).

Landau, D., 'South African Social Rights Jurisprudence and the Global Cannon: A Revisionist View' in R. Dixon and T. Roux (eds.), *Constitutional Triumphs, Constitutional Disappointments: A Critical Account of the 1996 South African Constitution's Local and International Influence* (Cambridge: Cambridge University Press, 2018).

Landau, D. and R. Dixon, 'Constitutional Non-transformation? Socioeconomic Rights beyond the Poor?' in K.G. Young (ed.), *The Future of Economic and Social Rights* (Cambridge: Cambridge University Press, 2019).

Langford, M., 'The Justiciability of Social Rights: From Practice to Theory' in M. Langford (ed.), *Social Rights Jurisprudence: Emerging Trends in International and Comparative Law* (Cambridge: Cambridge University Press, 2008).

Leventhal, G.S., 'What Should Be Done with Equity Theory? New Approaches to the Study of Fairness in Social Relationships' in K.J. Gergen, M.S. Greenberg and R.H. Willis, *Social Exchange: Advances in Theory and Research* (St. Louis, MO: Plenus Press, 1980).

Levi, M., 'A State of Trust' in V. Braithwaite and M. Levi (eds.), *Trust and Governance* (New York: Russell Sage Foundation, 1998).

Liebenberg, S., 'Direct Constitutional Protection of Economic, Social and Cultural Rights in South Africa' in D.M. Chirwa and L. Chenwi (eds.), *The Protection of Economic, Social and Cultural Rights in Africa: International, Regional and National Perspectives* (Cambridge: Cambridge University Press, 2016).

'The Participatory Democratic Turn in South Africa's Social Rights Jurisprudence' in K.G. Young (ed.), *The Future of Economic and Social Rights* (Cambridge: Cambridge University Press, 2019).

Luhmann, N., 'Familiarity, Confidence, Trust: Problems and Alternatives' in D. Gambetta (ed.), *Trust: Making and Breaking Cooperative Relations* (Oxford: Basil Blackwell, 1988).

Mansbridge, J., 'Social and Cultural Causes of Dissatisfaction with U.S. Government' in J.S. Nye, Jr., P.D. Zelikow and D.C. King (eds.), *Why People Do Not Trust Government* (Cambridge, MA: Harvard University Press, 1997).

Mantouvalou, V., 'In Support of Legalisation' in C. Gearty and V. Mantouvalou (eds.), *Debating Social Rights* (Oxford: Hart, 2010).

Matteucci, S.C. and S. Halliday, 'Social Rights, the Welfare State and European Austerity' in S.C. Matteucci and S. Halliday (eds.), *Social Rights in Europe in an Age of Austerity* (Abingdon: Routledge, 2017).

Mbazira, C., 'Uganda's Hybrid Constitutional Protection of Economic, Social and Cultural Rights' in D.M. Chirwa and L. Chenwi (eds.), *The Protection of Economic, Social and Cultural Rights in Africa: International, Regional and National Perspectives* (Cambridge: Cambridge University Press, 2016).

Miller, P.B., 'Dimensions of Fiduciary Loyalty' in D.G. Smith and A.S. Gold (eds.), *Research Handbook on Fiduciary Law* (Cheltenham: Edward Elgar, 2018).

Morel, N. and J. Palme, 'Financing the Welfare State and the Politics of Taxation' in B. Greve (ed.), *The Routledge Handbook of the Welfare State* (Abingdon: Routledge, 2013).

Moy, P. and M.H. Hussain, 'Media Influences on Political Trust and Engagement' in G.C. Edwards III, L.R. Jacobs and R.Y. Shapiro (eds.), *The Oxford Handbook of American Public Opinion and the Media* (Oxford: Oxford University Press, 2011).

Newton, K., 'Social and Political Trust in Established Democracies' in P. Norris (ed.), *Critical Citizens: Global Support for Democratic Government* (Oxford: Oxford University Press, 1999).

Nissenbaum, H., 'Will Security Enhance Trust Online, or Supplant It?' in R.M. Kramer and K.S. Cook (eds.), *Trust and Distrust in Organizations* (New York: Russell Sage Foundation, 2004).

Nolan, A., 'Introduction' in A. Nolan (ed.), *Economic and Social Rights after the Global Financial Crisis* (Cambridge: Cambridge University Press, 2014).

Norris, P., 'Conclusion: The Growth of Critical Citizens and Its Consequences' in P. Norris (ed.), *Critical Citizens: Global Support for Democratic Government* (Oxford: Oxford University Press, 1999).

Nye, Jr., J.S., 'Introduction: The Decline of Confidence in Government' in J.S. Nye, Jr., P.D. Zelikow and D.C. King (eds.), *Why People Do Not Trust Government* (Cambridge, MA: Harvard University Press, 1997).

Nye, Jr., J.S. and P.D. Zelikow, 'Conclusion: Reflections, Conjectures and Puzzles' in J.S. Nye, Jr., P.D. Zelikow and D.C. King (eds.), *Why People Do Not Trust Government* (Cambridge, MA: Harvard University Press, 1997).

O'Cinneide, C., 'Legal Accountability and Social Justice' in N. Bamforth and P. Leyland (eds.), *Accountability in the Contemporary Constitution* (Oxford: Oxford University Press, 2013).

'The Problematic of Social Rights – Uniformity and Diversity in the Development of Social Rights Review' in L. Lazarus, C. McCrudden and N. Bowles (eds.), *Reasoning Rights: Comparative Judicial Engagement* (Oxford: Hart, 2014).

'The Potential and Pitfalls of Intersectionality in the Context of Social Rights Adjudication' in S. Atrey and P. Dunne (eds.), *Intersectionality and Human Rights Law* (Oxford: Hart, 2020).

O'Neill, O., 'Trust, Trustworthiness, and Accountability' in N. Morris and D. Vines (eds.), *Capital Failure: Rebuilding Trust in Financial Services* (Oxford: Oxford University Press, 2014).

O'Regan, K. and N. Friedman, 'Equality' in T. Ginsburg and R. Dixon (eds.), *Comparative Constitutional Law* (Cheltenham: Edward Elgar, 2011).

Offe, C., 'How Can We Trust Our Fellow Citizens?' in M.E. Warren (ed.), *Democracy and Trust* (Cambridge: Cambridge University Press, 1999).

Oliver, D., 'Accountability and the Foundations of British Democracy – the Public Interest and Public Service Principles' in N. Bamforth and P. Leyland (eds.), *Accountability in the Contemporary Constitution* (Oxford: Oxford University Press, 2013).

Patterson, O., 'Liberty against the Democratic State: On the Historical and Contemporary Sources of American Distrust' in M.E. Warren (ed.), *Democracy and Trust* (Cambridge: Cambridge University Press, 1999).

Pettit, P., 'Republican Theory and Political Trust' in V. Braithwaite and M. Levi (eds.), *Trust and Governance* (New York: Russell Sage Foundation, 1998).

Pierson, P., 'Coping with Permanent Austerity: Welfare State Restructuring in Affluent Democracies' in P. Pierson (ed.), *The New Politics of the Welfare State* (Oxford: Oxford University Press, 2001).

Porter, B., 'Enforcing the Right to Reasonableness in Social Rights Litigation: The Canadian Experience' in M. Langford, C. Rodriguez-Garavito and J. Rossi (eds.), *Compliance with Socio-economic Rights Judgments: Making It Stick* (Cambridge: Cambridge University Press, 2017).

Roach, K., 'The Challenges of Crafting Remedies for Violations of Socio-economic Rights' in M. Langford (ed.), *Social Rights Jurisprudence: Emerging Trends in International and Comparative Law* (Cambridge: Cambridge University Press, 2008).

Rosevear, E., R. Hirschl and C. Jung, 'Justiciable and Aspirational Economic and Social Rights in National Constitutions' in K.G. Young (ed.), *The Future of Economic and Social Rights* (Cambridge: Cambridge University Press, 2019).

Rudolph, T.J., 'Political Trust as a Heuristic' in S. Zmerli and T. van der Meer (eds.), *Handbook on Political Trust* (Cheltenham: Edward Elgar, 2017).

Scholz, J.T., 'Trust, Taxes, and Compliance' in V. Braithwaite and M. Levi (eds.), *Trust and Governance* (New York: Russell Sage Foundation, 1998).

Shapiro, S., 'The Grammar of Trust' in J. Pixley (ed.), *New Perspectives on Emotions in Finance: The Sociology of Confidence, Fear and Betrayal* (Abingdon: Routledge, 2012).

Sheffrin, S.M. and R.K. Triest, 'Can Brute Deterrence Backfire? Perceptions and Attitudes in Taxpayer Compliance' in J. Slemrod (ed.), *Why People Pay Taxes* (Ann Arbor: University of Michigan Press, 1992).

Shue, H., 'The Interdependence of Duties' in P. Alston and K. Tomasevski (eds.), *The Right to Food* (Leiden: Martinus Nijhoff Publishers, 1985).

Steinmo, S.H., 'American Exceptionalism Reconsidered: Culture or Institutions?' in L.C. Dodd and C. Jillson (eds.), *The Dynamics of American Politics: Approaches and Interpretations* (Boulder, CO: Westview Press, 1994).

Steyler, N., 'Towards Understanding and Combating the Crime of Corruption in Africa' in C.M. Fombad and N. Steyler (eds.), *Corruption and Constitutionalism in Africa* (Oxford: Oxford University Press, 2020).

Sunstein, C.R., 'Against Positive Rights' in A. Sajó (ed.), *Western Rights? Post-Communist Application* (The Hague: Kluwer Law International, 1996).

Svallfors, S., 'Political Trust and Support for the Welfare State: Unpacking a Supposed Relationship' in B. Rothstein and S. Steinmo (eds.), *Restructuring the Welfare State: Political Institutions and Policy Change* (London: Palgrave MacMillan, 2002).

'Introduction' in S. Svallfors (ed.), *The Political Sociology of the Welfare State: Institutions, Social Cleavages and Orientations* (Stanford, CA: Stanford University Press, 2007).

Sydow, J., 'Understanding the Constitution of Interorganizational Trust' in C. Lane and R. Bachmann (eds.), *Trust within and between Organizations: Conceptual Issues and Empirical Applications* (Oxford: Oxford University Press, 1998).

Trüdinger, E.M. and U. Bollow, 'Evaluations of Welfare State Reforms in Germany: Political Trust Makes a (Big) Difference' in S. Zmerli and M. Hooghe (eds.), *Political Trust: Why Context Matters* (Chichester: ECPR Press, 2011).

Tyler, T.R. and P. Degoey, 'Trust in Organizational Authorities: The Influence of Motive Attributions on Willingness to Accept Decisions' in R.M. Kramer and T.R. Tyler (eds.), *Trust in Organizations: Frontiers of Theory and Research* (Thousand Oaks, CA: Sage Publications, 1996).

Underkuffler, L.S., 'Fiduciary Theory: The Missing Piece for Positive Rights' in E. Criddle et al. (eds.), *Fiduciary Government* (Cambridge: Cambridge University Press, 2018).

Uslaner, E.M., 'Tax Evasion, Trust, and the Strong Arm of the Law' in N. Hayoz and S. Hug (eds.), *Tax Evasion, Trust and State Capacities* (Bern: Peter Lang, 2007).

'Corruption, the Inequality Trap and Trust in Government' in S. Zmerli and M. Hooghe (eds.), *Political Trust: Why Context Matters* (Chichester: ECPR Press, 2011).

Van der Meer, T.W.G., 'Political Trust and the "Crisis of Democracy"' in *Oxford Research Encyclopedia of Politics* (Oxford: Oxford University Press, 2017).

Warburton, J., 'Corruption as a Social Process: From Dyads to Networks' in P. Larmour and N. Wolanin (eds.), *Corruption and Anti-corruption* (Canberra: Australian National University Press, 2013).

Warren, M., 'Trust and Democracy' in E.M. Uslaner (ed.), *The Oxford Handbook of Social and Political Trust* (Oxford: Oxford University Press, 2018).

Warren, M.E., 'Democratic Theory and Trust' in M.E. Warren (ed.), *Democracy and Trust* (Cambridge: Cambridge University Press, 1999).

'Introduction' in M.E. Warren (ed.), *Democracy and Trust* (Cambridge: Cambridge University Press, 1999).

'What Kinds of Trust Does a Democracy Need? Trust from the Perspective of Democratic Theory' in S. Zmerli and T.W.G. van der Meer (eds.), *Handbook on Political Trust* (Cheltenham: Edward Elgar, 2017).

Weinstock, D., 'Trust in Institutions' in D. Archard et al. (eds.), *Reading Onora O'Neill* (Abingdon: Routledge, 2013).

Young, K.G., 'The New Managerialism: Courts, Positive Duties, and Economic and Social Rights' in V.C. Jackson and Y. Dawood (eds.), *Constitutionalism and a Right to Effective Government?* (Cambridge: Cambridge University Press, 2022).

Yowell, P., 'Empirical Research in Rights-Based Judicial Review of Legislation' in K. Ziegler and P. Huber (eds.), *Current Problems in the Protection of Human Rights: Perspectives from Germany and the UK* (Oxford: Hart, 2013).

Ziemele, I., A. Spale and L. Jurcēna, 'The Constitutional Court of the Republic of Latvia' in A. von Bogdandy, P.M. Huber and C. Grabenwarter (eds.), *The Max Planck Handbooks in European Public Law*, Vol. 3 (Oxford: Oxford University Press, 2020).

Journal Articles

Ackers, L., E. Ioannou and J. Ackers-Johnson, 'The Impact of Delays on Maternal and Neonatal Outcomes in Ugandan Public Health Facilities: The Role of Absenteeism' (2016) 31 *Health Policy and Planning* 1152.

Akech, M., 'Abuse of Power and Corruption in Kenya: Will the New Constitution Enhance Government Accountability' (2011) 18 *Indiana Journal of Global Legal Studies* 341.

Albertyn, C. and B. Goldblatt, 'Facing the Challenge of Transformation: Difficulties in the Development of an Indigenous Jurisprudence of Equality' (1998) 14 *South African Journal on Human Rights* 248.

Alemanno, A., 'The Emergence of the Evidence-Based Judicial Reflex: A Response to Bar-Siman-Tov's Semi-procedural Review' (2013) 1 *Theory and Practice of Legislation* 327.

Allett, J., 'New Liberalism & the New Property Doctrine: Welfare Rights as Property Rights' (1987) 20 *Polity* 57.

Andersen, M.K., 'Why Corruption Matters in Human Rights' (2018) 10 *Journal of Human Rights Practice* 179.

Anderson, C.J. and Y.V. Tverdova, 'Corruption, Political Allegiances, and Attitudes toward Government in Contemporary Democracies' (2003) 47 *American Journal of Political Science* 91.

Anderson, R.D., A. Jones and W.E. Kovacic, 'Preventing Corruption, Supplier Collusion, and the Corrosion of Civic Trust: A Procompetitive Program to Improve the Effectiveness and Legitimacy of Public Procurement' (2019) 26 *George Mason Law Review* 1233.

Atrey, S., 'The Intersectional Case of Poverty in Discrimination Law' (2018) 18 *Human Rights Law Review* 411.

Bachmann, R. and A. Inkpen, 'Understanding Institutional-Based Trust Building Processes in Inter-organizational Relationships' (2011) 32 *Organization Studies* 281.

Baier, A.B., 'Trust and Antitrust' (1985) 96 *Ethics* 231.

Barbalet, J., 'A Characterization of Trust, and Its Consequences' (2009) 38 *Theory and Society* 367.

Bar-Siman-Tov, I., 'Semiprocedural Judicial Review' (2012) 6 *Legisprudence* 271.

'The Dual Meaning of Evidence-Based Judicial Review of Legislation' (2016) 4 *The Theory and Practice of Legislation* 107.

Bauhr, M. et al., 'Lights on the Shadows of Public Procurement: Transparency as an Antidote to Corruption' (2020) 33 *Governance* 495.

Baumgold, D., 'Trust in Hobbes' Political Thought' (2013) 20 *Political Theory* 1.

Becker, L., 'Trust as Noncognitive Security about Motives' (1996) 107 *Ethics* 43.

Bellamy, R., 'The Democratic Qualities of Courts: A Critical Analysis of Three Arguments' (2013) 49 *Representation* 333.

Bellia, Jr., A.J., 'Promises, Trust, and Contract Law' (2002) 47 *American Journal of Jurisprudence* 25.

Bilchitz, D., 'Giving Socio-economic Rights Teeth: The Minimum Core and Its Importance' (2002) 119 *South African Law Journal* 484.

'Towards a Reasonable Approach to the Minimum Core: Laying the Foundation for Future Socio-economic Rights Jurisprudence' (2003) 19 *South African Journal on Human Rights* 1.

Bittner, C., 'Casenote – Human Dignity as a Matter of Legislative Consistency in an Ideal World: The Fundamental Right to Guarantee a Subsistence Minimum in the German Federal Constitutional Court's Judgment of 9 February 2010' (2011) 12 *German Law Journal* 1941.

Blair, M.M. and L.A. Stout, 'Trust, Trustworthiness, and the Behavioral Foundations of Corporate Law' (2001) 149 *University of Pennsylvania Law Review* 1735.

Blidook, K., 'Media, Public Opinion and Health Care in Canada: How the Media Affect "The Way Things Are"' (2008) 41 *Canadian Journal of Political Science* 355.

Bovens, M., 'Analysing and Assessing Accountability: A Conceptual Framework' (2007) 13 *European Law Journal* 447.

Brand, D., 'Judicial Deference and Democracy in Socio-economic Rights Cases in South Africa' (2011) 3 *Stellenbosch Law Review* 614.

Breach, L., '*Fiducia* in Public Law' (2017) 48 *Victoria University of Wellington Review* 413.

Brinks, D.M. and V. Gauri, 'The Law's Majestic Equality? The Distributive Impact of Judicializing Social and Economic Rights' (2014) 12 *Perspectives on Politics* 375.

Brodsky, G. and S. Day, 'Beyond the Social and Economic Rights Debate: Substantive Equality Speaks to Poverty' (2002) 14 *Canadian Journal of Women and the Law* 184.

Caldeira, G.A. and J.L. Gibson, 'The Etiology of Public Support for the Supreme Court' (1992) 36 *American Journal of Political Science* 635.

'The Legitimacy of the Court of Justice in the European Union: Models of Institutional Support' (1995) 89 *American Political Science Review* 356.

Chang, E.C.C. and Y. Chu, 'Corruption and Trust: Exceptionalism in Asian Democracies?' (2006) 68 *The Journal of Politics* 269.

Chanley, V.A., T.J. Rudolph and W.M. Rahn, 'The Origins and Consequences of Public Trust in Government' (2000) 64 *Public Opinion Quarterly* 239.

Chayes, A., 'The Role of the Judge in Public Law Litigation' (1976) 89 *Harvard Law Review* 1281.

Chilton, A. and M. Versteeg, 'Rights without Resources: The Impact of Constitutional Social Rights on Social Spending' (2017) 60 *Journal of Law and Economics* 713.

Christodoulis, E.A., 'Paradoxes of Sovereignty and Representation' (2002) 1 *TSAR* 108.

Citrin, J. and L. Stoker, 'Political Trust in a Cynical Age' (2018) 21 *Annual Review of Political Science* 49.

Conaglen, M., 'The Nature and Function of Fiduciary Loyalty' (2005) 121 *Law Quarterly Review* 452.

Cook, K.S. and R.M. Emerson, 'Power, Equity and Commitment in Exchange Networks' (1978) 43 *American Sociological Review* 721.

Cook, K.S. et al., 'The Distribution of Power in Exchange Networks: Theory and Experimental Results' (1983) 89 *American Journal of Sociology* 275.

Cooray, A. and F. Schneider, 'Does Corruption Promote Emigration? An Empirical Examination' (2016) 29 *Journal of Population Economics* 293.

Contiades, X. and A. Fotiadou, 'Social Rights in the Age of Proportionality: Global Economic Crisis and Constitutional Litigation' (2012) 10 *International Journal of Constitutional Law* 660.

Cotterrell, R., 'Trusting in Law: Legal and Moral Concepts of Trust' (1993) 46 *Current Legal Problems* 75.

Criddle, E.J., 'Fiduciary Foundations of Administrative Law' (2006) 54 *UCLA Law Review* 117.

Cross, F.B., 'The Error of Positive Rights' (2001) 48 *UCLA Law Review* 857.

'Law and Trust' (2005) 93 *Georgetown Law Journal* 1457.

Das, T.K. and B.S. Teng, 'The Risk-Based View of Trust: A Conceptual Framework' (2004) 19 *Journal of Business and Psychology* 85.

Davies, P., 'What Is Evidence-Based Education?' (1999) 47 *British Journal of Educational Studies* 108.

Davis, D.M., 'Adjudicating the Socio-economic Rights in the South African Constitution: Towards "Deference Lite"?' (2006) 22 *South African Journal on Human Rights* 301.

Davis, S., 'The False Promise of Fiduciary Government' (2014) 89 *Notre Dame Law Review* 1145.

De Fine Licht, J., 'Do We Really Want to Know? The Potentially Negative Effect of Transparency in Decision Making on Perceived Legitimacy' (2011) 34 *Scandinavian Political Studies* 183.

'Transparency Actually: How Transparency Affects Public Perceptions of Political Decision-Making' (2014) 6 *European Political Science Review* 309.

Dixon, R., 'Creating Dialogue about Socioeconomic Rights: Strong-Form versus Weak-Form Judicial Review Revisited' (2007) 5 *International Journal of Constitutional Law* 391.

Dixon, R. and J. Suk, 'Liberal Constitutionalism and Economic Inequality' (2018) 85 *The University of Chicago Law Review* 369.

Dommett, K. and W. Pearce, 'What Do We Know about Public Attitudes towards Experts? Reviewing Survey Data in the United Kingdom and European Union' (2019) 28 *Public Understanding of Science* 669.

Du Plessis, M. and A. Coutsoudis, 'Considering Corruption through the AllPay Lens: On the Limits of Judicial Review, Strengthening Accountability, and the Long Arm of the Law' (2016) 133 *South African Law Journal* 755.

Dworkin, R., 'Judicial Discretion' (1963) 60 *The Journal of Philosophy* 624.

Dworkin, R.M., 'The Model of Rules' (1967) 35 *The University of Chicago Law Review* 14.

'Social Rules and Legal Theory' (1972) 81 *The Yale Law Journal* 855.

Ebadolahi, M., 'Using Structural Interdicts and the South African Human Rights Commission to Achieve Judicial Enforcement of Economic and Social Rights in South Africa' (2008) 83 *New York University Law Review* 1565.

Edlund, J., 'Trust in the Capability of the Welfare State and the General Welfare State Support: Sweden 1997–2002' (2006) 49 *Acta Sociologica* 395.

Edlund, J. and A. Lindh, 'Institution Trust and Welfare State Support: On the Role of Trust in Market Institutions' (2013) 33 *Journal of Public Policy* 295.

Egbue, N.G., 'Africa: Cultural Dimensions of Corruption and Possibilities for Change' (2006) 12 *Journal of Social Sciences* 83.

Egidy, S., 'Casenote – The Fundamental Right to the Guarantee of a Subsistence Minimum in the *Hartz IV* Decision of the German Federal Constitutional Court' (2011) 12 *German Law Journal* 1961.

Emerson, R.M., 'Power-Dependence Relations' (1962) 27 *American Sociological Review* 31.

'Power-Dependence Relations: Two Experiments' (1964) 27 *Sociometry* 282.

Eskridge, Jr., W.N., 'Pluralism and Distrust: How Courts Can Support Democracy by Lowering the Stakes of Politics' (2005) 114 *The Yale Law Journal* 1279.

Fabre, C., 'Constitutionalising Social Rights' (1998) 6 *The Journal of Political Philosophy* 263.

Farnsworth, S.J., 'Congress and Citizen Discontent: Public Evaluations of the Membership of One's Own Representative' (2003) 1 *American Politics Research* 66.

Feldman, D., 'Democracy, the Rule of Law and Judicial Review' (1990) 19 *Federal Law Review* 1.

Ferraz, O.L.M., 'The Right to Health in the Courts of Brazil: Worsening Health Inequities?' (2009) 11 *Health and Human Rights Journal* 33.

'Harming the Poor through Social Rights Litigation: Lessons from Brazil' (2011) 89 *Texas Law Review* 1643.

Fineman, M.A., 'The Vulnerable Subject: Anchoring Equality in the Human Condition' (2008) 20 *Yale Journal of Law and Feminism* 1.

Finn, P., 'Public Trust and Public Accountability' (1994) 3 *Griffith Law Review* 224.

'Public Trusts, Public Fiduciaries' (2010) 38 *Federal Law Review* 335.

Flannigan, R., 'The Fiduciary Obligation' (1989) 9 *Oxford Journal of Legal Studies* 285.

'Fiduciary Control of Political Corruption' (2002) 26 *Advocates' Quarterly* 252.

'Contesting Public Service Fiduciary Accountability' (2016) 36 *University of Queensland Law Journal* 7.

'Fiduciary Accountability for Public Service Opportunism' (2018) *Public Law* 241.

Fox-Decent, E., 'The Fiduciary Nature of State Legal Authority' (2005) 31 *Queen's Law Journal* 259.

Fox-Decent, E. and E.J. Criddle, 'The Fiduciary Constitution of Human Rights' (2009) 15 *Legal Theory* 301.

Frankel, T., 'Fiduciary Law' (1983) 71 *California Law Review* 795.

'Fiduciary Law in the Twenty-First Century' (2011) 91 *Boston University Law Review* 1289.

Fredman, S., 'Providing Equality: Substantive Equality and the Positive Duty to Provide' (2005) 21 *South African Journal on Human Rights* 163.

'Redistribution and Recognition: Reconciling Inequalities' (2007) 23 *South African Journal on Human Rights* 214.

'Substantive Equality Revisited' (2016) 14 *International Journal of Constitutional Law* 712.

Freeman, D.C., 'Note: The Poor and the Political Process: Equal Access to Lobbying' (1969) 6 *Harvard Journal on Legislation* 369.

Fuller, L., 'The Forms and Limits of Adjudication' (1978–1979) 92 *Harvard Law Review* 353.

Gabriel, O.W. and E.M. Trüdinger, 'Embellishing Welfare State Reforms? Political Trust and the Support for Welfare State Reforms in Germany' (2011) 20 *German Politics* 273.

Gangl, A., 'Procedural Justice Theory and Evaluations of the Lawmaking Process' (2003) 25 *Political Behavior* 119.

Ganty, S., 'Poverty as Misrecognition: What Role for Antidiscrimination Law in Europe?' (2021) 21 *Human Rights Law Review* 962.

Garcia, P.J., 'Corruption in Global Health: The Open Secret' (2019) 394 *The Lancet* 2119.

Getzler, T., '"As If." Accountability and Counterfactual Trust' (2011) 91 *Boston University Law Review* 973.

Gibson, J.L., G.A. Caldeira and V.A. Baird, 'On the Legitimacy of National High Courts' (1998) 92 *American Political Science Review* 343.

Gibson, J.L., G.A. Caldeira and L.K. Spence, 'Measuring Attitudes toward the United States Supreme Court' (2003) 47 *American Journal of Political Science* 354.

Gold, A.S., 'Purposive Loyalty' (2017) 74 *Washington and Lee Law Review* 881.

Granovetter, M., 'Economic Action and Social Structure: The Problem of Embeddedness' (1985) 91 *American Journal of Sociology* 481.

Granovetter, M.S., 'The Strength of Weak Ties' (1973) 78 *American Journal of Sociology* 1360.

Gray, J.A.M., 'Evidence Based Policy Making' (2004) 329 *British Medical Journal* 988.

Greenawalt, K., 'Discretion and Judicial Discretion: The Elusive Quest for the Fetters That Bind Judges' (1975) 75 *Columbia Law Review* 359.

Greschner, D. and S. Lewis, '*Auton* and Evidence-Based Decision-Making: Medicare in the Courts' (2003) 82 *The Canadian Bar Review* 501.

Grimes, M., 'Organizing Consent: The Role of Procedural Fairness in Political Trust and Compliance' (2006) 45 *European Journal of Political Research* 285.

Grimmelikhuijsen, S., 'Linking Transparency, Knowledge and Citizen Trust in Government: An Experiment' (2012) 78 *International Review of Administrative Sciences* 50.

Hall, M.A., 'Law, Medicine, and Trust' (2002) 55 *Stanford Law Review* 463.

'The Importance of Trust for Ethics, Law, and Public Policy' (2005) 14 *Cambridge Quarterly of Healthcare Ethics* 156.

Hardin, R., 'The Street-Level Epistemology of Trust' (1993) 21 *Politics and Society* 505.

'Trustworthiness' (1996) 107 *Ethics* 26.

'Liberal Distrust' (2002) 10 *European Review* 73.

Harding, M., 'Manifesting Trust' (2009) 28 *Oxford Journal of Legal Studies* 245.

'Responding to Trust' (2011) 24 *Ratio Juris* 75.

'Trust and Fiduciary Law' (2013) 33 *Oxford Journal of Legal Studies* 81.

Hawkins, B. and J. Parkhurst, 'The "Good Governance" of Evidence in Health Policy' (2016) 12 *Evidence & Policy* 575.

Hawkins, B. and A.A. Rosete, 'Judicialization and Health Policy in Colombia: The Implications for Evidence-Informed Policymaking' (2019) 47 *Policy Studies Journal* 953.

Head, B.W., 'Three Lenses of Evidence-Based Policy' (2008) 67 *The Australian Journal of Public Administration* 1.

'Reconsidering Evidence-Based Policy: Key Issues and Challenges' (2010) 29 *Policy and Society* 77.

'Toward More "Evidence-Informed" Policy Making?' (2016) 76 *Public Administration Review* 472.

Hibbing, J.R. and E. Theiss-Morse, 'Process Preferences and American Politics: What the People Want Government to Be' (2001) 95 *American Political Science Review* 145.

Hirschl, R., 'From Comparative Constitutional Law to Comparative Constitutional Studies' (2013) 11 *International Journal of Constitutional Law* 1.

Hogg, P.W., 'The *Charter* Revolution: Is It Undemocratic?' (2001) 12 *Constitutional Forum* 1.

Holton, R., 'Deciding to Trust, Coming to Believe' (1994) 72 *Australasian Journal of Philosophy* 63.

Jackman, M., 'Charter Review as a Health Care Accountability Mechanism in Canada' (2010) 18 *Health Law Journal* 1.

'The Future of Health Care Accountability: A Human Rights Approach' (2016) 47 *Ottawa Law Review* 441.

Jones, A., 'Combatting Corruption and Collusion in UK Public Procurement: Proposals for Post-Brexit Reform' (2021) 84 *Modern Law Review* 667.

Jones, K., 'Trust as an Affective Attitude' (1996) 107 *Ethics* 4.

Jowell, J., 'Judicial Deference: Servility, Civility or Institutional Capacity?' (2003) *Public Law* 592, 598.

'The Legal Control of Administrative Discretion' (1973) *Public Law* 178.

Jung, C., R. Hirschl and E. Rosevear, 'Economic and Social Rights in National Constitutions' (2014) 62 *American Journal of Comparative Law* 1043.

Karlan, P.S., 'Foreword: Democracy and Disdain' (2011) 126 *Harvard Law Review* 126.

Kibet, E. and C. Fombad, 'Transformative Constitutionalism and the Adjudication of Constitutional Rights in Africa' (2017) 17 *African Human Rights Law Journal* 340.

King, J.A., 'The Pervasiveness of Polycentricity' (2008) *Public Law* 101.

Kisakye, A.N. et al., 'Regulatory Mechanisms for Absenteeism in the Health Sector: A Systemic Review of Strategies and Their Implementation' (2016) 8 *Journal of Healthcare Leadership* 81.

Klatt, M., 'Positive Rights: Who Decides? Judicial Review in Balance' (2015) 13 *International Journal of Constitutional Law* 354.

Klein, A., 'Judging as Nudging' (2008) 39 *Columbia Human Rights Law Review* 351.

Kogler, C. et al., 'Perceptions of Trust and Power Are Associated with tax Compliance: A Cross-cultural Study' (2023) 11 *Economic and Political Studies* 365.

Landau, D., 'The Reality of Social Rights Enforcement' (2012) 53 *Harvard International Law Journal* 189.

'A Dynamic Theory of Judicial Role' (2014) 55 *Boston College Law Review* 1501.

'Choosing between Simple and Complex Remedies in Socio-economic Rights Cases' (2019) 69 *University of Toronto Law Journal* 105.

Langa, P., 'Transformative Constitutionalism' (2006) 17 *Stellenbosch Law Review* 351.

Langford, M., 'Domestic Adjudication and Economic, Social and Cultural Rights: A Socio-legal Review' (2009) 6 *International Journal on Human Rights* 91.

Leib, E.J. and Galoob, S.R., 'Fiduciary Political Theory: A Critique' (2016) 125 *The Yale Law Journal* 1820.

Leib, E.J., D.L. Ponet and M. Serota, 'A Fiduciary Theory of Judging' (2013) 101 *California Law Review* 699.

'Translating Fiduciary Principles into Public Law' (2013) 126 *Harvard Law Review Forum* 91.

Lenard, P.T., 'The Political Philosophy of Trust and Distrust in Democracies and Beyond' (2015) 98 *The Monist* 353.

Levi, M. and A. Sacks, 'Legitimating Beliefs: Sources and Indicators' (2009) 3 *Regulation & Governance* 311.

Levi, M., A. Sacks and T. Tyler, 'Conceptualizing Legitimacy, Measuring Legitimating Beliefs' (2009) 53 *American Behavioral Scientist* 354.

Lichuma, C.O., 'Economic Wrongs and Social Rights: Analyzing the Impact of Systemic Corruption on Realization of Economic and Social Rights in Kenya and the Potential Redress Offered by the Optional Protocol to the International Covenant on Economic, Social and Cultural Rights' (2018) 5 *Transnational Law Review* 63.

Liebenberg, S., 'The Value of Human Dignity in Interpreting Socio-economic Rights' (2005) 21 *South African Journal on Human Rights* 1.

'Participatory Approaches to Socio-economic Rights Adjudication: Tentative Lessons from South African Evictions Law' (2014) 32 *Nordic Journal of Human Rights* 312.

'Participatory Justice in Social Rights Adjudication' (2018) 18 *Human Rights Law Review* 623.

Liebenberg, S. and B. Goldblatt, 'The Interrelationship between Equality and Socio-economic Rights under South Africa's Transformative Constitution' (2007) 23 *South African Journal on Human Rights* 335.

Lindstrom, M., 'Social Capital, Political Trust and Purchase of Illegal Liquor: A Population-Based Study in Southern Sweden' (2008) 86 *Health Policy* 266.

Marien, S. and M. Hooghe, 'Does Political Trust Matter? An Empirical Investigation into the Relation between Political Trust and Support for Law Compliance' (2011) 50 *European Journal of Political Research* 267.

McLean, K., 'Meaningful Engagement: One Step Forward or Two Back? Some Thoughts on *Joe Slovo*' (2010) 3 *Constitutional Court Review* 223.

Meßerschmidt, K., 'Evidence-Based Review of Legislation in Germany' (2016) 4 *The Theory and Practice of Legislation* 209.

Michelman, F.I., 'The Constitution, Social Rights, and Liberal Political Justification' (2003) 1 *International Journal of Constitutional Law* 13.

Miller, P.B., 'Justifying Fiduciary Duties' (2013) 58 *McGill Law Journal* 969.

Milovanovitch, M., 'Fighting Corruption in Education: A Call for Sector Integrity Standards' (2013) 5 *World Bank Law Review* 367.

Moellendorf, D., 'Reasoning about Resources: *Soobramoney* and the Future of Socio-economic Rights Claims' (1998) 14 *South African Journal on Human Rights* 327.

Monahan, P.J., 'Judicial Review and Democracy: A Theory of Judicial Review' (1987) 21 *UBC Law Review* 87.

Moseneke, D., 'The Fourth Bram Fischer Memorial Lecture: Transformative Adjudication' (2002) 18 *South African Journal on Human Rights* 309.

Mubangizi, J.C. and P. Sewpersadh, 'A Human Rights-Based Approach to Combating Public Procurement Corruption in Africa' (2017) 10 *African Journal of Legal Studies* 66.

Mureinik, E., 'Beyond a Charter of Luxuries: Economic Rights in the Constitution' (1992) 8 *South African Journal on Human Rights* 464.

Murphy, K., 'The Role of Trust in Nurturing Compliance: A Study of Accused Tax Avoiders' (2004) 28 *Law and Human Behavior* 187.

Nam, E.Y. and M. Woo, 'Who Is Willing to Pay More Taxes for Welfare? Focusing on the Effects of Diverse Types of Trust in South Korea and Taiwan' (2015) 44 *Development and Society* 319.

Natelson, R.G., 'The Constitution and the Public Trust' (2004) 52 *Buffalo Law Review* 1078.

Nolan, R.C., 'Controlling Fiduciary Power' (2009) 68 *Cambridge Law Journal* 293.

Oliver, K., T. Lorenc and S. Innvaer, 'New Directions in Evidence-Based Policy Research: A Critical Analysis of the Literature' (2014) 12 *Health Research Policy and Systems* 34.

O'Neill, O., 'Accountable Institutions, Trustworthy Cultures' (2017) 9 *Hague Journal on the Rule of Law* 401.

Pabst, A., 'Rethinking Evidence-Based Policy' (2021) 255 *National Institute Economic Review* 85.

Peters, A., 'Corruption as a Violation of International Human Rights' (2018) 29 *European Journal of International Law* 1251.

Pieterse, M., 'Coming to Terms with Judicial Enforcement of Socio-economic Rights' (2004) 20 *South African Journal on Human Rights* 383.

'What Do We Mean When We Talk about Transformative Constitutionalism?' (2005) 20 *SAPR/PL* 155.

'Resuscitating Socio-economic Rights: Constitutional Entitlements to Health Care Services' (2006) 22 *South African Journal on Human Rights* 473.

'Eating Socioeconomic Rights: The Usefulness of Rights Talk in Alleviating Social Hardship Revisited' (2007) 29 *Human Rights Quarterly* 796.

Pillay, A., 'Towards Effective Social and Economic Rights Adjudication: The Role of Meaningful Engagement' (2012) 10 *International Journal of Constitutional Law* 732.

'Economic and Social Rights Adjudication: Developing Principles of Judicial Restraint in South Africa and the United Kingdom' (2013) *Public Law* 599.

Pixley, J., 'Impersonal Trust in Global Mediating Organizations' (1999) 42 *Sociological Perspectives* 647.

Rave, D.T., 'Politicians as Fiduciaries' (2013) 126 *Harvard Law Review* 671.

Ray, B., 'Engagement's Possibilities and Limits as a Socioeconomic Rights Remedy' (2010) 9 *Washington Global Studies Law Review* 399.

'Proceduralisation's Triumph and Engagement's Promise in Socio-economic Rights Litigation' (2011) 27 *South African Journal on Human Rights* 107.

Reich, C.A., 'The New Property' (1964) 73 *The Yale Law Journal* 733.

Roach, K., 'Dialogic Remedies' (2019) 17 *International Journal of Constitutional Law* 860.

Roach, K. and G. Budlender, 'Mandatory Relief and Supervisory Jurisdiction: When Is It Appropriate, Just and Equitable?' (2005) 5 *South African Law Journal* 325.

Rodriguez-Garavito, C., 'Beyond the Courtroom: The Impact of Judicial Activism on Socioeconomic Rights in Latin America' (2011) 89 *Texas Law Review* 1669.

Rose, C., 'The Limitations of a Human Rights Approach to Corruption' (2016) 65 *International and Comparative Law Quarterly* 405.

Rose-Ackerman, S., 'Regulation and Public Law in Comparative Perspective' (2010) 60 *University of Toronto Law Journal* 519.

Rothstein, B., M. Samanni and J. Teorell, 'Explaining the Welfare State: Power Resources vs. the Quality of Government' (2012) 4 *European Political Science Review* 1.

Rothstein, B. and J. Teorell, 'What Is Quality of Government? A Theory of Impartial Government Institutions' (2008) 21 *Governance* 165.

Rudolph, T.J., 'Political Trust, Ideology, and Public Support for Tax Cuts' (2009) 73 *Public Opinion Quarterly* 144.

Scheppele, K.L., 'A Realpolitik Defense of Social Rights' (2004) 82 *Texas Law Review* 1921.

Scholz, J.T. and M. Lubell, 'Trust and Taxpaying: Testing the Heuristic Approach to Collective Action' (1998) 42 *American Journal of Political Science* 398.

Scholz, J.T. and N. Pinney, 'Duty, Fear, and Tax Compliance: The Heuristic Basis of Citizenship Behavior' (1995) 39 *American Journal of Political Science* 490.

Sekalala, S., H. Masud and R.T. Bosco, 'Human Rights Mechanisms for Anti-corruption, Transparency and Accountability: Enabling the Right to Health' (2020) 13 *Global Health Action* 1.

Seligson, M.A., 'The Impact of Corruption on Regime Legitimacy: A Comparative Study of Four Latin American Countries' (2002) 64 *The Journal of Politics* 408.

Seyd, B., 'Exploring Political Disappointment' (2016) 69 *Parliamentary Affairs* 327.

Shapiro, M., '"Deliberative," "Independent" *Technocracy v. Democratic Politics*: Will the Globe Echo the E.U.?" (2005) 58 *Law and Contemporary Problems* 341.

Shapiro, S.P., 'The Social Control of Impersonal Trust' (1987) 93 *American Journal of Sociology* 623.

Sitkin, S.B. and N.L. Roth, 'Explaining the Limited Effectiveness of Legalistic "Remedies" for Trust/Distrust' (1993) 4 *Organization Science* 367.

Slavin, R.E., 'How Evidence-Based Reform Will Transform Research and Practice in Education' (2020) 55 *Educational Psychologist* 21.

Sossin, L., 'Boldly Going Where No Law Has Gone Before: Call Centres, Intake Scripts, Database Fields, and Discretionary Justice in Social Assistance' (2004) 42 *Osgoode Hall Law Journal* 363.

Stacey, R., 'Dynamic Regulatory Constitutionalism: Taking Legislation Seriously in the Judicial Enforcement of Economic and Social Rights' (2017) 31 *Notre Dame Journal of Law, Ethics and Public Policy* 85.

Svallfors, S., 'Government Quality, Egalitarianism, and Attitudes to Taxes and Social Spending: A European Comparison' (2013) 5 *European Political Science Review* 363.

Sunstein, C.R., 'Social and Economic Rights? Lessons from South Africa' (2000) 11 *Constitutional Forum* 123.

Titmuss, R.M., 'Welfare "Rights", Law and Discretion' (1971) 42 *The Political Quarterly* 113.

Tsoukas, H., 'The Tyranny of Light: The Temptations and the Paradoxes of the Information Society' (1997) 29 *Futures* 827.

Tweheyo R. et al., '"Nobody Is after You; It Is Your Initiative to Start Work": A Qualitative Study of Health Workforce Absenteeism in Rural Uganda' (2017) 2 *BMJ Global Health* 1.

Tyler, T.R., 'Social Justice: Outcome and Procedure' (2000) 35 *International Journal of Psychology* 117.

'Trust and Law Abidingness: A Proactive Model of Social Regulation' (2001) 81 *Boston University Law Review* 361.

Tyler, T.R., J.D. Casper and B. Fisher, 'Maintaining Allegiance toward Political Authorities: The Role of Prior Attitudes and the Use of Fair Procedures' (1989) 33 *American Journal of Political Science* 629.

Tyler, T.R. and P. Degoey, 'Collective Restraint in Social Dilemmas: Procedural Justice and Social Identification Effects on Support for Authorities' (1995) 69 *Journal of Personality and Social Psychology* 482.

Underkuffler, L.S., 'Property, Sovereignty, and the Public Trust' (2017) 18 *Theoretical Inquiries in Law* 329.

Veriava, F., 'The Limpopo Textbook Litigation: A Case Study into the Possibilities of a Transformative Constitution' (2016) 32 *South African Journal on Human Rights* 321.

Waldron, J., 'The Core of the Case against Judicial Review' (2006) 115 *The Yale Law Journal* 1346.

Wallace, A. and J. Goodman-Delahunty, 'Measuring Trust and Confidence in Courts' (2021) 12 *International Journal for Court Administration* 1.

Wang, D.W.L., 'From Wednesbury Unreasonableness to Accountability for Reasonableness' (2017) 76 *Cambridge Law Journal* 642.

Warburton, J., 'Corruption, Power and the Public Interest' (1998) 17 *Business & Professional Ethics Journal* 79.

Weinstock, D., 'Building Trust in Divided Societies' (1999) 7 *The Journal of Political Philosophy* 287.

Wesson, M., '*Grootboom* and Beyond: Reassessing the Socio-economic Jurisprudence of the South African Constitutional Court' (2004) 20 *South African Journal on Human Rights* 284.

'Discrimination Law and Social Rights: InterSections and Possibilities' (2007) 13 *Juridica International* 74.

'Equality and Social Rights: An Exploration in Light of the South African Constitution' (2007) *Public Law* 748.

'Disagreement and the Constitutionalisation of Social Rights' (2012) 12 *Human Rights Law Review* 221.

Wiseman, D., 'Competence Concerns in Charter Adjudication: Countering the Anti-poverty Incompetence Argument' (2006) 51 *McGill Law Journal* 503.

'The Past and Future of Constitutional Law and Social Justice: Majestic or Substantive Equality?' (2015) 71 *The Supreme Court Law Review* 563.

Yamin, A.E. and O. Parra-Vera, 'How Do Courts Set Health Policy? The Case of the Colombian Constitutional Court' (2009) 6 *PLoS Medicine* 147.

Young, M., 'Social Justice and the *Charter*: Comparison and Choice' (2013) 50 *Osgoode Hall Law Journal* 669.

Zucker, L., 'Production of Trust: Institutional Sources of Economic Structure, 1840 to 1920' (1986) 8 *Research in Organizational Behavior* 53.

Webpages

Afrobarometer, 'South Africans' Trust in Institutions and Representatives Reaches New Low' (24 August 2021), https://news.gallup.com/poll/4732/supreme-court.aspx.

Al-Ali, Z. and M. Dafel, 'Egyptian Constitutional Reform and the Fight against Corruption' (2013), www.constitutionaltransitions.org/wp-content/uploads/2017/05/1_Al-Ali_Dafel_Egypt_Corruption.pdf.

Crown Commercial Service, 'Publication of Central Government Tenders and Contracts: Central Government Transparency Guidance Note' (November 2017), section 9.1, https://assets.publishing.service.gov.uk/government/uploads/system/uploads/attachment_data/file/996108/Withdrawn_Guidance_Publication_of_New_Central_Government_Tender_documents__and_Contracts_2017__1___1_.pdf.

Engelbert, A. and M. Kaltenborn, 'Corruption and Social Rights Accountability' (2019) Institute of Development Research and Development Policy Working Paper No. 213, www.econstor.eu/handle/10419/202093.

Gallup, 'Supreme Court Trust, Jobs Approval at Historical Lows' (29 September 2022), https://news.gallup.com/poll/402044/supreme-court-trust-job-approval-historical-lows.aspx.

Gallup, 'Trust in Government' (2022), https://news.gallup.com/poll/5392/trust-government.aspx.

Gedan, B.N. and S. Canton, 'Radical Transparency: The Last Hope for Fighting Corruption in Latin America' (1 April 2022), https://gjia.georgetown.edu/2022/04/01/radical-transparency-the-last-hope-for-fighting-corruption-in-latin-america%EF%BF%BC/.

Houreld, K., 'U.S. Suspends Aid to Kenyan Health Ministry over Corruption Concerns' (9 May 2017) *Reuters*, www.reuters.com/article/us-kenya-health-corruption-idUSKBN1851RY.

Igunza, E., 'Coronavirus Corruption in Kenya: Officials and Businesspeople Targeted' (24 September 2020) *BBC*, www.bbc.co.uk/news/world-africa-54278417.

International Council on Human Rights Policy, *Corruption and Human Rights: Making the Connection* (2009), https://assets.publishing.service.gov.uk/media/57a08b6540f0b64974000b10/humanrights-corruption.pdf.

Ipsos, 'Doctors Become the World's Most Trusted Profession' (12 October 2021), www.ipsos.com/en/global-trustworthiness-index-2021.

Macharia, J., 'Kenya Minister Urged to Resign over Medical Scam' (8 May 2012) *Reuters*, www.reuters.com/article/ozatp-kenya-corruption-20120508-idAFJOE84709Z20120508.

Mance, H., 'Britain Has Had Enough of Experts, Says Gove' (3 June 2016) *Financial Times*, www.ft.com/content/3be49734-29cb-11e6-83e4-abc22d5d108c.

Migiro, K., 'Donors Want Their Money Back in Kenyan Education Scam' (11 June 2011) *Thomson Reuters Foundation News*, https://news.trust.org/item/20110617115200-fytp5.

Mijatović, D., 'Corruption Undermines Human Rights and the Rule of Law' (19 January 2021) Council of Europe, www.coe.int/en/web/commissioner/-/corruption-undermines-human-rights-and-the-rule-of-law.

Möllering, G., 'Understanding Trust from the Perspective of Sociological Neoinstitutionalism: The Interplay of Institutions and Agency' (Max Planck Institute for the Study of Societies, Discussion Paper 05/13, 2009), www.ssoar.info/ssoar/bitstream/handle/document/37397/ssoar-2005-mollering-Understanding_trust_from_the_perspective.pdf?sequence=1.

'Net1 under FBI Investigation for Corruption in SA' (4 December 2012) *BusinessTech*, https://businesstech.co.za/news/it-services/27861/net-1-under-fbi-investigation-for-corruption-in-sa/.

OECD, 'Preventing Corruption in Public Procurement' (2016), www.oecd.org/gov/ethics/Corruption-Public-Procurement-Brochure.pdf.

'Building Trust to Reinforce Democracy: Summary Brief Presenting the Main Findings from the OECD Trust Survey' (2022), www.oecd.org/governance/trust-in-government/oecd-trust-survey-main-findings-en.pdf.

Office of the United Nations High Commissioner for Human Rights, 'Realizing Human Rights through Government Budgets' (2017), www.ohchr.org/sites/default/files/Documents/Publications/RealizingHRThroughGovernmentBudgets.pdf.

Office for National Statistics, 'Trust in Government, UK: 2022' (2022), www.ons.gov.uk/peoplepopulationandcommunity/wellbeing/bulletins/trustingovernmentuk/2022.

Ortiz, I. and M. Cummins, 'Austerity: The New Normal: A Renewed Washington Consensus 2010–24' (Initiative for Policy Dialogue, Working Paper, October 2019), http://policydialogue.org/files/publications/papers/Austerity-the-New-Normal-Ortiz-Cummins-6-Oct-2019.pdf.

'End Austerity: A Global Report on Budget Cuts and Harmful Social Reforms in 2022–25' (Initiative for Policy Dialogue, September 2022), https://assets.nationbuilder.com/eurodad/pages/3039/attachments/original/1664184662/Austerity_Ortiz_Cummins_FINAL_26-09.pdf?1664184662.

Porter, B., 'Rethinking Progressive Realization: How Should It Be Implemented in Canada?' (SRAC, 2015), www.socialrights.ca/documents/publications/Porter%20Progressive%20Implementation.pdf.

Rahman, K., 'Anti-corruption Measures in Constitutions' (2021) Transparency International, https://knowledgehub.transparency.org/helpdesk/anti-corruption-measures-in-constitutions.

Sachs, A., 'Economic and Social Rights and the Right to Health: An Interdisciplinary Discussion Held at Harvard Law School in September, 1993' (Harvard Law School Human Rights Program, 1995), http://hrp.law.harvard.edu/wp-content/uploads/2013/08/EconomicandSocialRightsandtheRighttoHealth.pdf.

Section 27, 'The 2012 Limpopo Textbook Crisis: A Study in Rights-Based Advocacy, the Raising of Rights Consciousness and Governance' (September 2013), www.section27.org.za/wp-content/uploads/2013/10/The-2012-Limpopo-Textbook-Crisis1.pdf.

'South Africa's Net1 Falls on News of US Justice Department Probe' (4 December 2012) *Reuters*, www.reuters.com/article/us-net1ueps-investigation-idUKBRE8B30QS20121204.

Transparency International, 'Literature Review: Corruption as a Driver of Migration' (22 December 2015), https://knowledgehub.transparency.org/assets/uploads/helpdesk/Literature_review_corruption_and_migrations.pdf.

'The Ignored Pandemic: How Corruption in Healthcare Service Delivery Threatens Universal Health Coverage' (March 2019), www.transparency.org.uk/publications/ignored-pandemic.

'Track and Trace: Identifying Corruption Risks in UK Public Procurement for the COVID-19 Pandemic' (2021), www.transparency.org.uk/sites/default/files/pdf/publications/Track%20and%20Trace%20-%20Transparency%20International%20UK.pdf.

Vrushi, J. and R.M.B. Kukutschka, 'Why Fighting Corruption Matters in Times of COVID-19, Corruption Perceptions Index 2020: Research Analysis' (28 January 2021) Transparency International, www.transparency.org/en/news/cpi-2020-research-analysis-why-fighting-corruption-matters-in-times-of-covid-19.

Walker, R., 'Welfare Policy: Tendering for Evidence' in Davies, Nutley and Smith; United Nations Economic Commission for Europe, 'Guidelines on Evidence-Based Policies and Decision-Making for Sustainable Housing and Urban Development' (2020), https://unece.org/DAM/hlm/documents/Publications/2020_Guidelines_on_evidence-based_policies.pdf.

INDEX

CAMBRIDGE STUDIES IN CONSTITUTIONAL LAW

Books in the series

Trust, Courts and Social Rights: A Trust-Based Framework for Social Rights Enforcement David Vitale

The Collaborative Constitution Aileen Kavanagh

Non-Statutory Executive Powers and Judicial Review Jason Grant Allen

The Law as a Conversation among Equals Roberto Gargarella

Micronations and the Search for Sovereignty Harry Hobbs and George Williams

Fundamental Rights and the Legal Obligations of Business David Bilchitz

Courting Constitutionalism: The Politics of Public Law and Judicial Review in Pakistan Moeen Cheema

Ruling by Cheating: Governance in Illiberal Democracy András Sajó

Local Meanings of Proportionality Afroditi Marketou

Property Rights and Social Justice: Progressive Property in Action Rachael Walsh

Carl Schmitt's Early Legal-Theoretical Writings: Statute and Judgment and the Value of the State and the Significance of the Individual Lars Vinx and Samuel Garrett Zeitlin

Remedies for Human Rights Violations: A Two-Track Approach to Supra-national and National Law Kent Roach

Europe's Second Constitution: Crisis, Courts and Community Markus W. Gehring

A.V. Dicey and the Common Law Constitutional Tradition: A Legal Turn of Mind Mark D. Walters

Administrative Competence: Reimagining Administrative Law Elizabeth Fisher and Sidney A. Shapiro

Legal Sabotage: Ernst Fraenkel in Hitler's Germany Douglas Morris

Proportionality in Action: Comparative and Empirical Perspectives on the Judicial Practice Edited by Mordechai Kremnitzer, Tayla Steiner and Andrej Lang

Constitutional Dialogue: Democracy, Rights, Institutions Edited by Geoffrey Sigalet, Grégoire Webber and Rosalind Dixon

The Veiled Sceptre: Reserve Powers of Heads of State in Westminster Systems Anne Twomey

Vigilance and Restraint in the Common Law of Judicial Review Dean Knight

The Alchemists: Questioning Our Faith in Courts as Democracy-Builders Tom Gerald Daly

Australia's Constitution after Whitlam Brendan Lim

Building the Constitution: The Practice of Constitutional Interpretation in Post-Apartheid South Africa James Fowkes

Dimensions of Dignity: The Theory and Practice of Modern Constitutional Law Jacob Weinrib

Reason of State: Law, Prerogative, Empire Thomas Poole

Bills of Rights in the Common Law Robert Leckey

The Guardian of the Constitution: Hans Kelsen and Carl Schmitt on the Limits of Constitutional Law Translated by Lars Vinx with an introduction and notes by Lars Vinx

Parliamentary Bills of Rights: The Experiences of New Zealand and the United Kingdom Janet L. Hiebert and James B. Kelly

Lawyering for the Rule of Law: Government Lawyers and the Rise of Judicial Power in Israel Yoav Dotan

Balancing Constitutional Rights: The Origins and Meanings of Postwar Legal Discourse Jacco Bomhoff

Judges on Trial: The Independence and Accountability of the English Judiciary Shimon Shetreet and Sophie Turenne

Proportionality and Constitutional Culture Moshe Cohen-Eliya and Iddo Porat

The Politics of Principle: The First South African Constitutional Court, 1995–2005 Theunis Roux

The New Commonwealth Model of Constitutionalism: Theory and Practice Stephen Gardbaum

Searching for the State in British Legal Thought: Competing Conceptions of the Public Sphere Janet McLean

Judging Social Rights Jeff King

Proportionality: Constitutional Rights and their Limitations Aharon Barak

Parliamentary Sovereignty: Contemporary Debates Jeffrey Goldsworthy

For EU product safety concerns, contact us at Calle de José Abascal, 56–1°, 28003 Madrid, Spain or eugpsr@cambridge.org.

www.ingramcontent.com/pod-product-compliance
Lightning Source LLC
LaVergne TN
LVHW011810200926
848484LV00005B/1139